I0661174

The Complete Scottish Sketches
of R. B. Cunninghame Graham:
'A Careless Enchantment'

Compiled from the original sources
and edited by

Lachlan Munro and
W. R. B. Cunninghame Graham

EDINBURGH
University Press

Edinburgh University Press is one of the leading university presses in the UK. We publish academic books and journals in our selected subject areas across the humanities and social sciences, combining cutting-edge scholarship with high editorial and production values to produce academic works of lasting importance. For more information visit our website: edinburghuniversitypress.com

© editorial matter and organisation Lachlan Munro and W. R. B. Cunninghame Graham, 2024, 2025
© the text, Edinburgh University Press, 2024, 2025

Edinburgh University Press Ltd
13 Infirmary Street
Edinburgh EH1 1LT

First published in hardback by Edinburgh University Press 2024

Typeset in 10.5/12 Adobe Sabon by
Cheshire Typesetting Ltd, Cuddington, Cheshire

A CIP record for this book is available from the British Library

ISBN 978 1 3995 3308 9 (hardback)
ISBN 978 1 3995 3309 6 (paperback)
ISBN 978 1 3995 3310 2 (webready PDF)
ISBN 978 1 3995 3311 9 (epub)

The right of Lachlan Munro and W. R. B. Cunninghame Graham to be identified as editors of this work has been asserted in accordance with the Copyright, Designs and Patents Act 1988 and the Copyright and Related Rights Regulations 2003 (SI No. 2498).

Contents

Acknowledgements

This book has been compiled with the generous assistance and local knowledge of Paul Wilson of the Gartmore Heritage Society, Hugh Edmond MBE of Fintry and Pat Thomson of the Balfron Heritage Group. Also, the expertise and support of Atilio Martínez, and Eduardo Macrae Moir, in Argentina.

We would also like to acknowledge the help and advice of Professor Laurence Davies of King's College London, Professor Alan Riach of the University of Glasgow and Graham's great-great nephew and biographer, James Jauncey.

Dedicated to the memory of
Professor Cedric Watts (1937–2022)

'A gentleman and a scholar'

'Were we invited to recommend a model of graceful, vigorous and eloquent English, we could mention few modern examples better calculated to instruct and inspire.'

THE SATURDAY REVIEW

'Judged upon their style, they rank among the best things ever written in this country ... little works of art that place the writer by the side of the great story-tellers of France and Russia. In a few pages Mr Cunninghame Graham conjures up the colour, the idiosyncrasy, the soul of a whole people.'

THE OBSERVER

'One of the very best writers in the English language.'

THE NATION

'Graham was probably the greatest literary artist of his day in Scotland.'

THE SCOTSMAN

'The most neglected of the interesting writers in English of the past 100 years.'

PAUL BLOOMFIELD

'The fiery, dandyish, Quixotic Graham might have been invented by some unlikely collision between Oscar Wilde, John Buchan, and Hugh MacDiarmid.'

RODERICK WATSON

'There is no living writer quite like him, and, although a liking for his books is a taste in itself, it is one which should certainly be acquired.'

VITA SACKVILLE-WEST

'By fits and starts, Graham is a great writer. There is nothing that is not great about him.'

BASIL DE SÉLINCOURT

'He is a combination of Byron and Don Quixote.'

ANDREW C. LONG

'The rain-in-the-air-and-on-the-roof mournfulness of Scotch music in his time-past style, snap-shots – the best verbal snapshots ever taken I believe.'

T. E. LAWRENCE

'If anybody were to ask me who was the best English writer of whom a general reader could name offhand the fewest books, I should say Mr. Cunninghame Graham.'

THE SCOTTISH DAILY EXPRESS

'R. B. Cunninghame Graham does not write romances being himself a romance, but his exquisite travel narratives and short stories have by their fastidious craftsmanship earned for him a unique position in Scottish Letters.'

GEORGE MALCOLM THOMSON

'Mr. Cunninghame Graham, an engaging blend of dandy, dreamer, and buccaneer, is a gentleman of various foibles and accomplishments. Too volatile for any one continent, he has travelled far in every direction, and has written books that are mines of wit and humour and bewildering information.'

SIR WILLIAM ROTHENSTEIN

'Cunninghame Graham is a man to buy. His work bears reading many times.'

THE OBSERVER

'He was, all in all, the most brilliant writer of that or of our present day.'

FORD MADOX FORD

'For forty years or so Cunninghame Graham has been caviar to the general and to the few one of the best writers in the world. His fastidious dexterity defies the common and escapes every category of the select.'

THE OBSERVER

'Graham was an artist who cared for words and their effects. Always delicate and almost faery.'

GLASGOW WEEKLY HERALD

'I valued Cunninghame Graham beyond rubies. We will never see his like again.'

HUGH MACDIARMID

'Every book is a history book. Every author stands on the shoulders of the past.'

LACHLAN MUNRO

Editors' Note

The title of this book is ironic: Cunninghame Graham was by no means careless, but as a reviewer in *The Observer* noted, 'The art is always concealed ... there is no sense of conscious effort'.[1] However, some might question why such a volume is necessary since in 1982 Professor John Walker published an excellent and long-overdue anthology of Graham's Scottish sketches[2] in a noble attempt to re-engage the reading public with one of Scotland's sadly neglected sons.[3] However, Professor Walker's book is long out of print, and perhaps, when interest in Graham has been reawakened, the time has come to reintroduce these works. But there are other reasons.

First, after Graham's death, all the anthologies of his sketches, including Walker's selection, were derived from Graham's own anthologies, which Graham and his editor, Edward Garnett,[4] had selected from articles, the majority of which had originally appeared in literary magazines,[5] and there were omissions.[6] Not only that,

---

[1] *The Observer*, 16 October 1910, p. 5.

[2] *The Scottish Sketches of R. B. Cunninghame Graham*, ed. John Walker (Edinburgh: Scottish Academic Press), 1982.

[3] Reviewing the book, Nancy Curme wrote: 'The inexplicable neglect of R. B. Cunninghame Graham's works must by now be almost as well known as the same works remain neglected, and this includes his Scottish writings.' Nancy Curme, 'R. B. Cunninghame Graham: The Scottish Sketches', *Scottish Literary Journal*, 1983, p. 25.

[4] Edward Garnett (1886–1937), English literary editor for T. Fisher Unwin, Duckworths and Jonathan Cape. He advanced the careers of many famous writers, including Joseph Conrad, D. H. Lawrence and John Galsworthy, who described him as a man who 'has done more for English fiction than any living critic, and for less recognition'. John Galsworthy, 'Note on Edward Garnett', *Forsytes, Pendyces and Others* (London: Heinemann, 1935), p. 262.

[5] Six others, 'Beattock for Moffat', M'Kechnie v. Scaramanga', 'Miss Christian Jean', 'Christie Christison', 'A Princess' and 'The Falkirk Tryst', which, because of their subject matter, or use of dialect, were not published in magazines, but which Graham and Garnett considered had merit, were published in his anthologies.

[6] Walker's anthology included thirty-four works.

there were in some cases, textual and titular differences between the original pieces and the anthologised works.

Second, Graham's 'Scottish' sketches were originally widely dispersed throughout his huge canon of over 250 (supposedly) non-political works,[7] written over a period of almost forty years, and Walker grouped them thematically: for example: 'Landscapes and Places', 'The Scottish Character' and 'The Scots Abroad', etc. This gave the first-time reader a way into Graham's work, but also allowed Walker to select what he considered the best pieces, or, more importantly, to omit those he thought had less literary merit. Graham, however, was by temperament a polemicist, and remained a deeply political writer. Consequently, presenting them thematically, valuable as it was, could not address the historical context of the works, nor Graham's motivations, and the campaigning, aristocratic iconoclast was obscured. Your current editors have thus approached their task, not as *littérateurs* (for which they possess few credentials), but, like Graham himself, as historians, to provide factual background where possible, not only to make the works more accessible, but to cast a new light on Graham's memories of a bygone age – 'perfectly poised short stories, sharp, ironic, compassionate vignettes of Scottish life'[8] – a thoroughly original legacy, quite unique in all of Scottish literature.

For the first time, this book records Graham's Scottish 'sketches' chronologically, from the original sources, good, and indifferent, in an attempt to trace his literary and political development. However, for any editor to claim that their compilation is complete gives a hostage to fortune, with the danger that something, previously missed, in some defunct and long-forgotten journal, might suddenly pop up and sour the claim. That, we believe, is a risk worth taking.

Conscientious readers will quickly realise that Graham made no concessions in his writing to the uneducated, and frequently displayed an aristocratic disdain for mass readership.[9] One might be forgiven for concluding that with so many references and asides, he was playing to his strengths as a well-read, urbane gentleman, or had a tendency to show off. Thus, in compiling these works, we have

---

[7] They comprise approximately one-fifth of his total literary output. Graham also wrote fourteen history books, over 100 political works for small socialist journals, and fifty Introductions and Prefaces to the works of others.

[8] Alan Riach, *Scottish Literature: An Introduction* (Edinburgh: Luath Press, 2022), p. 353.

[9] Frank Harris wrote of Graham's audience, 'good readers are almost as scarce as good writers'. Frank Harris, *Contemporary Portraits* (Series 3) (New York, 1920), p. 57.

added footnotes, intended to illuminate Graham's use of Scottish and foreign words, colloquialisms, and his more obscure references and allusions. He also had an annoying habit of breaking his own spell by self-indulgent digressions, a reviewer describing one such work as, 'a narrative full of gesture, interrupting itself'.[10] However, these distractions decreased over time, and he settled into a less polemical, and more ruminative writing style.

Choosing what qualifies as 'Scottish' is occasionally difficult when dealing with Graham.[11] Part of his uniqueness lay in his cross-cultural experiences, and a sometimes uncontrollable urge to transport his readers off to foreign climes, in the middle of some reverie, but as V. S. Pritchett wrote: 'it freshened the "fug" for a while and let the foreign air in',[12] and as Ronald Fraser wrote: 'The Scots alone have enough turbulence in their blood to appreciate the doings of Gauchos, Indians and jaguars'.[13] With these words, we are looking at another unique part of Graham's legacy, the avoidance of over-indulgent nostalgia, when the shutters were opened to reveal a wider world. For example, the first piece is set entirely in Spain, one is set in Africa, three others almost entirely in Argentina. These have been included on the basis that (to paraphrase Rudyard Kipling) 'what should they know of Scotland who only Scotland know',[14] and they will hopefully illuminate 'the soldier of fortune and the wandering scholar'[15] nature of the Scots themselves, while others, where the characters simply administer lonely outposts in the Sahara, have been omitted.

There are also many repetitions; his 'flauchtered feals', his 'linns', his '*Scotissimus Scotorums*', and, of course, his mists. However, it should be remembered that these works were spread out over almost forty years, and few contemporary readers would have noticed.

---

[10] 'The Unlucky Number', *Saturday Review*, 29 September 1900, p. 400.
[11] Graham included a sketch entitled 'Aunt Eleanor' (*The English Review*, February 1911, pp. 446–51), in his own anthology, *Scottish Stories* (1914), but Walker did not, and your current editors concur.
[12] V. S. Pritchett, 'New Literature', *London Mercury*, January 1938, p. 339.
[13] Ronald Fraser, 'The Riddle of Don Roberto', *Sunday Times*, 28 November 1937, p. 9.
[14] 'The English Flag' by Rudyard Kipling. Graham despised Kipling's imperialism and jingoism, and in a letter to Graham, dated 26 January 1899, Garnett described Kipling as '*the* enemy'. Manuscript Collection of Admiral Sir Angus Cunninghame Graham, NLS.
[15] Hamish Henderson, 'Who Remembers Cunninghame Graham?' (1952) *Alias, MacAlias: Writing on Songs, Folk and Literature* (London: Polygon 1992), p. 319.

As an addendum, we have also included a small selection of Graham's other Scottish works, which convey impressions of landscapes and people, or contain historical or antiquarian interest, and also a biography of his long, varied, and adventurous life.

Lachlan Munro and Robin Cunninghame Graham

Introduction

'The truth is, Mr. Cunninghame Graham on the platform
is an impatient idealist; Mr. Cunninghame Graham in the
study, is to a great extent, a patient realist.'[1]

There is much to be gained from immersing oneself in Graham's
eccentric prose, but his works are not for everyone, certainly not
the impatient reader, nor those who seek a coherent, well-plotted
story with a happy ending. In 1913, a reviewer in *The Manchester
Guardian* commented: 'It is a delight to read Mr. Cunninghame
Graham's sketches, but a tantalising delight. Tantalising because he
is like a fiddler always preluding a tune and never quite striking into
it.'[2] In 1900, an unnamed reviewer in *The Saturday Review* wrote:
'Mr. Cunninghame Graham is not altogether a good story-teller:
indeed, he is not exactly a story-teller at all. He has a remarkable power of calling up an atmosphere, as if by a kind of careless
enchantment.'[3] As Hubert Bland wrote: 'He rarely has a story to
tell, but he always has an impression to create, and he creates it
vividly with unerring accuracy.'[4] In 1932 another critic wrote: 'He
has seldom told what we call a story. They are brilliant scenes and
characters, described by someone endowed with exact observation
and a perceptive sympathy with wild and unusual types of men and
women.'[5]

This accuracy was not to everyone's taste; even a critic in *The
Saturday Review*, which published the large majority of his works,
described Graham as 'a disconcerting writer'.[6] Certainly, as with

---

[1] *The Nation*, 24 January 1914, p. 718.
[2] 'New Books', *Manchester Guardian*, 25 November 1913, p. 5.
[3] 'The Unlucky Number', *Saturday Review*, 29 September 1900, p. 400.
[4] Hubert Bland, 'New Novels', *New Statesman*, 20 December 1913, p. 343.
[5] 'A Knight of the Word', *Manchester Guardian*, 5 October 1932, p. 7.
[6] *The Saturday Review*, 27 December 1913, pp. 813–14. The critic added:
    'Graham does not have the pride of his class nor the treacly sentiment of so
    many of his fellow-Scots.'

his political views, his writings divided opinion. In 1912, a critic in *The Nation* described him as 'One of the very best writers in the English language',[7] while earlier that year, another described him as 'a stableyard humourist'.[8] Graham's works, however, have had many admirers, including George Bernard Shaw, Joseph Conrad, President Theodore 'Teddy' Roosevelt, T. E. Lawrence (of Arabia), G. K. Chesterton, Hugh MacDiarmid, Compton Mackenzie and John Galsworthy, to name but a few. His chosen medium, however, has always been difficult to explain. As one anonymous critic wrote:

> Sketches, stories, studies, or what do you call them? Is Mr. Graham a novelist or an essayist; is he bent on picturesque reminiscence or on preaching? In truth we do not know, and do not believe Mr. Graham knows either.[9]

In an attempt to differentiate between the short story and the sketch, George Scott Moncrieff wrote that there was never a satisfactory distinction, 'mainly depending on the individuals' requirement for a plot',[10] and certainly, the large majority of Graham's works are plotless. Wendell Harris described his works thus:

> The difficulty of knowing precisely what to call these brief pieces of prose is a reflection of Graham's uncertain appeal as a writer. Graham does not write short stories as that genre has come to be understood, nor yet the older form, the tale. In general, his pieces are not only too descriptive to be either, but too little plotted to be short stories and too tight to seem tales. 'Sketches' is the best term, sketches which often give equal attention to the narrative and the descriptive. Though the majority are clearly based on his own experience, they seem too distanced to be direct autobiography and too personal to be heavily fictionalized autobiography. The most successful are so not because they achieve the status of true short stories but on their own somewhat mysterious terms.[11]

Graham's shorter writings could contain elements of the sketch, short stories and even essays, through which they move seamlessly, all in the same work, or in the words of his biographer, Laurence Davies: 'The essayist squeezes the impressionist, who in turn squeezes the storyteller; the bed is very crowded. Graham had much he wanted to

---

[7] 'Book of the Month', *The English Review*, April 1912, p. 163.
[8] A. E. Randall, 'Views & Reviews', *New Age*, 21 March 1912, p. 496.
[9] 'Thirteen Stories', *Outlook*, 6 October 1900, p. 313.
[10] George Scott Moncrieff, 'Cunninghame Graham and a Contemporary Critic', *Outlook & The Modern Scot*, May 1936, p. 27.
[11] Wendell V. Harris, 'R. B. Cunninghame Graham', *English Literature in Transition*, 1880–1920, vol. 30, issue 2, 1 January 1987, pp. 222–3.

say, and seemed to want to say it all at once.'[12] Withal, there has never been a Scottish writer from his background, class, and international experiences, who has attempted to capture the character of the land and the people of Scotland so honestly and so vividly.

———

Graham's 'sketches' can best be recognised by their subject matter and structure. At the beginning of his writing career, they commenced with diatribes on what he considered the debasement of Scottish culture, and so-called 'progress'. Later, these changed into long vivid descriptions of nature (displaying a knowledge of flora and of horses), followed by some gist or meditation, often switching between discourse and narration, and what Cedric Watts described as 'panorama terminating in close-up'.[13] Watts believed that 'his better tales are frequently those which employ the oblique narrative form, so that the comments are assimilated to the personality of the teller of the tale-within-the-tale'.[14] They often carried a peremptory *punch* at the end, or simply stopped, a snapshot of a continuum; as Graham himself recorded, 'I liked the manner of his going off the stage'.[15] This would become another feature of his long writing career, leaving the reader to ponder and decipher a meaning or a moral. However, should readers gain the impression that he lacked humour, the Scottish author Richard Curle wrote of him:

> In his eye there was already the twinkle of the coming joke. For Don Roberto had his jokes with everybody, jokes bound up, so to speak, with the personality of the hearer, and by reminding you of them at once he helped create that feeling of comradeship which was one of his charms.[16]

The origins of his unusual writing style can be dated to his early political journalism for small socialist publications. As a natural

———

[12] Laurence Davies, 'R. B. Cunninghame Graham: The Kailyard and After', in *Studies in Scottish Literature*, vol. 11, issue 3, p. 164.
[13] Cedric Watts, *R. B. Cunninghame Graham* (Boston: Tayne Publishing, 1983), p. 50.
[14] Watts, *Joseph Conrad's Letters to Cunninghame Graham* (Cambridge: Cambridge University Press, 1969), p. 30.
[15] Cunninghame Graham, Preface to *Brought Forward* (London: Duckworth, 1916), p. x.
[16] Richard Curle, 'Adventurous Men', in *Caravansary and Conversation* (London: Jonathan Cape, 1937), p. 37. Curle was made executor of Joseph Conrad's estate.

polemicist, and a fighter for justice, while a Liberal MP, and the first
declared socialist in parliament, he attacked every aspect of contemporary society, particularly parliament, the hypocrisy of empire, and
the landed elites (of which he was part), and occasionally reported
on foreign labour disputes, particularly in Hispanic regions. This
required description, and description quickly became more satisfying
than polemic. In 1890, during his time in parliament, Graham had
a small piece published in *Time*[17] entitled 'Horses of the Pampas',
which he described as 'rambling and incoherent reminiscences of a
life I have lived'. These memories had been prompted by a letter from
a friend in Argentina, which caused his thoughts on the 'Eight Hours
Bill' to become 'vaguer and dimmer'. Here was the first occasion
on which he wrote nostalgically of his earlier life in South America,
which could hardly be more different from his present circumstances.
The piece was described by Watts and Davies as:

> An essay which, while recalling affectionately the way of life that Graham
> had seen in South America, lamented its inevitable demise. Perhaps his
> attack on the ugliness of industrial civilization does have a tenuous con-
> nection with the Eight Hour Bill ... but it is clear that for the first but
> certainly not the last time, Graham's memories have taken control. His
> career as a writer, indeed, is the story of an irrepressible rememberer
> trying to discipline his reminiscences without sacrificing their subversive
> power.[18]

Eventually, after relinquishing his parliamentary seat in 1892, and
three years in the political wilderness, he was able to exploit these
emotions, and to salvage another unpaid career, as a travel writer and
nostalgic commentator, for more prestigious publications.

Graham's literary breakthrough occurred in 1895 with the publication of a guidebook entitled *Notes on the District of Menteith*,[19]
which ran to three reprints. Most significantly, *The Saturday Review*
extolled it as:

---

[17] A short-lived socialist journal published by Belfort Bax. It was reprinted in
Graham's first anthology, *Father Archangel of Scotland* (London: Adam &
Charles Black, 1896), pp. 146–65.

[18] Watts & Davies, p. 155.

[19] The *Aberdeen Journal* proffered that it was 'not a guide book in the ordinary
sense at all', but 'a delightful monograph on Menteith', and went on to describe
it as: 'this bright, attractive, and sparkling little volume'. 'Cunninghame
Graham's Guide Book', *Aberdeen Journal*, 2 September 1895, p. 6. Taylor
believed that due to Graham's celebrity, his slim volume was widely reviewed.
Taylor, p. 225.

The wittiest little book to come out in a long time [...] Mr. Graham has found his vocation. We hope that he will cease to "fash"[20] himself with politics and give us many another book small or great but, like this, discursive, poetical, full of ingenious reflection and pleasant distortion of history.'[21]

He was then recruited to *The Saturday Review* as a regular contributor by the owner and editor, Frank Harris, who later proclaimed: 'What a crew of talent to get together on one paper before they were appreciated elsewhere – [H. G.] Wells and [Bernard] Shaw, Chalmers Mitchell, D. S. McColl, and Cunninghame Graham.'[22]

Graham continued his association with the journal after Harris sold it in 1898, and contributed regularly up until 1913, with occasional contributions between 1924 and 1926, and a final piece in 1931. It had been by a stroke of luck (and personal contact)[23] that he became a regular contributor, and it was the prestige of '*The Saturday*', that made and sustained his literary reputation. As Anne Taylor wrote:

While his political articles had much of the force and style of his later work, very few of his contemporaries, and fewer still of what have to be termed his social equals, took the *Labour Elector, Justice*, or *The People's Press*. *The Saturday Review* was a different matter: discussed in the London clubs and, if not always read, at least laid out on the table in the library of every country house in Britain.[24]

Graham's previous literary output had been marginal, and somewhat chaotic, but now, contributing to this prestigious 'Tory' periodical,[25] although he would be obliged to frame his social and political criticism

---

20 Scots: Trouble/bother/worry/annoy.
21 'Notes on the District of Menteith', *The Saturday Review*, 21 September 1895, p. 437.
22 Harris, p. 47.
23 Harris, who had worked as a cowboy in the US Midwest, socialised with Graham in the same London circles, and they rode together in Hyde Park: 'We had many points of contact; we were both outlaws by nature; both eager to live to the utmost, preferring life to a transcript of it.' Harris, p. 48.
24 Taylor, p. 235.
25 Read by the very people that Graham most despised and criticised. In 1899, an unnamed reviewer for *The Saturday Review* patronisingly wrote of him: 'Many heresies may be forgiven or at least ignored for the sake of brilliant individuality in a humdrum age, and though we do not take the man seriously, we owe homage to the master of style. Indeed, were we invited to recommend a model of graceful, vigorous and eloquent English, we could mention few modern examples better calculated to instruct and inspire.' *The Saturday Review*, 29 April 1899, p. 533.

more subtly, it undoubtedly lent a new respectability and kudos to his writing and political reputation, which it had hitherto lacked in the eyes of the public, and particularly his peers.

Constrained from writing socialist propaganda, for a new and more conservative readership, and accepting that his inventive story-telling abilities were limited, Graham had little choice but to write reflective memoirs from his travels, which were simply a development of his early foreign news reports. These were known as 'middles'[26] – descriptions of locations that he had experienced at first hand, knew about, or was interested in, in South America, Morocco and later, Scotland, and might sit between factual works by others, such as 'Maori Tattooing' or 'African Cannibals'.

As for his imaginative talents, Graham eschewed what he termed 'invention', stating:

> It is (I think) a general belief, that every writer draws his matter straight from the fountain of his brain, just as a spider weaves his web from his own belly. This may be so, especially with folk of much invention and no imaginative power ... It may be that which I refer to as invention they style imagination.[27]

Therefore, while attempting to meet the public taste for exotic locations and adventure, he was now obliged to reach into his own experiences for inspiration, and to employ his emotionally reserved impressionistic skills to make his accounts more realistic. Fortunately, he possessed an extraordinary facility for recollection, and a felicity of expression, that could conjure convincing, often startling exotic settings and incidents, and like his 'ould Colonel', he 'had an eye intil him like a hawk',[28] for 'the trifling actions of which life was composed'.[29] In 1932, Pritchett most succinctly summed up Graham's unique individual style: 'He has invented a new manner

---

[26] Infrequent literary essays placed between reviews and news items. Watts describes them as 'stories, essays reminiscences and descriptive pieces – particularly if, during this heyday of European imperialism, they dealt with remote and exotic regions'. Watts, *Cunninghame Graham*, p. 32. A contemporary reviewer described Britain's fascination with travel, 'The spirit of vagabondage possesses the nation. Call it what you will, *Reiselust*, or go-fever, we are most of us subject to this malady.' *Outlook*, 6 May 1899, p. 455.

[27] Cunninghame Graham, *His People* (London: Duckworth, 1906), p. ix. He expressed very similar sentiments in *Faith* (1909), pp. xi–xii.

[28] Cunninghame Graham, 'A Veteran', *Saturday Review*, 14 April 1900, p. 455.

[29] Cunninghame Graham, 'At Dalmary', *Saturday Review*, 4 December 1909, p. 689.

of telling stories – by word painting, and his crash and subtlety of language are splendid.'[30]

Having experimented with, and no doubt gained confidence from recording his foreign experiences, it might have been assumed that Graham could have easily transferred these developing literary skills to Scotland, but it would not be a simple transition. Scotland was an old country whose turbulent history and startling incidents were now in the distant past, which only survived in history books and local traditions. He mourned the passing of the spontaneous life he had known in South America, but the life he had known in Scotland, and was witnessing again, was of an entirely different nature – domesticated, unheroic, often squalid – thus, conjuring up romance or exoticism would not be an option, unless they lay in that remembered or imagined past. He was thus obliged to rely purely on nostalgia, seeking out links 'with days of glory long departed', among the population and the landscape, occasionally spicing them with South American memories and reflections.[31] As David Daiches wrote, 'The combination of observation and memory on the one hand with a hauntingly imaginative sense of the past on the other, gives a special flavour to his evocations of Scottish scenes and Scottish manners',[32] while Walker wrote that Graham's literature 'possesses a spiritual quality which transcends the simple narrating of biographical facts'.[33] In 1925, a critic in the *Times Literary Supplement* wrote: 'No writer, not even Stevenson, has a greater gift of catching in a phrase the flavour of a landscape.'[34]

Consequently, with a few notable exceptions, all of Graham's Scottish works were derived from his personal experiences. This was particularly true of his descriptions of nature, and his portraits of characters in and around his erstwhile home district of Menteith in the Forth Valley, which form their own sub-genre. These were typically set in the time-laden interiors of grand, musty houses,

---

[30] V. S. Pritchett, 'A Reviver of Chivalry in English Prose', *Current Literature*, LIII, October 1932, pp. 470–2.

[31] Graham liked to draw parallels between Scotland and foreign lands as disparate as Mexico, Morocco and Afghanistan. A reviewer wrote, 'In *Notes on the District of Menteith* he talks pleasantly about atavism and things traditional and pantheistic'. 'The Stewartry of Menteith', *Times Literary Supplement*, 5 March 1931, p. 166.

[32] David Daiches, 'Preface' to *The Scottish Sketches of R. B. Cunninghame Graham*, p. vii.

[33] John Walker, 'Cunninghame Graham and the Critics: A Reappraisal', *Studies in Scottish Literature* vol. 19, no. 1, January 1984, p. 108.

[34] 'Meditations on an Ancestor', *Times Literary Supplement*, 28 May 1925, p. 362.

located in enclosed and shadowy landscapes, or dilapidated farm-steads that he owned:

> The last examples of the old Scotland which has sunk below the waves of Time. Perhaps not an example to be followed, but yet to be observed, remembered, even regretted in the great drabness of prosperity which overspreads the world.[35]

Here then is Graham's unique contribution to Scottish literature, his memoirs of a local gentry, eccentric relatives, wily farmers, ine-briated Highlanders, fractious villagers, nit-picking infants, funer-als, nostalgic emigrants and creatures of folklore – a recognisable, eclectic, heterogeneous community – in a world lit only by fire, now melted into the misty region of the past.

---

[35] Cunninghame Graham, 'Caisteal-Na-Sithan', *Saturday Review*, 15 April 1911, p. 455.

The Sketches

1896–9

Figure 1 'Trootie'.

'I dedicate this little work to Mr. Wilkie, of Balfron,
known to the world as "Trootie". This I do because,
being himself a shadow of the time before the railway
snorted across our moors, he should know most of the
shadows as they come and go over the countryside.
Already the shadow of St. Rollox's chimney,[1] so to speak,
reaches almost to Inverness, and in the time to come there
will be no place for such as "Trootie" in the land.'

R. B. Cunninghame Graham
'Dedication' in *Notes On The District
of Menteith* (1907 edition)

---

[1] St Rollox Locomotive Works at Springburn, North Glasgow.

It may appear curious that the first 'Scottish' sketch is set in Spain, but it is entirely appropriate. The majority of Graham's works were set in the Hispanic world, particularly in South America among his beloved gauchos, and his works set only in Scotland form a minority.[2] However, he frequently blurred borders, and often flipped between Scotland and warmer climes. As a Scot with a proud Spanish heritage,[3] he used the position of the 'outsider-insider' to bring a fresh perspective to everything he wrote about, in a way that is unique in the Scottish literary canon.

Most of Graham's works carry a political message, and here, after his usual meandering preamble, we are engaged in a meditation on the vagaries of history, and of futile sacrifice. However, there are also early portents of recurring themes in his work, particularly his conviction that capitalism and Calvinism had pernicious effects upon Scottish life. He mourned the loss of an older, more heroic type of Scot,[4] and his attack on imperial abuses and racism, would soon find a fuller and more strident expression in his satirical and vitriolic diatribes against the British Empire[5] during the jingoistic build-up to Queen Victoria's Diamond Jubilee of 1897. Withal, there is another half-hidden message; that despite their religious differences, Catholic Scots and Protestant Scots, constitute a different tribe from their near neighbours, and that history and culture had created a stronger bond than the more ephemeral divisions over matters of faith.

Despite fallacious and extravagant claims,[6] and should readers be left with the impression that Graham himself followed the Catholic faith, he had been raised as an Anglican, and during his 1886 election campaign, he declared himself 'a Protestant'.[7] Indeed, his grandfather had donated the funds to build the first Free Church of Scotland (Wee

---

[2] Graham wrote thirty-five sketches about Spain, and fifty set in South America.

[3] Graham's mother, Anne Elizabeth, was the youngest daughter of Admiral Charles Elphinstone Fleeming of Cumbernauld and Doña Catalina Paulina Alessandro, of Cadiz.

[4] What Graham often referred to as the 'pre-Culloden type'.

[5] 'Fraudesia Magna', parts I and II, *Saturday Review,* 21 March and 4 April 1896, '"Bloody Niggers"', *The Social Democrat,* April 1897, and 'Expansion of Empire', *Sunday Chronicle,* 13 June 1897. This goes some way to explaining his unpopularity as a writer among certain classes. An American critic wrote: 'Writing of this sort is not likely to make an author a popular prophet in his own country.' Ben Ray Redman, 'Old Wine in New Bottles', *New York Herald Tribune,* 28 October 1929, p. 12. Graham's name never appeared in *Who's Who?*

[6] 'Cunninghame Graham', *Catholic Herald,* 23 April 1937, p. 2.

[7] *Coatbridge Express,* 7 July 1886, p. 2. In his most famous book, *Mogreb El Acksa,* when asked by his bemused Muslim captors if he was a Christian, he replied "No, I'm a U.P." (United Presbyterian).

Free) kirk in their home village of Gartmore.[8] Graham's attitude to religion was complex, and despite his wife Gabrielle's mystic faith,[9] his own quirky interest in what he saw as religion's more pagan aspects, his Jesuit missionaries and a fascination with 'religious enterprises pursued under disadvantageous circumstances',[10] he remained a sceptical agnostic.[11]

DE HERETICO COMBURENDO[12]

Anthologised in *Father Archangel of Scotland* (London: Adam & Charles Black, 1896), pp. 65–78.

VALLADOLID,[13] from Belad el Walid – that is, in Arabic, the Land of Walid, once the capital of Spain, and now a dull, decaying town in Old Castille, on the Pisuerga.

Few places even in Spain recall more forcibly the past. On every side a plain stretching for miles, to the north the mountains dimly visible, on the south and east and west plains, and more plains.

No commerce, little traffic, few modern buildings except a court for the *pelota* (the national game of ball), to which the inhabitants draw your attention with pride as evidence of coming prosperity. Even the bull ring seems decaying. No bicycles, but few advertisements, and these chiefly of things that no one can have any use for.

Still, an air of ancient splendour hangs about the town. In the arcaded plazas many a heretic has purged his contempt by fire, and gone, perhaps to heaven, perhaps from fire to fire. In every street a ruined palace, at every turn a house in which lived some one known in history; an air that only having been a capital ever imparts. In the Plazuela del Ochavo, where the Emperor Charles V. pardoned the

---

[8] Graham mentions a conflict between the churches in Gartmore in two of his sketches.

[9] She initially used the name 'Gabrielle Marie' while posing as French, but she later took on a Spanish persona, and used 'Gabriela'.

[10] Cunninghame Graham, *Father Archangel of Scotland and Other Essays* (London: Adam & Charles Black, 1896), p. 3.

[11] Keir Hardie's close colleague, David Lowe, wrote of Graham: 'Although he was at times, both in public and private expression, ostensibly and perversely pagan, in contradistinction to the Christianity in evidence around him, yet he had a soft side for the older form of Christian faith.' David Lowe, 'When Graham Said Good-Bye to Gartmore', *Evening Times*, 18 March 1938, p. 3.

[12] Latin: 'Regarding the burning of heretics'.

[13] The largest town in north-west Spain.

Comuneros,[14] still stands the house, with its window bars not yet repaired, where Philip II. was baptized. The bars were cut to show the infant to the people.

Just the sort of town in which one might expect to find a Scottish and an English Catholic College. Philip, of pious memory (in Spain), found them both. Perhaps his motives were political, perhaps religious. Who in England can judge the motives of Spain? As easily as a Spaniard can judge the morals of England. Climate, I take it, influences both, as it does judgements. Mary, in England 'bloody,' in Spain is 'pious.' Claverhouse,[15] a fiend in Ayrshire, is a hero in the Highlands. Still we owe Philip gratitude for his two colleges, if only to remind us that we too were persecutors.

In a long rambling street the Scottish college stands. The natives (of the poorer sort) speak of the College as *el colegio de los Escorozeces*, giving the word an extra syllable, perhaps for euphony. Still they are good Christians, and this is the highest praise men of their kind in Spain can give.

Hard by the College Cervantes lived and wrote the second part of *Don Quixote*; close by Columbus died poor and broken-hearted; not far off dwelt Gondomar.[16] A bit of Scotland lost in Castille, and yet a place no Scotsman (even a Presbyterian) should behold unmoved.

Many in Scotland are the tales of suffering and persecution that Protestants endured, but never does one hear of the tyranny that forced a Scottish Catholic to seek his education at Douay, Valladoid and St Omer. How many Scotsmen have heard of the Scoto-Spanish College? How many have visited it? Yet thoroughly to comprehend the faith sufficient to move mountains and extirpate humanity in man, which reigned in Scotland in times past, it must be visited. Much has the Odium Theologicum[17] to answer for in Scotland and other lands. How admirable, when thinking of it, appears the simple faith of the savages of whom some traveller relates that of whatever faith the missionary was, into the hot stone oven straight he went.

Passing the ponderous door, set in a horse-shoe arch, the present melts away. On every side the past looks down on one. A flagged and vaulted corridor leads to a long refectory, with the table set, as

---

[14] An uprising of the citizens of Castile against the rule of Charles V, between 1520 and 1521. At its height, the rebels controlled the cities of Valladolid, Tordesillas, and Toledo.

[15] John Graham of Claverhouse 'Bonny Dundee' (1648–89), a Scottish nobleman and soldier, who served King Charles II against the Lowland Covenanters.

[16] Don Diego Sarmiento de Acuña, Count of Gondomar (1567–1626). Spanish ambassador to the court of King James VI and I, from 1613 to 1622.

[17] Latin: Theological hatred. A term commonly used by Graham in his writings.

in the 'Cena' of Leonardo,[18] with bread, and jugs of rough Valencian pottery. Mary Queen of Scots looks through the gloaming from the wall; Semple of Semple (a pious founder) faces her.[19] Out of every corner Scottish Jesuits of the past seem to appear. Across the passage seem to emerge the shades of Scottish priests, who in their lifetime had lurked in Scottish castle and Elizabethan manor-house, and occupied the secret chamber in the houses of the English and Scottish Catholics. At once the air of rest and quiet seems to suggest the College as a fitting place in which to rear up men to minister to scattered Catholic communities in Aberdeenshire, Lochaber, and Strathglass.

Scholars – some twenty, chiefly peasants' sons from Aberdeenshire; priests – three or four; lastly, the Rector. Only in *Redgauntlet*[20] and in books of Jacobites does such a priest exist. I fancy the Rector of the Scottish Castilian College is the last surviving type. Scotissimus Scotorum, a Scot of Scots, tall, thin, and sinewy, a Highlander, a scholar, and linguist, withal a gentleman, with the gentility that Presbyterianism seems to have crushed out of the modern Scotsman. In talking with him one seems to see what sort of men the Scotsmen of the past had been before the Bawbee[21] and the Bible had altered them. Something quite unlike Scotland in the urbanity of the man; a sort of being, as it were, in community with the rest of Europe, instead of, as at present, condemned to fellowship with only Germans (High and Low), Dutchmen, and Scandinavians; people who, excellent no doubt, have nothing of the Slave or Latin interest about them. Just the kind of man who in old days was charged with missions by the Pope, 'the King of Spain,' or Mary Queen of Scots, to save the somewhat scabby, if faithful sheep who still remained in Scotland. If the world had only gone on right (or wrong) Father M'Donald had been enthroned at Edinburgh, at Brechin, or St. Andrews, 'a fayre prelate,' with cope and chasuble,[22] crosier and ring of amethyst on his forefinger, with candle, bell and book, and power to curse the heretic and lift the finger in the attitude so dear to bishops, of malediction. As it is, a Scoto-Spanish priest and gentleman speaking Castilian faintly tinged with Gaelic, and dinning[23] education and religion into fledgling Scoto-Spanish or Hispano-Scottish priests.

---

[18] 'The Last Supper'.
[19] Robert Sempill (1505–76), a resister of the Scottish Reformation of 1560.
[20] *Redgauntlet* (1824). An historical novel by Sir Walter Scott.
[21] A Scottish halfpenny.
[22] Vestments.
[23] Scots: Hammering/instilling.

Nature or fate is, very prodigal of men, not in the way of turning out many, fitted to excel in anything but cheapening bicycles, but in another fashion. When in a million a man is born to rule the Church, lead men, or to direct a country, ten to one that fate or nature sets him to do that which a million others could have done as well as he, and leaves the task to fools.

Over the Scottish College hangs an air of Scotland, but not of Scotland of to-day, but of that older Scotland that was poor and furnished soldiers and adventurers to all the rest of Europe; that Scotland which vanished after Culloden, and has been replaced by factories and mines, progress and money, and an air of commonplace, exceeding all the world.

Not looking over carefully at the writing of St. Thomas of Aquinas, the autograph of Her of Avila,[24] the relics (all authentic), the rich groined roof so finely arched, or even the curious wooden flooring of the church, unique in Spain, I say farewell to my compatriots and out into the street, thanking my stars for the chance of having seen that which enabled me to reconstruct the Scotland of the past more vividly than by perusing libraries.

In the Calle Real de Don Sancho, as close to the Scottish College as Gretna is to Carlisle, stands the Colegio de los Ingleses. Founded, like the other, by Philip II., the English College was designed to commemorate the triumph of the Invincible Armada. The 'Invincible' is long dispersed; its sailors from Biscay and Catalonia have left their bones on Achill[25] and upon the Hebrides; all of it has disappeared with the exception of here and there a rusty anchor, but here and there a darker cheek in Galway or a brighter eye amongst the ponies of the coast. Had it succeeded, without doubt to-day we had all been Catholics, and the poor Catholic gentleman of Garstang, mentioned by Froude,[26] had been relieved from the obligation of going on Sunday to 'take wine' with the vicar at the parish church. The College still remains, apparently unchanged since its foundation.

The work begun by Campion, Parsons, and their fellows, still goes on. The corridors through which they paced, reading their breviaries, remain identical. The pupils (more ruly, let us fain hope, than their predecessors, of whom the Jesuit fathers had to complain at Rome) still sit down in the self-same stone refectory.

In England how few remember the disgraceful page of history that the fantastic tortures and the martyrdoms of the Jesuits in the pictures

---

[24] St. Teresa (1515–82).
[25] An island off the coast of County Mayo in Ireland.
[26] James Anthony Froude (1818–1894). English historian, novelist, and biographer.

hanging on the wall attest. Let them rest on, secure at least in one thing, that the torments that a hard world inflicts on their descendants defy the limner's[27] power to put up in pictures, even with a knowledge of perspective.

If the Scots College had an air of Scotland, so the English College has an air of prosperous England; but how unlike the other. The self-same architecture, the self-same iron-studded doors, the altars in the style of Churriguera[28] in the chapels, where saints and angels float in a sea of gilded gingerbread, identical, but still an outwards air and inward grace making them different, as Thurso is from Yeovil.

Why is it that the races English and Scotch have never really amalgamated? So close, so like, both wizened by the same east wind, tormented more or less by the same Sunday, and yet unlike, and so the colleges. St. George and Merrie England. No one in his widest fits of patriotism ever talked of Merrie Scotland. Did Knox kill merriment, even as Macbeth did murder sleep? Loyal, abstemious, business-like, haggis-eating, tender, disagreeable, true, a Scotsman may be, but merry never.

An air of Oxford pervades the English College, all seems so prosperous, so old-established, and so English. The well-stocked library, with its rows of fine old Spanish, Latin, and English books clothed in white vellum, lettered on the backs in strange old-fashioned hands; the comfortable reading-desks and well-warmed room, all spoke of England. Not that there were not things unusual to be seen in English colleges. The pictures on the wall of English Catholics, martyred for conscience' sake by so-called freedom-loving Englishmen, gave a different note. There are particulars it pleases me to dwell on. Pleasant to slap one's chest and say, 'I am an Englishman;' to think that in my country every faith is free, from Christianity to Obi worship, free and untrammelled as long as it observes the laws of decency and of the Stock Exchange. It pleases me to think that the cruel Duke of Alva racked and burnt and scourged the Protestants of Holland, Elizabeth of England was not a jot inferior to him in her dealings with English Catholics. It is to be allowed that Catholics shall have the copyright of persecution? Perish the thought; Christians of all denominations have shown their love to one another by the rack and the stake. Certain it is that Pizarro and Cortez[29] depopulated empires, but they at least imagined that their mission in the Indes (after the gold was

---

[27] Painters.
[28] In the Rococo style of the Spanish architect and sculptor José Benito de Churriguera (1665–1725).
[29] Francisco Pizarro González (1471–1541), Hernán Cortés de Monroy y Pizarro Altamirano (1485–1547). Spanish conquistadors.

found) was to convert the Indians. Besides, the Spanish butcheries ceased with the sixteenth century. Ours have continued almost to the present day. Where are the natives of Tasmania, the Australian blacks, the greater proportion of the Maories? Is it to believed that we exterminated these men out of our desire to save souls?

After the martyrs' pictures the chief glory of the place is the image of the Blessed Virgin richly carved in wood. Powerful in miracles (*muy milagrosa*[30]) the people of the town affirm her, and why should any doubt it? During the sack of Cadiz the heathen soldiers (so runs the Spanish story) of the Count of Essex tore this virgin from her shrine, and to display their Christian toleration hacked off her arm and drew it through the streets tied to a string. After the sack, and when the pagans had returned to England, what could an English College do better than show its faith by offering an asylum to the poor image maltreated by the English who in England denied the faith? So in procession they received her, with music, incense, and with acolytes, and placed her where she stands to-day, blackened with age, but comely and most miraculous.

Each name upon the lists on the refectory wall has had its tragedy. Tichbornes and Babingtons, Englefields and Catesbys,[31] jostle one another. They set one thinking on the past, and the way in which all history is written to suit the conscience of the conquerors. The world has always readily come out to greet the conqueror with trumpets and with flowers; but he has always had to conquer first. The names upon the walls are the names of beaten men, and speak of causes long forgotten. Neither racks nor calumny can further harm them, and in their time they had their fill of both. Therefore I take it that without incurring *scandalum magnatum*[32] a man may drop his literary tear upon their memory. At any rate, if freedom has been won by martyrdom, to the Campions, Garners, and the rest we owe as much as to men who perished at Smithfield[33] or upon the moors of Galloway. And if they did not snuffle through the nose, or take the names of Hebrew worthies, instead of calling themselves plain George or John, they were as truly martyrs, and their state, for all I know, as gracious.

So out into the deserted sandy street, between the *tapia* walls, to muse upon the colleges, and to reflect that had not stake and rack

---

[30] Spanish = Quite miraculous.
[31] Catholic martyrs. The latter led the planned regicide of James VI & I, in the 'Gunpowder Plot'.
[32] Latin: A great scandal.
[33] Execution site in London, adjacent to St Bartholomew's Hospital.

and red-hot pincers proved so efficacious, perchance the England of to-day had been as Catholic as Belgium.

* * * * *

In his 'Introduction' to his anthology of Graham's Scottish sketches, Professor Walker divided them into three periods. The first, 1896–7, he described as: 'a bitter portrayal of the defects of the Scottish character somewhat in the naturalistic manner of George Douglas Brown's *The House With the Green Shutters*'. The next two decades, up to 1916, saw the bulk of Graham's Scottish works, in which Walker perceived a more settled portrayal of people and places, and the third period, which dealt with mythology and sentimentality.[34] However, Walker made no attempt to explain these distinct phases by putting them into an historical context, which is peculiar, because there are obvious explanations to hand.

The first, and most distinctive group, contains only three of Walker's so-called 'bitter portrayals', of which 'A Survival' (1896) was the first (and the first Scottish sketch for *The Saturday Review*), followed by 'Salvagia', and 'Heather Jock' (1897). However, Graham was quite explicit in each that his motivations were protests against, and subversions of, the popular literary taste of the time, the writings of 'The Kailyard[35] School' (1880–1914), which was reaching the height of its huge popularity around this time. Thomas Knowles described this literary genre as 'characterised by the sentimental and nostalgic treatment of parochial Scottish scenes, often centred on the church community',[36] and appealing to 'the amiable, respectable, slightly cosy church folk'[37] represented in the works of J. M. Barrie, S. R. Crockett and Ian MacLaren, among others. The genre has had many critics over the years,[38] with criticism ranging from George

---

[34] *The Scottish Sketches of R. B. Cunninghame Graham,* edited by John Walker (Edinburgh: Scottish Academic Press, 1982), p. 11.

[35] 'Cabbage patch', or more appropriately, 'kitchen garden'. The disparaging epithet was first coined by Robert Louis Stevenson's friend, the English poet and critic, W. E. Henley. J. H. Millar, *A Literary History of Scotland* (London: Fisher Unwin, 1903), p. 511.

[36] Thomas Knowles, *Ideology, Art & Commerce: Aspects of Literary Sociology in the Late Victorian Scottish Kailyard* (Gothenburg: Universitatis Gothoburgensis, 1983), p. 13.

[37] William Power, *Literature and Oatmeal* (London: Routledge, 1935), p. 161.

[38] The first serious critic of the genre had been the novelist and literary critic Margaret Oliphant, who, in 1889 greeted 'the springing up of this literature which may justly be called provincial with dismay'. Margaret Oliphant, 'The Window in Thrums', *Blackwood's Edinburgh Magazine*, August 1889, p. 265.

Douglas Brown's contemporary description of 'the sentimental slop of Barrie, and Crockett',[39] to George Blake's description of S. R. Crockett's works as 'sentimental sludge',[40] and to the Kailyard literature in general, which 'presented the English and American reader with a picture of a country as a sort of collection of picturesque rural parishes peopled by "pawky" and/or "nippy" characters'.[41] Christopher Harvie analysed them as social escapism,[42] and Gillian Shepherd assessed them as parables, perfectly suited to the mood and taste of the times: 'it is not far-fetched to claim that they were in a sense dictated by their readers. They are the product not only of three individuals but also of an era.'[43]

Graham's criticisms were more trenchant and immediate. On the surface, it appeared that his first main objection was linguistic, as expressed in the Preface to his first anthology, *Father Archangel of Scotland* (1896), where he referred to 'that all-sufficient cloak of kailyard Scotch spoken by no one under heaven, which of late has plagued us',[44] an accusation which he repeated in 'A Survival', below. However, it was not only the artificiality and misuse of the Scots language that angered him; Graham's main objections went deeper, and can be divided into two inextricably linked strands.

The first strand was the most directly 'political'. For a man who had spent the previous ten years fighting for the underdog and the industrial poor, his political experiences had shown him a grimy, industrial, impoverished, violent side of Scotland, which cried out for reform, even revolution. George Blake claimed that the Industrial Revolution had:

> Knocked the old Scotland sideways, with a violence in both the process and the consequences unexampled … A really dramatic, often beastly, revolution was taking place. And what had the Scottish novelists to say about it? The answer is – nothing, or as nearly nothing as makes no

---

[39] G. D. Brown to Ernest Barker, 24 October 1901, quoted from James Veitch, *George Douglas Brown* (London: H. Jenkins, 1952), p. 153.

[40] George Blake, *Barrie and the Kailyard School* (London: Arthur Barker, 1951), p. 51.

[41] Ibid. pp. 15–16

[42] Christopher Harvie, *Scotland and Nationalism* (London: Routledge, 2004), p. 99.

[43] Gillian Shepherd, 'The Kailyard', in *The History of Scottish Literature*, vol. 3., edited by Douglas Gifford (Aberdeen: Aberdeen University Press, 1988) p. 311. There were also many imitators.

[44] Cunninghame Graham, Preface to *Father Archangel of Scotland* (London: Adam & Charles Black, 1896), p. ix.

matter. They might as well have been living in Illyria as in the agonized country of their birth.[45]

Kailyard literature, in Graham's view, was depicting sentimentalised, picturesque and cosy communities, disguising life's harsh realities, and ameliorating calls for the radical change that he so desired. Harvie attempted to explain this incongruity and the popularity of the Kailyard writings in the context of an increasingly industrialised Scotland.

A society beset by terrifying social problems was *threatened* by realism ... exacerbated by the deep-seated evils of poverty and overcrowding generated by Scotland's pell-mell industrialisation. To expose these would be revolutionary; it would also break the discipline of puritanism by mentioning the unmentionable ... The Kirk enforced silence out of conviction, the middle class out of fear. The bogus community of the Kailyard was an alternative to the horror of the real thing.[46]

Any 'revolutionary' opportunity to subvert the genre might have been attractive to Graham, but he did not attempt this by depicting the poverty, deprivation, drunkenness and overcrowding in Scotland's industrial towns; that would have required vivid description, which, from his position as a landowner, would have sounded crass and patronizing.[47] Instead, he chose the more available option of deconstructing and parodying the bucolic lifestyle in his own familiar 'kail-yard' of Menteith, in a manner that Watts described as 'tactical'.[48] In the following piece, 'A Survival', there is an unmistakable delight in Graham's attempted sabotage, by what Watts and

---

[45] George Blake, *Barrie and the Kailyard School* (London: Arthur Barker, 1951), pp. 8–9.

[46] Christopher Harvie, *Scotland and Nationalism* (London: Routledge, 2004), p. 99. William Power described the social conditions of the time in industrial Scotland as 'beyond the scope of realism'. William Power, *Literature and Oatmeal* (London: Routledge, 1935), p. 165.

[47] A reviewer wrote of him, 'Mr. Graham is only a diver into the slums, not a dweller in them', *The Manchester Guardian*, 11 November 1902, p. 4. However, in June 1892, a socialist friend, John Burns, visited Glasgow to support Graham's unsuccessful election campaign in Camlachie, and Graham took him around the streets and into houses in the city's East End between 11 pm on a Saturday night, and 2 am on the Sunday morning, to show him extraordinary scenes of drunkenness and deprivation. A tearful Burns was heard to exclaim: 'My God, does Scotland stand where it did?' and, 'My God, no wonder these people drink', *Glasgow Evening News*, 13 June 1892, p. 3.

[48] Watts, p. 50.

Figure 2 The ruins of Offrance farm by the River Forth.

Davies called: 'his nostalgia for the pre-civilised',[49] as he undermined the concept of the Protestant work ethic, and the perceived orderliness of Scottish rural life.

A SURVIVAL[50]

The Saturday Review, 3 May 1896, pp. 542–4.
Anthologised in *Success* (London: Duckworth, 1902), pp. 1–9.

TO be a Scotchman nowadays is to fill a position of some difficulty. It is expected by the respectable public when a Scotchman takes his pen in hand, that no matter what his antecedents, education, or predilections may be, he is bound to set down his thoughts in language as unintelligible as possible to the average Englishman.

---

[49] Cedric Watts and Laurence Davies, *Cunninghame Graham: A Critical Biography* (Cambridge: Cambridge University Press, 1979), p. 267.

[50] This story of the indolent Highlander, and the ramshackle farm, was repeated almost word for word in *The Gateway* in 1916, as 'Transplanted in Vain' (see below). The attack on the 'Kailyard' was however replaced by an attack on capitalism.

It is in vain to plead that our greatest writers in the past used what they considered was the English language. It is quite useless to draw attention to the fact that Hume, Smollett and Sir Walter Scott, together with Adam Smith and Dugald Stewart, when treating of ordinary affairs, endeavoured (perhaps unwisely) to render themselves intelligible to all men.

Dunbar,[51] our greatest poet, used an English but little different from that of Chaucer, who, by the way, he acknowledged as his master. Bishop Douglas did not translate Virgil into the patois of his day. Master Robert Henryson,[52] the author of "Robin and Makyne," one of the few pastorals that can be endured by those whose lives are passed outside towns, is easy to understand. Drummond of Hawthornden[53] rarely if ever employs a Scottish word. Carlyle, it is true, made for himself a language and a philosophy, but neither seems likely to endure. Indeed it may be that it is chiefly as a humourist (in spite of Mr. Morley,[54] who does not sin in that respect himself) that he will be most remembered.

Be all that as it may, the fact remains that the modern Scottish writer to be popular in England must write in dialect. If he must live (and write) he has, I presume, to adopt the ruling fashion, and write of weavers, idiots, elders of churches, small farmers' wives, and others of those without whom, according to Jesus the son of Sirach,[55] a city cannot be inhabited, and who chiefly maintain the state of the world. Now, though I have no skill of the jargon which it has pleased the band of Levites who write of these worthy people to evolve, it must not be thought that I depreciate the aforementioned weavers, ministers, and elders, or even the idiots. Rather do I compassionate them, in that they have been dragged into publicity and their language distorted by the above-mentioned sons of Levi; so that I verily believe there is not a henwife, weaver, idiot, elder, or ploughman in the conglomerate of granite, pudding-stone, and peat moss known as Scotland who would recognize himself in the dress which the British public has been eager to welcome him. Neither would I have

---

51 William Dunbar (1459–1530), Scottish 'makar', closely connected to the court of King James IV.
52 Robert Henryson (no dates), Scottish Renaissance poet.
53 William Drummond of Hawthornden (1585–1649), Scottish poet.
54 John Morley, first Viscount Morley of Blackburn (1838–1923), a distinguished Liberal politician and statesman, and biographer of Gladstone, whom Graham despised. However, like Graham, Morley opposed imperialism and the Boer War, and supported Home Rule for Ireland.
55 The Wisdom of Sirach (or Ecclesiasticus) is a non-canonical collection of Jewish ethical teachings from the early second century bc contained in the Apocrypha.

Englishmen believe is the entire Scottish nation composed of ministers, elders, and precentors.[56] I should explain that a precentor is a
man employed to put the congregation out in a Scottish church by
starting hymns and psalms on the wrong notes, and in a key which it
is impossible for the majority to compass.

The modern way of looking at a native of North Britain differs
considerably from what used to be the fashion. In the blithe times
of clans and borderers, of Wardens of the Marches, of battles and
mosstroopers,[57] each Scotchman was an enemy to England.

Generally in stricken fields, you Southern folk discomfited us by
reason of your archers and your horses, with their riders sheathed in
armour. Upon the borders we had the advantage of you, as you had
cattle for us to steal, houses for us to burn, and money and valuables
to carry off. We having none, you were not in a position to retaliate
efficiently. A little later we pushed our forays further south, even to
London, giving you a king (and such a king!) and a whole tail of
needy courtiers, all with authentic pedigrees and empty purses.

Your people, not unnaturally, began to hate us, as indeed was
reasonable; for hitherto our plunderings had been confined to
Cumberland, but now we put the capital itself to sack and pillage.

From this time date the Sawneys and Sandies,[58] the calumnies about
our cuticle, and those which stated that we were so tender-hearted
that we scrupled to deprive of life the smallest insect which we have
about our persons. About that time you found our cheek-bones out,
observed that we were all red-haired and blew our noses without
handkerchiefs to save expense. You noted down the exiguity of our
"Pund Scots", our love of sixpence (which we called saxpence), and
you learnt the word "bawbee."

So far so good; but still you pushed discovery to whisky, haggis,
predestination, and other mysteries of our faith and cookery. The
bagpipes burst upon you (with a skirl), and even Shakespeare set
down things about them which I only do not quote because I do not
wish to make gentlewomen afraid. Then came the road to England,
that we chiefly used, all others in our country being only fit for par-
tridges, but that well-worn and beaten down just like the road to hell.

All this continued more or less the same till George in pudding
time appeared to rule us. Then all things changed, and a new race of
Scotsmen dawned on the English vision. Perhaps not quite unnaturally

---

[56] The Scottish equivalent of a Jewish cantor, a person who leads congregational
a capella singing.

[57] Disbanded Scottish soldiers from 'The War of the Three Kingdoms'
(1644–51), who took to brigandage along the border with England.

[58] The diminutives of 'Alexander', once a common forename among the Scots.

to many Scotsmen of that day a foolish prince of their own kith and kin seemed preferable to a foolish prince from Hanover. Then came the risings in '15 and in '45, and the half of Scotland which the Englishman knew less of then than now he knows about the natives of Arauco came into sight. It appeared that every native of North Britain did not cant or cheat with prayer, and seek to make his fortune. A few half-naked, ill-armed men made England reel, and the measure of the terror that they caused can be appreciated by the savageness of the butcheries after Culloden.

Still, from that time we conquered you and forced you step by step to take us at our Scottish valuation, until to-day it seems that we are about to impose even our language on you.

Progressing step by step, the position of a Scotsman has been altering in England. From mosstrooper and thief we rose by slow degrees to the dignity of impecunious courtiers; then became known as pious business men, ready to cheat and pray on all occasions; but still ridiculous. Our want of wit amazed you, for you did not know we wondered at your lack of humour. So to the days of Walter Scott we bettered our position. Then he rose and threw a glamour over Scotland which was all his own. We then appeared as thread-bare heroes, fighting for our kings, our hills, our haggises, and whatsoever else was dear to us. True, we were poor, but then our poverty was so romantic. Scott though, like all men of genius, saw that not every Scotsman was cut from the same piece; and as a counterfoil to the romantic chief, the pale-faced, slightly-bilious Master, and the Highland soldier, he looked about and found his low comedians, without whose presence all tragedy must halt.

Your Piddlewhinkies and McSneeshins[59] say that Scott was Tory, Jacobite, unpatriotic, unpresbyterian, and other things which pain us to reflect on. They say (your Rev McOffertories) that Scotchmen were not like the types that Scott depicted, and in proof of what they say call on the public to read their valued works. All this, for aught

[59] Pettifoggers, naysayers, and anti-patriots. 'McSneeshins' = 'From the beginning the McSneeshin clan have been the greatest enemy Scotland has known. The Spanish saying runs, "There is no worse thief than the thief in your own house" ("*no hay peor ladron, que el de casa*"). Scotland has suffered bitterly, if not from thieves, at least by traitors in her house. They, one and all, disguise it as they may, were but mere pensioners of England, taking her money quite contentedly, so that, as Murray, Morton, and many other Scottish noblemen, they were allowed to browse upon the spoils of the monasteries, and to preserve their power and their position of pre-eminence inviolate. All were McSneeshins to a man, and anti-patriots, content to do the bidding of a foreign potentate, as long as a full mess of beef and beer supplied the absence of the soul that they hard bartered for it.' Cunninghame Graham, 'McSneeshin', *Scots Independent*, January 1931.

I know, may be quite true; for literature, like other things, is subject to the fashion. Still I maintain that in the Scotland of to-day there yet remain some types which differ from the types set forth by Kailyard novelists. Of course I know that virtue which has long left London and the South still lingers about Ecclefechan.[60] I know a Scotsman is a grave, sententious man, oppressed with the difficulty of the jargon he is bound to speak, and weighed down by the sense of being a North Briton. I know he prays to Mr. Gladstone and Jehovah, time about, finds his amusement in comparing preachers, can read and write, and does so, buys newspapers, tells stories about ministers, and generally deports himself in a manner which would land a weaker man in idiocy within a fortnight.

What I object to is the assumption that the "douce"[61] and Presbyterian, "pawky" three-per-centling of the kailyard men has quite eclipsed the pre-Culloden type. I say it lingers in spite of Butcher Cumberland,[62] in spite of School Board education, kodaks, bicycles, excursion trains, cheap knowledge, magazines, and Liberal politics; it lingers if only to disprove Darwinism. No doubt the average Scotchman is all he is depicted; the land is his, he is the type (and what a type!), he sets his Bethel up,[63] he preaches, psalmodizes, cracks his jokes, invests his money, takes what he thinks an intelligent view of public matters duly distorted for him by the newspaper. Still he is not all the nation after all.

The men who named the hills, the streams, the stones; who hunted, fished, and fought; who seemed to come out of the mist; who followed like dumb, faithful, foolish dogs the foolish Stewarts,[64] and fought against the brutal Hanoverians to their own undoing, have now and then a type, even to-day, which strikes me much as if we came across a ghost. All that still lingers from another age is really what we call a ghost; a ghost perhaps of happier, perhaps freer times, when men were less tormented about nothing than they are to-day. Even in Scotland, I contend, there still exists some few remains of the pre-Knoxian and pre-bawbee days, though fallen into oblivion.

Not far from where I live there lives a worthy man, a Scot of Scots, Scotissimus Scotorum, who has made his money by some kind of

---

[60] Thomas Carlyle's birthplace.
[61] Scots: Respectable.
[62] Prince William Augustus, Duke of Cumberland (1721–65). The third and youngest son of King George II, who commanded the British troops at the Battle of Culloden.
[63] The pillar Jacob set up in honour of God, following a dream of angels (Genesis 28).
[64] Graham is using the original name of those of the Royal House of Stuart, ignoring the French spelling.

sweating;[65] but still a kindly soul, and full of views on everything but trade, which is a thing apart and sacred. A Liberal of course – that is, a Liberal wishing to drag down all men over him – but a Tory of the Tories to all below his own estate; but still a kindly soul. A moral man, if such a one there be, thinking all sins but fornication venial. A teetotaler – that is for others – but himself taking at times his glass of whisky for the reasons which have been so cogently set forth by St. Paul the Apostle of the Caledonians.

My friend lives in a house to which is joined a small estate called Inverquharity. Now, though a Radical, nothing pleased him so much as to be designated territorially as Inverquharity,[66] and to put round the county that he is a sort of cousin to the Marquess of Glenfalloch. These inconsistencies give zest to life, and go some way towards redeeming even North Britain from the awful load of dulness [sic] which the kailyard men depict and seem to revel in. One of the themes the worthy sweater, now turned "bonnet" laird,[67] delights to dwell on is that race has little influence on mankind, and that if you take a Highlander and place him in the same conditions as a kailyard Scot, he straight becomes identical in thought and ways with those around him. The discussion of such questions with such a man is difficult. What the true Scotsman wants is argument, and it angers him as much if you agree with him as if you argue and confute his argument. If you agree, you are a hypocrite; and arguing only shows your narrow-mindedness. Therefore the safest thing is to keep silence. One day he broached the theory that the crofters of the Hebrides were really fond of work, and most industrious, and that their idleness came chiefly from lack of opportunity to work. "See," he remarked, "in Manitoba how they improve when they are far away from landlord tyranny." All landlords in my friend's opinion are tyrants, and though he likes to meet them individually and dine with them, if they have titles, in the bulk they are anathema. Sometimes I fancy he only tolerates myself because I am an idiot at the business. Of course there is no tyranny in trade, and if a strike occurs, why none so loud as he to call for extra police and soldiers; for commerce, as we know, came down from heaven and never can do wrong. However, after a discussion, he asked me if I knew a farm of his, the Offerance[68] of Inverquharity. I knew the place, a little farm, with hideous little house four windows

---

[65] The use of 'sweated labour', i.e., employing those who work long hours for low pay.
[66] Locally, Scottish landowners were named after their estates or farms.
[67] A small landowner.
[68] 'Offrance Farm'. One of five farms containing that name, all owned by Graham himself. *Valuation Roll*, Parish of Drymen, 1895–6.

and a door, with slated roof, and with two spruces ragged with the wind which sweeps over our favoured land, on either side the house. A little garden in which nothing grew but gooseberries and currants, known to the Scotch as "berries." A barn, a byre, and a horse-mill, with its top just like a mushroom, and with four wide openings on purpose to give the horses colds whilst working. And over all that air of dreary desolation which the lack of flowers and care, with the excess of wind and rain, give to a Scottish homestead. Withal not ill appointed; the fields well drained and top-dressed, the fences in repair, the gates well painted, and the whole place made uglier than necessary by the excess of modern improvements.

Though a small place, nothing about the Offerance was done by hand. The crops were tortured into the ground by Yankee sowers, and tortured out again by other artful machines when ready to be reaped. Of course the fences were all wire, and barbed, and no path existed in the fields. For some reason unexplained, the tenant of this earthly paradise was just about to leave it. The worthy owner proceeded to propound his theory about the crofters, and concluded by announcing that he intended to get a crofter family from the Hebrides to take the place.

It seemed to me that if he must have islanders he might as well have brought them from Tahiti as from the Hebrides, but I said nothing. The matter slipped my memory, under the pressure of dressing and undressing, taking railway tickets, missing trains, attending churches, theatres, reading speeches and share lists, talking of art and science with others to the full as ignorant of both as myself, and in the exercise of the futilities during the course of which we find one day our hair is grey, our teeth decaying, and death near at hand.

It happened that when riding to a hill farm I had to pass the Offerance. It seemed a little changed, though certainly inhabited. Before the door a fire of peats was burning, on which a kettle, hung to three birch poles, essayed to boil. Before the fire sat, dressed in rags, two children, searching each others heads[69] as diligently as if they had been scriptures. An air of desolation of a different sort to that I had known before hung o'er the place. The fences were all broken, the ground untilled, and little paths traversed almost every field, where short cuts were made. The gates were off their hinges, and in one instance the want supplied by a broken cart. The stock reminded me of the animals one sees about an Arab's tent or Indian's wigwam. Two skinny ponies, with their feet hobbled with ropes which left the flesh all raw, were feeding on the weeds. Some Highland cattle and

---

[69] Looking for lice and nits.

a goat or two, some sheep, and quite a pack of mangy sheepdogs comprised the lot.

Close to the house a tall, athletic man, half drunk (but not as drunk as to have lost his senses), wrapped in a plaid,[70] and with a mat of rough black hair which fell over his small grey eyes, stood looking at a woman and a girl planting potatoes on what is called the system of the lazy bed. That is, instead of ploughing the ground, you dig it lightly with a spade, turning the turf on one side, then put in the potatoes and rearrange the turf. The plan is excellent for saving trouble, and exhausts the soil as quickly as can be desired. In these degenerate days we seldom get a chance to see it done. "Good heavens!" I thought, "this is a crofter family."

The man looked up, and, seeing me, came to the road, and, after having tried to take my horse's bridle, poured out a flood of Gaelic. I understood but little of it, except that he was glad to see me, and the word "Tighearnas," which he repeated frequently. It means a chief, and is used like "captain" by the gipsies on a racecourse when they want to flatter you. His hat was in his hand, and so he stood, protesting, bareheaded in the drizzling rain. In a mixed jargon composed of broken Gaelic and that sort of idiot English that we use when we cannot make our meaning clear to foreigners, I told him not to be a fool and asked him to put on his hat. He answered "Neffa!"; and, though I found that he could speak English pretty well, he beckoned his wife to come and speak. She said: "Donald is from Wester Ross; he does not like the digging, but Inverquharity is very pleased with him; he puts up such a bonny prayer." This with the singsong accent that Highlanders use when speaking English.

I felt sure he did not like either the digging or the ploughing or any form of work, knowing the species, so I asked if he liked the place, and why he would not put his hat on. "Och aye," he said, "Offerance of Inverquharity is a pretty place, and a pretty name it has whatever." Strange as it may appear, the uncouth syllables sounded quite different when pronounced by him. His wife went on to say that Donald never put his bonnet on before a gentleman; and though he did not like the digging, if I proposed to shoot the coverts[71] at any time I would find Donald was a first-rate beater.

After the semi-sacrament of whisky money had duly passed between us, I rode away amid a shower of what I think were Gaelic blessings.

---

[70] Gaelic: A rectangular length of twilled woollen cloth, sometimes self-coloured, but more often of a chequered or tartan pattern, which was formerly worn as a mantle or outer garment, predominantly in the rural areas of Scotland.

[71] Concealed game birds.

Turning, I saw the Offerance through the rain; black but uncomely, ragged, wind-swept – a picture of the Scotland which has almost disappeared. Sloth was not altogether lovely, but prating progress worse. I might have left the place quite discontented even with mankind, had I not recollected that the world is to the young, and noted that the children's diligence had been rewarded, and that one was handing something to the other with quite an air of triumph.

*****

The second strand, to which Graham objected, was that the Kailyard authors had depicted only a small fringe of the population and reduced those they represented to sad stereotypes that their English neighbours were all too ready to accept, an offence against Graham's wish to see the Scot depicted as hero, albeit that these heroes now seem confined to the past. Stereotypes serve the interest of power, and the inward-looking, parochial, narrow, bucolic passivity of the Kailyard writers' depictions, in Graham's anti-capitalist and home-rule agenda, would have suited the unitary state's agenda very well. Thus, the next sketch, 'Salvagia' (1896), ironically lampooned how the Scots had been depicted. Any piety and respectability in Scottish rural life was false, a hypocritical veneer which many contemporary readers would have instantly recognised. This was a graceless, vulgar kailyard, neither dystopian nor lapsarian, but an exaggerated, satirical attempt at social realism, in a location that he knew well. It is a parody of a 'Kailyard' setting, a stony place, full of stony people, sterile, unmerciful; a place of Holy Willies, where the residents showed little or no emotion, and any gentler qualities were well concealed.

This work was a very deliberate counter-blast against what Graham believed was emasculating and debasing Scotland into a cosy parochial backwater, but there is something else at work. G. K. Chesterton observed in Robert Louis Stevenson's Scottish stories that Stevenson, like many Scots, was proud of the extremities of Scottish landscape, character, and history, which others might have found harsh and cruel:

> Indeed, stories of this kind are told by Stevenson with a deliberate darkening of the Scottish landscape and exultation in the ferocity of the Scottish creed. But it would be quite a mistake to miss in this a certain genuine national pride running through all the abnormal artistry; and a sense that the strength of the tribal tragedy testifies in a manner to the strength of the tribe.[72]

---

[72] G. K. Chesterton, *Robert Louis Stevenson* (London: Hodder & Stoughton, 1927), p. 125. In 1900, a reviewer of Graham's *Thirteen Stories*, wrote, 'Take

This underlying 'anti rational primitivism' in Graham's depictions is a device that is meant to shock, or at least discomfit the reader, to inject a note of harsh reality, to deliberately de-romanticise Scottish rural life, but with much of his work, there is also a strong underlying pathos.

SALVAGIA

The Saturday Review, 12 September 1896, pp. 279–80.
Anthologised in *The Ipané* (London: Fisher Unwin, 1899), pp. 130–40.

ALMOST the most horrible doctrine ever enunciated by theologians is, in my opinion, the attribution of our misfortunes to Providence. An all-wise power, all merciful and omnipresent, enthroned somewhere in omnipotence, having power over man and beast, over earth and sky, on sea and land, able (if usually unwilling) to suspend all natural laws, seated above the firmament of heaven, beholding both the evil and the good – discerning, we may suppose, the former without much difficulty, and the latter by the aid of some spectroscope at present not revealed to men of science – sees two trains approaching on one line, and yet does nothing to avert the catastrophe or save the victims. Withal, nothing consoles humanity for their misfortunes like the presence of this unseen power, which might do so much good, but which serenely contemplates so many evils.

I have often thought that, after all, there is but one idea at the bottom of faiths, and that, no matter if the divinity is called Jehovah, Allah, Moloch, Dagon,[73] or the Neo-Pauline Providence of the North Britons, the worshippers seem to esteem their deity in proportion as he disregards their welfare.

Some have maintained that the one common ground of all the sects was in the offertory;[74] but most recent reflection has convinced me that the impassibility of Providence provides a spiritual, if unconscious, nexus which unites in one common bond Jews, Christians (whether Coptic, Abyssinian, Greek, or Roman), Mohammedans, Buddhists, the Church of England with that of Scotland, and the multitudinous

---

Robert Louis Stevenson's love of the sun and the open air, his quick eye for the picturesque, his love of adventure, and his preference for the gentleman savage over the civilised cad; and substitute for Stevenson's gallant optimism Thomas Carlyle's fierce dogmatic temper and his hopeless fight against cant – and you have something of Mr. Graham's literary personality.' *Pall Mall Gazette*, 26 October 1900, p. 4.
[73] Gods of the Canaanites and Mesopotamians.
[74] Collection money.

sects of Nonconformists, who, scattered over two hemispheres, yet hate one another with enough intensity to enable mankind to perceive that they have comprehended to the full the doctrines of the New Testament.

It may be that the knowledge that the aforesaid Moloch is reputed to have endowed mankind with free will to work out their own salvation consoles some people for his neglect to exercise the power he is supposed to have of preventing suffering altogether. This leads a man somewhat deeper that it is expedient for him to show that he is going. If omnipotent, how then bound by natural laws, and if bound by any laws, wherein the common sense of abrogating them for individuals?

I know a little village in the country, generally described in old Italian maps under the title of "Salvagia,"[75] where the providential scheme is held in its entirety. Nothing, at first sight, proclaims the fact why a great power should specially concern itself about the village. Still, is it not the case that, as a rule, blear-eyed, knock-kneed young men imagine that they touch the heart of every woman who pities their infirmities? Do not red-haired and freckled, cow-houghed maidens usually attend a fancy ball attired as Mary Queen of Scots, and think their fatal beauty deals destruction on the sons of men, unconscious that their lack of charm preserves them safe from those temptations by means of which alone virtue can manifest itself? That which holds good of individuals often applies to people in the bulk. So of my village in Salvagia. A straggling street, looking upon a moor, bordered by slated living boxes, each with its "jaw-box"[76] at the door and midden at the back, its ugly strip of garden without flowers, in which grew currants, gooseberries, with nettles, docks, potatoes, and other fruits known to the tender North.

In every house is a picture of Dr. Chalmers[77] flanked by one of Bunyan, and a Bible ever ready on the table for advertisement, as when a minister or charitable lady calls, and the cry is heard of "Jeanie, rax the Bible doon, and pit the whisky bottle in the aumrie."[78] Two churches and two public-houses, and feud between the congregations of each church as bitter as that between the clients of the rival taverns.

---

[75] Something left over, at the edge = Scotland.

[76] Scots: A kitchen sink, or drainage facility.

[77] Thomas Chalmers FRSE (1780–1847), was a Scottish minister, professor of theology, political economist, a leader of the Church of Scotland, and first Moderator of the Free Church of Scotland.

[78] "Jeanie, reach me down the Bible, and put the whisky bottle in the medicine cabinet." This sentence may have been a deliberate subversion of Robert Burns's graciously pious domestic scene in his poem *The Cotter's Saturday Night*, in which 'Jenny' is the daughter of the house.

No whisky or no doctrine from the opposing tavern or conventicle[79] could possibly be sound. No trees, no flowers, no industry, except the one of keeping idiots sent from Glasgow, and known to the people as the "silly bodies." Much faith and little charity, the tongue of every man wagging against his neighbour like a bell-buoy on a shoal. At the street corner groups of men standing spitting. Expectoration is a national sport throughout Salvagia. Women and children are afraid to pass them. Not quite civilized, not quite savage, a set of demi-brutes exclaiming, if a woman in a decent gown goes past, "There goes a butch."

A school, of course, wherein the necessary means of getting on in life is taught. O education, how a people may be rendered brutish in thy name! Behold Salvagia! In every town, in every hamlet, even in the crofting communities upon the coast, where women till the fields and men stand idle prating of natural rights, the poorest man can read and write, knows history and geography, arithmetic up to the Rule of Three – in fact, sufficiently to overreach his neighbour.

Still, in the social scale of human intercourse the bovine dweller in East Anglia is a prince compared to him. How the heart shrinks, in travelling from London, when, the Border passed, the Scottish porter with a howl sticks his head into the carriage and bellows "Tackets – are ye gaeing North?" No doubt the man is better educated than his southern colleague, but as you see him once, and have to time to learn his inward grace, his lack of outward polish jars upon you. After the porter comes the group of aged men at Lockerbie, all seated in the rain, precisely as their forbears sat when Carlyle lived in Craigenputtock.[80] Then come barefoot boys selling the "Daily Mail," the "Herald," and "Review," till Glasgow in its horror and its gloom receives you, and you lose all hope.

Throughout Salvagia "Thank you" and "If you please" are terms unknown. In railway trains we spit upon the floor and wipe our boots on the cushions, just to show our independence; in cars and omnibuses take the best seats, driving the weaker to the wall, like cattle in a pen. In streets we push women into the gutters, "It's only just a woman" being our excuse. Our hearts we wear so distant from our sleeves that the rough frieze of which our coats are made abrades the cuticle of every one it touches. Our reverend novelists, 'tis true, have found out much about us, previously quite unsuspected by ourselves; but then their works are not for home consumption, but sell in England and America, where, I understand, they touch the cords of the Great National Heart, and loose the strings of the Great National Pocket.

---

[79] A secret religious meeting often held outdoors.
[80] The matrimonial home of Thomas Carlyle, near Dumfries.

Back to our village – "Gart-na-cloich," I think the name,[81] meaning the enclosure of the stones. Stony indeed the country, stony the folks, the language, manners, and all else pertaining to it. Even the Parameras[82] outside Avila, where every boulder is a tear that Jesus wept, is not more sterile. Not that Jesus had ever aught to do with Gart-na-cloich. The deity worshipped there is Dagon, or some superfetated[83] Moloch born in Geneva.[84]

In no Salvagian village is there any room for a gentle God, a God of love and pity. "Nane of your Peters; gie me Paul," is constantly in everybody's mouth, for every dweller in Salvagia is a theologian. Faith is our touchstone, and good works are generally damned throughout the land as savouring of Erastianism.[85] Only believe, that is sufficient. "Show me your moral man," exclaims the preacher, "and I will straight demolish him"; the congregation nod assent, being well convinced "your moral man" is not a denizen of Gart-na-cloich, or, if he was, that the profession of a "cold morality" on earth must lead to everlasting fire, in the only other world they hear of from the pulpit.

Our sexual immorality, and the high rate of illegitimacy, we explain as follows. Who would buy a barren cow or mare? Therefore, we cannot buy our wives or sell them, if they prove unprofitable, 'tis well to try them in advance, and as our law follows the Pandects of Justinian,[86] being more merciful to those who come into a hard world through no fault of their own than that of England, the matter is put right after a year or so, and all are pleased. That which a thing is worth is what it brings we teach our children from the earliest days; we inculcate it in our schools, at mart and fair, in church, at bed and board, and that accounts for the hide-bound view we take of everything.

Anger and love move us not much: we seldom come to blows after the fashion of the people in the mysterious region that we call "up about England." A stand-up fight with knock-down blows is not our way, not for the lack of courage but from excess of caution and the knowledge that we have intuitively that calumny kills further off than blows. How we get married is a mystery I have never solved, for no Salvagian ever seems heartily to wish for anything, or, if he does, is far too cautious to make his wishes known. Perhaps that is the reason why the Germans drive us out from business as easily

---

[81] A thinly disguised Gartmore.
[82] A mountain range in the province of Ávila, Spain.
[83] To conceive when a foetus is already present in the uterus.
[84] John Calvin (1509–64). Graham had a particular distaste for Calvinism.
[85] The doctrine that the state is superior to the church in ecclesiastical matters.
[86] The digest of writings on Roman law compiled by order of the Eastern Roman emperor Justinian I in the sixth century.

as the Norwegian rat expels the original black rat, or the European extirpates the natives of Australia.

Withal, we have our qualities, but well concealed, and only to be found after a residence of fifty years amongst us. In spite of kail-yard tales, we really snivel little, and cant not much more than our neighbours; and we have humour, though the kail-yarders record it not, for fear of troubling the Great Heart which only likes "a joke," and is impervious either to wit or humour. Sometimes we have a touch of pathos in our composition which startles, coming as it does from unexpected sources.

In Gart-na-cloich there dwelt one Mistress Campbell, a widow and the mother of four sons, all what we call "weel-doing" lads – that is, not given to drink, good workers, attenders at the church, and not of those who pass their "Sawbath" lounging about and spitting as they criticize mankind.

Going to church with us replaces charity – that is, it covers an infinity of things. A man may cheat and drink, be cruel to animals, avaricious, anything you please so that he goes to church; he still remains a Christian and enters heaven by faith alone. Our faith we take from "Paul," our doctrine from Hippo,[87] so that we need do nought but bow the knee to our own virtues, secure in our salvation.

No one could say that Mistress Campbell's cottage was neat or picturesque. No roses climbed the walls, nor did the honeysuckle twine around the eaves. For flowers a ragged mullein growing in a wall, a plant of rue, one of "old man," with chamomile and gillyflowers, did duty. Apple and damson trees round the "toon," the fruit of which was as bitter as a sloe. Beside the door the cheesestone with its iron ring, a "stoup" for water shaped like a barrel, a "feal" spade,[88] and a rusty sickle lying in the mud, gave promise of the interior graces of the house.

Inside the acrid smell of peat, with rancid butter, and the national smell of whisky spilt and left to dry, assailed the nostrils.

All round the kitchen stood press beds[89] in which the children slept. Before the fire grey woolen stockings dried whilst scones were baking, and underneath the table lay a collie dog or two snapping at flies.

The inner room had the peculiar musty smell of rooms which only serve for great occasions. Upon the walls a picture of Jerusalem set forth in a kind of uphill view, balanced by a sampler which may have been the Ten Commandments, the Maze of Hampton Court, the Fountains of Versailles, or almost anything you chose, according to

---

[87] St Augustine of Hippo (354–430).
[88] Scots: An implement for cutting turf or peat.
[89] Beds in an alcove.

the point of vision. Not tidy or convenient was the house, but still a home of the peculiar kind that race and climate made acceptable to the dwellers in it.

The widow's faith was great, her household linen clean, and her chief pride, after her sons, was centred in her cows, called in Salvagia "kye." She liked to sit in church and fall asleep, as pious people do during the sermon. Seated between her sons, her Bible in a handkerchief scented with lavender, she had the faith not merely able to move mountains, but with her Bible for a lever, had she but got a fulcrum, to move the world itself. She knew her church was right, the others wrong, and that sufficed her; and, for the rest, she did her duty to her sons and cows and to her neighbours.

Years passed by, the world wagged pretty much as usual in Gart-na-cloich; sometimes a neighbour died, and we enjoyed his funeral in the way we love with whisky, whilst we listened in the house of woe to the set phrases of the minister which use has constituted a sort of liturgy.

Winter succeeded summer, and day night, without a thing to break the dreary life we think the best of lives because we know no other.

Years sat lightly upon Mistress Campbell; for she had attained the time of life when countrywomen in Salvagia seem to mummify and time does nothing on them. Her sons grew up, her cows continued to give milk, the rent was paid in season. Nothing disturbed her life, and folk began almost to murmur against Providence for his neglect to visit her.

Then came a season with the short fierce spell of heat which goes before thunderstorm, and constitutes our summer. In every burn the children paddled, and in Glasgow honest burgesses went for their yearly wash to the region which they know as "doon the watter."[90]

A little river, in which before the days of knowledge kelpies[91] were wont to live, flows past the village.

Its glory is a pool (we call it linn) known as the Linn-a-Hamish. Here the pool below the stream spreads out and babbles over stones mostly worn flat by the action of the stream, as proverbs are worn smooth in the current of men's speech. The boys delight to throw these flat stones edgeways in the air, to hear the curious muffled sound they make when falling in the water, which they call a "dead man's bell." Alders fringe the bank, and in the middle of the pool a little grassy promontory juts out, on which cows stand swinging their tails, and meditate, to at least as good a purpose as philosophers. The linn lies dark and sullen, and a line of bubbles rising to the top

---

[90] The annual excursion to Clyde Coast holiday resorts.
[91] Mythical water horses.

shows where the current runs below the surface. In a lagoon a pike has basked for the last thirty years. In our mythology, one Hamish met his death in the dark water, but why or wherefore is uncertain. Tradition says that the place is dangerous, and the country people count it a daring feat to swim across.

There the four sons of Mistress Campbell went to bathe, and all were drowned. Passing the village, I heard the Celtic Coronach,[92] which lingers to show us how our savage ancestors [sic] wailed for their dead, and to remind us that the step which separates us from other animals is short. I asked a woman for whom the cry was raised. She answered, "For the four sons of Lilias Campbell." In the stupid way one asks a question in the face of any shock, I said, "What did she say or do when they were brought home dead?"

"Say?" said the woman; "nothing; n'er a word. She just gaed out and milked the kye."

* * * * *

The next sketch is the most remarkable of these three so-called 'bitter portrayals'. In 'Heather Jock',[93] Graham took his de-stereotyping to its logical, squalid conclusion, by injecting an outlandish reality and diversity into the Scottish character. It is also the quintessential Graham, flitting as it does between Scotland and Argentina, regretting the loss of another unique part of Scottish individuality, juxtaposed by the sometimes brutal realities of frontier life. However, the veracity of the final part of the sketch is in doubt, since this particular 'Heather Jock' had died in 1885, and Graham, having latterly dwelt in Texas, Spain and England, had permanently returned to Scotland in 1883, following the death of his father.

Graham's editor, Garnett, had advised him to omit the opening paragraphs, prior to republication in his 1899 anthology The Ipané, but Graham protested that it was impossible because, 'I am an essayist and an impressionist, and secondly a story teller but have the story telling faculty very weakly. Therefore if you cut out my reflections, nothing remains.'[94]

William Brodie, who was born in Paisley, started his working life as a weaver, and moved to Bridge of Weir, but finding it difficult to get paid work, he began travelling around southern Scotland singing his peculiar off-key songs at fairs to entertain children, wearing a

---

[92] Gaelic: A lament for the dead, a dirge, either sung, or played on the bagpipes.
[93] A soubriquet applied to several eccentric characters throughout Scotland.
[94] Cunninghame Graham to Edward Garnett, 6 August 1898, University of Texas.

bejewelled feathered headdress, and carrying a four-foot-long caduceus,[95] complete with bells. He did this for twenty-two years, until 1864, when he took to hawking small items such as boot laces and blacking door to door, by which means he kept himself and his wife from destitution.

Figure 3 William Brodie, 'Heather Jock'.

"HEATHER JOCK"

The Saturday Review, 30 January 1897, pp. 110–12.
Anthologised in *The Ipané* (London: Fisher Unwin, 1899), pp. 120–9.

---

[95] An ancient Greek or Roman herald's wand, typically one with two serpents twined round it, carried by the messenger-god Hermes or Mercury. It is frequently used as a symbol for medicine or a pharmacy.

"OÙ sont les chevaliers de jadis?"[96] Education is a cruel and falla-cious, though no doubt necessary, process. "Give me but polish," says the pebble, "and I should be even as is a diamond." But the pebble polished is still a pebble, and the diamond still sparkles in a higher planet.

To differ from the crowd, whether as a genius, an idiot, an inven-tor, or simply have a differently shaped beard from other men, will shortly be a crime. At present, out of pure philanthropy for our-selves, we seclude our madmen in prisons euphemistically called lunatic asylums. In the East the madman still walks the streets, as free as any other man, and gives his judgment on things he does not understand, like any other citizen. True, in the East there generally is the sun, and every evil with the sun is less.

There is no sun in Scotland, but not so long ago our semi-mad-men and our idiots philosophized about the world, taking the bitter and the sweet of life in public, just like the rest of us. The custom had its inconveniences; but, on the other hand, perhaps, was just as merciful as that which to-day shuts up every harmless, foolish creature within four walls to save the sane the pain of seeing them.

The wandering semi-madman was a feature in Scotch life. In ancient times he filled, to some degree, the function of a newspaper, retailing news distorted to the taste of those he catered for, after the fashion of the modern editor. Again, he was a sort of block on which men tried their wits, not always coming off the victor in the trial.

What reasons influenced William Brodie, bred a weaver at Bridge of Weir, in Renfrewshire, to first turn pedlar, or, as we say (Scoticé), "travelling merchant," and from that to transmigrate himself into a wandering singer and buffoon under the name of Heather Jock, are quite unknown. The status of the Scotch Autolycus[97] has no doubt charms. We do not look on pedlars with the disdain with which in England the trading class is viewed. Rather, we honour them for the use we have of them, knowing the Lord created them for some wise purpose of his own not yet made plain. Hucksters and merchants both are prone to sin, and as a nail sticks fast between the joinings of the stones, so sin sticks close between selling and buying: at least so Jesus son of Sirach[98] tells us, and though not canonical himself, his works are much esteemed in Scotland for their "pawkiness." But,

---

[96] French: "Where are the knights of yesteryear?" Graham's adaptation of a fif-teenth-century French poem, *Ballade des Dames du Temps Jadis* by François Villon.

[97] A cunning, shape-changing Greek mythological character.

[98] Joshua ben Sirach, a Jewish scribe who wrote The *Wisdom of Sirach*, also known as the *Book of Ecclesiasticus*, c. 200–175 bce.

being practical, we see as little honour in haggling for thousands as for halfpennies, and call men "merchants" whether they carry packs upon their backs or send out ships freighted with shoddy goods to sell to niggers.[99]

So no one asked his reasons, but accepted him just as he was, his headdress like an Inca of Peru stuck all about with pheasants' and peacocks' feathers, bits of looking-glass, adorned with heather, and fastened underneath his jaws with a black ribbon; with moleskin waistcoat; bee in his bonnet; humour in his brain; with short plaid trousers, duffel coat, and in his hand a crude Caduceus made of a hazel stick, in the centre a flat tin heart, set around with jingling bells, and terminating in a tuft of heather. In figure not unlike a stunted oak of the kind depicted in the arms of Glasgow, or such as those which grow in Cadzow Forest, and under which the white wild cattle feed, as they have done since Malcolm Fleeming slew one with his spear and saved the King.

The minstrel's features of the Western Scottish type, hard as flint, yet kindly, his eyes like dullish marbles made of glass, such as the children of Bridge of Weir call "bools," his hair like wire, his mouth worn open and his nose merely a trap for snuff. Hands out of all proportion large, and feet like planks, his knees inclining to be what the Scotch call "schauchlin,"[100] and imparting to his walk that skipping action which age sometimes bestows on those who in their youth have passed a sedentary life. A true *faux bossu*,[101] though without a hump, having acquired the carriage of a hunchback by diligence, or sloth. In fact, he seemed a sort of cross between a low-class Indian, such as one sees about a town in South Dakota, and an orang-outang which had somehow got itself baptized.

From Kilmalcolm, to Mauchline, from Dalry to Ayr, at a Kilwinning Papingo,[102] at races, meets, fairs, trysts, at country house or moorland farm, to each and all he wandered and was welcome.

His minstrelsy, if I remember right, was not extensive as to repertory, being comprised but in one dreary song about a certain "Annie Laurie," originally of a sentimental cast, but which he sang with humoursome effects of face, at breakneck speed, jangling his bells and jumping about from side to side just like a Texan cowboy in Sherman, Dallas, or some Pan Handle town during the process of a bar-room

---

[99] Graham is using this word in ironic mockery of racial attitudes, as in his anti-imperialist and anti-racist diatribes. See '"Bloody Niggers!"', *Social Democrat*, April 1897.

[100] Scots: Shambling.

[101] French: A fake hunchback.

[102] An ancient annual archery competition aimed at dislodging a wooden pigeon from Kilwinning Abbey tower, known locally as 'dinging doon the doo'.

fight, to dodge the bullets. At the end he signified his wish to lay him down to die for the object of his song, and did so, elevating, after the fashion of expiring folk, his feet into the air and waggling to and fro his boots adorned with what the Scotch call "tackets."[103]

Perhaps it was the dispiriting nature of the performance which drew sympathy from those men whose lives were uninspiring. They might have thought a livelier buffoon untrue to nature from his unlikeliness to themselves. What he had seen during his wandering life he treasured up, relating it, on invitation, to his hearers in the same way an Arab or a Spaniard quotes a proverb as if it was a personal experience of his own. Once in his youth "west of Dalry" he chanced to see a panorama of the chief incidents of Scottish history. What specially attracted his attention (so he said) was when the lecturer enlarged upon the fate of Rizzio:[104] "Man, he just depicted it so graphically ye fancied ye could hear the head gae dunt, dunt, dunting, as they pulled the body doon the stairs."

Our northern wit runs ghastly and dwells on funerals; on men at drinking parties, dead but quite the gentleman still sitting at the table;[105] sometimes on people drunk in churchyards; but always alternating, according to the fancy of the humourist, from one to the other of staple subjects for jesting, whisky, or death. But Heather Jock, like other memories of youth faded away, and the constant spectacle of much superior buffoonery in parliaments, in marts, at scientific lectures, literary clubs, and other walks of life, bore in upon me that all the world is but a pantomime, badly put on the stage by an incompetent stage manager, ourselves the mummers, and each man, according to the estimation he is held in by his fellows, the pantaloon.

One day in Tucuman,[106] amongst the orange gardens, mounting my horse, which for my personal safety I had to do with a bandage over his eyes and a foot tied to the girth, and thinking that the business of my life, which then consisted chiefly in going out by break of day to round my cattle up (*parar rodeo*, as the gauchos say), was not inferior after all to that passed in a European office – where men begin at twenty to enter nothings in a ledger, and old age creeps on them finding them bald-headed at the same task – I chanced to get some letters.

---

[103] Scots: Studs on the shoe sole.
[104] David Rizzio (1533–66). Italian private secretary and close confidant of Mary Queen of Scots, murdered in front of the Queen on the orders of her husband, Lord Darnley.
[105] See passim, 'Beattock For Moffat', below.
[106] A province in north-west Argentina.

The messenger who brought them, slowly got off his horse; his iron spurs, like fetters on his naked feet, clanked on the bricks on the verandah; he seemed perturbed – that is, as much perturbed as it is possible to be upon the frontiers – his hat was gone, around his head he wore a handkerchief which had been white when it left Manchester some years ago, his horse was blown and wounded, but still he stood impassively handing me a letter bag and asking after the condition of my health with some minuteness. Was he tired? "No, Señor, not over-tired." Would he take a drink? "Yes, to the health of all good Christians." Where was his brother who used to ride with him? "Dead, patroncito,[107] and I hope in Glory, for he died like a Christian, killed at the crossing of the Guaviyú by the infidel who came on us as we were crossing, with the water in our saddle skirts." This with a smile to make the unpleasant news more palatable in the delivery. Christian, I may explain, upon those frontiers is rather a racial than a religious status. All white men are *ex officio* Christians, with the possible exception of the English, who, as they listen to their mass mumbled in English, not in Latin, are less authentic. However, said the Gaucho (always with permission) he would saddle a fresh horse and with some friends go out and fetch the body.

Whilst he caught a horse – a lengthy operation when the horses have to be driven first to a corral and then caught with a lazo – I took the bag, with the feeling, firstly, that it had cost a man his life, and then with the instinctive dread which, when in distant lands, always attends home news, that some one would be dead or married, or that at least the trusted family solicitor had made off with the money entrusted to him for investment.

Nothing of this in the letters, only, as per usual in such cases, accounts of deaths and marriages of folk I did not know, of fortunes come to those I most disliked, and other matter of the regulation kind with which people at home are apt to stuff their letters to their distant friends.

One of the letters had a scrap of newspaper inside it, with the announcement of the death of Heather Jock. "At Bridge of Weir upon the 13th instant, William Brodie, at the age of eighty-two, known through the West of Scotland to all as Heather Jock."

So Heather Jock would strive no more with life, with people just as foolish if more wicked than himself, struggle no more against the difficulties of English concert pitch, and be with "Annie Laurie" and the other puny dead who erstwhile followed his profession. Then I remembered where I saw him last: at an old house in Scotland

---

[107] Spanish: Boss.

perched on a rock above the Clyde[108] and set about with trees, the avenue winding about through the woods and crossing a little stream on bridges made the most of by a landscape-gardener's art. I saw the yew trees under which John Knox is said to have preached and dealt with heresy and superstition, like the man he was, driving out the kindly Paganism which is so mingled with the Catholic faith, and planting in its stead the stern, hard, hyper-Caledonian faith which bows the knee before its God in a temple like a barn, and looks upon the miserable east end of Glasgow as a thing ordained by God. The tulip tree, the yellow chestnut, and the laurels tall as houses, all came back to me, the little garden with its curious stone vases and tall hollyhocks. I saw the river with its steamers always passing between the fairway marks, saw Dumbarton Castle on its rock and wondered how it could have been the seat of Arthur's Court as wise men tell us. Then it came back to me that one day upon the sands I found the outside covering of a cocoanut and launched it on the Clyde just opposite to where the roofless house of Ardoch[109] stood, and watched it vanish into nothing, after the fashion of an Irish peasant woman on the quay at Cork watching the vessel take her son away, and just as sure as she of the return.

Then it occurred to me that Heather Jock had been a different character from what he really was, and that there had been something noble and adventurous in his career. That he had, somehow, fought against convention, and preferred, after the fashion of Sir Thopas, to "liggen in his hood,"[110] and go about the world a living protest against the folly of humanity. But, God pardon me, for that was exegesis[111] lies, with finding out of hidden and mysterious esoteric motives for common actions, after the fashion which would astonish many, who, if they came to life again, would find those worshiping who, in life, were their most bitter enemies.

Nothing of moment was in the other letters, and when the neighbours mustered, armed with spears and rusty guns, lazo and bolas, but each man mounted on a first-rate horse and leading another to run away upon in case of danger, I mounted a "picazo,"[112] which I kept for such occasions, knowing he was a horse "fit for God's saddle," and taking his rifle with me unloaded, not for superior daring, but because I had no cartridges.

---

[108] Finlaystone, formerly seat of the Earls of Glencairn, and Graham's childhood home (1852–63). Now the seat of MacMillan of that Ilk.

[109] Graham's Scottish home from 1903 until his death.

[110] Lie in his cloak/sleep rough. From Geoffrey Chaucer's 'The Rime of Sire Thopas'.

[111] The critical interpretation of a religious text.

[112] A black horse with a white face.

Just at the crossing of the Guaviyú, close to a clump of "Espinillo de Olor,"[113] we found the body, cut and hacked about so as to be almost unrecognizable, but holding in the hand a tuft of long black hair, coarse as a horse's tail, showing the dead man had behaved himself up to the last like a true Christian.

At the fandango after the funeral, during the hot night, and whilst the fireflies flickered amongst the feathery tacuaras,[114] and lit the metallic leaves of the orange-trees occasionally with their faint bluish light, above the scraping of the cracked guitar, above the voices of the dancers when they broke from the chorus of the "Gato,"[115] above the neighing of the horses shut in the corral for fear of Indians, I seemed to hear the jangling of the dead fool's bells, and listened to the minstrelsy, such as it was, of the hegemonist of Bridge of Weir.

*****

Neil Munro believed that Graham had not taken his views on Scotland from real life, 'but from bookish conventions', describing his own outdated stereotypes – the Celt who is always admirable: 'touched with old-time graces and courtesies', and the Lowlander: 'a religious bigot, prone to ardent waters', which Munro believed had not existed in Scotland for generations.[116] Professor Walker pointed out:

> Nationalists of the 1930s [...] have tended to forget that in the early stages of his career [...] Graham had treated with a vitriolic realism the defects of the Scottish character and the abuses and vices of the national way of life.[117]

Stephen Graham fell into line with this view, when he wrote:

> For him, reality is Scotland; romance is South America. He is a bitter, sarcastic, even cynical, intellectual Scot, tearing and rending his own country when he thinks of it – but suddenly melted and sentimentalised by Spain. He writes of a decidedly real Scotland, but of an unreal, unearthly, romanticised, golden Spain. It is even touching, he cannot be critical of the Latin.[118]

---

[113] A species of flowering tree.

[114] A species of bamboo.

[115] Argentinian music and dance.

[116] Neil Munro, *The Looker-On* (Edinburgh: Porpoise Press, 1933), p. 305.

[117] John Walker, 'Cunninghame Graham and the Critics', *Studies in Scottish Literature* 19 (1984): p. 113.

[118] Stephen Graham, *The Death of Yesterday* (London: Ernest Benn, 1930), pp. 39–40.

This, however, could be interpreted quite differently. Graham's 'reality' (of which 'Salvagia' is the best example) demonstrated his gift for parody, an exaggerated reality of Scotland *now*, while his reality of South America and Spain, was, by necessity, *then*, and distance, in Graham's imagination, always lent enchantment. When in his future works, Scotland was remembered *then*, his tone is entirely different, and if it is not exactly 'golden', it has a benign and misty, ethereal quality, appropriate to its climate. Also, the only sketches that demonstrated this 'vitriolic realism' were the three above, written at the height of Kailyard popularity, and neither Munro, (Stephen) Graham nor Walker appreciated that in these three sketches, Graham was undoubtedly parodying, or exaggerating for political effect. Graham, however, would continue to pursue the anti-stereotype agenda in his subsequent Scottish sketches and portraits, albeit in a less overtly polemical way.

*****

Professor Walker omitted the following two sketches, perhaps because he did not consider them 'Scottish' enough. They tell of Graham's experiences aboard a ship which took him from New York to Scotland, then to Argentina, with a brief stop-over in Glasgow. They are a wonderful evocation of the rigours of voyages in less than seaworthy ships, and the hardships endured by passengers and crew alike, ending in a riotous festivity. They are also another swipe at the stereotypical respectable Scot, replaced by an altogether less savoury stereotype.

"S. S. ATLAS", Part I

The Saturday Review, 14 May 1898, pp. 652–3.
Anthologised in *The Ipané* (London: Fisher Unwin, 1899), pp. 68–76.

IT was a filthy autumn day in New York, with Fifth Avenue looking more than usually vulgar under the leaden sky, and the streets carpeted with rotting plane leaves, as I drove, jolting over the rough cobble stone, to a wharf near Dubrosses Ferry to go on board the "Atlas." The "s.s. Atlas" was a type of ship well known in the seventies, but more obsolete. In those days the "tramp" had scarcely made its appearance, and the liner was less frequent and less gorgeous than at present.

Vessels long, iron-built, flat sided, and coffin-like, of the "Atlas" type held an intermediate position. They looked for cargo where it might be reasonably expected, and took passengers to whom a long passage, rough food and poor accommodation were rendered indifferent through lack of means. The American agent had informed me that the fare from New York to Glasgow was £10, and that the vessel was a Scotch boat, in which I should find a Bible and whisky, and might expect to be in Glasgow in twelve days, if (so the agent said) the Lord was willing and the Scotsmen did not over-drink themselves. I had no deck-chair, the decks were an inch deep in coal dust, and the vessel went to sea at once. Leaving Sandy Hook we encountered the full force of a north-easterly gale, and I (the only passenger) retired at once to my athwartship bunk, to be miserable and endeavour to read the "Faerie Queene," my only book, and the only book aboard except the Bible and a bound-up volume of the "Reaper"[119] and some professional works. For weeks, as it appeared to me, "Burry Banes," rattle of ropes, racing of screw, banging of my portmanteau as it washed to and fro in a foot of water in the cabin, groaning of timbers, roaring of the wind, bellowing of the Blatant Beast[120] (in the "Faerie Queene"), shouting at the boatswain, pattering of naked feet upon the deck, then a fitful dozing, broken but by the rare visits of the steward with a "cup of arrowroot and whisky, sir," to tell me everything was battened down, and that the skipper had been sixteen hours on the bridge and looked like Lot's wife when she enjoyed her last wistful glance at Sodom.[121] Air stifling, lamp smoking, drops of moisture on every plank, a continuous dropping of water on to my pillow, rats running across the floor, a dense, steamy feeling which made one sleepy, crumbs of biscuits in the bedclothes, a futile tin basin floating in the cabin, a brandy bottle propped between a Bible and a sponge in the fixed washing-stand, guttering candles swung in gimbles, decks which seemed to rise and hit one in the face when staggering out in the rare intervals of the storm to see yards of bulwarks swept away, feeling ones ways between the seas, clutching a life-line to the engine-room to listen to the yarns of the chief engineer, a Greenock Ananias[122] of the first water, and bushy bearded as befitted one who had "gone out in '47,[123] second engineer aboard the craft what took out Rajah Brook."[124] Then back to bed, wet through, and back into a trance between waking and sleep, more brandy, arrowroot, more "Faerie Queene," more stifling, and the vessel labouring

---

[119] *The Reaper: The Organ of the Ayrshire Christian Union.* Published in Ardrossan, 1882–1908.

[120] A slanderous monster who defames aristocratic characters.

[121] Genesis 19. Turned to a pillar of salt.

[122] A liar.

[123] Took up gold prospecting in California in 1847.

[124] Sir James Brooke (1803–68), Rajah of Sarawak. A British soldier and adventurer who founded the kingdom of Sarawak in Borneo.

so heavily that when the copper cargo shipped at Copiano shifted on the fifth day out, it seemed that she lay almost upon her broadside in the sea. And still I liked the voyage, and even took pride in knowing we had sighted Rockall,[125] hoped in my heart of hearts we should sight Iceland, and yet was miserably seasick all day long, and all night long lay half awake, meditating on the adventures of Sir Satyrane, of Britomart, Parlante, and the Faire Florimell, and all the other characters of Spenser's masterpiece, who in some curious way seemed to become connected with the ship.

After the seventh day no cooking, galley fire put out and steward staggering in drunk, with a Bible in his hand, white-faced and frightened, "rubber" sea boots on, and a plate of cold salt horse and biscuit, and, of course, more whisky; fitfully came the strains of "Renzo"[126] as the crew set the fore topmast staysail, and in my berth I learned how "Reuben Renzo" shipped aboard a whaler, "Renzo, boys, Renzo," heard his adventures, cruel treatment by the mate, and was most interested to find that for a change his virtue was rewarded at last, and at the present time "he was the skipper of a sugar droger."[127] Weeks seemed to pass, and on a day the Captain, clad in dripping oilskins, looking in for a moment with a speaking trumpet in his hand, deigned to impart the information that we had a slant wind, and though the smoke stack had fetched loose, he reckoned to make Cape Clear,[128] "damn his eyes, forgive him, God, for swearing," in a few hours.

Now floated down to me the cheering melody of "New Orleans," with the inspiring chorus of, "Yah yer, ho, roll and go," and somewhat inconsequent but Demosthenic[129] envoy of "Hell to yer soul, is it tay that ye want," as the crew "set sail to steady her," as my familiar the steward, having discarded whisky, fear, and Bible, for the nonce,[130] and bearing hot sea-pie came in to say.

At last on deck, with Rathlin Island on the starboard beam, steaming towards the Mull [of Kintyre], a great sea change, no boats, bulwarks all washed away upon the weather side, doors torn off the hinges, the "fetched loose" smoke stack, coated white with salt, and stayed up in a clumsy fashion with some chains, rigging a mass of tatters, halyards flying loose, the jackstaff gone, the Captain haggard and red-eyed, the officers all cheerfully profane, the crew going about

---

[125] An uninhabitable granite rock situated in the North Atlantic Ocean.
[126] An English sea-shanty, also known as 'The Wild Goose'.
[127] A long-masted cargo boat, used in the West Indies.
[128] An island at the southern coast of Ireland.
[129] In the manner of the Greek statesman and orator, Demosthenes.
[130] Formal or literary: 'for now or for the moment'.

like men after a long debauch, but cheerily, as hauling in the main sheet they bent their backs, taking the time from a Long Island fisherman who did not pull the value of a cent, and hauled together, keeping time to the innumerable verses of that old world lyric of the seas, "Tom's gone to Hello." The Mull and Pladda, Lamlash Island, Cloch Lighthouse,[131] and the winding river with its fairway marks, Dumbarton Castle, and Dumbuck, Elderslie House,[132] and at last the Broomielaw, black decks, and step ashore in "Glesca" to find it "Sawboth,"[133] and be asked by the pious whisky seller, where I essayed to change a sovereign to pay my cab, if I was sure I was a "bona feede traveller."[134]

Ten days flew past at home with theatres, dress-clothes, good dinners, and the unaccustomed feel of comfort, so strange to those who but a week ago have been the inmates of a tramp. Ten days amongst the faces, once so familiar, but which to-day may look quite strange if we should meet in limbo, purgatory, or wheresoever it is the souls of travellers pass their appointed time. Ten days and back again upon the Broomielaw, rain, fog, and coal-dust, and the lights of whisky shops glaring like ogres' eyes upon the crowd, decks filthy, crew either half drunk or else disabled by disease; the skipper sulky, mates thinking about home and surly, the boatswain almost inaudible through a bad cold, and the poor draggled drabs[135] upon the shore looking like animated rag-shops in December gloom. Scuffling and cursing, creaking of blocks, throbbing of the screw, and then the vessel slides out into the foul-smelling, muddy drain they call the Clyde, slips past the shipyards, passes Blythswood, leaves the Cloch astern, runs past the Cumbraes, where the minister once used to pray for the adjoining islands, England and Ireland, leaves Pladda on the weather side, begins to dip and roll and sends me to my bunk to lie half stupid, torpid, a prey to nausea and foul smells, till the throbbing ceases, the heaving and the pitching stop, and going upon deck I see the sun and find that we are anchored in the Garonne[136] under a vineyard, and about a mile outside Pauillac. Here we intended to take in emigrants for the River Plate, the vessel, during ten days' rest in Glasgow having been whitewashed down below and fitted up with tiers of bunks after

---

[131] A distinctive lighthouse near Gourock, designed by Thomas Smith and Robert Louis Stevenson's grandfather, also Robert.
[132] Landmarks on the River Clyde. Elderslie House was the home of Graham's grandmother, Laura Speirs.
[133] Sabbath.
[134] Only *bona fide* travellers were entitled to purchase alcohol on a Sunday in an hotel.
[135] Sluttish women.
[136] A river in south-west France and northern Spain.

the fashion of those vans in which sheep make their railway journeys
and just as comfortable. Visions of tugs coming sweeping down the
yellow stream, crammed thick with people, all with Basque caps
and carrying bags, bundles, and the inevitable bird-cage, without
which no emigrant embarks. Glimpses of garboard strakes,[137] as the
tide sets, the steam launches round, and the emigrants rush to one
side chattering in Basque, clattering of donkey-engines[138] worked by
a grimy "greaser" and recollections of an interminable song about
"Oh mariniers, bon mariniers, à combien vendez-vous votre blé?"[139]
sung by black-haired and red-sashed men, working the cargo under
the direction of a much bejeweled stevedore. Then all the emigrants
crowd down below, kissing takes place, men hug their sweethearts, to
wed whom they are going foreign, and hope in ten years' time when
they return with dollars to find constant, unimpaired in virtue and in
face, with the same figure which the dim but treasured photograph
sets forth. A bell rings and the quartermasters clear the ship, the
friends who go ashore holding their handkerchiefs, dirty with tears,
to their red eyes, the friends on board waving their greasy hats, and
neither trying in the least to keep their feelings in, but weeping lustily
after the primitive and natural fashion which relieves a man and
makes him feel that his tears wash out his grief, making him happier
than those whom education, custom, prejudice, or what you will,
have forced to face their misery with dry eyes.

So past the Tour de Cordouan, and, after, Lisbon, where again the
ship took in another freight of human cattle, this time chiefly peasants
from the Galician hills, who emigrate en masse, leaving their villages
deserted and the houses closed, for wolves to scamper through the
deserted streets on winter nights. Then out into the "roaring forties,"
followed by a rising gale. Hell down below amongst the emigrants,
and no one on board who could speak French or Spanish, still less
Portuguese, except the wretched reader of "Faerie Queene." So
through those all-ways I weltered sick to death, when difficulties rose,
and jabbered with the unlucky peasants, who bore their sufferings
manfully, sitting on the deck all jammed together like sardines, from
grandmother to new-born infant, and almost every family hampered
with a great wicker bird-cage, though they were going to a land of
parrots, macaws, toucans, humming-birds, cardinals and flying spots
of jeweled rainbow, compared to which the birds of Europe all seem
made of sackcloth or of mackintosh; but were not Abana and Pharpar

---

[137] A wooden ship with thick planking forming a ridge along the side of the keel.
[138] Steam-powered winches for loading cargo.
[139] French: "Oh sailors, good sailors, for how much do you sell your wheat?"

superior to all the waters of Judea?[140] And it seems natural to man upon a journey to impede himself with all the living things he can, and to trail draggled birds, bound in their wicker servitude, beyond the seas. As he could no free man, body or soul, by all the strength of prayer and of example, St. Francis perhaps did well to open bird-cages and set their inmates free whenever he got the chance, and when they sainted him had I been there I should have urged against the arguments of the Devil's Advocate this fact, and pled that every rookery about the place, all larks, quails, pigeons, thrushes, black-birds, linnets, and starlings should have had a chance to register their vote. And then the gale subsided, and the old semi-tramp lurched at nine knots before the following seas, till in a day or two, we struck the north-east trades, carried them fair and light, and woke one morning in the dream world of sapphire sea, clear sky, and flying fish darting before the ship, Portuguese men-of-war[141] on every side of us, warm air, a feeling of content, a heavy roll, sails flapping against the rigging, now and then filling with a jerk as if they would tear out the bolt ropes, in fact, the magic of a fine day in a low latitude not to be represented to the mind by a curved line and straggling lettering, Tropic of Capricorn, as in a map.

*****

"S. S. ATLAS", Part II

The Saturday Review, 21 May 1898, pp. 676–7.
Anthologised in *The Ipané* (London: Fisher Unwin, 1899), pp. 76–83.

LIKE a white cloud we sighted Teneriffe, full thirty leagues away, passed close to Santa Cruz, left Lanzarote on our lee, coaled at St. Vincent, passed under San Antonio rising a piece of Africa lost in the sea, and then headed across the ocean towards Brazil. Christmas Day caught us somewhere: no doubt the longitude and latitude is still recorded in some forgotten log-book with the due "observations" and "remarks:" but we were Scotchmen and recked but little of such Erastian festivals,[142] although the emigrants performed a sort of mutilated mass upon the deck, a Biscayan schoolmaster mumbling his mystery from a prayer-book and the faithful gathered in a crowd a

---

[140] 2 Kings 5:12
[141] Jellyfish.
[142] Christmas was little-celebrated in Scotland, New Year being a more important festival.

little aft of the fore bitts,[143] whilst the West of Scotland crew pushed through them now and then to trim the sails or make their way into the forecastle. At times a perspiring fireman emerged out of the stoke-hole, a "sweat-rag" round his neck and lump of waste in his black hands, to breathe and see the show, sat looking for a minute as if the worshippers had been a tribe of savages, and then climbed down the ladder backwards, just pausing a moment as his head sunk below the combing of the hatch to mutter something reflecting on the Whore of Babylon.

Days followed starry nights and we began to know each other, and the officers and men having emerged out of their oilskins, and the watch and watch duty which made them north of 40°,[144] so to speak, fenced off from the mere landsmen and oppressed with work, they now began to take a patronising interest in the passengers and to chat freely with the emigrants, their deep-sea dignity laid to one side, perhaps because they could unbend more safely as no other sailors were about. The captain, who since then has risen to command big ships, to be commodore (I think) of a great line of steamers, and to retire upon a well-earned pension and laurels to Blackheath,[145] to bore himself consumedly on shore, and to regret the days, no doubt, when he commanded the "s.s. Atlas," was a pious, blaspheming Scotchman, built as it seemed to last for ever, hardy and wise, beard like a scrubbing brush, quick-tempered and good-hearted, a perfect seaman of what I may term the transition school,[146] having served all his early life in "wind-jammers," but "sceenteefic" in his way, and able, to deal with a scratch,[147] rough, skulking crew such as we had on board. The mates indefinite, all Glasgow men, well educated, reading "improving" books; one of them with a master's certificate, and all so boorish in demeanour that till you knew them it appeared that they were mad. Much is forgiven to North Britons, for they have drunk much, but why they should think that rudeness shows independence is not so clear, for above all men in the world they are the first to see a slight intended to themselves. The boatswain and quartermasters were all Englishmen, two of them old men-of-war's men, clean and tidy as old housemaids, and often on their watch off, on a fine night, I saw them washing their clothes amid the jeers of the Scottish crew, "who did not hold with it," and thought that water had only one use, to mix with whisky, and that that use was only made of it by fools, by

---

[143] The posts to which the mooring ropes are tied.
[144] From northern lands.
[145] A wealthy south-London suburb.
[146] Experienced in sail and steam-powered vessels.
[147] A crew that has not worked together before.

weaklings, by Englishmen. At night I sat and yarned with them, tried unsuccessfully to learn to splice, thinking the art might turn out useful in mending lazos, listened to their jokes and forgot most of them, but still remember something about the "'Mary Dunn' of Dover, a brig (I think) wot went to sea with three great bloomin' decks and 'ad no bottom." The crew appeared to be composed mainly of costermongers with a stray seaman here and there, 'longshoremen, and an occasional west Highland fisherman. The doctor (brother of a well-known portrait painter), who perchance may smile when he reads this, informed me that their habit was to come on board blind drunk, without a kit except a new jack-knife and new sea-boots, pitch the latter down the fore peak and fall themselves upon the top of them, lie prostate for a day or two, and then get up and ask him for "black-wash,"[148] of which he kept a mighty store, knowing the medicines by experience which were most likely to be useful in their case. The fishermen were quieter and had sea-chests, good stocks of clothes, and were sailors in a fashion, all having made a trip or two to sea. When sails were hoisted they always got close to the block, "lifted the shanty," you heave ho! and made as if they were about to pull like oxen, but stopped there, and if some three or four of them had clapped on to the same rope the sail would never have been set in the whole watch they pulled so "cartiously."

The Spanish and French emigrants were mostly Basque all wearing "boinas"[149] and "alpargatas,"[150] speaking dialects of the Basque tongue quite comprehensible to one another, and yet hating each other to the full as much as Irish and English, merely because an arbitrary line ran through the mountains where they all were born. A long, thin Bordelais called Pierre, but known as "Monsieur Pedro," because he spoke a little Spanish, ruled them like slaves, and when they fought knocked them about till they were quiet, at times coming aft to ask for medicines from the doctor with a grave face, often explaining with some detail that a woman was apparently ill with fever, but that he (Monsieur Pedro) thought that was untrue, and "the dam woman really make too much love." But love or fever to the doctor were all one (perhaps they are to every one) and Pierre used to go off contented with a seidlitz powder[151] and two pills. At night the emigrants danced to the strains of an accordion, sang "me gastan

---

[148] A lotion composed of calomel and lime water, used especially in the treatment of the skin lesions of syphilis.
[149] A traditional Basque beret.
[150] Canvas shoes with a hemp sole fastened with tapes.
[151] The generic name under which a commonly used laxative was sold.

todas"[152] to the guitar, or joined in chorus to the eighty verses of an old southern French song, known as "La Blonde," a damsel who was beloved by all "Les Chasseurs," but who incontinently flung herself away upon "a braconnier," perhaps because as the chorus used to set forth "Les braconniers sont dangereux et nombreux,"[153] – but why spy into the motives of a poacher and his wife?

The great Scotch festival found us off Fernando Noronha,[154] the little island off the coast where the Brazilian had a penal settlement. The day broke hot, and as we passed the island it loomed low, the palm trees standing in a sort of mirage so that they seemed to have no roots and float above the land like parasols, between the sand and sky.

How the crew got the liquor no one ever knew, but before twelve o'clock the ship was like a pandemonium or the east end of Glasgow on a fast day night.[155] From the stokehole came the sound of "Auld Lang Syne," the watch on deck were stupid, and the emigrants scattered before them like chickens before the gambols of a large Newfoundland pup. Just when the skipper came on deck, his sextant in his hand, ready to shoot the sun, a man walked up to him and said "Hoo are ye Captain? Ye ken although my feyther aye sat under Dr. Candlish[156] I'm a devil wi' the lasses, and so are ye yirsel." The captain who, since early morn had been boiling with fury, growled like a bear, told the man roughly to go forward and lie down, received an insolent reply, knocked the man down, and had him put in irons, then carried to a spare cabin and locked in, where he continued to howl "Auld Lang Syne" until he fell asleep. But by this time the decks were filthy, men falling down and sick all over them, the mates and engineers working like slaves, punching and kicking, driving the drunken crew below, until at last they were all got into the forecastle and a man planted at the door with a handspike to keep them in.

The day passed rather awkwardly, for though a special dinner had been prepared, a list of toasts drawn out, haggis and cock-a-leekie duly prepared, no one could eat it, for, till night fell, the mates, the passengers, doctor, purser, and such as the emigrants as were able were forced to work the ship; the doctor and myself steering occasionally and putting the helm invariably hard up, when it should have been put hard down, keeping the vessel yawing about as if we

---

[152] 'Me gustan todas', Spanish: 'I like them all'.
[153] French: 'The poachers are dangerous and numerous.'
[154] A chain of volcanic islands off Brazil's north-east coast.
[155] Friday.
[156] The Reverend Robert Smith Candlish (1806–73) was a leading figure in the establishment of the Free Church of Scotland. This indicated that the crewman had come from a strict Presbyterian background.

wished to write our names upon the sea. Next morning decks were washed, black eyes and broken heads attended to, the prisoner let out on promise of amendment and a search made to find how the men had got the drink. Nothing, of course, came out, and we pursued our voyage, touching at Rio, and half-way to the Plate ran into a Pampero,[157] which kept us out a day till one fine morning we sighted Lobos, slipped past Maldonado, left the English Bank upon our lee, passed close to Flores Island, anchored finally just underneath the "Mount." The Neapolitan who rowed me to the shore said that the "Atlas" looked to him like a coffin, but having spent so long aboard of her I cursed him for a fool, told him the blood of St. Januarius[158] would never liquefy if he went on like that, and turning saw the skipper leaning on the rail waving his hat and calling out "So long, don't forget New Year's Day." I said I would not and the "Atlas" passed out of my life, and what became of her the underwriters could possibly have told. Perhaps she was broken up for scrap iron, lost on a well-known shoal, sold for a tramp, and maybe dodges about between the Islands of the Chinese Seas, if she has not long ago foundered in the night after the fashion of so many of her class.

But anyhow my copy of the "Faerie Queene" still smells of cock-roaches, is spotted on the cover with salt water, some of the leaves are foxed, the title page is lost, and when I open it even the music of "Epithalamion"[159] is dumb, and in its stead I hear the swishing of the sea, feel the screw racing and the long-drawn-out notes of a "forebitter"[160] seem to quaver in the air, until I shut the book.

* * * * *

The following two sketches were Graham's attempts at pen-portraiture through the virtual monologues of his subjects, two lowly characters who represented two faces of the bucolic working class, the wandering Scot, and the sentimental, jovial drunk. Both speak in broad Scots, slightly modified for those who were not at home with the language, and both demonstrated Graham's extraordinary ear for dialect,[161] including repeated sentiments that demonstrated aged

---

[157] A cold polar air from the west, south-west or south on the pampas.
[158] The patron saint of Naples, whose blood is said to liquefy three times a year in a sealed glass ampoule in Naples Cathedral.
[159] A poem by Edmund Spenser, the author of 'The Fairie Queene', written to his bride, Elizabeth Boyle, and presented to her on their wedding day in 1594.
[160] A sea-shanty.
[161] An obituarist wrote: 'Although he was at Harrow and spent much of his life in England, Cunninghame Graham kept traces of his Highland accent [sic] and told stories in broad Scotch like a master.' 'Mr Cunninghame Graham Death in Buenos Aires', Manchester Guardian, 21 March 1936, p. 15.

forgetfulness, or the effects of alcohol. The writer's own occasional interjections render the class differences more apparent, but what is also apparent is Graham's affection for his subjects.

The first is Graham's conversation with a neighbour, and his rambling recollections of his youth in New Zealand, from where he had been forced to return home by nagging parents. On the surface, this piece is non-political, but Graham cannot resist a jibe at British hypocrisy and double-dealing.

"A PAKEHA"[162]

The Westminster Gazette, 31 January 1899, pp. 1–2.
Anthologised in *Thirteen Stories* (London: Heinemann, 1900), pp. 201–8.

Rain, rain, and more rain, dripping off the sodden trees, soaking the fields, and blotting out the landscape as with a neutral-tinted gauze. The sort of day that we in the land, "dove il dolce Dorico risuona,"[163] designate as "saft." Enter along the road to me a neighbour of some fifty to sixty years of age, one Mr. Campbell, a little bent, hair faded rather than grey, frosty-faced as we Scotsmen are apt to turn after some half a century of weather, but a glint of red showing in the cheeks; moustache and whiskers trimmed in the fashion of the late sixties; "tacketed" boots, and clothes, if not impervious to the rain, as little affected by it as the bark of trees. His hat, once black and of the pattern affected at one time by all Free Church clergyman, now greenish and coal-scuttled fore and aft and at the sides. In his red, chapped, and dirty, but grey-mittened hands a shepherd's stick – long, crooked, and made of hazelwood.

"It'll maybe tak' up, laird."[164]

"Perhaps."

"An awfu' spell o' it."

"Yes, disgusting."

"Aye, laird, the climate's sort o' seekinin'. I mind[165] when I was in New Zealand in the sixties, aye, wi' a surveyor, just at the triangulation, ye ken.[166] Man, a grand life, same as the tinklers,[167] here to-day

---

[162] Maori: Someone of European origin.
[163] Italian: 'Where the gentle Doric (speech) rings out' = Scotland.
[164] Scots: 'The weather might improve.'
[165] Scots: remember.
[166] Land surveying and mapping.
[167] Travellers/gypsies.

and gane to-morrow, like old Heather Jock. Hoot,[168] never mind your dog, laird, there's just McClimant's sheep, puir silly body, I ken his keel mark.[169] Losh[170] me, a bonny country, just a pairfect pairadise, New Zealand. When I first mind Dunedin it wasna' bigger than the clachan there, out by.[171] A braw place noo, I understan', and 'a the folk fearfu' took up wi' horse, driving their four-in-hands,[172] blood cattle, every one of them. There's men to-day like Jacky Price – he was a Welshman, I'm thinking, who I mind doing their day's darg[173] just like mysel aboot Dunedin, and noo they send their sons hame to be educated up aboot England.

"When? 'Oo aye, I went oot in the old *London* wi' Captin' Macpherson. He'd bin the round trip a matter o' fifteen times, forbye[174] a wee bit jaunt awhiles[175] after the 'blackbirds' (slaves, ye ken, what we called free indentured labourers) to the New Hebrides. The *London*, aye, 'oo aye, she foundered in the Bay (Biscay, ye ken) on her return. It's just a special providence I wasna' a passenger myself.

"Why did I leave the country? Eh, laird, ye may say.[176] I would hae made my hame out there, but it was just the old folks threap, threaping[177] on me to come back, I'm telling ye. A bonny toon, Dunedin, biggit[178] on a wee hill just for a' the wurrld like Gartfarran[179] there, and round the point a wee bit plain just like the Carse o' Stirling. Four year I wrocht[180] at the surveyin', mainly triangulation, syne[181] twa at sheepherdin', nane o' your Australian fashion tailing them a' day, but on the hame system gaen' aboot; man, I mind, whiles I didna' see anither man in sax weeks time."

"Then you burned bricks, you say?"

"Aye, I didna' think ye had been so gleg[182] at the Old Book. Aye, aye, laird, plenty of stra',[183] or may be it was yon New Zealand flax

---

168 Nonsense, tut-tut.
169 Coloured 'raddle' marking to distinguish flocks.
170 Lord!
171 'The Clachan of Aberfoyle.'
172 A carriage drawn by four horses.
173 Scots: Work.
174 Scots: Besides.
175 Scots: For a time.
176 You might well ask.
177 Scots: Nagging.
178 Scots: Built.
179 A nearby medieval mound.
180 Scots: Worked.
181 Scots: Then.
182 Scots: Quick of perception.
183 Exodus 5: 'Ye shall no more give the people straw to make brick, as heretofore: let them go and gather straw for themselves.'

stalk. The awfiest plant ye ever clapt your eyes on, is yon flax. I mind
when I first landed aff the old *London* she foundered in the Bay. It was
just a special interposition[184] ... but I mind I telt ye. Well, I was just
dandering[185] aboot outside the toon, and ettled to pu'[186] some of yon
flax; man, I wasna' fit; each leaf is calculated to bear the pressure of
aboot a ton. The natives, the Maories, use it to thack[187] their cottages.
A bonny place, New Zealand, a pairfect pairadise – six-and-thirty
years ago – aye, aye, 'oo aye, just the finest country in God's airth.

"Het? Na, na, nane so het as here in simmer, a fine, dry air, and
a bonny bright blue sky. Dam't, I mind the diggings opening tae.[188]
There were a wheen captins'. Na, na, not sea captins', airmy captins',
though they were plenty of the sea yins doon in the sooth, just airmy
captains' who had gone out and ta'en up land; blocked it ye ken far as
fae here to Stirlin.' Pay for it, aye, aboot a croon an acre, and a wee bit
conseederation to the Government surveyor just kept things square.
Weel, when the diggings opened, some of them sold out and made a
fortune.[189] Afu' place thae diggings, I hae paid four shillin' a pound
for salt mysel, and as for speerits, they were just fair contraband.

"And the weemin. Aye, I mind the time, but ye'll hae seen the
Circassian[190] weemen aboot Africa. Weel, weel, I'm no saying it's not
the case, but folk allow that yon Circassians are the finest weemin
upon earth. Whiles I've seen them tae, at fairs ye ken, in the bit
boothies, but to my mind there's naething like the Maories, especially
the half-casted yins, clean limbed, nigh on six feet high the maist o'
them. Ye'll no ken Geordie Telfer, him that was a sojer, he's got a bit
place o' his ain out by Milngavie.[191] Geordie's aye bragging, bostin'
aboot weemin that he's seen in foreign pairts. He just is of opeenion
that in Cashmere or thereabouts there is the finest weemin in the
world. Black, na, na, laird, just a wee toned and awfu' tall, ye ken.
Geordie he says that Alexander the Great was up aboot Cashmere
and that his sojers, Spartans I think they ca'ed them, just intromitted wi' the native weemin, took them, perhaps, for concubines, as
the Scriptures say, but ye'll ken sojers, laird; Solomon, tae, an awfu'
chiel[192] yon Solomon. The Maori men were na blate[193] either, a' ower

---

[184] In theology, the direct interposition of divine authority.
[185] Scots: Strolling.
[186] Scots: Attempted to pull.
[187] Scots: Thatch.
[188] The gold rush in New Zealand's South Island, 1850s–60s.
[189] The discovery of gold in central Otago in the early 1860s.
[190] The women of mainly Sunni Muslim peoples of the north-western Caucasus.
[191] A town in East Dunbartonshire, now a northern suburb of Glasgow.
[192] Scots: Lad.
[193] Scots: Shy.

sax fut high, some nigh on seven fut, sure as death, I'm tellin' ye. Bonny wrestlers, tae, man [,] Donald Dinnie got an unco tirl wi' ane o' them aboot Dunedin, leastwise, if it wasna Dinnie, it was Donald Grant or Donald McKenzie, or ane of they champions frae Easter Ross. Sweir[194] to sell their land tae they chaps, I mind the Government sent out old Sir George Grey, a wise like man, Sir George, ane o' they filantrofists. Weel, he just talkit tae them, ca'ed them his children, and said that they shouldna resist legeetimate authority. Man, a wee wiry fella', he was the licht-weight champion wrestler at Tiki-Tiki, just up and said, 'Aye, aye, Sir George,' though he wasna gi'en him Sir George, but some native name they had for him, 'we're a' your children, but no sic children as to gie our land for naething.' Sir George turnit the colour of a neep,[195] ane o' yon swedes, ye ken, and said nae mair."

"How did they manage it?"

"The Government just arranged matters wi' the chiefs. Bribery, weel a' weel, I'll no gae sae far as to impute ony corruption on them, but a Government, a Government, ye ken, is very apt to hae its way.

"Dam't, 'twas a braw country, a pairfect pairadise, I mind aince going oot with Captin' Brigstock, Hell-fire Jock they ca'ed him after they bushrangers. There was ane Morgan frae Australlia [sic] bail't up[196] a wheen folks, and dam't, says Captin' Brigstock, ye'll hae to come, Campbell. Shot him, yes, authority must be respected, and the majesty o' law properly vendeecated, or else things dinna thrive. It was in a wood of gora-gora we came on him about the mouth of day. Morgan, ye ken, was boiling a billy in a sort o' wee clearin', his horse tied to a tree close by, when Brigstock and the others came upon him. Brigstock just shouted in the name o' the law and then let fly. Morgan, he fell across the fire, and when we all came up says he, 'Hell-fire, ye didna' gie me ony chance,' and the blood spouted from his mouth into the boiling pan.

"Died, oo' aye, deid as Rob Roy. I dinna care to mind it. But a fine life, laird, nae slavin' at the plough, but every ane goin' aboot on horseback, and the bonny wee bit wooden huts, the folk no fashed[197] wi' furniture, but sittin' doon to tak' their tea upon the floor wi' their backs against the wall. That's why they ca'ed them squatters. They talk aboot Australlia [sic] and America, but if it hadna' been for the old folks I would hae made my hame aboot a place ca'ed Paratanga,

---

194 Scots: Reluctant.
195 Scots: Turnip.
196 Bushrangers of colonial Australia and New Zealand were said to 'bail up' their prey.
197 Scots: Bothered.

and hae taken up wae ane o' they Maori girls, or maybe a half-caste. Married, weel, I widna' say I hae gane to such a length. Dam't, a braw country, laird, a pairfect pairadise, I'm telling ye"; and then the rain grew thicker, and seemed to come between us as he plodded on towards the "toon."

* * * * *

The next piece was not anthologised, perhaps because of the bleakness of the doctor's jaundiced world view, but more likely because of the use of the Scots language. For those familiar with it, however, this is a wonderfully touching evocation of happiness, in the face of adversity and loss (albeit induced by alcohol), a perfect example of Scottish fatalism and nostalgia, which a New Year's celebration is guaranteed to provide. Again, Graham employs his 'authorial silent finish',[198] making no judgement on the subject or the scene, letting his readers cope with their own emotions.

"PAX VOBISCUM"[199]

The Westminster Gazette, 25 February 1899, pp. 1-2.

Rain falling on the station roof, on platform, bridge, on signal-box, upon the shining rails, enveloping everything with that North British clammy dampness which we Scotchmen recognise, and find (word illegible) like as a negro does the odour of the mangrove swamps. An air of blackness upon everything; a smell of whisky in the air; and in the waiting-rooms the fires black out, a Bible jacketed in American cloth[200] on the table, the chairs all broken, the floors befouled with spittle, and on the walls two notices – one that no smoking was allowed, and the other calling attention to the fact that God is Love.

   Putting his case of instruments upon the table, the doctor stepped out upon the platform, cursing the telegram that on New Year's Night had called him from his home. Pacing about and waiting for the train (the station, either Lochwinnoch, or else Dalry), he fell a-musing on his profession, on science, and the apparent uselessness of the daily fight with microbes, patching up people who had much better die, breaking to rich men that they had but six months of life, and on the

---

[198] Watts and Davies, *Cunninghame Graham,* p. 157. Neil Munro wrote of this device, 'I have learned to look for these conclusions in the minor key with expectancy'. Neil Munro, p. 304.

[199] 'Peace be with you' (plural).

[200] Oilcloth.

endless *Via Crucis*[201] of the hospital. The world seemed black to him, empty, cold, dreary – life a delusion, death a hard release, friends all deceivers, and mankind scarce worth the muscular exertion of a heart-felt curse. But as he reached the blackest corner of the damp-pervaded station, and was about to turn, out of the darkness a figure stepped. Clad in a worn-out "stan o' black"[202] which no doubt had served at funerals for fifty years, his boots mere "bauchles,"[203] and around his neck a woolen comforter, hands red and dirty, and with outstanding knotty veins like roots of trees, trousers frayed at the feet, an old Kilmarnock bonnet on his head, a bottle sticking from his pocket, and a rolled up and dirty copy of the Glasgow Weekly Mail peering out from another, the man drew near. The gaslight falling on his face showed him a grizzled, hard-featured North Briton of about seventy years of age. Swaying about a little unsteadily, after the fashion of a dancing bear, and stretching out a grimy, grey woolen mittened paw, in a raucous voice, he said, "Doctor – for I ken ye are a doctor – would ye mind gi'en us a shake o' the haun'? That's the richt feelin' at this time o' year, an' as for me, I feel jist at peace wi' a' mankind the night. Whisky? Oo aye, a body can whiles drink when it's a sair job for him getting ony meat. I live oot by, at Dreghorn,[204] ye ken, and hae jist cam through to see some auld freens at the New Year. A fine time the New Year, doctor; hoot, ye man feel naething but gude will to a' mankind. Na, na, man, I ken fine what I'm aboot.[205] For four or five nichts afore the New Year I had naether licht nor fire at hame, west by Dreghorn, ye ken. Seventy-two? Oo aye, seventy-two or ther-aboot – a man at my age is na' just so particular aboot a year or twa, ye ken. It's a dark eneuch place I'm gaun back to, doctor, but, man, I feel at pairfek peace wi' a' mankind, and feel naething but gude will to a' the world the nicht. An' I micht no, ye ken."

"How's that?" – "Weel, ye see, I was married just aboot the New Year, a wheen years back. Weemen, ye see, doctor, whiles gie ye a surprise. I mind oor meenister before I was marrit upon Jess – man, she was a bonny lass – he jist cam' doon – he cam' fower times – an' sees he, 'Andra,' says he (they ca' me Andrew Gilchrist), 'yon lass is no a gude yin, and ye manna[206] marry her.' But whin a man's got an idea intil his heid, it's no sae easy whiles to pit it oot.

---

[201] Way of the Cross.
[202] Sombre church-going or mourning clothes.
[203] Scots: loose slippers/worn out shoes.
[204] A village in North Ayrshire.
[205] Scots: I know very well what I'm doing.
[206] Scots: Mustn't.

"I couldna' richt mak' oot what he was meaning at the time, but I kent weel syn syne.

"Jess, she made a moonlight flittin' wi' Geordie Jardine, ane o' oor neeghboors, an' it was just a day or twa afore the New Year's Nicht. Aye, oo aye, doctor, thank ye, an' gie's yer haun; it doesna matter; she was na' worth the minding, or maybe I was sort o' dour wi' Jess, aiblins[207] she's tane the causeway;[208] puir wee lamb; ye canna help thae things.

"But gies yer haun, doctor. I'm just at pairfek peace wi' a' mankind, an' filled wi' naething but gude will to a' the wurld this nicht."

As he was speaking the train slid snorting into the platform, and the porters, shouting "This way for Dreghorn and Kilmarnock; any more passengers gaein' South?" bundled the philosophic septuagenarian into a third-class carriage.

For an instant there was light and noise, and for a moment everything seemed filled with life.

Then the train slipped noiselessly into the light, and darkness once again descended on the place.

---

[207] Scots: Perhaps.
[208] Died.

1900–3

'It seems to me, a world all void of grace must needs be
cruel, for cruelty and grace go not together.'[209]

Cedric Watts wrote:

After 1899 ... he [Graham] showed little development as an essayist and
short-story writer. The elegiac obituary study, the nostalgic traveller's
anecdote, the remembered glimpse of life in a Spanish settlement, the
brief character sketch of a soldier, a Spaniard, a Scot or a whore – these
subjects recur, and so does the mood of pawky wistfulness and almost glib
melancholy.[210]

However, Watts failed to take into account the next distinctive group
of Scottish sketches that occupy the years immediately after 1900
(what Walker described as Graham's 'middle period'), which are
entirely different in subject and character, and which, in their own
more subtle way, were an antidote to the writing of 'the Kailyard'.

It may be a coincidence that Graham's more overt and stark anti-
Kailyard texts ceased prior to the publication of George Douglas
Brown's classic anti-Kailyard novel: *The House With the Green
Shutters* (1901),[211] but no coincidence that his subject matter and
style radically altered after 1900, when Gartmore House was sold to
pay off his family debts,[212] perhaps reflecting ancestral guilt, but more
importantly, his own loss of mutuality with the neighbourhood and
his past. William Power described them as 'sketches [of] a twilight
Scotland, ennobled by tragedy and defeat',[213] although defeat *per
se* rarely featured in Graham's writings, unless it is the defeat by
modernisation of an older way of life. Certainly, they demonstrated
a less critical view of Scotland, dealing with landscapes and old-
world types, types who now (like himself), had gone, the railway

---

[209] Cunninghame Graham, *Thirteen Stories* (London: Heinemann, 1900), p. ix.
[210] Watts, p. 30.
[211] Ian Campbell wrote that Brown 'created a kailyard novel to subvert its values',
which is exactly what Graham did in 'Salvagia', and possibly for the same
reason, that it was – 'the compliment the author of *The House with the Green
Shutters* would have liked to pay his country'. Ian Campbell, *Kailyard: A New
Assessment* (Edinburgh: Ramsay Head Press, 1981), pp. 11–12.
[212] David Lowe, wrote of this period: 'In the turmoil of his impoverished condition, with the dark prospect ahead of having to sell part of his lands, his
thoughts hovered lovingly over his ancestral environments'. David Lowe, 'The
Old Scottish Labour Party', *Glasgow Evening Times*, 18 February 1938, p. 3.
[213] Power, p. 169.

being the sworn enemy of such people, and which was breaking the homogeneity of communities.[214]

These ruminative Scottish works were mostly set in and around his erstwhile home of 'the varied realms of fair Menteith',[215] an area of southern Perthshire, and parts of Stirlingshire, stretching along the valley of the River Forth as far east as Dunblane and including Kippen. The valley was once an arm of the sea, then, for millennia, a vast barren moor, until it was mostly cleared in the eighteenth century. It is a hybrid land, poised between the Highlands and the Lowlands, with strong characteristics and resonances of both. Like many hybrids, it had, and still has, its own distinctive character, a mixture of rich farmland, and at its western extremity, near Graham's old home of Gartmore, the remains of the boggy moor known as 'Flanders Moss'.[216] 'The Moss' is a recurring and brooding presence in many of the works that follow, it haunts the narratives, more ghostly because it produces a preponderance of mist, to which Graham frequently referred. From above it, mist is transformative, landmarks and man's presence disappear, leaving a primitive, unspoiled landscape, while inside it, one's imagination has free rein, which Graham obviously relished. It is frontier territory where, not far away, there are lonely lochans and ruined castles that allowed him to ponder on a deeper past, a past ignored by the Kailyard writers, a past where the Highlands and Lowlands were not so distinct, where 'broken' clansmen and caterans once made their raids, and drovers descended with their cattle on their way to market.

These middle works were typically set in grand, musty houses, amongst enclosed, shadowy landscapes, peopled by low-country gentry, local lairds and eccentric relatives, relics from the age of enlightenment, displaced by an age of entitlement. They represented a bygone gentility of a distinctly Scottish pattern, the kind of people whom in various articles and letters he called 'old style', people from his own class who occasionally still 'lingered' from a more gracious time, but who were ultimately doomed. They were descended from ancient local families, and they had rank in their rural communities,

---

[214] Campbell noted the huge impact on the attitude of mind that the coming of the railway imposed on rural communities. Campbell, p. 90. Ironically, it was the proximity of a railway station to Gartmore House that made Graham's frequent sojourns in London much more convenient. His later dwelling, Ardoch House near Helensburgh, was also very convenient to the railway.

[215] Charles Stirling Home Drummond Murray, *The Red Book of Menteith* (Edinburgh: 1880), p. xvii. According to this book, the earldom of Menteith stretched along the Forth to the Ochil Hills in the east.

[216] Associated with Flemish immigrants who were reputedly imported to drain the countryside. It is now a nature reserve.

and although as landlords they might sit uneasily in Graham's ideal world, unlike the parvenu landowners, their lineage (like his own) was predicated on paternalism, not exclusivity in land. They represented the values of tradition, decency and respect, a type rarely featured in Scottish writing. T. E. Lawrence described these works as: 'the rain-in-the-air-and-on-the-roof mournfulness of Scotch music in his time-past style [...] snap-shots – the best verbal snapshots ever taken I believe',[217] but they are nostalgic rather than sentimental,[218] and if Graham had not emphasised their Scottishness, they could just as easily fit into country houses in England. However, when added to the Heather Jocks, inebriated Highlanders, eccentric farmers and village roughs, Graham had broadened out the Scottish rural canvas into a recognisable, eclectic, heterogeneous community, and when they died, they left the world 'poorer for a type'.[219]

The contrast in atmosphere between his South American and his Scottish settings could hardly be greater; there is little 'sunshine' in the latter,[220] but the chiaroscuro is deceptive. Like his sketches of gaucho life, his 'structural nostalgia' is strongly in play, and there is a longing for a primordial birthright, to offset the compromising of purity and the destruction of cultural continuity and inheritance, corroded by time, and in danger of slipping into oblivion, irreversibly destroyed by the self-interest of the modern world. Graham is mostly remembered for his adventurous life and his portrayal of exotic locations, but these portraits, which document the bygone characters and graces of the Forth Valley deserve a special place in Scotland's heritage.

The first two sketches in this group, 'A Veteran', and 'A Relative', were published just before the sale of Gartmore House, but Graham was already aware of his imminent departure. They are quite unlike his previous works, where he relied on the words of his actors. Now, his nostalgic emotions were in full flow for the characters and places remembered from his youth. However, as usual, the Hispanic world is never far away.

*****

---

[217] *The Selected Letters of T. E. Lawrence*, edited by David Garnett (World Books, 1941), p. 343.

[218] Graham despised sentimentality, and wrote 'In dealing with Scotland and things Scotch, one should avoid sentiment, it destroyed those awful McCrocketts, and Larens, and is a snare to the pious chanting, hypocritical, hard, but at the same time sentimental, and whisky loving Scotchman. I am a Scotchman.' Letter from Graham to Edward Garnett, 25 May 1898.

[219] 'A Veteran', p. 456.

[220] 'True, in the East there generally is sun, and every evil with the sun is less.' Cunninghame Graham, 'Heather Jock', *Saturday Review*, 30 January 1897, p. 110.

Figure 4 Culcreuch Castle.

Graham became a master of the pen-portrait, particularly when describing the foibles and eccentricities of his extended family. These form another unique record of a bygone age among Scotland's minor landed gentry, subjects rarely dwelt upon by other writers. They are also remarkable for their honesty, and at times, ribaldry. One reviewer wrote: 'The tales are told with frankness bordering on license at times, because the author writes as he speaks, with brilliance and sparkle, but with a sublime disregard for proprieties.'[221] A reviewer in *The Spectator* remarked: 'Mr Cunninghame Graham is as plain in his language as he is independent in his opinions, and his readers who object to a spade being called a spade had better look elsewhere for their entertainment.'[222]

The elderly squire described in the following sketch was a senior cousin of Graham's, named Alexander Graham Speirs (1793–1877), second Laird of Culcreuch, an estate and castle near the village of Fintry in Stirlingshire. The estate had been bought in 1796 by

---

[221] 'The Over-Seas Library', *Yorkshire Herald*, 22 May 1899.
[222] 'Current Literature', *Spectator*, 24 June 1899, p. 887.

Alexander's grandfather, also Alexander Speirs, first of Elderslie (1714–82), a rich Glasgow 'Tobacco Lord', and passed to his fourth son, Peter (1761–1829). Peter had married Martha Harriet Graham, Graham's great-aunt, the third daughter of Graham's great-great-grandfather, Robert Graham of Gartmore (1735–97), the collector of taxes, and slave-owner in Jamaica. Their son, our subject, was briefly the 'Whig' MP for Paisley from 1835 to 1836, but he resigned, and was declared bankrupt in 1837, due to the failure of his cotton mill in Fintry. The castle stayed in the Speirs family until 1890. He is also the subject of Graham's sketch of 1910, 'The Craw Road', and mentioned in 'Loose and Broken Men' (1913).

A VETERAN

The Saturday Review, 14 April 1900, pp. 455–6.
Anthologised as 'The Colonel' in *Hope* (London: Duckworth, 1910), pp. 208–15.

THE railway, that sworn enemy of old-world types, has done more in the last fifty years to make the whole world common than all the international pilgrimages of all past times. So that search England, Scotland and Ireland all through, to-day you scarce shall find a man differing in any aspect of his mind or body from the next. But as a wounded bird or animal sometimes seeks concealment, in some place made difficult to find by obviousness, so chiefly is the eccentric to be sought in London and its purlieus.[223] But fifty years ago in wind-swept, ragged Scottish country houses not a few remnants of pre-railroad days still lingered on.

Scotland alone could have produced, and perhaps only Scotch people could have appreciated such a survival of the youth of the nineteenth century, as was the veteran. He bore his eighty years as lightly as an oak tree bears its centuries, and used to tell with a twinkle in his fierce, brown, blood-shot eye that an old gamekeeper had said that "the Colonel was born in the same year in which the saughs[224] were planted in the West Park, and that they were maistly a' deid at the tap." Tall and broad-shouldered, he seemed as if his fell of snow-white hair had bowed his shoulders as the snow bends down the topmost branches of an aged fir. Otherwise time had but little touched him. Years had not blunted the intensity of his hatred for a Free Churchman, a Tory, or a Highlander. Experience

---

[223] Surrounding areas.
[224] Scots: Willows.

had not taught him to tone down his restrictions on all who disagreed with him. The snows of eighty winters had not dimmed the fire of his glance. The very county-people said the "ould Colonel had an eye intil him like a hawk."

No eccentricity of dress betrayed the man born in the eighteenth century. Either the tailors of his youth had mildewed off or had become bankrupt, as their patrons one by one had preceded them to that land in which their craft will presumably not be required, or the Colonel's own good sense had impelled him to conform ostensibly at least to the degeneracy of the times in which he lingered. His collars may have been perhaps a trifle higher than those of the time in which he lived: the skirts of his heather mixture shooting-coat a trifle fuller than those worn in the sixties. So that except the fact of his large silver snuff-box, snuff-stained shirt, and red handkerchief, usually drying at the fire, when not in active service, these were the only outward protests against the flight of time.

Lost in a corrie of the hills, miles from a railway, surrounded on all sides by moors and still more moors, looking out upon a little loch, on which grew yellow and white water-lilies and in which fed tench, stood his ancestral tower. Hills towered at the back of it, and the tall firs of the "pinetum" kept out such little light as the small deep-set windows, all built in a recess, might have admitted. It's thick "harled"[225] walls, its "corby steps,"[226] the low hall-door, opening without a porch upon the ground, the high-pitched roof, and the air of gauntness over all, impressed the stranger sadly at first sight, as the house loomed greyly through the constant rain. Inside, three or four large and curly, but cross-tempered dogs greeted the visitor, showing their teeth at him, and walking up the stairs beside him, holding their tails out stiffly as the Arabs say a lion does, when in a forest in South Algeria he comes upon a man. The Kingswood furniture, the jars of rose leaves in china basins on the stairs, the apples in a cupboard by the hall, mixed with the snuff which lay like brown dew on all the furniture, produced an atmosphere, which only practice rendered tolerable. An old grey parrot in a bright brass cage, which bit at everyone as fiercely as an otter, the two green parroquets which flew about the rooms, occasionally alighting with a shriek on ladies' heads, rendered life livelier than was the wont of other country houses in the days of which I write. Few houses of the kind are left in these degenerate days, and men like the old Colonel have long since disappeared.

---

[225] Roughcast.
[226] 'Corbeled steps' = Stepped gable ends.

The long campaign of the Peninsula[227] had softened off his angles towards both French and Spaniard, but the long warfare of his life had left him still militant towards an Irishman or Kelt of any kind. Episcopalians were his detestation; on Catholics he looked with toleration, knowing that at the time he lived their power beyond the Tweed was small; but all the shades and little differences of Presbyterian dissent he lumped and damned in one fell swoop as hypocritical, giving no reason for his faith, but holding it and acting on it, after the fashion of his kind. Born when the echoes of the '45[228] were ringing (though faintly) through the land, he held the Stuarts in abhorrence, but yet hated the Hanoverians, whom he termed German Boors, and would, I fancy, have stood by Fletcher of Saltoun[229] (he who let fools make laws so long as he made the rhymes), had that illustrious Scoto-Roman flourished in his time. Nobody nowadays descants as he did on the divine right of monarchs to be hanged, dwells upon Robespierre's virtues, worships the Iron Duke,[230] or swears by Ebenezer Elliott[231] as did my ancient friend.

The incongruities of faith, these whimsicalities of creed the penny logic of the daily press has quite obliterated, whether to the greater glory of the Lord 'tis hard to say. But no such speculation came into the Colonel's mind, bothered his brain, or lost him for a single evening his after-dinner nap. Wine put upon the board, the great armchair wheeled to the fire, the red silk handkerchief duly set out to dry, his nostrils both well charged with snuff, the Colonel commonly embarked upon the tale of the French wars. The siege of Badajoz, the marches and the countermarches in the Castilian and La Manchan plains, the bivouac in the wild mountains of Leon, the tales of straying Frenchmen dipped in oil and set on fire, his meeting with the guerilla chief called the "Empecinado,"[232] the lines of Torres Vedras, all were brought out, together with some Val de Peñas,[233] which though he always said it was sour stuff, he never was

---

[227] 'The Peninsular War' in Spain (1808–14), under Wellington, against Napoleon. There is no extant record of Alexander's service in the Peninsular War, where he would only have been fifteen years of age at its start, nor that he ever achieved the rank of colonel, which was probably an honorary nickname.

[228] The 1745 Jacobite rebellion.

[229] Andrew Fletcher of Saltoun (1655–1716). Scottish writer, politician, and opponent of the 1707 Act of Union between Scotland and England.

[230] The Duke of Wellington.

[231] English poet (1781–1849), an opponent of the Corn Laws.

[232] El Empecinado (the Undaunted): Juan Martín Díez (1775–1825), a Spanish military leader and guerrilla fighter who was later executed by Fernando VII.

[233] A red wine from the province of La Mancha.

without since his campaigning days. Strange facts in natural history and in botany, lore about horses, odd reminiscences about Capra Hispanica[234] which he had seen in the Estrella Mountains, curious remarks about the bustard which he remembered in the Norfolk Broads; the hotch-potch of a fertile brain, helped by his eyes sharp as a lynx's and trained by eighty years of practice to pick up the trail of anything unusual, as an Indian's eyes pick up the footprint of a strange horse, he would unpack.

Fortune which smiles but seldom on interesting folk had treated him but scurvily. Some speculator had induced him to set up a mill.[235] Right in the middle of the rushy ragweed and thistle ornamented park the monster stood. Failure, which waits on all excursions made by gentlemen into the serious affairs of life, had from the outset marked it as his own. Now long deserted by its crowd of blear-eyed operatives, it stood a skeleton, the marauding boy having shattered all its windows, and the winter gales removed its slates. Still the walls stood four square, a monument to folly and ugliness, and in his walks abroad the Colonel stopping and leaning on his thistle-spud[236] would curse it from the bottom of his heart, with so much unction, as to show that our forces in the Peninsula must have maintained all the tradition of the Flemish wars. Radical member for Paisley in his youth, convenor of his county in his riper years, he lived a stirring, stormy life, endeavouring without success to pay off debts incurred by his luckless venture in the mill.

Friends he had many, but his relations as a rule were as anathema to him, especially his heirs.[237] Tradition, that useful entity, upon whose shoulders (as upon those of Providence) the humourist can throw so many of his griefs, some of his quiddities, and almost all his cranks, avers that for ten years before the Colonel's death, he never mended a fence, repaired a building, metalled a road or laid out anything to benefit those who by law should occupy his place. Sometimes (again tradition) he was heard to say, if God would only tell him the precise hour of his death, he would burn his house the night before he died.

---

[234] The Iberian ibex.
[235] This was incorrect. The mill was built by Alexander's father Peter, in partnership with Robert Dunmore, Laird of Ballindalloch. It stood near Culcreuch Castle, and part of the ruins can still be seen. After Alexander's bankruptcy in 1837, the Culcreuch Cotton Company was sequestrated, and finally closed in 1845.
[236] A long-handled garden trowel-cum-walking stick.
[237] On his death, the house passed to his niece, Baroness Anne Oliphant Speirs, third of Culcreuch (1838–1907).

Up to the end he rode his chestnut hack, at a slow canter up and down his avenue, attended country meetings, and preserved his senses to the last hour of his life. Death took him with his snuff-box in his hand, grim and prepared, although not pleased to go. He left the world poorer for a type, and when I pass the lonely tower in the glen, and skirt the park in which no longer either ragweed, docks or thistles bloom, I look at the tall saughs in the west park, and remark sadly that nowadays not only are they all "deid at the tap," but most of them are rotten, and not a few lie bald and sere,[238] their bark all peeling off in ribbons upon the upland grass.

*****

Graham was doubly related to the Speirs family, through his grand-mother, Frances Laura Speirs, who was the daughter of Archibald (second of Elderslie), and thus the niece of his brother, Peter Speirs (first of Culcreuch), father of 'The Colonel'. 'Laura' had thirteen siblings, including Thomas Dundas Speirs ('Eccentric Uncle Tom' 1805–92) who is the subject of the next sketch, and Helen Speirs (1801–1887) who lived in Leamington. She appeared as 'Aunt Eleanor' (*The English Review*, February 1911), but she does not feature in this collection.

If it were not already obvious, Graham was attracted to eccentrics, of which he had a fair share in his own extended family, and in this piece, Graham, describes his lecherous and dishevelled relative with surprising candour, but there is also genuine affection.

Inexplicably, this sketch was not anthologised until ten years after it first appeared in print, and several corrections to poor punctuation were made. It was, perhaps, considered too ribald and indecorous for late Victorian tastes, a critic in *The Spectator* describing Graham's writing style as 'Descending in a moment from a plane of distinction or poetical tenderness to the level of a guttersnipe; disgusting and delighting one on the same page ... and his Quixotic championship of the unsuccessful'.[239]

Equally inexplicably, it was also omitted from Walker's 1982 anthology, but it is one of Graham's most candid and 'rounded' Scottish works.

---

[238] Withered.
[239] 'His People', *Spectator*, 12 January 1907, p. 59.

A RELATIVE.

The Saturday Review, 28 July 1900, p. 109.
Anthologised as 'My Uncle' in *Hope* (London: Duckworth, 1910),
pp. 196–207.

THE folly of a fond mother had warped his life. No career was good
enough for my relative, so he, like a good son, remained without one
to the last day of his existence. Report had it that when young he
was a personable man, though whether from modesty or from the
difficulty of finding a painter skilled enough to depict him, no record
came down to my time of his appearance in the heyday of his youth.
When first I recollect him personal beauty was not what suggested
itself to the impartial observer of his countenance. "A lang backit,
sort o' bandy legit, duck footed body, wi' a' his duds[240] in rags, and
wi' his waistcoat hangin' a' in threads, I thocht he had been ane o'
they burglars frae aboot England," was the way in which a servant
girl described him to her mistress, upon whom my relative had called.
She added "he was aye keekin at the window, and when I turned
awa' he took me round the waist and ettled to kiss me, a dirty, snuffy
loon; ca' ye yon man a gentleman, I just ca' him naething better than
a tink."[241]

Certainly few were the sacrifices he made to outward grace. A
pair of hunting breeches, loose at the knees, grey worsted socks and
high-lows,[242] a tartan waistcoat (hangin' a' in threads), and round his
neck, summer and winter, he wore a worsted comforter. An ancient
Scottish chronicler relates that the spearmen of Upper Annandale
wore round their necks a similar adornment, and adds mysteriously
that they thus wore it, "not so much for cold as cutting." The latter
reason could have weighed but little with my relative, for history does
not relate he ever engaged in any wars, or ran much risk of cutting,
but for the finger nails of some west-country serving lass whose cap
he had pulled off as she was carrying coals or water up a stair.

Summer and winter, year in year out, he wore a tall silk hat, brushed
the wrong way, so that by accident or design it looked like a beaver.[243]
He kept it in its place by a piece of common twine, and seemed contented with the effect it produced on all and sundry who beheld and
marveled at it. Most commonly his shirt was scarlet flannel (which he
called flannen'), and sometimes when the rare northern sun peeped

---

[240] Scots: Clothes.
[241] Tinker.
[242] Short boots.
[243] A hat made of felted beaver fur. Fashionable until around 1850.

out for a week or two in August or July he wore a smockfrock over all, and walked about, a cross between an old-time southern counties hedger and a scarecrow; but still a gentleman. Both in and out of season he took snuff, daubing it on his face and clothes, carrying a supply of it loose in his pocket, as well as in a well-filled silver box; dropping it into tea and coffee, or in the soup, mixing it with the yolk of eggs, and turning tender stomachs by its omnipresence whilst he was in the house. Man doth not live by snuff alone, but yet my relative would, I believe, have given up his food rather than stint himself in this ingredient to his happiness.

Sent by his loving parents to a university, he certainly learned Greek, which to the astonishment of those who did know him well he quoted freely, especially when drunk. A horseman from his youth, although he looked more like a sack of coals upon a horse than like a man, he yet had hands of silk. Leaning well back upon the saddle his broken high-lows jammed into the stirrups as he had been in irons, he rode in the first flight,[244] sticking at nothing; or on a four-year-old would ride him through the streets, laughing and talking to himself as the unmade colt stumbled and slithered on the stones.

If his exterior was strange and wonderful, his inward spiritual graces were no less whimsical. Most people at first sight would have set down my relative as [stark] mad. Often in Scotland where personal originality is pushed to the verge of lunacy; where people cherish and cultivate those tricks of manner, gesture and deportment, which in most other countries men fight against, and though knowing they possess them deny them with an oath, it is not always safe to judge. Certain it is my relative, for the possessor of a shrewd brain and mordant wit, yet went as near to madness as was possible. A calculated madness though, and near allied[245] to that of those malevolent fools of history who, when the world laughed at them, returned the compliment by mocking at humanity. It seemed as if humanity itself was what my relative had set up as his target; not that he was a misanthrope, still less a woman-hater, for he liked company and sitting drinking at the dinner table after the antique Scottish fashion, and as for women [,] any created thing that wore a petticoat he turned the light of his snuffy countenance upon with Satyrlike content.

Few ever knew him guilty either of a kind or cruel action, but yet his humour was to offend, disgust, and above all revolt. So his sister's house, where he would pay long visits, he used to come dressed

---

[244] The leading horseman in a fox-hunt.
[245] This is a sly allusion to John Dryden's poem *Absalom and Achitophel* (1681): 'Great wits are to madness near allied/And thin partitions do their bounds divide'.

as I have described, or for a change, in what we call in Scotland "a stan o' black,"[246] with frilled white shirt and collar, the ends of which stuck up like gills, the whole surmounted by a hideous soft hat of the species known as [a] wideawake thirty of forty years ago, and made of tweed, sewn into many ridges, and lined with green or scarlet silk. In the poor maiden lady's drawing-room he sat, reading "Bell's Life,"[247] his feet stuck into slippers of a kind which in those days, I think, were made in Paisley, and in Paisley only [,] and called "bauchles," all down at heel, and the cheap leather cracked. All round him was a rampart made of snuff, which befouled every-thing, and so he sat talking and singing to himself, retailing Rabelaisian anecdotes, or singing songs half jocular and half indecent, for his own edification, and to pass the time. No one seemed to him half so good an audience as he was himself; at times he had long conversa-tions *sotto voce*, in which he held his best friends up to ridicule; or sometimes passed remarks on all and sundry before their faces, being half conscious, half unconscious what he said, and if remonstrated with, chuckling and laughing, and saying "Eh, did I though [?] [W]ell, well, where's the snuff-box, have any of ye seen my box?" His *sotto voce* psalmody was not much varied, and consisted chiefly of "Joseph Muggin's Party"[248] (all his friends he did invite), and an old Scottish lyric, "Jack and his Master," quite democratic in its sympathy, and setting forth at the end of each verse, that "Jack was as good as his master," which he gave in a crooning minor key, like that adopted by old Highland women spinning, or by a sea-man keeping the anchor watch aboard a tramp.

Mysterious business used to take him to Glasgow now and then, when he would lunch at a good club, and then sink out of sight no one knew where or why. His relations and his friends, after the manner of their kind [,] attributed all kinds of vices to him, though [,] if the truth were known, I fancy there was nothing more awful than a left-handed wife[249][,] perhaps some country girl, and a knock-kneed, "short-backit" family, in the dim regions of his family life. In spring [,] about the month of April [,] he regularly appeared in Leamington[250] to drink the waters in that ineffable stucco resort of Irish colonels and Scotch generals, partly because his sisters lived there, and partly on account of the fame the waters enjoyed in Dr. Jephson's[251] time. Although he

---

[246] See passim.

[247] *Bell's Life in London, and Sporting Chronicle.* Up to 1886, it was Britain's leading sporting newspaper.

[248] An eighteenth-century English folk song, a parody of 'Lord Lovel'.

[249] A Common Law wife of unequal social status.

[250] A spa town in Warwickshire.

[251] Dr. Henry Jephson (1798–1878), a society doctor who popularised the spa.

spoke the English language with nothing of his native country in his accent, but that faint intonation which reminds one of the air escaping from the chanter of a bagpipe, yet generally at Leamington, and with all those he looked on as stuck up, he discoursed in broadest Scotch. An English lady being displeased with the genial showers of our northern summer remarked to him "It always seems to rain whenever I come to Scotland," to which he answered "Yes, but it whiles rains when you do not come, Mem." It was his humour usually to address a man as "Mem," a lady by the style of "Sir," and end his sentences no matter what the sex of with him with whom he talked, "No, Sir; yes, Mem;" thus showing his contempt or his respect for both sexes quite impartially. At breakfast time he sat with his teacup making a ring upon the newspaper, silent but comminative, upon the extracts which he read, raising his snuff-smeared face at times to say, "I'll take aw egg. Yes Sir, No, Mem, I think I will take aw."

And so he passed his life in alternation between Leamington and the West of Scotland, growing each day more snuffy, more untidy, and more cynical. Then came a period of nomadism, and to his relatives' amazement they heard he had attached himself to a travelling circus; whether from love of some young lady whom in short petticoats and tights danced on a barebacked horse; from pleasure in the society of the horses or the clown, or simply from the amusement he derived from scandalising all his friends, no one could tell. But with the circus for a year or two he roamed about, appearing now and then, when it chanced, either in Yorkshire or in Scotland, to perform near to a country house where he was known, and dropping in for lunch. On such occasions his sharp wit and knowledge of the world atoned for his strange dress, his dirty habits, and the trail of snuff which, as a snail leaves slime upon a window pane, he left where'er he went.

But this phase like the others had its turn, and tired of his nomadic life he settled down at Largs.[252] There in the semi-fishing village semi-watering place he passed his time, sauntering about artistically draped in his white smock-frock or pinafore, worn over white duck trousers, muttering to himself, and cracking jests alone upon the beach.

A terror to the unprotected nursery-maids, a frequent visitor in church where he sat critically scanning the preacher with disfavour, putting a halfpenny into the plate, which in old-fashioned Scottish churches used to stand at the church door upon a pine or maple pillar simulating a stick of barley-sugar, and focusing all eyes upon himself by his loud criticisms.

---

[252] A town on the Firth of Clyde in North Ayrshire, thirty-three miles south of Glasgow.

But as the most of us have in our heart of hearts some person or another before whom our cynicism melts, our knowledge of the world becomes of no avail, and kindness, love, or custom, makes us regard them as perhaps a wayward dog regards its master whom it runs off from but returns to when hungry, so had my relative, hidden below the crust of snuff and whimsicality, with which he was well pitched inside and out, a feeling of regard, respect or something, for the older of his sisters, with whom he sometimes lived. No sentimental feeling seemed to unite them, in fact, his sister criticised with frank openness, reproved him for his sloth, for dirtiness and for other matters about which modern ladies do not often reprehend their brothers, but he took it in good part. He seldom ventured to indulge in any of his coarse sallies in her presence, whether restrained by fear or by affection no one knew. Towards his other sister he had no such scruples, and when she talked of hunting, being like himself a rider from her youth up, he used to say "To hear my sister talk you would think there never was a woman who could ride, and hardly any man."

Death in its foolish, blundering, inexorable way first took the hunting sister, who with her last breath enjoined upon her heirs not to allow a spavined horse[253] to take her to her grave. Her brother bore her loss quite philosophically, and as the hearse came to the door, exclaimed that the near leader had a thoroughpin,[254] and that his sister never could bear a hearse horse decked in petticoats.

After a year or two spent between snuff and newspapers by my relative, the other sister went. He gave no sign of grief, unless by taking a double dose of snuff, and at the funeral behaved himself more decently than was his custom. All through the lines of stucco villas, semi-detached, each with its garden plot and araucaria, its air of desolate respectability, and its tent in summer on its little lawn, the cortège took its way. My relative was more subdued than usual, but took his snuff at proper intervals, and talked a little with himself of horses he had known, and dogs which in their day had drawn more badgers than the degenerate dogs of modern times.

Under the elm trees in a quiet English churchyard, the rooks' nests swinging in the March east wind, the tardy buds of the late spring forming themselves like drops of amber on the twigs, the hard, old, upright, kindly Scottish lady's grave was dug. On the one side a cheap Carrara monument,[255] commemorating all the virtues of some prosperous citizen reared its head. Upon the other, a mouldering elm board with "affliction sore" marked out the grave of some

---

[253] A painful swelling of the fetlock.
[254] See previous note.
[255] Grey marble tombstone.

poor cottager. In his canonicals the clergyman mumbled his prayer, and on the coffin fell Warwickshire red loam. Friends and acquaintances walked off in pairs, leaving my relative almost alone before the grave. To say he was affected outwardly would be untrue, for he took snuff with regularity. But as I turned to go he drew from the recesses of his "stan o' black"[256] a rose all smeared with snuff, holding it in his hand, as a man holds a bird caught in a window, half cautiously as if he feared it might escape. Then stooping forward he laid it on the grass, and turning round said, "Did you spot the gurrl with the pink flowers in her hat?"

Fortune did not arrange I was to see his funeral, therefore I cannot say if in his coffin his relations had sense enough to place a snuffbox. If they omitted so to do, or if a spavined horse was in his hearse, their sin was great. For me he is a memory of childhood, so quaint, at times I think that I evolved him from my own brain could I not swear I saw him in the flesh, and testify to his strange mutterings, his singing to him-self, his quips, his cranks, his quiddities, and to his snuffy rose.

* * * * *

'*Beattock For Moffat* is a piece of writing that can never die.'

Ford Madox Ford, *The Death of Yesterday*

'At his best (e.g. "Beattock for Moffat") he rivals Maupassant, and, in fact, no writer of our time has equalled him in pictorial quality.'[257]

Stephen Gwynn

Considered by many to be Graham's finest Scottish 'sketch', hidden away inside one of his little-read anthologies, 'Beattock For Moffat' is a wonderful demonstration of Graham's understanding not only of Scottish dialect and its idioms, but of the character, habits and preoccupations of the lower orders.[258] Its true uniqueness, however, lies in the fact that it was taken from 'the fountain of his brain',[259] as it is highly unlikely that he personally witnessed such a scene in the 'Third

---

[256] See passim.

[257] Stephen Gwynn, 'Ebb and Flow: Mr. Cunninghame Graham', *Fortnightly Review,* 1 February 1933, p. 251.

[258] Graham's first biographer, Herbert Faulkner West, claimed to have found Graham's holograph to a friend in a copy of *Beattock to Moffat* at Ardoch which read, 'With hope she will perfect herself in the study of a language that she ought to have learned at her mother's knee'. 'Three Fugitive Pieces'. Talk by West to the Scottish P.E.N. Club, 12 June 1959, p. 8.

[259] Cunninghame Graham, *His People* (London: Duckworth, 1906), p. ix.

Class' carriage of any train. We are, however, left to ponder what his legacy might have been if he had continued to exercise and develop the inventive skills demonstrated here.[260]

At first glance it appears to be a simple tale of touching humanity of a sick man's wish to return home to die. Behind this deeply humane character-study there is, most obviously, an evocation of national and cultural differences, particularly the Scots inclination towards dark humour and an optimistic fatalism, although it is also about town versus country attitudes. It is Graham's most sentimental work, but his sceptical, critical, documentary eye prevents a descent into mawkishness.

BEATTOCK FOR MOFFAT.

Anthologised in *Success* (London: Duckworth, 1902), pp. 139–54.

The bustle on Euston platform stopped for an instant to let the men who carried him to the third class compartment pass along the train. Gaunt and emaciated, he looked just at death's door, and, as they propped him in the carriage between two pillows, he faintly said, "Jock, do ye thing I'll live as far as Moffat? I should na' like to die in London in the smoke."

His cockney wife, drying her tears with a cheap hem-stitched pocket handkerchief, her scanty town-bred hair looking like wisps of tow[261] beneath her hat, bought from some window in which each individual article was marked at seven-and-sixpence, could only sob. His brother, with the country sun and wind burn still upon his face, and his huge hands hanging like hams in front of him, made answer.

"Andra," he said, "gin ye last as far as Beattock, we'll gie ye a braw hurl back to the farm, syne the bask[262] air, ye ken, and the milk, and, and – but can ye last as far as Beattock, Andra?"

The sick man, sitting with the cold sweat upon his face, his shrunken limbs looking like sticks inside his ill-made black slop suit, after considering the proposition on its merits, looked up, and said, "I should na' like to bet I feel fair boss,[263] God knows; but there, the mischief of it is, he will na' tell ye, so that, as ye may say, his knowledge

---

[260] The fact that the sketch did not appear in a journal prior to publication in an anthology, might indicate that Graham was initially concerned about its reception.

[261] Fibres of flax, hemp, or jute.

[262] Scots: Very dry.

[263] Scots: Exhausted.

has na commercial value. I ken I look as gash as Garscadden,[264] Ye mind, Jock, in the braw auld times, when the auld laird just slipped awa', whiles they were birlin' at the clairet. A braw death, Jock ... do you think it'll be rainin' aboot Ecclefechan? Aye ... sure to be rainin' aboot Lockerbie. Nae Christians there, Jock, a' Johnstones and Jardines, ye mind?"

The wife, who had been occupied with an air cushion, and, having lost the bellows, had been blowing into it till her cheeks seemed almost busting, and her false teeth were loosened in her head, left off her toil to ask her husband "If 'e could pick up a bit of something, a porkpie, or a nice sausage roll, or something tasty," which she could fetch from the refreshment room. The invalid having declined to eat, and his brother having drawn from his pocket a dirty bag, in which were peppermints, gave him a "drop,"[265] telling him that he "minded he aye used to like them weel, when the meenister had fairly got into his prelection in the auld kirk, outby."

The train slid almost imperceptibly away, the passengers upon the platform looking after it with that half foolish, half astonished look with which men watch a disappearing train. Then a few sandwich papers rose from the dust almost to the level of the platform, sank again, the clock struck twelve, and the station fell into a half quiescence, like a volcano in the interval between the lava showers. Inside the third class carriage all was quiet until the lights of Harrow shone upon the left, when the sick man, turning himself with difficulty, said, "Goodbye, Harrow-on-the-Hill.[266] I aye liked Harrow for the hill's sake, tho' ye can scarcely ca' yon wee bit mound a hill, Jean."

The wife, who, even in her grief, still smarted under the Scotch variant of her name, which all her life she pronounced as "Jayne," and who, true cockney as she was, bounded her world within the lines of Plaistow, Peckham Rye, the Welch 'Arp ('Endon way),[267] and Willesden, moved uncomfortably at the depreciation of the chief mountain in her cosmos, but held her peace. Loving her husband in a sort of half antagonistic fashion, born of the difference in type between the hard, unyielding, yet humourous and sentimental Lowland Scot,

---

[264] 'Gash as Garscadden' = Looking grim, but in fact dead. From a popular tale of the eighteenth century, when the Laird of Garscadden (now part of Glasgow) died during a drinking bout. According to tradition, a guest on his right leaned over to the guest on his left and whispered: "Garscadden's looking awfu' gash the night', to which the latter whispered back: "Whisht man! Garscadden's been wi' his Maker the last half oor, but no' a word for fear o' spoiling the enjoyment o' the evening."

[265] A 'pan drop', a hard white mint sweet.

[266] Where Graham attended the private school.

[267] The Brent Reservoir, adjacent to the north London suburb of Hendon.

and the conglomerate of all races of the island which meet in London and produce the weedy, shallow breed, almost incapable of reproduction, yet high strung and nervous, there had arisen between them that intangible veil of misconception which, though not excluding love, is yet impervious to respect. Each saw the other's failings, or, perhaps, thought the good qualities which each possessed were faults, for usually men judge each other by their good points, which, seen through prejudice of race, religion and surroundings, appear to them defects.

The brother, who but a week ago had left his farm unwillingly, just when the "neeps were wantin' heughin' and a feck o' things requirin' to be done, forby a puckle sheep wantin' keelin,'[268] to come and see his brother for the last time, sat in that dour and seeming apathetic attitude which falls upon the country man torn from his daily toil and plunged into a town. Most things in London, during the brief intervals he had passed away from the sick bed, seemed foolish to him, and of a nature such as a self-respecting Moffat man, in the hebdomadal[269] enjoyment of the "prelections" of a Free Church minister could not authorise.

"Man, saw ye e'er a carter sittin' on his cart, and drivin' at a trot, instead o' walkin' in a proper manner alongside the horse?" had been his first remark.

The short-tailed sheep dogs, and the way they worked, the inferior quality of the cart horses, their shoes with hardly any calkins[270] worth the name, all was repugnant to him.

On Sabbath too, he had received a shock, for, after walking miles to sit under the "brither of the U.P.[271] minister at Symington," he found Erastian hymn books in the pews, and noticed with stern reprobation that the congregation stood to sing, and that, instead of sitting solidly whilst the "man wrastled in prayer,"[272] stooped forward in the fashion called the Nonconformist lounge.

His troubled spirit had received refreshment from the sermon, which, though short, and extending to but some forty-and-five minutes, had still been powerful, for he said:

"When you wee, shilpit[273] meenister – brither, ye ken, of rantin' Ferguson out by Symington – shook the congregation ower the pit

---

[268] 'Turnips required topping, many chores to be dealt with, as well as a few sheep to be marked with raddle.'
[269] Weekly.
[270] Metal cleats on the front of horseshoes to prevent slipping.
[271] United Presbyterian Church.
[272] Epistle to the Colossians 4:12.
[273] Scots: Thin, puny.

mooth, ye could hae fancied that the very sowls in hell just girned.[274] Man, he garred the very stour to flee aboot the kirk, and, hadna' the big book been brass banded, he would hae dang the haricles fair oot."[275]

So the train slipped past Watford, swaying round the curves like a gigantic serpent, and jolting at the facing points as a horse "pecks" in his gallop at an obstruction in the ground.

The moon shone brightly into the compartment, extinguishing the flickering of the half-candle power electric light. Rugby, the station all lit up, and with its platforms occupied but by a few belated passengers, all muffled up like race horses taking their exercise, flashed past. They slipped through Cannock Chase, which stretches down with heath and firs, clear brawling streams, an out-post of the north lost in the midland clay. They crossed the oily Trent, flowing through the alder copses, and with its backwaters all overgrown with lilies, like an "aguapey"[276] in Paraguay or in Brazil.

The sick man, wrapped in cheap rugs, and sitting like Guy Fawkes, in the half comic, half pathetic way that sick folk sit, making them sport for fools, and, at the same time, moistening the eye of the judicious, who reflect that they themselves may one day sit as they do, bereft of all dignity of strength, looked listlessly at nothing as the train sped on. His loving, tactless wife, whose cheap "sized" handkerchief had long since become a rag with mopping up her tears, endeavoured to bring round her husband's thoughts to paradise, which she conceived as a sort of music hall, where angels sat with their wings folded, listening to sentimental songs.

Her brother-in-law, reared on the fiery faith of Moffat Calvinism, eyed her with great disfavor, as a terrier eyes a rat imprisoned in a cage.

"Jean wumman," he burst out, "to hear ye talk, I would jist think the meenister had been a perfectly illeeterate man, pairadise here, pairadise there, what do ye think a man like Andra could dae daunderin'[277] aboot a gairden naked, pu'in soor aiples frae the trees?"

Cockney and Scotch conceit, impervious alike to outside criticism, and each so bolstered in its pride as to be quite incapable of seeing that anything existed outside the purlieus of their sight, would have made the carriage into a battle-field, had not the husband, with the authority of approaching death, put in his word.

---

[274] Whined.
[275] 'He made the dust fly around the church, and if the bible hadn't been secured by brass straps, he would have made the insides (entrails) come out.'
[276] A South American tributary.
[277] Scots: To stroll or walk aimlessly.

"Whist, Jeanie wumman, Jock, dae ye no ken that Odium-Theologicum[278] is just a curse – pairadise – set ye baith up – pairadise. I dinna' even richtly ken if I can last as far as Beattock."

Stafford, its iron furnaces belching out flames, which burned red holes in the night, seemed to approach, rather than be approached, so smoothly ran the train. The mingled moonlight and the glare of the iron-works lit the canal beside the railway, and from the water rose white vapours as from Styx or Periphlegethon.[279] Through Cheshire ran the train, its timbered houses showing ghastly in the frost which coated all the carriage windows, and rendered them opaque. Preston, the catholic city, lay silent in the night, its river babbling through the public park, and then the hills of Lancashire loomed lofty in the night. Past Garstang, with its water-lily-covered ponds, Garstang where, in the days gone by, catholic squires, against their will, were forced on Sundays to "take wine" in Church on pain of fine, the puffing serpent slid.

The talk inside the carriage had given place to sleep, that is, the brother-in-law and wife slept fitfully, but the sick man looked out, counting the miles to Moffat, and speculating on his strength. Big drops of sweat stood on his forehead, and his breath came double, whistling through his lungs.

They passed by Lancaster, skirting the sea on which the moon shone bright, setting the fishing boats in silver as they lay scarcely moving on the waves. Then, so to speak, the train set its face up against Shap Fell, and, puffing heavily, drew up into the hills, the scattered grey stone houses of the north, flanked by their gnarled and twisted ash trees, hanging upon the edge of the streams, as lonely, and as cut off from the world (except the passing train) as they had been in Central Africa. The moorland roads, winding amongst the heather, showed that the feet of generations had marked them out, and not the line, spade and theodolite, with all the circumstance of modern road makers. They, too, looked white and unearthly in the moonlight, and now and then a sheep, aroused by the snorting of the train, moved from the heather into the middle of the road, and stood there motionless, its shadow filling the narrow track, and flickering on the heather at the edge.

The keen and penetrating air of the hills and night roused the two sleepers, and they began to talk, after the Scottish fashion, of the funeral, before the anticipated corpse.

---

[278] See passim.
[279] Two of the five underworld rivers in Greek mythology.

"Ye ken, we've got a braw new hearse outby, sort of Epescopalian lookin', we' gless a' roond, so's ye can see the kist.[280] Very conceitly too, they mak' the hearses noo-a-days. I min' when they were jist auld sort o' ruckly[281] boxes, awfu' licht, ye ken upon the springs, and just went dodderin' alang, the body swinging to and fro, as if it would flee richt oot. The roads, ye ken, were no nigh hand so richly metalled in thae days."

The subject of the conversation took it cheerfully, expressing pleasure at the advance of progress as typified in the new hearse, hoping his brother had a decent "stan' o' black," and looking at his death, after the fashion of his kind, as it were something outside himself, a fact indeed, on which, at the same time, he could express himself with confidence as being in some measure interested. His wife, not being Scotch, took quite another view, and seemed to think that the mere mention of the word was impious, or, at the least, of such a nature as to bring on immediate dissolution, holding the English theory that unpleasant things should not be mentioned, and that, by this means, they can be kept at bay. Half from affection, half from an inborn love of cant, inseparable from the true Anglo-Saxon, she endeavoured to persuade her husband that he looked better, and yet would mend, once in his native air.

"At Moffat, ye'd 'ave the benefit of the 'ill breezes, and that 'ere country milk, which never 'as no cream in it, but 'olesome, as you say. Why yuss, in about eight days at Moffit, you'll be as 'earty as you ever was. Yuss, you will, you take my word."

Like a true Londoner, she did not talk religion, being too thin in mind and body even to have grasped the dogma of any of the sects. Her Heaven a music 'all, her paradise to see the king drive through the streets, her literary pleasure to read lies in newspapers, or pore on novelettes, which showed her the pure elevated lives of duchesses, placing the knaves and prostitutes within the limits of her own class; which view of life she accepted as quite natural and as a thing ordained to be by the bright stars who write.

Just at the summit they stopped an instant to let a goods train pass, and, in a faint voice, the consumptive said, "I'll almost lay a wager now I'd last to Moffat, Jock. The Shap, ye ken, I aye looked at as the beginning of the run home. The hills, ye ken, are sort o' heart-some.[282] No that they're bonny hill like Moffat hills, na', na', ill-shapen sort of things, just like Borunty tatties,[283] awfu' puir names too, Shap Fell

---

[280] 'With glass all round so you can see the chest (coffin).'
[281] Scots: Rattling.
[282] Cheering, encouraging.
[283] Potatoes grown in 'lazy-beds'.

and Rowland Edge, Hutton Roof Crags, and Arnside Fell; heard ever
ony body sich like names for hills? Naething to fill the mooth; man,
the Scotch hills jist grap ye in the mooth for a' the world like speerits."

They stopped at Penrith, which the old castle walls make even
meaner, in the cold morning light, than other stations look. Little
Salkeld, and Armathwaite, Cotehill, and Scotby all rushed past,
and the train slackening, stopped with a jerk, upon the platform, at
Carlisle. The sleepy porters bawled out "change for Maryport," some
drovers slouched into carriages, kicking their dogs before them, and,
slamming to the doors, exchanged the time of day with others of their
tribe, all carrying ash and hazel sticks, all red faced and keen eyed,
their caps all crumpled, and their great-coat tails all creased, as if
their wearers had laid down to sleep full dressed, so as to lose no time
in getting to the labours of the day. The old red sandstone church,
with something of a castle in its look, as well befits a shrine close to
a frontier where in days gone by the priest had need to watch and
pray, frowned on the passing train, and on the manufactories, whose
banked up fires sent poisonous fumes into the air, withering the trees
which, in the public park, a careful council had hedged round about
with wire.

The Eden ran from bank to bank, its waters swirling past as wildly
as when "The Bauld Buccleugh"[284] and his Moss Troopers, bearing
"the Kinmount" fettered in their midst, plunged in and passed it,
whilst the keen Lord Scroope[285] stood on the brink amazed and
motionless. Gretna, so close to England, and yet a thousand miles
away in speech and feeling, found the sands now flying through the
glass. All through the mosses which once were the "Debatable Land"
on which the moss-troopers of the clan Graeme were used to hide
the cattle stolen from the "auncient enemy," the now repatriated
Scotsman mumbled feebly "that it was bonny scenery" although a
drearier prospect of "moss hags" and stunted birch trees is not to
be found. At Ecclefechan he just raised his head, and fairly spoke
of "yon auld carle, Carlyle,[286] ye ken, a dour thrawn[287] body, but a
gran' pheelosopher," and then lapsed into silence, broken by frequent
struggles to take a breath.

---

[284] Walter Scott, first Lord Scott of Buccleuch (1565–1611), was a Scottish nobleman and famous border reiver.
[285] Thomas Scrope, tenth Baron Scrope of Bolton (1567–1609), Warden of
the English West March. He captured the Scottish outlaw 'Kinmont Willie'
Armstrong, but Buccleuch's men freed him from Carlisle Castle.
[286] Thomas Carlyle (1795–1881). Scottish historian, essayist, and philosopher,
born in Ecclefechan, Dumfriesshire.
[287] Scots: Extremely obstinate.

His wife and brother sat still, and eyed him as a cow watches a locomotive engine pass, amazed and helpless, and he himself had but the strength to whisper "Jock, I'm dune, I'll no see Moffat, blast it, yon smoke, ye ken, yon London smoke has been ower muckle for ma lungs."

The tearful, helpless wife, not able even to pump up the harmful and unnecessary conventional lie, which after all, consoles only the liar, sat pale and limp, chewing the fingers of her Berlin gloves. Upon the weather-beaten cheek of Jock glistened a tear, which he brushed off angrily as it had been a wasp.

"Aye, Andra'" he said, "I would hae liket awfu' weel that ye should win to Moffat. Man, the rowan trees are a' in bloom, and there's a bonny breer[288] upon the corn – aye, ou aye, the reid bogs[289] are lookin' gran' the year – but Andra', I'll tak' ye east to the auld kirk yaird, ye'll no' ken anything aboot it but we'll hae a heart-some funeral."

Lockerbie seemed to fly towards them, and the dying Andra' smiled as his brother pointed out the place and said, "ye mind, there are no any Christians in it," and answered, "Aye, I mind, naething but Jardines," as he fought for breath.

The death dews gathered on his forehead as the train shot by Nethercleugh, passed Wamphray, and Dinwoodie, and with a jerk pulled up at Beattock just at the summit of the pass.

So in the cold spring morning light, the fine rain beating on the platform, as the wife and brother got their almost speechless care out of the carriage, the brother whispered, "Dam't, ye've done it Andra', here's Beattock; I'll tak' ye east to Moffat yet to dee."

But on the platform, huddled on the bench to which he had been brought, Andra' sat speechless and dying in the rain. The doors banged to, the guard stepping in lightly as the train flew past, and a belated porter shouted, "Beattock, Beattock for Moffat," and then summoning his last strength, Andra' smiled, and whispered faintly in his brother's ear, "Aye, Beattock – for Moffat?' Then his head fell back, and a faint bloody foam oozed from his pallid lips. His wife stood crying helplessly, the rain beating upon the flowers of her cheap hat, rendering it shapeless and ridiculous. But Jock, drawing out a bottle, took a short dram and saying, "Andra', man, ye made a richt gude fecht o' it," snorted an instant in a red pocket handkerchief, and calling up a boy, said, "Rin, Jamie, to the toon, and tell McNicol to send up and fetch a corp." Then, after helping to remove the body to the waiting room, walked out into the rain, and whistling

---

[288] Scots: Beard (corn silk).
[289] Red bog-moss (*sphagnum capillifolium*).

"Corn Rigs"[290] quietly between his teeth lit up his pipe, and muttered as he smoked "Aye richt gude fecht – man aye, ou aye, a game yin Andra', puir felly. Weel, weel, he'll hae a braw hurl onyway in the new Moffat hearse."

* * * * *

Perhaps there is no better example than this rambling soliloquy to demonstrate Graham's value to the world of Scottish letters. Garrulous, inconsequential, disconnected, yet accurately reflecting conversational Scots.

A FISHERMAN

Justice: *The Organ of Social Democracy*, 3 May 1902, p. 3.
Anthologised in *Success* (London: Duckworth, 1902), pp. 155–68.

The steamer scrunched against the pier, the gangway plank was drawn back slowly, and with as great an effort as it had weighed a ton, by the West Highland tweed-clad semi-sailors, semi-longshore men. The little groups of drovers separated, each following the fugle-man[291] to the nearest public house. The ropes were cast off from the belaying pins, and whisked like serpents over the slippery slime-covered boards: a collie dog holding on to one of them by its teeth was dragged to the very edge, amongst a shower of Gaelic oaths.

Then with a snort and plunge the "Islesman" met the south-west swell coming up past Pladda[292] from the Mull. The wandering Willie with his fiddle in a green baize bag, stripped off its cover, and got to work in the wild wind and drizzling rain, at reels, strathspeys, laments, and all the minor music which has from immemorial time been our delight in Scotland, although, no doubt, it is as terrifying to the Southerner as when the bagpipes skirl. His dog beside him, a mere mongrel, looking like a dirty mop, and yet with something half pathetic, half ridiculous about him, sat holding round his neck a battered can for pence. The fiddler, bandy-legged and dressed in heather mixture tweed, which gave out fumes of peat reek, snuff, and stale whisky, stood by the forebits, and round him clustered all the heterogeneous "heids and thraws"[293] of the population of the

---

[290] A well-known song by Robert Burns.
[291] A soldier who stands in front of a regiment to demonstrate and maintain time in drilling exercises.
[292] A small island off the south coast of Arran.
[293] Scots: In disorder or confusion.

West Highlands, Glasgow and Greenock, and the other towns upon the Firth of Clyde. Gently the steamer glided through the Kyles of Bute, left Toward Point on her port bow, and headed for Dunoon. And as she steamed along, passing the varied scenery of mist-capped mountain, and of stormy loch, the peaks of Arran in the distance like a gigantic saddle, hung outlined in the clouds. The passengers, for the most part, seemed to see nothing but each other's clothes and personal defects, after the fashion of so many travellers, who, with their shells of prejudice borne on their backs as they were snails, go out to criticise that which they could have seen to just as great advantage in their homes. Amongst them was a man dressed in a greasy "stan' o' black," who, at first sight, appeared to be what we in Scotland call a "goin' aboot body,"[294] and recognise[d] as having quite a status in the land. His clothes, originally black, had borne the labour, whisky, and rain of many a funeral. He did not seem a townsman, for he had that wizened, weather-beaten look which, once a sailor, never leaves a man this side the grave. At once you saw that he had made his bread in ships, or boats, or in some way upon that element on which those who go down to it in brigs "smell hell," as the old shellback[295] said who heard the passage in the Bible on the wonders of the deep.[296]

Hard bread it is; damned hard, as the old admiral told his sacred majesty, the fourth William, who asked him whether he had been bred up to the sea.

He,[297] at least, cared not an atom for the others on the boat, but seemed to know each inlet, stone, and islet on the coast. He carried a geranium cutting in a little pot, hedged around with half a newspaper to shield it from the wind, and as the sun fell on the hills of "Argyle's bowling-green,"[298] broke out into a rhapsody, half born of whisky and half of that perfervidness which is the heritage of every Scot.

"'There shall be no more sea,'[299] no a wise like saying of John, though he sort o' doited[300] in Patmos;[301] what had the body against the sea?"

"I followed it myself twal[302] year. First in an auld rickle o' a boat at Machrihanish, and syne wi' the herrin' fishers about Loch Fyne.

---

[294] Scots: A traveller/tinker.
[295] Someone who has crossed the equator.
[296] Psalm 107.
[297] Altered to 'The nonedescript' in the anthology.
[298] A name given to the promontory between Loch Goil and Loch Long.
[299] Revelation 21:1.
[300] Scots: Behaved foolishly.
[301] The Aegean island where John of Parmos received visions found in the Book of Revelation.
[302] Twelve.

Man, a gran' life the sea. Whiles I was sorry that I left it; but auri sacra fames,[303] ye mind. Nae mair sea! Set John up. But the mountains, the mountains will remain. Thank the Lord for the mountains."

No one responded to his remarks, he turned to me, observing that I looked an "eddicated man."

"Aye, ou aye, I mind I made a matter of five hundred pund at the herrin' fishin', and then, ye ken, I thocht I saw potentialities (gran' word, potentiality) of being rich, rich beyond the dreams of avarice, as that auld carle, Dr. Johnson, said. Johnson, ye ken, he that keepit a skule, and ca'ed it an academy, as auld Boswell said. A sort o' randy body yon Boswell, man, though he gied us a guid book. Many's the time I hae lauched[304] over it. Puir, silly devil, bit with an eye untill him like a corbie[305] for detail. Details, ye ken, are just the vertebræ of the world. Ye canna do without detail. What did I do? Losh[306] me, I had most forgot. Will ye tak' an apple? It'll keep doun the drouth.[307] Scotch apples are the best apples in the world, but I maun premise I like apples sour, as the auld leddie said.

"Na – weel, ye're maybe right, apples are sort o' wersh[308] without speerits. Bonny wee islands, yon Cumbraes, the wee yin just like a dunter's[309] heid, the big yin, a braw place for fishin'.

"Whitin' Bay,[310] ye ken, just beyond where the monument for they puir midshipmen stands. An awfu' coast, I mind three laddies, some five and thirty years syne,[311] from up aboot England gaein' oot in a lugsail boat from the Largs. Ane o' they easterly haars[312] cam' on. They just come doon like a judgment of God on the coast – ye canna escape them nor it. Aye weel, I'll no say no, a judgment, a special judgment o' divine providence, just fa's like a haar, fa's on the just and unjust alike. Na, na, I'm no meanin' any disrepeck to providence, weel do I ken which side my bannock's buttered. ... The laddies, the easterly wind just drave them aff the coast, in a wee boatie, and had it no' been ane o' them was a sailor laddie, they had ne'er a' won back. Wondrous are His ways, whiles He saves those that never would be missed, and whiles. ... Do I no believe in the efficacy of prayer.

---

[303] 'What do not you force mortal hearts [to do], accursed hunger for gold.' Virgil, *The Aeneid*, book 3:57.
[304] Scots: Laughed.
[305] Scots: Crow.
[306] Scots: Lord.
[307] Scots: Satisfy your thirst.
[308] Scots: Flavourless.
[309] Scots: A porpoise or dolphin.
[310] A place on the southern end of the island of Arran.
[311] Scots: Since.
[312] Scots: Thick coastal fogs.

Hoots aye, that is I'm no sure. Whiles a man just works his knees into horn wi' prayin' for what might profit him, that is, profit him in this world ye see, and providence doesna steer[313] for a' his prayin.' Whiles a man just puts up a sipplication for some speeritual matter, and the Lord just answers him before the man is sure he wants the object of his prayer.

"The Cumbraes, sort o' backlyin' islands, but the folk that live on them hae a guid conceit. Sort o' conceity, the bit prayer, the minister in Millport used to pit up for the adjawcent islands o' Great Britain and Ireland,[314] ye mind it, ye that seem to be a sort o' eddicated man.

"Yer lookin' at the bit gerawnium. Sort of tragical that gerawnium, if you regard the matter pheelosophically. I telt you that I aince made a bit o' money at the herrin' fishin'. Shares in a boat or twa. Man, I was happy then, a rough life the fishin', but vera satisfyin'. Just an element o' gambling aboot it that endears it to a man. Aye, ou aye, the sea, I ken it noo, I see why I lik'd the life sae weel. I felt it then though, just like a collie dog feels the hills, although he doesna ken it. I always fancy that collies look kind o' oot o' place in Glesca.

"A collie dog, ye ken, would rather hear a West Hielandman swear at him in Gaelic than an English leddy ca' him a' the pets in the world. It's no his fault, it's no the swearin' that he likes, but just the tone o' voice. A gran' language the Gaelic, profanity in it just sounds like poetry in any other tongue.

"Weel, a fisherman is just like a collie dog, he's rather hear the tackle run through the sheaves o' the blocks than a' the kists o' whis-tles[315] in the Episcopalian churches up aboot Edinburgh. And then the sea, dam't I canna tell why I still ettle[316] to get back to it. It took ma fayther, maist o' ma brithers, and the feck[317] o' a' ma folk. It's maybe that, it's the element o' uncertainty there again, but dam't I dinna rightly know what it is, except that when ye aince get the salt doon into the soul ye ken, ye canna get it oot again. That is, no' on this side the grave. I wouldna have left it, had it not been ma mither, threep, threepin'[318] on me ... aye, and the auri sacra fames.

"... Bonny the Largs looks, eh? Gin it's no the view of Cuchuillin,[319] the hills of Arran fae the Largs is the brawest view in Scotland.

---

[313] Scots: Stir, move.
[314] By reputation, the people of the Cumbraes were so independently-minded in former times that the local minister used to pray for 'the islands of the Great Cumbrae and the Little Cumbrae and the adjoining island of Great Britain'.
[315] Scots: A church organ. Episcopalian churches were known as 'whistle kirks'.
[316] Scots: Intend.
[317] Scots: Majority.
[318] Scots: A determined and persistent argument. To nag.
[319] Cúchulainn, a Celtic hero and demi-god.

That is for a man who likes the sea. But I see I'm wearyin' ye with ma clash.[320] Ye'd maybe like to see the *Herald*. ... I hae Bogatsky in my bawg: Bogatsky's 'Golden Treasury,'[321] but maybe its no greatly read in your body. Fine old-fashioned book Bogatsky, nae taint o' latter-day Erastianism aboot it. Na, na, I'se warrant ye the man compiled Bogatsky gied his congregation mony a richt shake abune the pit. Tophet,[322] ye ken, the real old, what I might ca' the constitutional Tophet, before they hung thermometers aboot the walls, in case the temperature gaed ower high."

The steamer, after plunging uneasily beside the pier at Largs for sufficient time to let a knot of drovers, each with his dog led by a piece of twine, and holding in their hands hooked hazel sticks, reel off towards the town, and to allow the passengers (who did not mark it) space to view the beauties of the place, the little river brawling through the town, and the long bit of sea-swept grass on which goats pasture fixed to chains, and get a living on the scanty herbage, eked out with bottles, bones and sardine tins, turned eastward once again towards the Clyde.

She ran past Fairlie, with its cliffs all clothed in oak and hazel copse, the passengers by this time being "michtily refreshed,"[323] as was the chairman of the curling Club at Coupar Angus, after his fifteenth tumbler, threw sandwich bags and bottles overboard, and took to dancing on the deck. The elders gathered into knots, talked politics, religion, or with much slapping of red hands upon their knees, enjoyed indecent tales, after the fashion of the Puritan, who though his creed enjoins a modest life, yet places no embargo on his speech. So it is said an Irishman in Lent, meeting a friend who remarked that he was drunk, rejoined, "Sure, God Almighty never set a fast upon a drink."

My philosophic friend and I watched the athletic sports, and when the lassies skirled[324] as partners pinched them, or in the joys of life, which manifests itself in diverse ways, and usually in some unseemly fashion when the two sexes meet, he wagged a moralizing head, and freely poured out his philosophy.

"Man Rabbie, ... ye'll hae Burns ... Rabbie kenned his country-men. A fine, free, fornicatin', pious folk we are. Man, Rabbie, kent us

---

[320] 'I see that I'm tiring you with my chatter.'
[321] *A Golden Treasury for the Children of God* (1746) by Karl Heinrich von Bogatzky (1690–1774).
[322] A site within the Valley of Hinnom where a cult of burning children as a sacrifice to Moloch was practised during the Judean monarchy (viz. 2 Kings 23:10; Jer. 7:32). Graham erroneously uses it as a name for Hell.
[323] Drunk.
[324] Scots: Screeched.

better than he kent himsel', I sometimes think. Aye, ou aye, ye canna mak a saint o' Rabbie. Saints, ye ken are weel enough in books. But sort o' weary bodies, they must hae been, the feck o' them. I didna tell ye though aboot the bit gerawnium. I hae it in the cabin, for fear they cattle micht sit doon on it; ye mind auld Walter Scott, the time he pouched[325] the glass George IV. Drank oot o', and then fair dang it into finders[326] on the road hame? Kind o' weak o' Scott pouchin' yon glass; a bonny carle, yon George, to touch folk for the King's evil[327] ... but ou aye, the gerawnium, I mind it.

"Ye see a' my potentialities of growing rich werena just realized. I wrocht[328] twa year in Glesca, ane in Edinburgh, syne sax in Brig o' Weir,[329] whiles takin' a bit flutter on the Stock Exchange. Rogues they fellies on the Exchange, ettlin' to mak' their siller without honest toil. Na, na; I ken what ye'r goin' to say – if I had won, I wouldna' hae misca'ed them. Pairfectly reasoned, sir; but then ye ken when a man loses, the chap that gets his siller is aye a rogue. Weel, weel, many's the time I wished masel back at Tobermory[330] in the bit boat, wi' the bonny wee-tanned lug, fishin', aye, fishin', like the Apostles. Weel, I ken why the Lord found his first followers amongst fishermen. Simple folk, ye see, and wi' the gamblin' element weel developed; no like yer hinds[331] – slave, slavin' at the ground – but oot upon the lake, yon sea of Galilee, ye mind; a sort o' loch, just like Loch Fyne, as I ae thocht. When ye sit in the boat, keepin' her full and by, fechtin' the sea, your eye just glancin' on the waves, it kind o' maks ye gleg to risk a wee.[332] Nae fears we'll get another preacher like the Lord; but if we did, there wouldna be a fisherman, from Tobermory doun to the Cruives o' Cree[333] that wouldna follow him. I'se warrant them. Dour folk, the fishers, but venturesome; and a' the time I wrocht aboot thae stinkin' towns, I ettled to get back. I aye went since a year to see our mither; she just stops aboot twa mile west of Tobermory, and I aye tak back ane o' they gerawniums in a pot. Why do I not stop there when I win back ye say? Aye, there's the mystery of it, the sort o' tragedy as I was tellin' ye when we came through the Kyles.

"Ye see ... spot yon lassie wi' the sunset hair o' the lang backit, short-leggit West Highland kind, built like a kyloe, just gars me think

---

[325] Pocketed.
[326] Scots: Broke it into pieces.
[327] Scrofula, an infection of the lymph nodes.
[328] Scots: Worked.
[329] Bridge of Weir, a town in Renfrewshire; the erstwhile home of 'Heather Jock'.
[330] The chief town on the Island of Mull.
[331] Scots: Farm servant.
[332] Scots: Responsive to taking a gamble.
[333] Fish traps on the River Cree in Dumfries & Galloway.

upon yon woman of Samaria[334] … I'm haverin' … weel, the fack is I canna stop at hame. Tak' a West Heilan' stirk[335] and put him in a park, doon aboot Falkirk, or in the Lothians, or maybe, at the first he doesna' thrive, misses the Heilan' grass maybe, and the gran' wind that blaws across the sea. Syne he gets habeetuated, and ye tak him back to the north, maybe he couldna bide. That's just ma ain case, sir.

"Weel do I mind the auld braw days; a herrin' never tasted sae weel as just fresh caught and brandered[336] in the boat. I mind yon seinin'[337] too, sic splores[338] we had, aye and a feck o' things come back to me when I am in the toon. The peat reek, and a' the comfortable clarty[339] ways we had, the winter nights, when the wind blew fit to tak' the flauchter feals[340] o' the old cottage. I mind them o't a'. That is, I danna care to mind."

As we talked, the steamer slipped past Wemyss Bay, left the Cloch Lighthouse on the left hand, and passed by Inverkip, slid close by Gourock, and then opened up the valley of the Clyde. Greenock with all its smoky chimneys rose in view, sending a haze of fog into the air. The timber in the ponds upon the shore surged to and fro against the railings as the steamer's swell lifted it slowly, and the settled down again to season in the mud. Dumbarton rock showed dimly and the river narrowed, the fairway marks showing the channel like a green ribbon winding through mud banks, as the vessel drew towards the pier.

Gathering their packages and parcels, and smoothing out their clothes, the passengers passed down the gangway, laughing and pushing one another in their haste to get away.

The man with the geranium in the pot still lingered, looking back towards the sea. Then gathering up his traps[341] and tucking his umbrella underneath his arm, prepared to follow them.

"Good-bye," he said, "we hae had a pleasant crack, I'll just be off and daunder up the toon. Doddered[342] and poor, and a wee thing addicted to strong drink, strong drink, ye ken, speerits, that maketh glad the heart of man,[343] neither a fisher nor a townsman, a sort o' failure as ye may say, I am. Good-bye, ye seem a sort o' eddicated

---

[334] The Samaritan woman who gave Jesus water. John 4.
[335] Scots: A young bullock.
[336] Scots: Cooked on a gridiron.
[337] Songs.
[338] Scots: Such parties/celebrations.
[339] Scots: Messy/mucky.
[340] Scots: Roof turfs cut with a 'flauchter' = turf spade.
[341] Personal luggage or belongings.
[342] Scots: Moving slowly, tottering.
[343] Psalm 104:15. 'And wine that maketh glad the heart of man.'

man. ... Na, na, I will na drop it, never fear. I brocht it a' the way from Tobermorey, and ye ken, sir, Greenock is no' a guid place for gerawniums after all.'

He stumbled out along the gangway plank, his rusty "stan o' black" looking more storm-worn and ridiculous than ever in the evening sun. Holding his flower-pot in his hand wrapped round with newspaper, he passed out of my sight amongst the crowd, and left me wondering if the flower in the pot would live, and he return, and die in Tobermory, by the sea.

✳ ✳ ✳ ✳ ✳

Early in life, Graham had developed an anti-Calvinism, which he associated with a rigid and hypocritical morality,[344] thus, the subject of this next tale, an uncompromising Presbyterian missionary in Africa would seem to be an ideal target for his mockery,[345] but other preoccupations are in play. The first was Graham's anti-imperialism, and the exploitation on native societies, most fully realized in an indignant, biting satire entitled '"Bloody Niggers"', published in the Marxist journal, *The Social-Democrat*,[346] in which he wrote:

> 'Niggers' who have no cannons, and cannot construct a reasonable torpedo have no rights. 'Niggers' whose lot is placed outside our flag, whose lives are given over to a band of money-grubbing miscreants have neither rights nor wrongs. Their land is ours, their cattle, fields, their houses, their poor utensils, arms, all that they have; their women, too, are ours to infect with syphilis, leave with child, outrage, torment, and make by consort with the vilest of our vile, more vile than beasts.

Graham also harboured a deep distrust of missionaries, and their baleful effects of on native societies, but, despite his professed religious scepticism, he maintained an interest in 'religious enterprises pursued under disadvantageous circumstances',[347] demonstrated particularly

---

[344] G. K. Chesterton wrote: 'Cunninghame Graham at my elbow, muttering in my ear in a soft but fierce fashion: "I never could stand a Protestant sermon". G. K. Chesterton, *Autobiography* (House of Stratus, 2001), p. 177.

[345] Tom Hubbard described it as 'a comic *Heart of Darkness*'. Tom Hubbard, 'Cunninghame Graham', *Cencrastus*, Autumn 1982, p. 42.

[346] Cunninghame Graham, '"Bloody Niggers"', *Social Democrat*, April 1897, pp. 104–9.

[347] Cunninghame Graham, 'Father Archangel of Scotland', *Nineteenth Century*, no. 34, September 1893, p. 385.

in his essays 'Father Archangel of Scotland', and 'A Jesuit',[348] but finding fuller expression in his book, *A Vanished Arcadia*.[349]

In his sketch 'In the Tarumensian Woods', he related how a priest had brought three members of a native family into his township, who were soon afflicted by lethargy and pains, and one by one they wasted away and died. After praising the piety and sacrifice of this priest, he also called him 'muddlehead', and suggested that the baptisms he had carried out had resulted in death. The priest, however, believed that the deaths were due 'to the exceeding compassion of the Almighty'. Graham concluded that 'the Jesuits did much good, mixed with some folly, as is incidental to mankind'.[350] Consequently, this respect disappeared, and we might contrast it with an uncompromising stance towards similar good works, written ten years later:

> Who does not feel as if a slug was crawling on his soul on reading in some missionary report of all their misdirected labours and their sufferings, and of the perils that they have endured, to turn some fine free race of savages ... into bad copies of our lowest class, waddling about in ill-made clothes and claiming kindred with us as brother 'Klistians' in the Lord?[351]

A CONVERT

The Saturday Review, 30 May 1903, p. 677.
Anthologised in *Progress* (London: Duckworth, 1905), pp. 218–36.

FROM Bathurst to S. Paul's Loanda:[352] right up and down the coast; in every bight; upon the Oil Rivers[353] down Congo way: in all the missionary stations, in which the trembling heathen had endured his ministrations; in factory and port: by all the traders and chance travellers, no one was more detested than the Reverend Archibald Macrae. All that is hard and self-assertive in the Scottish character, in him seemed to be multiplied a hundredfold. All that is kindly, old world and humorous: all that so often makes the Scot more easy to

[348] Cunninghame Graham, 'A Jesuit', *Saturday Review*, 3 August 1895, pp. 135–6.
[349] Cunninghame Graham, *A Vanished Arcadia* (London: Heinemann, 1901).
[350] Cunninghame Graham, 'In the Tarumensian Woods', *Nineteenth Century*, no. 36, August 1894, p. 252.
[351] Cunninghame Graham, *Progress and Other Sketches* (London: Duckworth, 1905), p. 4.
[352] From Gambia to Angola.
[353] The delta of the River Niger.

get on with than an Englishman, in the Reverend Archibald was quite left out. Dour and grey-headed, with a stubbly Newgate frill[354] under his chin; dressed in black broadcloth, with a white helmet shadowing his dark red mottled face, a bible and umbrella ever in his hand or tucked beneath his arm; (he said himself he "aye liked oxtering aboot the word o' God"[355]), he stood confessed, fitted to bring a sword rather than peace to everyone he met. Withal not a bad-hearted man, but tactless, disputatious, and as obstinate as a male mule. "I hae to preach the worrd, baith in an' out o' season, and please the Lorrd I'll do so", was his constant saw.[356]

From the earliest times, the tactless, honest and aggressive missionary has been a thorn in the flesh of everyone upon the coast of Africa. Consuls and traders, captains of men of war, all know and fear him, and most likely he has kept back the cause he labours for, more than a hundred slave traders have done. They kill and enslave the body, but such as was the Reverend Archibald enslave and kill the soul. His station far up a river which flowed sluggishly through woods of dark metallic foliaged trees, was called Hope House. Sent out from Norway all in sections, it had been set up just on the edge of a lagoon from which at evening a thick white vapour rose. A mangrove swamp reached almost to the door, the situation having been chosen by the Reverend Archibald himself to thwart the heads of his society, who not unnaturally wished it should be "located" in a more healthy spot. Painted a staring white, with bright green shutters, none of which fitted the windows they were supposed to shield, without a garden or patch of cultivated ground, Hope House stood out a challenge to the heathen either to come at once beneath the yoke of the Reverend Archibald and to embrace his demonology, or to entrench themselves more strongly in their befetished faith.

The Reverend Archibald lived what is called a virtuous life, that is, he did not drink, did not sell gin or arms upon the sly, and round about the precincts of Hope House no snuff and butter colour children played. Hard, upright and self-righteous, he stalked about as if cut out of Peterhead grey granite: a Christian milestone set up on the heathen way, with the inscription "that road leads to Hell". This he himself was quite aware of, and used to say, "Ye see I hae the word of God, and if the heathen dinna come to listen to it they will all burrn".

Still, disagreeable and wrongheaded as he was, the Reverend Archibald was in his way an honourable man. "Conviction", as he said a thousand times "should follow reasonable airgument".

---

[354] Whiskers grown under the jaw and chin, with no moustache.
[355] Carrying his Bible in his armpit.
[356] A saying.

He himself having from his earliest youth argued upon every subject in the heaven above, the earth beneath, and on the water, which may or may not be under the earth, was well equipped for battle with the comparatively lightly armed fetish-worshiper of the West Coast of Africa.

Seated in his black horsehair-covered chair, before his table with its legs stuck into broken bottles filled with paraffin to keep off the white ants, and with his bible covered in shiny cloth before him, the Reverend Archibald passed his spare time looking up texts wherewith to pulverise such of the infidel who in his neighbourhood had conscientiously resisted all his wiles and held by their old faith.

Often in reading over and again the minor prophets, so called, he would exclaim, "not on account of their less authenteecity, but simply because of the greater brevity of their prophecies", his Scottish mind was struck with the similarity of the scheme of life of which they treated and of those with whom he lived. "Yon Zephaniah, he was a gatherer of sycamore fruit ye ken,[357] would ha' done powerfu' work amongst the heathen on the coast" he would exclaim as he shut up his bible with a bang, and sat down to read "Bogatsky's Golden Treasury"[358] and smoke his pipe. His library was limited to the aforesaid "Golden Treasury" of damnatory texts, "Blair's Sermons",[359] and some books by Black,[360] which he read doubtfully, perceiving well that they set out a picture of no life known to the world, but because the scenes were laid in what he called "N.B".[361]

The frequent poring upon these treasures of the literary art, and ponderings upon the precepts of war to the knife with unbelievers, so faithfully set forth by the more ferocious writers in the Old Testament, together with his isolation from the world, had made him even narrower in mind than when he left his village in the east neuk of Fife. His blunt outspokenness and bluff brutality of manner, on which he prided himself beyond measure, thinking apparently that those who save the soul must of necessity wound every feeling of the mind, had set a void between him and all the other Europeans on the coast.

The washed-out, gin-steeped white men of the oil rivers turned from him with an oath when he adjured them to become Good Templars:[362] the traders from the interior when they dropped down the river in their steam launches or canoes, all gave Hope House the

---

[357] It was not Zephaniah who tended sycamores but the prophet Amos (Amos 7:14).
[358] See passim.
[359] Hugh Blair (1718–1800), a Scottish author and religious theorist.
[360] Alexander Black (1789–1827), a Scottish Free-Church theologian.
[361] North Britain (Scotland).
[362] An international temperance organisation.

widest of wide berths, after the experience of one who going to his station with his young wife from Europe was asked if he had "put away yon Fanti[363] gurrl, that was yer sort o' concubine ye ken". As for the natives who had come beneath his yoke, he treated them as he thought in a kindly way, after the fashion that in days gone by the clergy treated the laity in Scotland, that is, as people conquered by raiders from the Old Testament, making their lives a burden for the welfare of their souls. Still being, as are most missionaries, possessed of medicines and goodwill to use them when his flock fell ill, he had some reputation amongst those who had no money to go out and pay a fetish doctor on the sly. Upon the spiritual side, he was not quite so far removed in sympathy from those to whom he ministered; his God was a mere counterpart of the negroes' devil, and both of them were to be conciliated in the same way, by sacrifice of what the worshipper held dear. But in his dealings with his flock the Reverend Archibald Macrae took no account of isothermal lines. For him, mortality, not that he much insisted on it, holding that faith was more important, was a fixed quantity. These shifting and prismatic qualities of right and wrong, by him were seen identical, no matter if the spectrum used were that of Aberdeen or Ambrizette.[364] Occasionally, therefore, he and his flock were at cross purposes, for to the flock, it seemed an easy matter to give up their gods, but harder all at once to change the daily current of their lives.

Conviction, it is true, had followed upon reasonable, or at least upon reiterated "airgument", but when the Reverend Archibald spoke of what he called "a nearer approximation to the moral code of the Old Book", his catechumens[365] were apt to leave him and retire to the seclusion of the woods. Nothing contributed more to these backslidings than the vicinity of an unconverted chief known by the name of Monday Flatface who had his "croom'[366] five or six miles beyond Hope House upon the river side. The chief lived his own life after the way of his ancestors had lived before him, accepting gratefully from the Europeans their gin, their powder and sized cotton cloths, but steadfastly rejecting all their different faiths. All the exponents of the various sects had tried their hands on him without success. Priests from the neighbouring Portuguese settlements had done their best, flaunting the novel charms of purgatory before the simple negro's eyes, who up till then had known but heaven and hell.

---

[363] An archaic spelling applied to the Fante people who occupy the coastal regions of Ghana.

[364] The Portuguese name for a town and province in Angola.

[365] 'People under instruction.'

[366] Asante Twi: Hut.

The church of England backed by the stamp of its connection with the governing powers had tried its fortune on the chief, holding out hints of Government protection, but without effect. The Nonconformists, too, had had their turn, and sought by singing hymns and preaching to let in light upon the opinionated old idolater, and had all been foiled. Lastly, the Reverend Macrae who bore the banner of the Presbyterians, had attacked in force, bringing to bear the whole artillery of North British metaphysics, dangling before the chieftain visions of a future when his children brought into the fold, should be in spiritual touch with Aberdeen, be fed on porridge, and on Sawbath while away the afternoon in learning paraphrases and wrestling with the Shorter Catechism.[367] All had been in vain, and Monday Flatface while taking all that he could get in medicines, cotton clothes, Dutch clocks, and large red cotton parasols, was still a heathen, a polygamist; some said cannibal upon the sly, and regularly got drunk on palm-tree wine instead of buying gin after the fashion of his brethren who had come into the fold. But above all the rest the chief was hateful to the missionary in his character of humorist. Naturally, those who leave their country to propagate their individual faith are serious men, and the Rev. Archibald was no exception to the rule. Your serious man has from the beginning of the world added enormously to human misery. Wars, battles, murders and the majority of sudden deaths are all his work. Crusades for holy sepulchers, with pilgrimages to saints' tombs, leagues and societies to prevent men living after the fashion they consider best, were all the handiwork of serious men. A dull, gold-dusted-over world it would have been by now, had not a wisely constituted all-seeing Providence, in general denied brains in sufficient ratio to energy, or allowed success invariably to wait on iteration. So when Chief Monday Flatface took the Reverend Archibald's exhortations to amend his present naughty life, forsake his fathers' gods and straight dismiss his wives he had himself with care selected, choosing them fat but comely, and such as best anointed all their persons with palm oil, as a mere joke, the missionary's fury knew no bounds. Had he but tried to persecute, or stepped an atom beyond what the general sentiment of the European traders sanctioned, the missionary would have been pleased. In the one case the dignity of persecution, hitherto withheld, would like an aureole shone above his head, and in the other a complaint to the nearest British governor would have procured a gunboat to bombard the village of the chief. But nothing of the sort occurred, and the old chief persisted in still flourishing like

---

[367] The Westminster Shorter Catechism was written in 1646 and 1647 by a synod of English and Scottish theologians and laymen. It is widely used by non-conformist denominations.

a green mangrove tree, and stopping up his ears to all the arguments of the Reverend Archibald Macrae. Often they met and talked the matter out in "Blackman English", eked out with Fanti and with Arabic, of which both polemists just knew sufficient to obscure the arguments upon their disagreeing faiths. Still, as so seldom happens in the case of well-matched enemies, a sort of odd respect, mingled with irritation, gradually grew between the adversaries. Naturally neither the chief nor yet the missionary advanced a step towards the conversion of the other infidel. Their simple, bloody creeds, softened in one case by the increase of indifference which even in East Fife has modified the full relentlessness of the Mosaic dispensation,[368] and on the other by the neighbourhood of European forts and factories, gave them a starting point in common, on which they could agree. Each looked upon the other as a keen sportsman looks on some rare bird or beast, which he hopes one day may fall before his gun, but which he wishes to escape from every other sportsman in the world except himself. Often the chief would ask the missionary to work a miracle to satisfy his doubts. Sorely the Reverend Archibald at times was tempted to display magnesium wire, or to develop photographs, in short to bag his game by pseudo-thaumaturgic[369] art; but having the true sportsman's instinct, always refrained, entrenching himself safely behind his dictum that "conversion should ensue after reasonable airgument". The chief, on his part, was quite ready to be baptized if he could see some evidence of the missionary's supernatural power: holding quite reasonably that "airgument" did not quite meet the case in questions of faith. Still he had promised that if he should ever change his mind none but the Reverend Archibald should admit him to the fold.

So on the rivers and the coast, things jogged along in the accustomed way: steamers arrived and hung outside the bars, fleets of canoes came down from the remoter streams to trade, and in the open roadsteads lighters took the goods and krooboys staggered through the surf, whilst objurgating[370] Scottish clerks, note-book in hand, counted the barrels and the bales. The sun loomed through a continual mist, and sheets of rain caused a white vapour to enshroud the trees, whose leaves seemed to distil a damp which entered to the bones. The traders strove with whisky and with gin to fight off fever and to pass the time, till they could make sufficient money to go home and rear their villas near their native towns.

---

[368] The divine ordering through Moses of the affairs of the world.
[369] Having been brought about by supernatural powers or magic.
[370] Scolding.

Years passed, and up and down the coast, at factories and gar-
risons; upon the hulks, and amongst travellers who coming from the
interior stayed at Hope House forced by necessity to ask for hospitality, a rumour made its way. Over their gin, or stretched out smoking
in their hammocks during the long hot hours after the second breakfast, traders and merchant skippers, Scotch clerks and the occasional
globe-trotters who waited for steamers in the various ports to take
them home to write their ponderous tomes upon the countries they
had seen as a swallow sees the lands he passes over in his winter
hegira,[371] all agreed that a great change had come upon the Reverend
Macrae. Not that his outward man had altered, for his beard still
bristled like a scrubbing-brush; his face with years and long exposure
to the sun had turned the colour of "jerked" beef; his clothes still
hung upon him as rags hang upon a scarecrow in the fields, and still
he faithfully "oxtered aboot the word of God", although the book
itself, originally given to him by his mother in East Fife, had grown
more shiny and more greasy with the lapse of years. But certainly a
change had come to the interior man. Occasionally and almost as it
were apologetically he would quote texts from the New Testament,
and in his steel grey eye the gleam as of a gospel terrier was softened
and subdued. Though he was still as ardent to convert the heathen
as before, his methods were more human, and to the amazement of
everyone upon the coast, he sometimes said "perhaps the patriarchs
were whiles sort of a' rash in their bit methods wi' yon Canaanites".

The miserable converts saw the change with joy, and convert-like
were quick to take advantage of it, and revert by stealth to practices
which before the Reverend Archibald would instantly put down.
They dared to appear on Sawbath at Hope House without the "stan
o' black"[372] with which the Reverend Archibald had provided them.
Only the women clung tenaciously to European dress, cherishing in
special their red parasols; but holding them invariably turned from
the sun which beat upon their well-oiled faces, melting the palm oil,
and causing it to drop upon their clothes.

Traders and brother missionaries came by degrees to drop into
Hope House to smoke and talk, and to endeavour to find out the
reason for the change. But as the Reverend Archibald never spoke
about himself their curiosity might have been fruitless had not a
brother worker on his journey home asked for an explanation saying
that as thought: "the Lord himself often worked changes in the heart
of man for providential ends". Dressed in pyjamas of grey woollen
stuff, his feet stuck into carpet slippers, and seated in a hammock

---

[371] The emigration of Muhammed from Mecca. A flight.
[372] See passim.

which he kept swinging with his toes, the Reverend Archibald after thrice spitting in contemplative fashion on the floor, and after having killed a mosquito on his forehead with a bang, looked round and started on his tale.

"Ye see", he said, "ma freends, as the Arabs say, we are a' in His hands. That which has been the pride of a man's life – in my case it was airgument – may prove at last to be a stumbling block, for we are all as worrms in His hand. Airgument, airgument, a weel discussed and reasonable airgument, was aye ma' pride. By it, I thoct to do a mighty worrk before the Lorrd. But He, nae doot for reasons of His ain, has made me see the error of my ways, that is, has shown me that that there are things man's reason canna touch".

He paused and wiped the sweat from off his brow, spat thoughtfully, sighed once or twice, and having asked his friends if they would take Kop's ale[373] or ginger beer, resumed his parable.

"Ye mind old Monday Flatface? Many's the crack on speeritual matters we have had, the chief and I, in days gone by. Sort o' teugh[374] in opinions the chief, a weary body for a man to tackle, and one I hoped wi' the Lord's grace to bring into the fold. Aye, aye, ye needna' laugh, I ha'ena pit ma raddle[375] on him as ye a' know yet. May be though mon, ae keel-mark[376] would do us baith. Weel, weel, the chief and I had bargained that if he got grace I should baptize him; a bonny burdie he would hae lookit at the font wi' his sax wives. Polygamy, ye ken, has its advantages, for I would have convertit a seven at once. One evening I was just got through wi catechising some of the younger flock, when doon the river can an afu' rout[377] o' drums, tom-toms, ye ken, and horns a' routing, and the chief's war-canoe tied up opposite the hoose. The chief came out, an' I was thinkin' of some text to greet him wi' airgument, ye ken (I think I tellt ye), when I saw at once there was something wrong. He lookit afu' gash, and wi'oot a worrd, he says, 'Big wife she ill, think she go die, you pray piece for her, and if she live, you pour water on my head.' I told him that was no way at all we Christians did things, but I would come and see his wife and bring some medicine and try what I could do. A' the way up the river the drums went on, man, it fair deaved[378] me, and when we reached the 'croom' in a' my twenty years' experience of the coast, I ne'er saw sic a sight. Baith men and women were a' sounding

---

[373] A non-alcoholic beer.
[374] Scots (pronounced tchyooch): Tough.
[375] A dye used to mark sheep.
[376] See passim.
[377] Scots: A loud noise.
[378] Scots: Annoyed with noise or talk.

horns, blowing their whistles, and shaking calabashes full of peas. The ground was red wi' blood, for the misguided creatures had sacrificed sheep, poultry and calves; an awfu' waste o' bestial ye ken, forby sae insanitary, and as ye say not the slightest use. At the chief's hut the wives and children made an awfu' din, roarin' and gashin' themselves wi' knives, just like the priests of Baal in the Old Testament. Right in the middle of the floor lay the 'big wife' insensible, and as I judged in the last stage of a malignant fever. The chief holdin' me by the airms says 'Save her, pray to your God for her, and if she lives I will believe'.

"Humanity, hymanity, shame to me as a Christian, that I say it, but 'tis just the same no matter if the skin is white or black. We a' just pray when we are wantin' onything, and when we've got it dinna thank the granter o' the prayer.

"I pushit through the folk, and felt the woman's pulse and syne prisin' her mouth open a bit wi' a jack-knife I gied her some quinine Then I knelt doon and wrestled in prayer wi' a' ma heart for the tears just rolled off the old chief's face. Sair I besought the Lord to show His power if He thought fit to do so, but prayer ye ken is often answered indirectly, and as the night wore on the chief aye askit me 'Will your God heed you?' and the woman aye got worse. An awful position for a minister of God to be placed in as ye may understand. Syne Flatface roused himsel' and saying, 'I will call then upon my God and sacrifice to him after the manner of my fathers', stotted[379] outside the house. The drums and whistles and the horns raised a maist defeaning din, and in the hut the smell of perspiration and palm oil was sort o' seekenin'. After a spell o' prayer the chief came in, sweatin' and ashen grey, his hands bound up and carrying a finger which he had chappit off upon the alter of his gods. It garred me skunner when he laid it on the sick woman's breast and once again I sunk upon my knees prayin' the Lord to hear the heathen's prayer. Ye ken, mon, his faith in his false gods, was just prodeegious, and I felt that a sta[u]nch Christian had been lost in the old man. Long did I wrestle till aboot the dawn, but got nae answer, that is directly, and the woman aye got worse. Just as the day was breaking, and the false dawn appearing in the sky, the chief said 'I will pray again, and once more sacrifice'. When he came in he stottered in his gait and laid another finger beside the other, on his wife. Ma heart just yearned to him, and I yokit[380] prayin' as if I had been askin' for my ain soul's grace, and syne our prayers were heard".

As he talked on the night had worn away, the frogs ceased croaking and the white tropic mist which comes before the dawn had drifted

---

[379] Scots: Staggered.
[380] Scots: Started a spell of work.

to the house and shrouded all the verandah in its ghastly folds. Long shivers of the tide crept up the river, oily and supernatural-looking, and little waves lapped on the muddy banks making small landslips fall into the flood, with an unearthly sound. The listeners shivered over their temperance drinks, and once again the Reverend Archibald began.

"Maist like she had the turn, it might have been the effect of the quinine, or of the prayers, or it may be the Lord had looked in appro-bation on the sacrifice. I canna say, but from that time the woman mended, and in a week was well. Ah ... Flatface, weel no, he's still a heathen, though we are friends, and whiles I think his God and mine are no so far apart as I aince thoucht."

He ceased, and from the woods and swamps rose the faint noises of the coming day, drops fell from the iron roof upon the planks of the verandah with a dull splashing sound; the listeners shaking the mis-sionary by the hand disappeared, and he[,] looking out through the mist was comforted by the confession of his weakness and his doubts.

*****

'Well, but they are gone, and with them the bridled bear
[barley] and the pink haver [oats], and the potato plot
that looked as gay as any flower-garden with its blossoms.
I sometimes fancy that the very birds are gone, all but the
crows and the gleads [kites]. Well, and what then? Instead
of us all, there is one shepherd man, and it may be a pair
of small lads, and many, many sheep.

And do you think Sir, that God allows of such
proceedings?'

Samuel Taylor Coleridge

Land ownership, especially in the Scottish Highlands and Ireland, had been the cornerstone of Graham's campaigns to become a Member of Parliament, at a time when the Highland crofters were bringing their plight to public attention. During the late eighteenth century, and well into the nineteenth, Highland glens were systematically depopulated by landowners, to make way for sheep and the deer-forest, creating a public outcry and legislation, but the damage had been done, and tens of thousands had been forced into emigration, or into the sweatshops of smoky cities in the south.

It is not known when Graham visited this location, Loch Shiel in the western Highlands, but the population, after some resistance by the womenfolk, had been cleared in 1842, ten years before Graham was born.

THE LAROCH[381]

The Saturday Review, 19 September 1903, p. 357.
Anthologised in *Progress* (London: Duckworth, 1905), pp. 237–43.

The grass-grown-over "founds"[382] and the grey crumbling dry stone wall of what had been a house, stood in an island of bright, close-grown grass. About the walls sprang nettles and burdocks and in chinks tall mulleins[383] stood out like torches, veritable hag-tapers[384] to light the desolation of the scene. Herb robin, and wild pelargonium with pink mallows, straggled about the ruined garden walls. A currant bush all run to wood with grozets[385] and wild rasps still strove against neglect. In the deserted long kail patch, heather and bilberries had resumed their sway. Under the stunted ash, a broken quern and a corn-beetling[386] stone grown green with moss, spoke of a time of life and animation, simple and primitive, but fitting to the place. On every side the stone-strewn moor stretched to the waters of the loch, leaving a ridge of shingle on the edge. The hills were capped with mist, that lifted rarely, and only in the summer evenings, or in the winter frosts, were clear and visible. Firs, remnants of the Caledonian forest, sprang from the rocky soil and stood out stark, retiring sentinels of the old world, a world in which they, the white cattle, the wild boar and wolf, were fellow-travellers; and from which they lingered, to remind one of the others who had disappeared. The birch trees rustled their laments, sadder than those of earthly chanters, or of the strains of a scarce heard strathspey coming down through the glens with a west wind. The rowans on the little stony tumuli showed reddening berries, as they turned their silvery leaves towards Loch Shiel.[387] All was sad, wild and desolate, the soft warm rain drawing up from the ground a mist, which met the mist descending from the sky, and hung a curtain over the rocks, the strath, the loch and everything, and glistened greyly on the wet leaves of trees. A leaden sky, seen vaguely through the rain, and broken to the west by "windows", seemed to shut out the narrow glen from all the world, confining it in plates of lead; lead in the skies, and in the waters of the sullen loch.

---

[381] Gaelic: làrach = A ruined building.
[382] Foundations.
[383] The great mullein (*Verbascum Thapsus*).
[384] An ancient form of torch made from dried mullein stalks, soaked in tallow, and used in ceremonies such as funerals.
[385] Scots: A green gooseberry.
[386] Grinding.
[387] A long and narrow freshwater loch situated twelve miles west of Fort William.

Desolation reigned, where once was life, and where along the loch smoke had ascended, curling to heaven humbly from the shielings thatched with reeds, with heather and with whins, the thatch kept down with birchen poles, fastened with stones, and on whose roofs the corydalis and the house leek[388] sprang from the flaughter feals.[389] But now no acrid peat reak made the eyes water, or pervaded heart and soul, with the nostalgia of the North, that North ungrateful, hard, and whimsical, but loveable and leal; where man grows like the sapucaya nut,[390] hard rinded, rough and angular, but tender at the core. All, all were gone, gone to far Canada, or to the swamps and the pine-barrens[391] of the Carolinas, to Georgia, to New Zealand, nothing but Prionsa Tearleach's[392] monument, set like a lighthouse on the shores of a dead sea, the sea of failure, seemed to remind one that the pibroch had once resounded through the glens. Heather and tormentil, with cotton grass, that seemed to have preserved the feather of some bird extinct for ages, eye-bright and knapweed, hare-bells and golden rod, prunella, meadowsweet, with bog asphodel on the yellow springy turf near swamps, and foxgloves in the woods, all blossomed, and thought not on the departed children who had plucked them when the strath held men. It may be that the plants regretted the lost children's hands that gathered them, and were their only mourners, for thought must linger somewhere, if only amongst flowers.

In the old plough-marked ridges of the forsaken crofts, the matted ragweed grew, to show the land had once been cultivated. Nature smiled through the middle mist, which shrouded loch and hill as in derision of the changes which mankind had suffered, and looked as tolerantly upon the tourists, waterproofed to the ears, as she had gazed upon the clansmen, who must have seemed as much a part of her as the roe, who peeped out timidly from the birch thickets, to watch the steamboat puffing on the lake.[393] Yet still about the laroch a hum of voices hung, or seemed to hang to anyone who listened with ears undeadened by the steamhooter's bray; voices whose guttural accents seemed more attuned to the long swish of waves and moaning of the wind, than those which, in their throaty tone, mingle with

---

[388] (*Sempervivum tectorum*), a plant commonly found on cottage roofs, which is also known as 'Stone-crop'.

[389] See passim.

[390] A nut grown only in Brazil and Guyana.

[391] Large pine forests.

[392] Gaelic: Prince Charles Edward Stuart; a reference to the monument to the Raising of the Clans at Glen Shiel in 1745.

[393] A mail boat service, which also carried tourists, began on the loch in 1893, most notably on *The Clanranald II* which plied the loch from 1900 until 1953.

nothing but the jangle of a street. Voices there were that spoke of a dead past, when laughter echoed through the glens – the low-tuned laughter of a silent race. Voices that last had sounded in their grief and tears, as the rough roof tree fell, or worse, was left intact, as the owners of the house turned for a last look at their shielings on the solitary strath.

An air of sadness and of failure, as if the very power, which placed the ancient owners on the soil, had not proved powerful enough to keep them there, hung on the hills, and brooded on the lake. A Keltic sadness, bred in the bones of an old race, which could not hope to strive with new surroundings, and which the stranger has supplanted, just as the Hanoverian rat drove out his British cousin and usurped his place. Land, sky and loch spoke of a vanished people and their last enterprise; their first and last, when far Lochaber almost imposed a king on England, pushed on his fortunes, shed its blood for him, and when beaten and desperate he fled for life, sheltered him in the greyness of its mists. But in the soul-pervading futile beauty which hung over all, the laroch gave as it were a key-note, as the tired vapour-ridden sun at times blinked on it, and shone upon its ruined walls. It seemed to speak of mournful happiness and of the humble joys of those who felt the storm, the sunshine, the rain, as their own trees and rocks had felt them, dumbly but cheerfully, and who, departing, had left no record of themselves, but the poor rickle[394] of grey stones, or the faint echo of their hearts, heard in the notes of a strathspey quavering down the glens,[395] and mingling with the south-east gale. The silence of an empty land, from which the people had been driven sore against their will, and had departed to make their fortunes, and to mourn their stony pastures to the third generation[396] and the fourth, oppressed one, whilst the winds echoed through the corries, as if seeking someone to talk with about days gone by.

On the peat hags the struggling sunbeams glistened, lighting them up for a brief moment, as the flaming chimney of an ironwork, in a manufacturing town, breaks through the vapour of the slums, and lights the waters of some dark canal, giving an air as of an opening of the mouth of hell, black and unfathomable. The stunted willow and dwarf alder fringed the margin of the rushy streams, which gurgled in deep channels, forming small linns, on which the white foam flecked the tawny peat water, or breaking into little rapids, brattled[397]

---

[394] Scots: A loose, carelessly thrown together pile.
[395] This is Graham's third repetition.
[396] An allusion to God's punishment for iniquity in Exodus, Numbers and Deuteronomy.
[397] Scots: A loud clatter.

amongst round pebbles, or again sank out of sight amongst the sedge of flags. Their tinkling music was unheard, except perhaps in ears which had grown blunted with the roar of cabs. Perchance it was remembered as a legend heard in childhood is remembered faintly in old age. Straggling across the hills, the footpaths, long disused, lay white amongst the heather, the stones retaining still a smoothness made by the feet of those who, in their deer-skin moccasins, had journeyed in the past from the lone laroch to other larochs, which once had been homesteads dear to the dwellers in them, and to-day were silent and forgotten as the half-subterranean dwellings of the Picts.[398]

Still the sweet gale gave out its aromatic scent, the feathery bracken waved, the hills towered up to the sky, flecked here and there with snow, and nature seemed to call to the departed clans, telling them to return and find their land unchanged. She called to ears long dead, or rendered unresponsive in their new homes, for nothing broke the silence of the glens, but the harsh cry of the wild geese, flying unseen amongst the middle region of the mist, calling on high the coronach[399] of the departed and the dead.

* * * * *

Pollybaglan is a description of the landscape around a semi-der-elict farm on the Flanders Moss, on the banks of the Forth, and Graham's tenant, Mr James Mitchell of Polybaglot.[400] Again, the vernacular speech between landlord and tenant was by no means exaggerated, and Graham seemed very familiar and at ease with it. However, notwithstanding the farmer's exaggerated claim, Graham was pointing to other hidden depths. The first, a small point, was the farmer's address to his landlord, which, although acknowledging Graham's status, smacked of intimacy, of a freedom to speak, perhaps Graham's way of demonstrating an ancient democratic spirit among the locals (and himself) that he admired.[401] The second

---

[398] The Picts are incorrectly remembered as only building subterranean and half-subterranean dwellings (see *British Dwarfs* by David MacRichie, *Archaeological Review*, vol. 4, 1889).

[399] See passim.

[400] Gaelic: *poll-a-bagailt* = 'Stream with the clusters of nut bushes'. Also called 'Pullabag-land' on a map of 1779. The arable land was a narrow strip along the banks of the River Forth.

[401] Graham's great-niece, Jean Cunninghame Graham, wrote, 'Scottish lairds had nearly always been on friendly terms with their estate workers, feeling them to be equals; there was none of the English "feudal" relationship which produced the patronising breed of landowners that were sometimes found in the South.' Jean Cunninghame Graham, *The Gaucho Laird* (Long Riders Guild Press, 2004), p. 47.

Figure 5 The ruins of 'Polybaglot' Farm by the river Forth.

depth was the very nature of the description, particularly the simile, exposing a sensitivity of perception, which we might not expect to be exchanged between two Scottish men of differing social rank. The last was the most extraordinary, wherein the farmer described how time had become distended in this alien environment. It had become magical, otherworldly, which was analogous with the experience of the late seventeenth-century mystic, the Reverend Robert Kirk, inside Doon Hill (not two miles away). In this, Graham was of course suggesting another depth, the depth of folk belief, and if not actual belief, a spiritual connection to landscape and tradition, a desire to believe, to commune. As he recorded elsewhere, 'Faith it is said consists of the belief in something that we know to be untrue'.[402] In retrospect, the farmer was a mouthpiece for Graham's interest in the mystical, which was starting to find fuller expression in his works.[403]

---

[402] Cunninghame Graham, Introduction to *The Secret Commonwealth of Elves, Fauns and Fairies* (1933) (New York: Dover Books 2008), p. 6.
[403] Ibid., p. 7.

POLLYBAGLAN

The Speaker, 28 November 1903, pp. 214–15.
Anthologised in *Progress* (London: Duckworth, 1905), pp. 251–9.

ALONE it stood, outside the world, remote and desolate, washed by a sea of heather, just where the sluggish Forth, meandering slowly like a stream of oil through Flanders Moss, had formed a grassy link, but not of those which, as the saying went, were worth a knight's fee[404] in the north.

In times gone by, the moss which in most places marches with the Forth, leaving a narrow ribbon of green turf, had been drained off, and floated down the stream, exposing in its in its place some acres of stiff clay and a dull whitish scaur.[405] In these, the steading stood like some lacustrine[406] dwelling, on the river's edge, shut from the world of moss. Moss, moss, and still more moss, which rose piled like a snow wreath to the west, and south, and east, whist on the north the high clay bank sank steep into the flood.

The drumly[407] water flowed between banks of peat, through which at intervals a whitish clay peeped out, like strata in a mine. Slowly it flowed in many windings towards the sea, cutting the Flanders Moss across, receiving, as it went, the streams which gurgled deep below the surface of the ground, forming canyons in miniature and issuing out to join the river through a dense growth of bulrushes, rank growing coltsfoot, and low alder bushes. The deep black pools on which the foam brought by the current slowly whirled round and round before it took its course down stream were menacing in their intensity of gloom. Rarely the sun fell right upon them, and when it did its light ever appeared to pierce the water, which seemed to turn it back again, as if the bottom held some mystery down in its amber depths. Perhaps in ages past some Celtic fishers, paddled their coracles, had chosen out the place to build their cottary,[408] remote from all mankind and inaccessible. But having chosen, with the instinct of their race, they gave a name to it which, strange and incoherent to the Saxon ear, to them was typical of the chief feature of the place. Stream of the ragweed it was dubbed by the rude settlers, perhaps when all Moss Flanders was a forest, stretching to the sea. And still the ragweed grew luxuriantly in the stiff soil, commemorating the keen eyes of the

---

[404] An area of land considered sufficient to support a medieval knight.
[405] Stratum.
[406] A plain formed by an ancient lake.
[407] Scots: Muddy, perhaps troubled.
[408] Cottery, Scots: A cottar's holding.

first settlers, although the meaning of the name had long been lost, and twisted by the Anglo-Saxon tongue past recognition by the Celt.

The road which wound about the white clayey soil between the banks of moss which shut out the horizon was laid on faggots, and in places drew so near the river's bank that a cart's body passing seemed to overhang the stream. Such as it was, this track was the sole link with the unquiet world which had its being on the far side of the great moss. But that the quiet of the mossland farm should not too easily be broken by swift contact with mankind, the path ran up and down to every house upon the moss, making strange zigzags and parabolas, till it emerged at last on the high road. Carts in the winter time sunk to their axles, whilst in summer horses' feet stuck in the cracks formed in the sub-baked earth.

But though the road was bad, to make communication still more difficult at intervals rough farm gates barred the way. Hung loosely, and secured by rusty back-band chains of carts, or formed of barked and crooked oak poles stuck into horseshoes in a rugged post, they either forced you to dismount, and pull laboriously each bar from its confining horseshoe, or tempted you to open them on horseback, when their schauchling[409] hinges and bad balance usually drove them on your horse's hocks as you essayed to pass.

When all the obstacles were overcome and you had reached your goal and slithered through the clay which formed the fields between the river and the moss, the world seemed leagues away. That is, the ancient world in which men plough and reap and sow, watching the weather as a fisherman watches the shaking of his sail, possessed one, and real things resumed their sway, whilst agiotage[410] and politics, with arts and sciences, fell to their proper value in the great scheme of life. The scanty crop of oats, growing like rice in water which seemed to lie eternally in the depressions of the clay, although the dwellers in the farm averred that it "seeped bonnily awa' at the back en',"[411] became as all-important as the Stock Exchange. The meagre turnips and potatoes, drooping and blackening with disease, between whose furrows persicaria and fumitory grew, moved one's compassion, and excited admiration for the men who, in the fight with Nature, wrung a livelihood from such unfruitful soil. Fences there naturally were none, but piles of brushwood fastened with rusty wire to ragged posts did duty for them, whilst broken ploughs, and carts which had seen weary service on the clayey roads, stood in the gaps and did as well as gates.

---

[409] Scots: Shambling/tottering/awkward.
[410] Financial dealings, e.g., the Stock Exchange.
[411] 'Later in the year the water dispersed.'

Some scattered drain-pipes lying in the fields looked like the relics of a battlefield of agriculture, in which the forces of the modern world had been defeated in the contest with the moss.

But road and drain-pipes, thatched farmhouse and broken fences, stunted crop and wind-hacked ash tree growing by the farm were but the outward signs, whilst the interior significance lay in the billowing moss, the sluggish river, and the background of the lumpy hills, which from the steading seemed to rise sheer from the heathy sea.

Vaguely the steading and the cultivated land stood out for progress; the broken carts and twisted ploughs seemed to stretch out their hands to Charing Cross; but moss and mountain, river flowing deep, the equisetum growing on its banks, and the sweet gale, its leaves all wet with mist, reminded one that the forgotten past still lived in spite of us.

Deep in the soughing[412] of the wind, waving the heath with furrows and shaking out the dry brown seeds on the black soil, came sighs of a race whose joys were tinged with melancholy, and in the mists that crept along the faces of the hills its spirit seemed to brood, making the dwellers in the land appear as out of place as a poor Indian dressed in a torn frock coat and with an eagle's feather stuck in a hard felt hat looks in a frontier town.

The tussocks of the heather were not made for boots to tread upon, nor the few acres of poor soil, redeemed at many times their worth fee simple, to be sown in a fourfold rotation, or to have top dressing and bone manure shot from an agricultural machine upon their clay. A pair of Highland garrons[413] ought to have scratched the surface of the ground, yoked to some pristine plough by ropes which cut into their chests, or harrowed with a thorn bush, and the broken implements which lay about but seemed to accentuate the undying presence of an older world. But as the place in which a man is set to live always proves stronger than his race or creed, the dweller in the farm, though not a Highlander, had put on all the exterior and not a few of the interior graces of the Celt.

Tall and shocked-headed and freckled on the red patches of skin which a rough crop of beard and whiskers left exposed, his eyes looked out upon the world as if he had a sort of second sight begot of whisky and loneliness. His monstrous hands hung almost to his knees.[,] which in their turn stuck forward in the way a horse's hock sticks back, but for all that he crossed the moss as lightly as a mountain hare springs through the snow before a collie dog. Although his feet, encased in heavy boots, looked more adapted to the muddy

---

[412] Scots: Sighing.
[413] Ponies.

roads which wound through his domain than for the heather, he seemed to have become, during his life-long sojourn in the place, as light of foot as any clansman on whose feet in the old times the dun deer's hide was tied to form a moccasin. The country people said that he was "afu' soople for his years," which may have been some five and forty, or, on the other hand, threescore, for nothing told his age, and that he was a "lightsome traveller," not that his travels ever carried him more than ten miles from Pollybaglan, but then with us to travel is to walk. Withal a swimmer, an unusual thing amongst the older generation in Menteith.

"Ye ken, man laird, whiles I just dive richt to the bottom o' a linn, and set doon there; ye'd think it was the inside o' the Fairy Hill. Trooties, ye ken, and saumon, and they awfu' pike, a' comin' round ye, and they bits of water weeds, waggin aboot like lairch trees in the blast.[414] I mind ae time I stoppit doon nigh aboot half an hour. Maybe no just sae much, ye ken, but time gaes awfu' quick when ye're at the bottom o' a linn."

These talents and his skill in walking on the moss, together with his love of broken carts and gates, did not perhaps go far towards making him an agriculturalist such as a landlord loves, but looking back into the past, although his rent was often in arrear, he laid up, so to speak, and quite unconsciously, a real treasure for his laird, which, though moth may corrupt, no thief would waste his time breaking through to steal, as it lies gathering dust on the top shelf of someone's library.

And as the older life had entered into the body of the Lowland "bodach,"[415] making him seem a Highlander in all but speech, so had it filled the air of the oasis in the peaty moss that the dry reeds upon the river banks were turned into chanters, and gave out their laments for the forgotten namers of the land.

Well did they call it by the name Menteith, the district of the moss,[416] for moss invaded the whole strath, filling the space which once had been a sea with waves of heather and bog asphodel. Stretching from Meiklewood it kissed the Clach-nan-Lung. Lapping the edges of the hills upon the north and south shores of the heathy sea, it put a peaty bridle on the Forth, and from its depth at evening and at morn rose a white vapour which transformed it into a misty archipelago, upon whose waves the lonely steading rode, like the enchanted islands which old mariners descried, only to lose again into the fog at the first shift of wind. Birch trees and firs reflected on the mirage of the mist

---

[414] Larch trees in the wind.
[415] Gaelic: An old man.
[416] Although uncertain, the name is most likely derived from the Gaelic 'moine' = moor, and the River Teith that flows into the Forth near Stirling.

floated like parachutes, and heath and sky were joined together by the vapoury pall which brooded on the moss, billowing and boiling as if some cauldron in the bowels of the earth was belching forth its steam. Fences were blotted out, roads disappeared, and from the moss strange noises rose, as Forth lapped sullenly up against the bank where Pollybaglan stood.

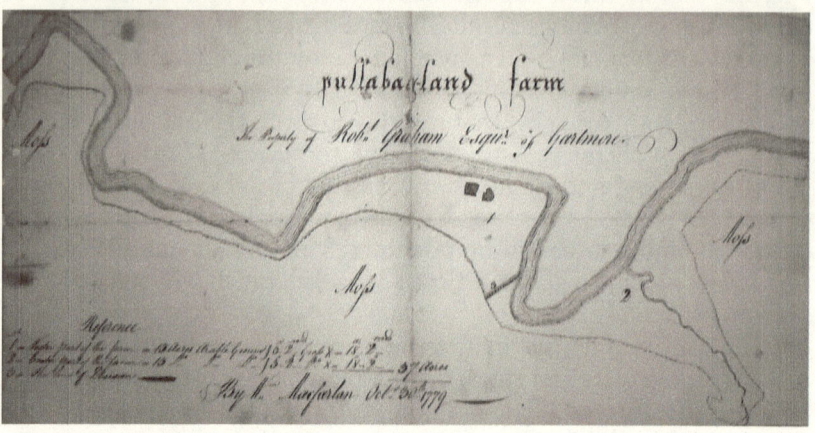

Figure 6

* * * * *

This next sketch, like *Polybaglan* (above), is another of Graham's pen-portraits of one of his tenants, Andrew Graham, which is infused with warmth and respect.

It opens with the memory of their first meeting in Gartmore House and Graham's description of his tenant's appearance and his habitually bleak outlook, which Graham called 'making poor mouth'. However, Graham had inherited the Gartmore Estate during one of the worst agricultural depressions of the nineteenth century, and farmers were suffering real financial hardship. He then describes the tenant's desolate farm, Tombreak, which lies on a hill to the north of Balfron. Despite his grumbling, Andrew was a capable stockman, able to turn a profit from his travelling to cattle markets, and was a well-known and well-liked figure in the locality.

As with *A Retainer* (below), Graham seems to have thought of his tenant as indestructible, and so Andrew's death, while travelling to such a market, was as inexplicable as it was unexpected. Graham laments that through his death, 'Andra' 'took away with him some of my life'. Yet, as with *The Beggar Earl* (below), he does not end with Andra's death, but by musing what had become of his collie and his pony.

Figure 7 Farming on 'The Moss' 1898.

A TRAVELLER

The Speaker, 19 December 1903, pp. 293–4.
Anthologised in *Progress* (London: Duckworth & Co., 1905),
pp. 260–8.

HE stood, a square, grey figure in the hall, and, looking upward at the
pictures of somewhat grim-visaged ancestors in their full-bottomed
wigs,[417] said, "Bonny scenery, aye, bonny scenery." The criticism was
as novel as it was unexpected, and was the introduction to a bickering
friendship which extended over years.

His greasy cap and crisp grey hair which melted into one another,
hodden grey clothes[418] and greenish flannel shirt, but with one touch
of colour in his bright red cheeks, like apples tinged with frost made
him look like stone which, in the district where he lived, was known
as the "auld carlin wi' the bratty plaid."[419]

"Laird, I hae travel't it, yes fack as death, richt through frae up
aboot Balfron."[420]

A man may make a circuit of the world in a short space of time as it
seems good to him, and yet not earn the title of a "soople traveller,"

---

[417] Full-length.
[418] See passim.
[419] Scots: 'the old peasant with the ragged shawl'.
[420] 'Sir, I have walked it, sure as death, all the way from above Balfron.'

for "travelling" means to walk. Thus we refer to pedlars by the name of "travelling merchants," and tramps as "gaen aboot"[421] or "travelling bodies," saving thereby their pride and ours, and not contributing to wear out shoe-leather any the faster by the mere application of the word. But, still, in using it we usually extend our pity to the traveller, who is a sort of survival of the times when all men rode, if only on West Highland ponies schauchling through the mud. Used by a poor man it generally infers that he is going to ask a favour, or by a tenant to his landlord, that the times are hard.

"Laird, I just travel't it. Thank ye, nae soddy[422] laird," and as he spoke, he drained a good half tumbler of raw whisky to the dregs, in such a quiet, sober, and God-fearing way, it seemed an act of prayer.

Of all the tenant farmers whom it has been my luck to meet and chaffer with, none could exceed the traveller in making a poor mouth.[423] Seasons were always backward, markets bad, the sheep had foot-rot or the fluke, the "tatties" were diseased – "Man, laird! I felt the smell of yon field out by Gartchurachan whenever I cam forward to the trough-stone, ye ken, fornent the Hosh."[424]

The act of God was instant at his farm, tirling the slates or hashing up the rhones leaving the sarking bare, so that snaw bree seepit thro' upon the stirks.[425] "I just tak shame to pit horse in that rickle o' a stable. And a' the grips are fair dune in the byre. Laird, I just biggit a' the steadin', that is, I drave the stanes and drainit a the land to ye. Siccan a farm for pipes! Man, I hae pit in more than ten thousand since back 'en, and still she's wet, wet as Loch Lomond. I'm just tellin' ye, ye'll may be hae to tak it back and try it yersel', for I'm just beat wi' it. ... What? tak it off my hands at Martinmas! Na, na, I'll fecht awa' in it, though I'll hae to hae a wee reduction, or maybe a substantial ane, just to encourage me to carry on my agricultural operations. Aye, dod aye, I'm sayin' it."[426]

---

[421] Scots: Travelling around.
[422] Scots: Soda water (in whisky).
[423] Complaints for sympathy or gain.
[424] Scots: Before the harvest.
[425] 'rattling and moving the slates, or ruining the roof guttering, leaving the wooden boards exposed, so that the melted snow drips onto the young bullocks'.
[426] 'I'm ashamed to put a horse in that ramshackle stable, and all the guttering in the barn is beyond repair. Sir, I had just built the steading, I smashed the rocks and drained the land for you. Such a farm for drainage pipes! Sir, I have put in more than ten thousand since last year, and still the ground is wet, wet as Loch Lomond. I'm just telling you, you'll perhaps have to repossess it. I'm exhausted by it. ... What? Take it off my hands in November! No, no, I'll fight on, though I'll have to have a small rent reduction, or maybe a substantial one,

His farm was grey and square, with the house planted down upon the road, leaving an angle which ran out from the farmyard, planted with cabbages and with some flowers which wrestled with the wind. No tree grew near the place, which, high and desolate, stood solitary, exposed to the full fury of the south-west wind. An air of neatness without homeliness pervaded everything. Carts with their shafts upright stood under sheds, and on a rope, stretched from stable to byre, hung braxy[427] sheep, their bodies black and shrunken, their skins new flayed and pink[,] fluttering around like kites.

But if the roadside farm was dreary in itself, a mere corral of coarse grey stones topped by blue slates, the distant hills atoned for all shortcomings in the fore-ground of the view.

From the high moorland platform where Tombreak seemed to be stuck down like a child's house of bricks, the Grampians rose, making a semi circle to the north and west. Lumpy, and looking like misshapen vegetables, monstrous and brown, their chain was broken here and there by peaks, and here and there by mountain burns which glistened on their sides as streaks of foam gleam white upon a horse's flanks. Ben Ledi and Schehullion [sic] to the east, and Stuc-a-Chroin, Ben Vorlich, Ben A'an, and Ben Venue, nearer Ben Dearg and Craigmore, and to the west Ben Lomond rising solitary, as a vast blue cone about whose top floated a vapoury cloud, as if the soul of the volcano long extinct hovered about its once accustomed haunts, stood sentinels, frowning down on the mossy strath, set with its lumpy hillocks grown with stubby oak, and on the still blue lake with the grey priory and the castled isle.[428] Far to the north snow-capped Ben More, with its twin paps, peeped out between the shoulders of the bolder hills, showing its beauties timidly, and at the faintest shift of wind retreating back into the mist – that veil which shrouds the Highlands in its mystery, shutting them off for ever from the south.

Below the farm the village of Balfron straggled, a long grey ribbon in the mist. Nearer it showed a Scottish village bare of flowers, but cosy in its clartiness,[429] in which barefooted children ran about and played at "bools,"[430] wiping their noses on their coat sleeves, or went to school wearing their boots uneasily, as ponies from the far off islands of the north hobble along in the first dignity of shoes.

---

just to encourage me to carry on my agricultural operations. Yes, God yes, that's my statement.'

[427] An incurable infectious disease, which causes sudden death in sheep.

[428] The Island of Inchtalla with the ruined castle of the Earls of Menteith, which Graham purchased from his kinsman, James Graham, the Duke of Montrose, and which is still owned by the Cunninghame Graham family.

[429] Scots: Muckyness.

[430] Scots: Marbles.

Above the village with its ancestral trysting tree clamped round with iron hoops,[431] its antiquated toll-house, now turned sweetshop, and in whose windows fly-blown toffy and flat-looking ginger beer winked at the passer-by, who knew, perhaps, that there was liquor more alluring to be had inside – the Campsies rose, a wall of green, broken only by the Corrie of Balglas.[432] Their grassy sides and look of pastoral quiet made a sharp contrast with the Highland hills, only ten miles away. The two hill ranges were as far apart as is a northern shepherd wrapped in his plaid and "sheltering a wee" behind a rock whilst his dog slumbers at his feet, his coat all wet with mist, and a gull-followed southland ploughman labouring at his craft.

Upon the plateau, with the hills to north and south, the wind raged ceaselessly, and many a weary mile upon the moors after his sheep my tenant must have "travelled" before his face took on the dark red polish which staring out from his grey aureole of hair and Newgate frill,[433] looked like a red bottle in a chemist's window when you passed him in the gloaming on the road. Long contact and familiarity with sheep had given him something of the grace of a West Highland wether,[434] which he resembled somewhat in his mind, for, in a land in which most men are cautious, not delivering their souls without due hedging, manward and Godward, as befits a Scot, he stood out easily the first. Prudence in his case almost amounted to a mania, so that in any case a bargain must have been a torture to him, for if he lost, he naturally cursed God and man, and if he gained by it, bewailed himself for having lost the chance of getting better terms. No word he spoke without a qualifying clause. Thus the best harvest ever known to man, to him was "no that bad," and a fine Clydesdale horse "a bonny beast, but no well feathered on the pastern joints."[435] No Ayrshire cow but was "a wee thing heich abune the tail,"[436] which dictum he would modify, and, sighing, say, "but we are a' that," and thus humanity and all the race of cows were either justified or stood arraigned,[437] according to your taste.

As was to be expected from a man so gifted for success amongst the men with whom he lived, he was "well doing," that is he had amassed

---

[431] Up until 1798, it was site of 'jougs', hinged iron collars chained to a wall or post, used as an instrument of punishment. They are mentioned in John Guthrie Smith's *Strathendrick and Its Inhabitants From Early Times*, published in 1896.

[432] A precipitous gouge out of the north side of the hills.

[433] See passim

[434] Scots: A male sheep castrated before sexual maturity.

[435] Not ideally shaped at the joints on the lower part of the leg above the hooves.

[436] Scots: A little high above the tail.

[437] Absolved or put on trial.

some little money, chiefly by "travellin'" about to cattle markets and picking up cheap beasts. In fact, he was an instance of the Scots proverb, that "the gangin' foot aye picks up something,[438] if it is but a thorn." No one who saw him walin'[439] his way across the moors leading his collie by a piece of common string, with his long hazel shepherd's crook thrust through his arms behind his back, making him look like a trussed fowl, or driving home some of his purchases through a mist upon the muddy roads, could ever think of him and death as having anything in common that should one day make them friends. So like the stubby oaks he looked, which grew in the Park Wood upon his farm, and which themselves had braved a thousand tempests and a hundred pollardings, that he seemed likely to endure as long as they. But your cursed cold, or heart disease, or his neglect in taking whisky at set hours, or something which no doctor could foresee, proved his undoing, and he departed "travellin'" to a tryst, his collie following at his heels, and his long shepherd's staff in hand, willing and eager for the coming deal.

Tough, knarred,[440] and kindly, with his apple cheeks and his thick fell of crisp grey hair, his hodden clothes and cheery smile, no matter whether he had got the best of his opponent in a bargain, or the worst, he took away with him some of my life and the kind memories of the whole countryside aboot Balfron.

Ben Lomond and Ben Ledi still lookdown upon the carse; in the Park Wood the twisted oaklings rustle in the breeze, and by Tombreak the wind sweeps ceaselessly.

"Andra" is gone, his collie dog perchance comes to another whistle, and his roan Iceland pony mare maybe ekes out her life in a fish hawker's cart; but her lost owner, I would like to think, there in the spheres is "travellin'" if only "goin' aboot," for it may well be that they hold no trysts where he dwells now; but still I know that it is ill to stay "the gangin' foot"[441] after a lifetime on the road.

---

[438] 'A Gangin' Fit's Aye Getting'. Scots: A motivated worker always get the reward.
[439] Scots: To select from amongst alternatives.
[440] Scots: Sturdily built.
[441] Scots: 'It is difficult to halt the restless foot.'

1904–10

'Snow in Menteith' is probably Graham's most beautiful evocation of his native locale. These closely observed, vivid remembrances of a winter landscape are particularly remarkable, as he claimed 'I never took a note on any subject under heaven, nor kept a diary'.[442]

Like the mists, which will increasingly creep into his narratives, the snow is transformative, blotting out mankind's presence and returning the landscape to a primitive past, or, as he never tired of telling his readers, an arm of the sea, which it once was. Mankind is superfluous, in fact we are rather shocked when 'woodmen … like interlopers strayed from a pantomime' make a fleeting appearance in this scene of beauty and sparkling, muffled nature.

SNOW IN MENTEITH

The Speaker, 30 January 1904, pp. 425–6.
Anthologised in *Progress* (London: Duckworth, 1905), pp. 244–50.

All the familiar landmarks were obliterated. The Grampians and the Campsies had taken on new shapes. Woods had turned into masses of raw cotton, and trees to pyramids of wool, with diamonds here and there stuck in the fleece. The trunks of beeches stood out black upon the lee, and on the weather side were coated thick with snow as hard as sugar on a cake. Boughs of firs and spruces swayed gently up and down under the weight of the snow, which bent them towards the ground.

Birches were covered to their slenderest twigs with icicles. Only the larches, graceful and erect, were red, for on their feathery branches snow could not find a resting-place. On the rough bark and knotted trunks of oak trees feathery humps bulged out, through which protruded shoots with sere brown leaves still clinging to them, and on them ruffled birds sat moping, twittering in the cold.

A new and silent world, born in a night, had come into existence, and over it brooded a hush, broken but by the cawing of crows, which fabulated as they flew, perhaps upon the strangeness of the pervading white.

---

[442] Quoted in C. Lewis Hind, 'R. B. Cunninghame Graham', in *More Authors and I* (London: John Lane, 1922), p. 76.

Even in Eden, in the days before man's fall and woman's mother-hood, all was not purer than the fields and moors under their burden of the carpet formed of the myriad of scintillating flakes.

But in the copses and the shaws of oak and birch a change had come, more wondrous even than the transformation of a piece of rough grey coral, as it sinks prismatic and transfigured by the water, dropped gently from a boat upon the beach of a sunlit lagoon.

The trees, congealed and tense, stood silent, quivering and eager for the embrace of the keen frost, their boughs all clad first with a thistle-down of cold, and then towards the tips with diamonds fashioned to their shape through which the shadow of their bark just faintly gleamed, whilst, here and there, there sparkled facets rarer and brighter than the gems of the Apocalypse.[443] A murmur born of stillness lost itself against the blackness of a clump of firs, and yet was all apparent and persisting as if the spirit of the frost, looking out from the north, was murmuring a self-approving blessing of his work. The sharp air hung the breath in a grey cloud against the sky; nature was silent, and a rabbit, loping through the bush, stirred the soft echoes of the snow-clogged weeds, leaving behind a trail which seemed gigantic, with its brown markings, made by the impress of its furry feet melting the new-fallen snow. In the dark woodland burns the wreaths of snow blocked all the streams, and in the silent pools, congealed and swept clean by the wind, the little trout loomed twice their natural size in the refracted light which penetrated through the ice. The roe-deer and hares and the great capercailzies,[444] sending a shower of sparkling particles from the dark fir trees when they took their flight, seemed to have come into their own inheritance; the woodmen, plodding heavily, their axes thrust beneath their armpits, and their hands deep buried in the pockets, looked like interlopers strayed from a pantomime into the transformation scene of frost. The wind amongst the sedges of the shallow pool in the sequestered clearing where the rabbit-eaten ash copse straggled down close to the water's edge discoursed the only music of the spheres to which our ears are tuned, and whistled in the rowans, swinging their hanging spathes of bark against their boles for its accompaniment.

Out of the hummocks of the withered grass it caught the frosted bracken, twirling it round and round upon itself, and leaving at the roots a circle in the snow which seemed the footprint of some strange new northern animal, brought by the magic of the night from the far realms of frost.

---

[443] Revelation 21:19–20.
[444] A large woodland grouse.

But if the hills and woods had all become unrecognisable, the mantle of pure white spread on the earth formed a blank page on which nothing could stir without a record of its passage being writ at least as permanently as was the passage of its life.

Badgers, who had adventured out for food, left their strange bear-like tracks in woods where no one had suspected that they lived. Roe, plunging through the crisp white snow, made a round hole marked at the bottom with their cloven feet, and leaving at the edge a faint red trace of blood.

The birds, in their degree, imprinted traces clear and distinct as those their ancestors had left in rocks from the time when the world was all a snowfield or all tropics, or all something different from what it is, as wise geologists, quarrelling with each other as they were theologians, write in ponderous tomes.

Even the field mice pattering along left tiny trails like little railways as they journeyed from their warm nests to visit one another and interchange opinions on the strange new scene.

Round holly-trunks sat rabbits, mere round balls of fur, eating the bark and scuffling to and fro, leaving well-beaten paths towards their burrows, at whose mouth some sat and washed their faces in the snow.

Across the frozen pond, upon whose surface lay a thin rime of frost, a fox had left his footsteps, frozen hard, mysterious as fresh Indian sign found by some solitary hunter on the head waters of the Rio Gila,[445] and as ominous. Birds as they flew their shadows deeper than at noonday on the sand, so deep they seemed to bite into the snow, as if it were determined that no living thing should pass above it and not leave a mark.

But as the desert is an open book to the Indian tracker, whose eye remarks the passage of each living thing in the faint marks it leaves upon the grass, so did the snow reveal all secrets to the most inexperienced eye.

Even when it had cleared away the grass remained black and downtrodden, and looked burned by every footstep that it passed.

But if it changed the woods to palaces of silver and of diamonds, the hills to Alpine ranges, and the fields to vast white chess-boards, blotting out the roads, which it filled solid to the hedges, what a change wrought about the moss! The Flanders moss that once had been a sea became an ocean, for as the peat-hags and the heather turned to waves, and as the sun lit up their tips with pink, they seemed to roll as if they wished once more to wash the skirts of the low foothills of the

---

[445] The Gila River is a 649 mile-long tributary of the Colorado, flowing through New Mexico and Arizona.

carse.[446] Foaming and billowing along, they turned the brown peat moss set with its bushes of bog myrtle and lean, wiry-growing heather into an Artic sea – a waste of desolation, brilliant and desolate, and upon which the sun reflected with a violet tinge. As the waves seemed to surge around the stunted pines and birches, all looked dead, extinct, and as remote from man as when the Roman legions camping on the edge of the great moss constructed their lone camp,[447] last outpost of the world on this side of the Thule[448] of the frowning Grampians to the north. As night fell slowly on the drear expanse of white, Ben Lomond, catching the last reflection of the setting sun, turned to a cone of fire, and at its foot the pine woods of Drumore stood out intense and dark as if cut out of blackened cardboard, and by degrees the hills and woods melted away into a vapoury mist.

Then, from the bosom of the moss came a hoarse creaking as a heron, rising slowly into the keen night air, after a day of unproductive fishing by the black frozen pools of the slow Forth, flapped heavily away.

* * * * *

Watts and Davies wrote that between 1900 and 1914, 'Graham soon discovered the rather narrow technical and imaginative limits within which he wrote most effectively, and within them he displayed increasing proficiency', although he occasionally fell into the trap of being 'too literary', as in the next sketch.[449] It does, however, have a certain charm and a ring of authenticity. The house Graham describes so fondly is, of course, his beloved Gartmore, which he had been obliged to sell five years earlier.

FATE

The Saturday Review, 25 March 1905, pp. 377–8.
Anthologised in *His People* (London: Duckworth, 1906), pp. 191–200.

IN a long corridor of an old Georgian house, lit by a skylight and by a window over the hall door, there hung a piece of needlework in a dark rosewood frame. In silk, some lady of the family had worked a

---

[446] Scots: Low land along a river.
[447] Bochcastle Roman fort at Callander, on the banks of the River Teith.
[448] Thule (Latin from Greek) = the location farthest north mentioned in ancient Greek and Roman literature and cartography.
[449] Watts and Davies, p. 205.

Figure 8 Upper landing, Gartmore House, 1898.

landscape setting forth the district and the house in which the picture hung. It stood four square and looked out on the east, across the moss which once had been a sea. On either side of the great strath ran lines of hills, one rough and heather-clad, as when just at their feet the Romans were rolled back, the other smooth and green, and sloping off towards the south. The moss itself was brown and on its face the shadows came and went, chasing each other as the hours pursue eternity, leaving no trace where they had passed.

Trees stood about the house and in the pictured needlework; in one case stiff and formal, looking like ineffectual monuments of grief in cemeteries, and in the other whispering in the wind, labouring and groaning in the storm, and in the sunshine all alive with bees.

The careful needlewoman had displayed each stone and window in the house; colouring those black which had been closed during the operation of the window tax,[450] and had dwelt lovingly on walls and pediments. The range of hills under her magnifying steel had changed to mountains, and a small lake had come into existence supplied with water from the fountains of her brain. Right carefully she had devised

---

[450] A property tax based on the number of windows in a house. In Scotland, the tax was applied from 1748 until 1798.

the cedars, with the beech avenue, the sycamores, the weeping yew, and the stiff terrace upon which the house was set, whilst every post in all the fences was portrayed both with elaborate stitching and with circumstance.

Just as much inkling of perspective was employed as to make all unnatural, and yet on looking at it, you felt it had been done with tenderness, and the contriver must have put her soul into the task.

Such artless works sometimes more nearly touch the heart than the most airy flights of genius, when the place represented has been dear to the beholder and the artist; for places, unlike men, can never vary, and time itself breeds no satiety of love.

The faint, fresh smell of the fir trees in the wet, the scent of dampness rising from the moss and the perfume of bracken, sweet and sharp, must have been present always to the worker as she sat sewing at her window seat, whilst gazing at the rain.

Time does not mellow needlework as it does pictures, yet still it gives it interest, and as the colours fade and ends of silk grow rough, it seems a soul is born in them which speaks to us out of its nothingness bringing us somehow nearer to the dead.

So it hung on, getting a little yellower, more flyblown, and with the varnish scaling from the rosewood frame and the gold falling off in particles from the interior rim, as winter damp and summer sun succeeded year by year in the long corridor of the old Georgian house. Birds sat upon it now and then, and bats occasionally hid themselves between it and the wall, and darted out again as fearlessly as if the lonely passage had been an alley of wood. Nothing appeared less likely than that a tragedy should be unrolled with it as background, or as the world, in which after the fashion of the greater world outside the frame, birth, life and death should pass all unperceived.

Life was serene as usual in the corridor, whilst the dust gathered on the picture frames and clung upon the looking-glasses as frost clings on a cabbage leaf in the autumn after a cold night. The house itself, buried in woods, woods and more woods, stood lonely and in the avenues guttered and channelled by the winter rains, the grass grew rank. The terraces were pitted here and there with holes made by the rabbits in their play, who left a little heap of sand outside them, to which occasionally clung brown silky fur.

The roedeer, venturing from the copses, strayed in the summer nights and belled close to the windows; and the soft flying owls wafted from tree to tree like kites, or hooted litanies from the tall larches, whilst, from the woods and mosses rose the faint noises which at night wake recollections of the time when men and animals perchance all spoke one tongue.

The charm of desolation had descended on the place, and the rare lights and few inhabitants seemed to be lost in nature, which invaded them, swallowing them in her amplitude as the stray vegetation swallows up a church deserted by the Jesuits out on the Chaco or in Paraguay. Gnomons[451] had fallen from sundials, and the stone slabs of terrace steps yawned open: from some of them sprang ferns, whilst on the coping of the walls the moss grew tenderly. The ponds were half grown up with flags and bulrushes. Great banks of sand and mud stretched into them, brought by the burns in winter, and on them feathers stuck, looking like snow-flakes and fluttering in the wind. All was so quiet that the mast[452] falling from the beech sounded like raindrops pattering upon ice or on a window-pane.

Nothing disturbed the quiet of the place, which slowly seemed to fall to ruins and to become more beautiful each day. Then, on a summer morning when the swallows darted through the trees, hawking at flies and on the grass the squirrels ventured timidly to play, springing upon the overhanging boughs at the first sudden noise, a bubble seemed to swell below the glass and force it out-wards at the corner of the frame. It grew mysterious and white, next turned a rusty brown, then was forgotten as the days slipped past, each one so like the other that the flight of time was imper-ceptible, darkness succeeding light as stealthily as the owls floated through the wood, lighting like thistle-down on the elastic branches of the trees.

Weeks passed and still the mystery was unsolved, only beneath the envelope of fluttering motion now and then was seen, as if a spirit prisoned in its cell stirred faintly, struggling to free itself from matter and to escape into the sky. But no one marked it much, for tragedies may be enacted at one's elbow, and none the wiser; for indeed, most tragedies seem comic to the looker-on, who does not comprehend the motive, and takes the sufferer for a mere ill-bred person, who might have lived and died, just like the rest of us, had he had common sense.

So the bees hung about the lime trees, making their music in the flowers, the cedars' branches swayed like windmills' sails, and in the thickest of the woods, the capercailzie crowed, flapping their wings with a strange hollow sound which echoed through the trees, like negro tomtoms by night up some mosquito-haunted river on the

---

[451] The upright part of a sundial that casts a shadow.
[452] Old English: *mæst* = the fruit of the oak, beech, chestnut, and other trees.

coast, or like the mournful drum which Bernal Diaz[453] heard during
the siege of the great temple of Tenochtitlán.[454]

Then, on a morning in late June, when the soft air just curled
the rising mist from off the moss into tall pillars such as rise in a
simoom,[455] one who had looked by chance at the old needlework in
passing saw that the tragedy had taken place.

The temple's veil was rent,[456] and fallen asunder, and underneath
the glass a brown and fluffy moth had come into the world, been
born, had stirred, just fluttered and had died, seeing the air it could
not fly in, feeling the life within it, which fate that laughs at all things,
moths and men alike, said it should never taste.

To wish it peace, it who had not known trouble, were in vain, and
for repose, its wings had never fluttered in the air. Care, sorrow, love,
hate, pain, revenge, and still less avarice, or ambition by which the
fool and not the noble fall, it shall know none of, and probably would
not have felt in its brief joyous life.

But to be cabined in a cage of glass, to suffer the "peine forte et
dure"[457] of death pressing, for no committed crime, poor, fluttering
fairy round the lamp of life, 'twas hard. How brief your pleasures and
how innocent, merely to play about the corridors of the old melancholy house to prove your wings, and then to soar into some fir tree
on the lawn, equipped at once with all the lore inherited from those
your ancestors in Eden, who flitted through cypresses of that fair
garden on the Tigris, and then after a day or two, at most a month,
to love, to rove at night amongst the trees, to fall at the first frost or
heavy shower, and lie amongst the needles of the pines without a
single crime upon your conscience, tender as your wings.

Alas, poor fellow, would-be flutterer in the realms of the hard
world, perhaps the fate presiding at your birth who with her unkind
shears cut off your destiny, was kind. Who knows? You might have
come to ruin or mishap, e'en you who surely had no unkind thought
in your minute and microscopic brain.

Circling about at night, thinking no evil, after the fashion of your
clan, a candle light which to your complex eyes might have appeared

---

[453] Bernal Díaz del Castillo (c. 1492–1584) A Spanish conquistador, who was
a soldier in the conquest of Mexico under Hernán Cortés. Graham wrote
a biography of him: *The Life of Bernal Diaz del Castillo* (London: Eveleigh
Nash, 1915).

[454] The ancient capital of the Aztec empire in Mexico.

[455] A hot, dry, wind blowing in the desert, especially in Arabia.

[456] Matthew 27:51.

[457] French: 'hard and forceful punishment'. The ancient punishment of having
heavier and heavier stones placed upon the chest until a plea was entered, or
death resulted.

a sun, vast, round, and vivifying, might have attracted you and left you writhing agonised and maimed, a prey to children who in their rage for self-improvement, or from the cruelty which we who have no wings bear in our blood as the true sign of the great curse our common Maker set upon us at the Fall, transfixed you with a pin.

Perils we know not of and which have never entered our dull brains, so ill attuned to all the mysteries of your world, may have awaited you. Some pestilence which no physician of our kind has diagnosed might have attacked and struck you blind, crippling your flight or rendering you unsightly to the companions of your merry little world. This might have been, or the fell spider with his web of fated filaments entangled your soft wings and drawn you struggling to his den, cut off your life and fed upon your flesh, for these are dangers even we who know so little of your lives can comprehend. From these your fate has freed you, making you equal to great Cæsar, Hannibal, to Alexander, both to the greatest and the least of all mankind, by the mere fact that you have lived.

Rail not at fate, poor iridescent moth, although the hues upon your wings were meant to shine at twilight as you flickered through the trees with just as fair a lustre as the most gorgeous butterfly who hovers in the sun on the Tijuca's[458] slopes can ever boast. Do not repine although no snowflake would have floated from the sky more delicately than the unfollowable pulsations of your wings would have conveyed you through the twilight air in your brief honeymoon with life. You will not know the joy of liberty, tender and innocent in its conception, as moths alone conceive it, out of created things. Let no cursed man of science with his dog Latin and apocalyptic[459] Greek dispel my ignorance, telling me that the family of moths is as rapacious as the vulture or the crow. I'll not believe it, but will mourn thy fate, condemned to see for a brief moment all the beauties of the light, never to flit at evening in the dark recesses of the trees. Poor pilgrim to a world unworthy of your innocence, who lived and died so quickly, surely you solved at once the mysteries which we live for a lifetime and still never grasp. My fellow-sufferer by fate, you, who left instantly the world in which we tarry longer instants, with as scant comprehension of our lives perhaps as you, do not forget us prisoned in our glass; but in the limbo where you flutter now, think that a fellow-moth remembers you, just as you lived and died, with your soft body, iridescent wings, and sharp antennæ.

* * * * *

---

[458] The mountains of the city of Rio de Janeiro, Brazil.
[459] The disclosure or revelation of great knowledge.

The bi-lingual journal *Guth Na Bliadhna* (Voice of the Year), was rooted in the the 'Celtic Revival', and fused culture, language and political nationalism. Founded by the Honourable Ruaraidh Erskine of Marr (1869–1960), it was published between 1904 and 1925. In 1908, it became the rallying point for a group of London Scots, leading to the formation of a new nationalist organisation called initially *Comunn nan Albannach*, which became better known as the Scots National League (SNL),[460] which Erskine had modelled on Arthur Griffith's Sinn Féin. Erskine himself had been born in Brighton, but raised in Edinburgh, and as a young man, in his late teens and early twenties, he was a leading light in the Legitimist League of Great Britain and Ireland, promoting the legitimacy of the lost House of Stuart. Introduced to the Gaelic language by his nanny, in 1901 he attended Gaelic lessons in Beauly, and achieved fluency and a love of the language, which would shape his development of language-activism and Scottish nationalism.

Despite their mutual support for Scottish independence, there seems to be no strong links between Graham and Erskine, possibly because of Erskine placing Catholicism and Gaelic at the centre of his political agenda.[461] However, Graham wrote three pieces for Marr's journal (one of which had no Scottish or 'Celtic' content[462]), and this is the first. It is a combination of his fondness for local legend around a place that he clearly knew, and a peculiar environmental monism.

Described on old maps as *Tiobairt na Reil* (the Well of the Star), it was assumed that it lay at the summit of the Duke's Pass, but as an active spring, it lies half-hidden, adjacent to an ancient Roman track and subsequent drove road, to the south of Loch Venachar, far away from destructive tourism. However, the spot is reputedly where the 3rd Earl of Menteith, William 'Graham of the Hens', was slain in 1547 by Donald, commander of the Appin Stewarts. Thus, the derivation might come from *Tiobair-na-Iorghuill*, meaning 'The Well of the Fray'.

---

[460] After the First World War, it was re-established as the Scots National League (SNL), which Hugh MacDiarmid described as 'the most promising nationalist organization that has been formed in Scotland since the Union'. *Contemporary Scottish Studies* (London: Leonard Parsons, 1926), p. 246. The SNL was distinctly 'separatist', but in 1928, it was instrumental in amalgamating the three 'home rule' organisations to form the National Party of Scotland.

[461] Erskine, who envisaged political union between Scotland and Ireland, insisted that origins of the British Union of 1707 lay in the Reformation, and that John Knox was a 'traitor', who led a 'rascal multitude', who had sold their country, its culture, and its faith to the English. Erskine, 'Knox and the Rascal Multitude', *Guth na Bliadhna*, vol. 1, book 2, 1904, p. 128.

[462] 'Dagos', *Guth na Bliadhna*, August 1906, vol. 3, pp. 216–30.

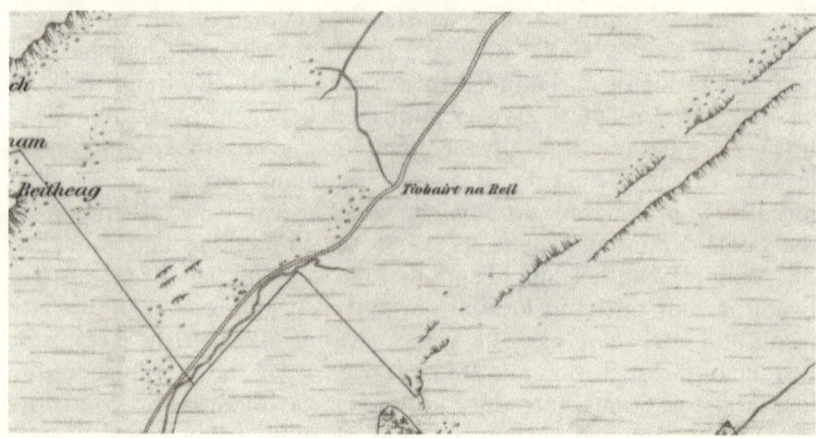

Figure 9

TOBAR NA REIL

Guth Na Bliadhna, May 1905, pp. 155–61.
Anthologised in *His People* (London: Duckworth, 1906), pp. 236–45.

RIGHT at the summit of the pass it lies, nothing above it but the sky. On every side the billowing heath-clad hills engirdle it about. Flat stones encircle it, and on its surface water spiders walk. Red persicaria, with wax-like stalks and ragged leaves, grows by its edge. Below it stretches out a vast brown moss, honeycombed here and there with black peat hags, and a dark lake[463] spreads out, ringed on one side with moss, and on the other set like a jewel in a pine wood, with a white stretch of intervening sand. On it are islands with great sycamores and chestnuts, stag-headed but still vigorous, and round their shores the bulrushes keep watch like sentinels. Mists rise from moss and lake and creep about the corries of the hills, blending the woods and rocks into a steamy chaos, vast and unfathomable, through which a little burn unseen, but musical, runs tinkling through the stones. So at the little *bealach*[464] the well lies open to the sky, too high for the lake mists to touch it, as it looks up at the stars.

They say that on a certain day in mid-summer, a star when at its zenith shines into the well. Which the star is, if Rigel or Algol or Aldebdran with his russet fire, is clean forgotten, for nowadays tradition has scant place in men's imagining. He who looks on the water

---

[463] The Lake of Menteith.
[464] Gaelic: High pass.

at the fateful hour, and sees the star reflected in the well, acquires again the ancient universal tongue, by which in ages past men and the animals held speech. For him the language of the birds becomes intelligible. The trees that groan or whisper in the breeze divulge their lore, and disclose all that they have seen in their long peaceful lives. Fish in the rivers and the lakes have no more dread of him, and, rising to the surface of the linns, tell him the marvels of the deep, whilst snakes and lizards, with newts, the moles and bats, impart their troubles or their joys, making their little secrets plain, by the strange virtues of the mystic star transmitted through the well.

There is no record of any one who, having drunk, obtained the power and straightway got into communication with all animals and things. No doubt if at the appointed hour the fountain had turned all to gold, a town would have arisen on the pass, and Baal's priesthood or an aristocracy would have reserved the right to drink and gaze upon the well, and temples of Algol or Aldebaran would have sprung up as if by magic from the hill. But man, who lives an outcast from all living things, cut off by pride and want of sympathy from beasts and birds, and careless of his own connexion [sic] with the world except so far as it may bring him the twin curses, wealth and power, which have combined to make him vile, cared not for such a gift. So trees and animals and beasts, with stones and streams, watched vainly every recurring year throughout the centuries for some adventurer who should break through the bonds which held the self-crowned monarch of the world in silence, condemned for ever to live dumb but to his own kind's speech, whilst on all sides secrets he never dreamed of were waiting to be heard. So as a Highlander went past, driving his cattle from the low country in Menteith, or in the summer evenings a group of men wrapped in their plaids, with curly hazel shepherd's sticks, and carrying long single-barreled Spanish guns, trotted along the steep and winding path, their deerskin shoes making no sound upon the stones, the rabbits sitting at their holes watched them expectantly. The birds upon the branches turned their round heads and looked towards the well. The trees and plants and heather on the hill seemed to sigh softly in the summer air, as if inviting them to halt until the mystic star should rise, then drink and break the spell.

But they, absorbed in the affairs of life, which lead men onward prisoners to the grave, discoursed of hogs and pownie-beasts, of trysts and markets, and of the price of hirsells[465] and of queys.[466] At times they stopped and drank, but never lingered, scooping the water in

---

[465] Scots: A flock of sheep.
[466] Scots: A two-year-old cow.

their palms or in their *cuachan*[467] of birch-wood hooped with silver, drawing their hands across their mouths, and sometimes murmuring, "Aye, och aye, they say that when a body drinks here, when the stars are up, he learns a vast o' things, that's why they ca' it *Tobar na Reil*, but I mind lying here aince o' a summer's nicht, sleeping ye ken, after some awqua[468] that I had doon by at old McKurston's, and never learned a thing".

And whilst they talked, the trees and stars, half-sleeping in the cold moon's light, listened but drowsily, and all they heard was Angus answer Finlay, "Och aye, McKurston just keeps the finest awqua that I ever drank no more, Finlay McLachlan," and his compeer and fellow driver, looking up whilst kneeling by the spring, would answer sapiently, "And neither did I too". And so the well slept on, having for its one tragedy the fight between the Grahams of Menteith, and Stuarts on a raid from Appin, whose leader's head, struck by a sword-cut from his body at a blow, rolled down the pass, calling out imprecations even after death.[469]

With the exception of this brief tragedy, history the well has none. Its very name means nothing to the men who now inhabit, where once its namers dwelt. The legend lives as a tradition, to be laughed or wondered at, according to the attitude of mind of him who hears it, for education has new superstitions of its own, which have expelled those of the older race. Who that to-day, when all flee from responsibility as from the plague, would incur the burden of the sorrow of the trees, the winds, the beasts, for man aspires not to equality but to command, by which, when he possesses it, he straightly becomes an outcast from his kind.

Yet, had it been but for the pleasure of another sorrow to his life, 'tis strange that no one quenched his thirst, for joy is transient, whilst sorrow lives for ever, and to prove sorrows yet unknown might have stirred some one with imagination, had there been any such a traveller on the road which winds by Glenny to the valley of the Teith.[470] And yet the district set with *Sith-bhrughan*[471] and with traditions of a fairy causeway in the lake, a borderland of races in the past, a frontier where the Lowland hob and Highland pixie met on neutral ground, to dance upon the green, seemed to invite experiment, and call for its

---

[467] Gaelic: A goblet or bowl.
[468] Whisky.
[469] See above. This incident was recounted in Walter Scott's *Tales of a Grandfather*.
[470] A tributary of the River Forth.
[471] Gaelic: 'Fairies of the little tumulus or mound'. Doon Hill between Gartmore and Aberfoyle.

Columbus to explore a newer world than that he saw in Guanahani[472] from his caravel.

A gentle world in which no hatred reigns; where envy and all malice are unknown, where each one tells his secret to his friend unwittingly, because the speech they use is universal and without volition, and not as ours, confined to persons and articulate. The speech that lives in the clear water of the well, at the conjuncture of the star, has no vocabulary, no rules, no difficulties, but he who has it, speaks as does the wind, and saying nothing in particular, is understood of all. Thus it can never lie, or lead astray, and so is valueless to us, as valueless as gold upon a desert island, with no one to enslave.

No one has claimed it since the first framers of the legend paddled their coracles upon the lake; no one will claim it, or ever think but for an instant of the treasure waiting to be grasped. Red-deer and roe and kyloes[473] on the hills are all born free of it, and swallows from the south need no interpreter, but straightway tell their travels to the birds who but a week ago have left the pole, or to the weasels and the wrens who never wandered more than a mile or two from where they saw the light, they find themselves as much at home amongst the scrubby copse, as they were, only a month ago, in cane brakes and in palms.

But if the birds and beasts, the trees and grasses and the stones, mourn the estrangement and the want of faith of man, so does mankind feel vaguely its own loneliness amongst created things with which it cannot have communication, and before which it always must be dumb. What tender idylls moss and lichens could unfold, if only some one of the passers by throughout the centuries had learned their speech, and taught his children, taking them, as the most sacred duty in his power, upon the star's appearance in its round, to drink and learn, and thus transmit their knowledge to their children, making them all hereditary dragomen[474] by right divine, betwixt their race and the creation of the beasts.

Drink and admire, the motto says, upon the well in far Marrakesh set among its palms. Above the fountain, built by some pious pilgrim, who perhaps had felt the desert's thirst and reared this monument to the one God – He who alone brings comfort in the sands – the horse-shoe arch is blue with pottery. Intricate patterns marked in lustrous tiles cross and recross each other, and arabesques repeat some pious saw or play upon God's name. Over the humble fountain on the pass unknown to fame, the skies are canopy, and the stars set in them,

---

[472] An island in the Bahamas where Columbus first made landfall.
[473] Highland cattle.
[474] Interpreters, translators and guides in the Near East.

Figure 10 The Well of the Star.

celestial glow-worms of the firmament, which mark the hours the pas-sers-by neglect. No pious pilgrim there has hedged about the spring with masonry; no sculptured stone relates its virtues, for it serves but as a drinking-place for roe, who as they drink admire and give their thanks instinctively, wiser by far than man. No one remembers the lone well among the heath or cares for it, but to smile scornfully at the old simple legend of the past. In all the district where it lies, few know its bearings, and for the name, refer to it "as a sort o' Gaelic fash aboot a star; I mind my feyther kent the meaning o' it," dismissing it at once as "juist a haver, auncient but fair redeeklous, an auld wife's clishmaclaver," beneath the notice of an "eddicated man."[475]

---

[475] 'A sort of Gaelic bother about a star, I remember my father knew the meaning of it … just nonsense, old and ridiculous, an old woman's idle gossip, of no interest to serious people.'

So it sleeps quietly upon the pass just where the road descends to Vennachar[476] and rises from Menteith. Winds sweep the bents and rustle in the ling, setting the cotton-grass a-quivering, bowing the heads of the bog asphodel, and carrying with them the sharp perfume of the gale, sweeter and homelier than the spice of Araby.

In the dark mirror of the lake below, the priory and the castle hang head downwards, and on the bullrushed shore the wavelets break amongst the stones. The earl's old pleasance, now neglected, is a park for cows, its few surviving sycamores have withered at the top, and soon will follow those who planted them into the misty region of the past.

The well, the star, the scrubby oak copse on the hill, the old Fingalian road, distinct in moonlight, or in the morning after frost, for time itself appears unable to efface the taint man's footsteps leave upon the ground, remain and call to the chance passer-by to stop and drink at the conjunction of the star. They call in vain, and nature in the breeze still raises its lament, uncomprehended by the ears of man, who, in his self-forged fetters, fails to understand.

*****

The following is one of the best examples of Graham's monologues in Scots. Though not a natural speaker of Scots himself, again he was quite at home with it, and his use of Scots in his writings feels authentic, but this is particularly strong, too strong even for the majority of Scots to understand. Unusually the subject of this sketch is one of the 'the "douce" and Presbyterian, "pawky" three-per-centling' men of commerce, of whom Graham was usually so dismissive, who is outwitted by a wily Greek ship's captain. It also shows an unusual understanding of merchant shipping and maritime law for a landlubber like Graham. However, its real oddity is the contrast between the exotic foreign locations to which the subject travels, and his parochial speech and attitudes.

M'KECHNIE V. SCARAMANGA

Anthologised in *Progress* (London: Duckworth, 1905), pp. 199–217.

"MAN, an awfu'-like thing yon law o' general average. Dod aye, I mind aince being the matter of a hundred pound oot by it."[477]

---

[476] Loch Venachar, a lake in the Trossachs.
[477] 'It's an awful thing that Law of General Average. God, yes, I remember once making a loss of one hundred pounds because of it.' (The Law of General

He paused, and spat reflectively into what he, having traded in his youth to Portland Maine, St. John's, and Halifax, knew as a cuspidor.[478] His whole appearance showed him at first sight a man who for the most part of his life had sailed out of Aberdeen or Peterhead.

His iron-grey hair was thin upon his head, and made a halo round his brick-dust face, on which the sun, the storm, and whisky of full fifty years had done their worst. His beard was stiff and bristly, and grew high upon his cheek, and underneath the chin, looked like the back of a wild boar or porcupine. His upper lip was shaved and blue, his teeth stained yellow with tobacco juice. Thick tufts of bristles overhung his eyes and sprang from out his ears, and his enormous hands, once muscular and hard with hauling upon ropes, although immense, were soft and flabby, though still freckled by the sun which tanned them in his youth. Upon his middle finger was tattooed a ring, and round his wrist a bracelet which he tried hard to hide by pulling down his cuff. Not that he was ashamed of it, or ever for an instant posed for anything but what he was, but, as he would explain, "Mistress M'Kechnie thocht it didna' look genteel. A woman's clavers,[479] aye ou aye; but then, ye see, Mistress M'K. raises a wild-like turley-wurley whiles, aboot a feck o' things that dinna matter, for I say when a man has got the siller[480] that is the principal." And certainly he had the siller, for from a mere tin kettle of a tramp, bought upon credit and in which the saying was if you should drop a marlin-spike it would go through her plates, he had attained to the possession of a fleet which peopled every sea.

But though good luck, which he referred to as the "act of Providence," had thus befriended him and seated him in his own private room in the great office, which he once likened to a liner's cabin, the highest praise in his vocabulary, he yet remained at heart the self-same pawky, pious, superstitious, and hard-fisted sailor man that he was when he first sailed in a whaler to the Arctic seas from Peterhead. His friends and his contemporaries knew him as Andrew Granite, whether because of his resemblance to the stone, his character, or simply from his birthplace, or from all combined, no one was

---

Average is a principle of maritime law, whereby, in an emergency, all stakeholders in a trading venture proportionately share any losses resulting from a voluntary sacrifice of part of the ship or cargo, to save the whole.)

[478] A spittoon.

[479] 'My wife believed that I didn't look genteel. A woman's foolish talk, oh yes, but then, you see, my wife raises a commotion about lots of small things that don't matter, for I believe, that when a man has money, that is more important.'

[480] Scots: Silver/money.

sure. But from the Clyde to Timor-Laut,[481] whenever any of his ships was spoken and ran up her number, a smile went round extending from the forecastle to the bridge, and some old shell-back was pretty safe to say, "One of old Andrew's coffins, damn them, a Granite liner; yes, by God; sink like a stone in some place some day, or run upon a shoal marked in no blooming chart; Andrew will grab the insurance money, and then go off to kirk."

Withal he was a genial, simple, whisky drinking, pious, and not unkindly man, with all the low-class Scotsman's love for law and pride in never being over-reached, and with a gift of story-telling which a long life at sea had sharpened and improved.

His conversation ran on bottomry, on jettison, demurrage, barratry[482] ("a grand word yon," he would explain), and barnacles. Much had he got to say about Restraint of Princes and the like, of berth notes, back freights, charter party, cession clause, frustration of adventure, and as to whether frost and rats fell under act of God, or might be held as perils of the sea. Much did he like to dwell upon "diceesions o' the Coorts," quoting with unction Stamforth v. Wells, Hadley v. Baxendale, and Vogeman v. Parkenthorpe, with comments of his own upon the judges, with much about the lunar and the calendar in the vexed question of the "Charter" month, much of the usages of trades and ports, all which he held "redeeklous," deeming them part and parcel of a scheme against the Granite Line. An elder of the kirk "outby Bearsden,"[483] where, as he said, "he stopped,"[484] he yet believed that Providence was a malicious demon on the watch to do him damage, sending foul winds and snapping shafts of screws, blowing off heads of cylinders and heating brasses in an arbitrary way, as if the power referred to had nothing else to do but to watch him and his affairs through a celestial magnifying glass which he kept screwed into his eye after the fashion of a watchmaker when looking at a watch.

The house "outby"[485] where Andrew Granite "stopped" was built of such well-hewn and finely pointed stone as to resemble plaster, so neat were all the joints, so sharp the edges, and though substantial, did not seem designed to live in, but rather as a model from some exhibition of what no house should be. Roofed with dark blue metallic-looking slates, it stood in its own carriage-sweep, which, laid

---

[481] A district that covers half of the north-eastern part of Penang Island, including George Town.
[482] Technical seafaring words concerning legal responsibility for a cargo.
[483] A church-elder in a northern suburb of Glasgow.
[484] Scots: Lived, resided.
[485] Scots: Outside but adjacent.

with furnace slag in lieu of gravel, formed as it were a yellow ochre river flowing between the bulwarks of green grass which bounded it, and which, as the possessor said, were "trimmed square by the lifts and braces and ran down sheer into the tide." He used to add that "in a ship, ye ken, ye canna let minavellings[486] lay aboot, an' for a gairdner ye couldna' get a better man nor steadier than an auld sailor, if ye can keep him frae the drink."[487]

Laurels and rhododendrons, the latter "bonny heebrids," as the seafaring "Gairdner" called them, stunted and withered by the wind, stood ranged beside the avenue in rows, each with its Latin nickname dangling from a wire upon a piece of tin, as if it was convicted of some crime against its fellows and was doing penance for its sins. Cast-iron hoops contrived to look like withies bordered the road; and to make all things sure, enamelled plates with the inscription "Parties are requested to keep off the grass" reminded people to be cautious how they walked. A battlemented lodge and wrought-iron gate with a huge gilt monogram upon the top stood sentinels at the edge of the domain. Clumps of young spruce trees were disposed at intervals to break the wind, which bent them over opposite the side it blew, and stripped them bare where they caught all the fury of the blast.

The inside of the villa was suitable to its exterior grace.

Plate-glass and varnished yellow pine gave it a sort of likeness to a ship. White fluffy mats lay on the floors, and on the walls were water-colours, so well finished and so smooth that they could easily have been mistaken for the best kind of chromo-lithographs.

Wax fruit and feather flowers, and hummingbirds, looking dis-torted ghosts of their bright selves, were stuck about upon the man-telpieces, covered with glass shades. A banner-screen with a ship worked in crewels stood before the fire, which in a bright steel grate burned till the twelfth of May, and then until October was replaced by coloured paper shavings so contrived as to present the appear-ance of a waterfall. Mistress M'Kechnie, a large, high-coloured lady, dressed in black silk and girt about the neck with a gold chain from which a watch was hung which dangled loose or else was stuck into the waistband of her gown, sat in her "droring-room" in state. A large medallion of her lord, with a stout wisp of his stiff hair fashioned into a cable round the edge, was pinned upon her breast. It showed him at the age of thirty, grim and ill-favoured, and had

---

[486] Obscure. Possibly a mispronunciation of 'Mandevilla', a genus of tropical and subtropical flowering vine.

[487] 'For a gardener, you couldn't do better than an old sailor, if you could keep him away from alcohol.'

been taken in the port that he called "Ryo" by an artist who he said had been "an awfu' clever chiel",[488] and certainly should have been heard of in the world of art for his stout realism and adherence to the truth.

The owner of the house sat in his sanctum, which, like the cabin of a ship, had small round windows, and was adorned with books, bound in morocco bindings, which he never read, and with a coloured photograph of her he always called "Mistress M'K." and stood in awe of; for she came of "weel-kenned folk," and had some tocher and a temper which was not always safe "to lippen to."[489]

With cigars lighted, his friends about him and their glasses filled, Mr. M'Kechnie used to give full play to his imaginative mind on many subjects which had appealed to him during the course of his career as law pleas about ships, soundings in various ports, the absence of all lights on certain coasts, the charms of ladies he had known about the world and his success with them, and other things of a like nature which he discussed more freely when certain that his wife had gone to bed.

One tale led to another, but the tale that his friends all loved the best was one he never failed to tell after his second tumbler of stiff toddy, when, with his feet in carpet slippers worked in yellow beads, and with a fox's head in blue in high relief upon the instep, he would light a Trichinopoly cigar, and after, with the story-teller's instinct, having forced his friends to press him, take up his parable.

"Hae ye all got your glasses filled? Weel-aye-I am a sort o' temperate man masel', but speerits, ye ken, are a fair panawcea, that is when taken moderately." To such a proposition no self-respecting Scotsman has an objection, and they all used to fill, and, "paidlin' "with their ladles, inhale the fumes of the hot spirit, puff their cigars, and wait expectantly. "Ye see, ma freens, law is a kittle sort o' gear, especially sea law, as mony o' ye ken I know fu' feel. But the maist awfu' thing is what they ca' yon general average ay juist fair redeeklous. Ye ken what Mr. Scrutton says – he's an M.A. and LL.B. and has juist written the maist compendious work on contrack of affreightment as expressed in charterparties – a pairfeck vawdy-mecum.[490] Ane ye ca' Mackinnon helpit him, and between the twa they lay ye aff a'maist a'thing that can arise between a charterer and a shipowner upon the sea.

---

[488] Scots: A very clever lad.
[489] 'She came from well-known people, and had a dowry and a temper, which was not always trustworthy.'
[490] An ideal pocket manual (*vade mecums*).

"Charter-party, sort o' dog Lay tin, carta partita they ca't. In the auld days they juist wrote it in duplicate on a single sheet o' paper, and then divided it by indented edges, each part fitted to the other. That's hoo they got the name, indenture.[491]

"A feck o' things ye'll find in Scrutton's book, ma freens, sort o' auncient like. Whiles when I havna' much to do I tak' it doon and lauch, man I lauch ower it till ma heid juist whummles like a sturdy sheep. Oo aye ye're richt – I'm sort o' wandered.[492]

"Weel aweel, I'll tell ye now about a wildlike tulzie[493] I had aince with a lash o' Dawgos a' aboot yon cursed general average. Man, it was this wey, ye ken – whiles I juist wonder that a man like Scrutton – Mackinnon is na blate[494] either – does na' dae something to get the law changed. Na, na, ye could na' richtly look for it; it's the man's bread, ye ken. Aye, I'll heave roond, I'm subject to thae digressions; so was Sir Walter Scott and others I could mention. Ye mind aboot the seventy-twa, or it may be the seventy-five, freights were fairly high and shipowners were ettlin' to mak' some siller.[495] Bad times we are havin' noo – yon cuttin' prices, I juist ca' it cuttin' throats – but in the seventy-five – that's it – I had a boat was gaein' oot to Smyrny wi' a feck o' cotton goods.

Somehow or other she just snappit her screw shaft, and if she had na' just by a special providence come across a tramp out o' the Hartlepools she micht have wandered aboot yon islands just like Ulysses – him thae raise sic' a dirl aboot in Homer;[496] for, ye ken, I ha'e a sort o' tincture o' the humanities.

"The tramp just gi'ed her a tow in to Saloneeky. Losh me, then there cam' the salvage racket, the maist infernal intrikit affair ye ever saw. A man juist has to go to the slauchter like a lamb, if aiver a ship makes fast a cable to any o' his boats. Scrutton has it textually, that unless the charter amounts to a demise but I'll no deave[497] ye wi' technicalities. Ye'll get it in Sepia v. Rogers, or Hubbertey v. Holts, and when ye hae it, mickle[498] wiser may ye be.

"Fill up, men, it winna' hurt ye, and there's plenty mair ... ah yes, yon maitter o' the salvage was sort o' seekenin'."

---

[491] 'Charter party' = imitative-Latin, for *charta partita* (a two-part contract).
[492] 'Sometimes, when I'm not busy, I take it from the shelf and laugh, I laugh over it until my head overturns, like a sturdy sheep. Oh yes, you're quite right – I'm getting confused.'
[493] Scots: A wrangle or a dispute.
[494] Scots: Shy.
[495] Scots: Attempting to make some money.
[496] Scots: Him they make such a fuss about in Homer.
[497] Scots: See passim.
[498] Scots: Little.

"The worst thing, though, was that the freighters were a' upon me for demurrage.[499] Sirs me, I was fair gyte, and I juist yokit on Scrutton (the vawdy-mecum, ye mind) as if it had been the Holy Scriptures. Ma heid fair dirled[500] wi' Sangivetti v. Postlethwaite and a heap o' cases very much resembling mine. I thocht I had a bit issue anent the cesser clause, and awa' I went to my awgents in West George Street. I laid my case before them, and they lauch't at me fair lauch't. They told me the point was clear that I stood liable. Man, I whiles[501] think the very elements are a' against the shipowner. What wi' they cursed strikes drawin' awa' the trade, the employers' liabeelity, and the infernal intrikitness o' the law, a body hasna' got a chance.

"Ye'll mind, Geordie, when we went tae sea thegither, sax-and-forty years ago it was maist a' wind jammers in thae days?"

The crony thus interpolated took his black oily Burmah cigar out of his mouth and grunted, "I mind weel. A man juist signed for his salt horse and his salt pork, nane o' your tin-bag then," and, after looking at the ceiling, spat into the fire.

"Aye, that's so, a sailor man was a richt felly then. Nane o' yer comin' aboard withoot an airticle o' kit except a knife and a pair o' seaboots, and slingin' the latter doon the forepeak and fa'ing drunk upon them.

"Na, na, we a' had oor bit kists wi' plenty dunnage in them[502] – and as for your employers' liabeelity set them up – a sailor man juist took his ain life in his hand."

Geordie having grunted something about a long yarn and a rope-maker, Andra' came, as he said, back to his course, and once again took up his tale.

"I juist cabled oot orders to my awgent in Awthens to proceed to Saloneeky to arrange for chartering a vessel to tak' the stuff on to Smyrny; the body juist agreed wi' the captain o' a Greek schooner, ane they ca'ed Scaramangy, heard you ever sic' a name?

"His craft was ane o' they Levantyne-built bits o' things, awfu' gay wi' paint, a kind o' gin-palace afloat, ye ken the things, Geordie? She lookit weel, and my awgent cabled me that, wi' God's blessing, he hoped she would do the trip to Smyrny in aboot three days. I couldna' thole yon 'God's blessing' in the cablegram. A man has his ain releegious opinions – ye mind I'm an elder in the U.P.[503] kirk

---

[499] A charge payable to the owner of a chartered ship for failure to load or discharge the ship within the agreed time.

[500] Scots: Spun.

[501] Scots: Occasionally.

[502] 'We all had our ship-board belongings in our sea-chests.'

[503] United Presbyterian.

outby Milngavie (ye canna' get the richt doctrine here in Bearsden, a mere puir imitation o' the Episcopawlians, a sort o' strivin' after being genteel, I ca' it); but business, ye see, is business. Besides, thae things are better understood, taken for read, as they ca' it up at Westminister.

"Yon blessing in the cablegram cost me a maitter o' some saxteen shillin' the rates were awfu' high in thae times, ye mind. Saxteen shillin' just expended in a manner I ca' redeeklous, for the Almighty must ha' kent that I was putting up ma ain bit supplication when the cash was at stake.

"Yon Scaramangy had a wild-like crew on board; man, they Greeks dinna sail shorthanded, I'se warrant them. Thirteen Dawgos forby himsel', and the bit schooner not above three hundred tons. Heard ye the like?

"I canna' bide a superstitious man, for I aye haud nae ane should stand between a man and Him; if a man wants Him, let him gang straucht, I say – through the Auld Book. Anyhow, Scaramangy had his Madoney a sort o' shrine, ye see-aft o' the mainmast, and a bit licht burnin' awa' before it nicht an' day; an' awfu' waste o' can'le. Weel aweel – anither Trichinopoly[504] ye'll na-aiblins anither tot.[505] What! yer done? Geordie, rax me the ginger snaps. Scaramangy – I didna' see him; but I hae seen his like a thoosand times, maist-like dressed in longshore togs, wi' ane o' thae Maneely straws,[506] an' alpacy jacket, an' white canvas shoes ye'll mind the rig. Maist o' them has a watch-gaird on them like the cable o' a battleship; ye canna' tell a gentleman nooadays, wi' everybody wearin' their bloody Alberts. No a'thegither bad-like sailors are they Greeks; sort o' conceity whiles the way they paint their bits o' schooners and their barquentines; maist o' them yallow, wi' a bit pink streak, whiles a blue ane, and sure to hae a figure-head, some o' they Greek goddesses. – No, Geordie, Sapho was no' a goddess she was a poetess, a queer-like ane tae, just went fair demented ower a felly they ca'ed But I'm havering – the humanities, ye ken, tak' an awfu' grip on a man.

"Scaramangy was most certain to hae had a wee bit curly Maltese dog on board – I canna' bide them, rinnin' aboot yap, yappin' and filin'[507] the decks. Set them up; for ma ain pairt, I like a cat, or maybe a mongoose – na, na, man, no a monkey – dirty brutes, the hale rick ma tick o' them; seem to gae into a decline tae soon as ye pass the

---

[504] An Indian cheroot.
[505] Scots: 'You won't perhaps have another drink.'
[506] Manilla straw hat.
[507] Fouling.

forties.[508] Man, I mind ane, I traded a coat and a bit Bible for him wi'
a missionary in the Cameroons. Puir brute, we had na' sighted the
Rock of Lisbon, comin' hame, afore he started hostin'.[509] I had him
in the cuddy, and ettled to mak' him tak' some Scott's Emulsion. It
would na' dae, and we had juist to commit his bit body to the deep,
the same as a Christian, just off the Wolf Rock. I dinna' care to mind
it. I lost my ain Johnny the same way. Man, I felt it sae, I should hae
liked to hae the wee deevil stuff t, but his mother said it would be
heathenish.

"Nae doot o' it, yon Scaramangy would foul some other body's
cable when he lifted anchor, and find his throat halliards unrove –
they're apt to use them for a warp, ye ken, or some other kind o'
deevilment; but, anyhow, to sea he went in half a gale o' wind.

"There must hae been an awfu' hagger-snash o' tongues, bad as the
Tower o' Babel, on board the *Aidonia*; that's what they ca'ed her thae
Levantynes canna' dae a thing without."

Set o' curly-heided Dawgos, with their silver earrings and sashes
rowld round their hurdies – I canna' stan' a sailor man wi' a sash on
him, it looks sae theatrical.

"What happened only the Lord Himself and Scaramangy really ken.
The Lord, for a' He kens, never lets on He hears, and Scaramangy
was a naitural accomplished liar frae his birth.

"What he said was, that a pairfect hurricane burst on him, soon as
he'd pit to sea. He couldna' get the topsails aff o' her, as nane o' his
dodderin' deevils daur to gae aloft. So he juist watched them blow
clean oot o' the boltropes, and shortened the lave o' his sails the best
he could by a special interposeetion o' Providence he didna' lose ony
o' his heidsails, though nae doots but he deserved tae.

"He says he and his cattle were in the awfu'ist peril that they ever
experienced in their lives, the schooner almost on her beam ends, and
the seas fair like to smother her.

"In the nick o' time, what think ye he did, man?" 'Ran for some
harbour,' 'lie to a bittie'; na, na, nae frichts o' him. He juist pit up
a bit sipplication to his Madoney in the companion, and promised
her (as if the painted bitch could hear him) that if she took him safe
to Smyrny, that he would sacrifice something valuable as a sign o'
gratitude. Heard ye the like o' that?

"God's truth, it mak's me mad to think aboot it the folly o' the
thing and the gratuitous waste o' valuable property.

---

[508] Between latitudes 40°S and 50°S.
[509] Scots: Coughing.

"Anyhow, he doddered in to Smyrny some gait or ither, and what d'ye think he done? He an' his men – aye, Geordie, nae doots he had the dawg along wi' them – went barefit oot to a shrine they had, and returned thanks to Him who stills the waves – that is, when He has a fancy tae.

"I dinna altogether disapprove o' that, for, prayer, ye ken, is usefu' whiles. Samuel pit up his sipplication to the Lord before he hewit yon Agag, and Joshua when he smote thae Canaanites, and even Paul – a gran' man Paul, sort o' pawky too lifted a prayer when he was in juist sich a situation as was yon Scaramangy.

"Scaramangy and his Dawgos, when they had done their prayer, went aboard again, unbent their mainsail, and took it ashore and burnt it on the beach. Mad, ye say, Geordie – mad, aye, mad enough, but no on business matters.

"Ye can't think what they did then?

"They gaed awa' up to the British Consulate, and tabulated their claim, under the law o' general average, for the value o' the mainsail; for the deevils said, had they no made their vow, the Madoney wouldna' have interfeired, and the vessel would maist certainly hae been lost. No blate, yon Scaramangy but mercy me, whatna' a conception o' natural laws he must have had! Fancy the Madoney expawtiating in the heavens, watching a storm like a fisherwife watching for her man when an easterly gale springs up, and no to be propeetiated without the promise o' an offerin'!

"After I got the cable, I fair sprang oot o' the hoose, and awa' to West George Street, to my awgents, and they tel't me Scaramangy was domiciled furth o' Scotland, and the case would have to be heard at Smyrny.

"It was juist held that whereas Captain Scaramangy, bein' in peril on the deep, and havin' done everything within his power and in the compass o' good seamanship to save his ship – ma God! – and being at the point o' daith, had recourse to prayer. Furthermore, the Coort bein' o' opinion that the vessel must have foondered had there not been an interposeetion o' a Higher Power, decides that Captain Scaramangy took the proper course, and that his prayer and his vow being both heard and considered favourably by the Madoney, that she thocht fit to save the vessel and the crew.

"Therefore, the Coort held that the vow was instrumental in the first degree, and that the jettison o' the mainsail – which of course wasna' a richt jettison at all was necessary, and that the shippers were all bound to bear their due proportion o' the loss.

"Appeal – nae frichts o' me. It cost me, one way and another, mair than a hundred pound. Appeal – na, better to lose than to lose mair; that's a Greek proverb at least I think so, and no a bad yin.

"Yer gauntin', men; weel, weel, good nicht to ye Geordie, rax me doon Scrutton fae aff the top shelf – there's juist a pint or twa anent yon cursed general aiverage I should like to look at before I turn in for the nicht."

* * * * *

Graham's second essay for Erskine's *Guth Na Bliadhna* was 'The Grey Kirk'. Although unnamed, it is an impression of St Bride's Kirk, the parish church of the town of Douglas in South Lanarkshire, the burial place of the chiefs of the Douglas family. The use of this location is an excuse for Graham to reflect upon medieval chivalry and border warfare, but also to bring in Spanish themes, as the remains of the Black Douglas, who was killed in Spain in 1330 while attempting to take Robert the Bruce's heart to the Holy Land on pilgrimage, are buried there.

THE GREY KIRK

Guth Na Bliadhna, February 1906, pp. 25–8.
Anthologised in *His People* (London: Duckworth, 1906), pp. 246–52.

IN a grey valley between hills, shut out from all the world by mist and moors, there lies a village with a little church.

The ruined castle in the reedy loch, by which stand herons fishing in the rank growth of flags, of bulrush and hemp-agrimony which fringes it, is scarcely greyer than the hills. The outcrop of the stone is grey, the louring clouds, the slated roofs, the shingly river's bed and the clear water of the stream. The very trout that dart between the stones, or hang suspended where the current joins the linn, look grey as eels.

Green markings on the moors show where once paths the border prickers[510] followed on their wiry nags led towards the south, the land of fatted beeves and well-stored larders, clearly designed by Providence or fate to be the jackman's[511] prey, but long disused, forgotten and grassed over, though with the ineffaceable imprint of immemorial use still clear.

Dark, geometrical plantations of black fir and spruce deface the hills, which nature evidently made to bear a coat of scrubby oak and birch. Wire fences gird them round, the posts well tarred against the weather, and the barbed wire so taut that the fierce

---

[510] Knights.
[511] An attendant/retainer.

winds might use them as Eolian harps, could they but lend themselves to song.

A district which the wildness of the past has so impressed, that the
main line of railway steals through its corries and across its moors
as it were under protest, and where the curlew mocks the engine's
whistle with his wilder cry.

The village clusters round the kirk, as bees crowd round their
queen, the older houses thatched. Their coping-stones carved with a
rope, remain to show how, in the older world, their rustic architects
secured their roofs against the blast.

No doubt the hamlet grew between the castle and the church. The
jackman of the chief, the sacristan[512] and kindly tenants of the church,
ready and near at hand to put on splent and spur, and able to take
lance or sprig of hyssop in their hand at the first tinkle of the bell or
rout[513] of horn.

The castle in the loch has dwindled to a pile of stones, from which
spring alders, birches and sycamores, whose keys hang yellow in the
wind, unlocking nothing but the sadness of the heart, which marks
their growth, from the decay of the abandoned keep.

A modern mansion set with its shrubberies and paltry planted
woods, where once the Caledonian forest sheltered the wild white
cattle in its glades, seems out of place in the surrounding grey. Its
lodge, with trim-cut laurels and with aucubas and iron gate, run in
a foundry from a mould, is trivial, comfortable and modern; and the
low sullen hills appear to scorn it in their fight with time, for they
remain unchanged from the bold time of rugging and of rieving, when
spearsmen, not a pensioned butler, kept the gate.

The crumbling and decayed stone wall, secluding jealously the
boggy meadows of the park, shuts off the modern mansion with
its electric light, its motor-cars, its liveried servants and its air of
castellated meanness, from the old houses huddling in the wynd.
They look towards the chapel with its high-pitched roof, its squat
round tower with crenellated top and its sharp windows pointed
like a lance.

It seems to gaze at them, as if it felt they were the only links that
time has left it with its old own world. The eye avoids the modern
buildings in the town, the parish church, four square and hideous,
with windows like a house, and from the hills falls on the chapel and
is satisfied. Only in some old missal, with the illustrations by some
monk adscribed to his small round of daily cares, can you behold its
equal, as it stands desolate and grey.

---

[512] A church officer who looks after the vestry.
[513] See passim.

The chapel of a race of warriors, men dark and grey as is the stone of which its walls are built, once a lone outpost of the great mother fort in Rome, it lingers after them, sheltering their tombs and speaking of their fame. Instinctively one feels that once its doors stood open, just as it were a mosque or church in lands where faith continues the whole week, and men pray as they eat or sleep, just when they feel inclined, and naturally as birds.

In the green churchyard, whose grassy hillocks wave it like a sea, the long grey tomb-stones of the undistinguished dead appear like boats that make towards some haven, laying their courses by the beacon of the tower.

The church itself floats like a ship turned bottom upwards on the grassy sea. Its voyage is ended, and the men who once clattered in armour in its aisles and through its nave now sleep below its flags. A maimed ritual and a sterner creed prevail, and those who worship in the church have shown their faith by laying down encaustic tiles over the spur-marked stones on which their forebears jingled in their mail. A fair communion table of hewn stone, smug and well-finished and with the wounds upon the bleeding heart all stanched (as one would think), stands where the altar stood, cold and uninteresting, a symbol of the age. Non ragioniam;[514] on every side, lie those who, in their time, carried their wars across the border, and on the bridge at Rome charged on the people who pressed round them, just as they would have charged in Edinburgh, had any other clan presumed to take the croon of the old causeway of the High Street, and brought upon themselves an excommunication from the Pope.

Stretched under canopies of stone they lie, looking so grim and so impenitent, that one is sure they must be satisfied with their present-ments, if, looking down on their old haunts, they see their images. Many are absent who would have filled a niche right worthily, Tineman and the Black Knight of Jedburgh and others of the house, who, in their time, shook Scotland to the core. But in the middle of the aisle, in leaden caskets hooped with iron and padlocked, lie two hearts. One, that of Archibald who belled the cat.[515] The other heart has travelled much, and in its life beat higher with all generous thoughts than any of its race.

---

[514] Italian: 'Let us not speak'; an allusion to a line from Canto III of *Inferno* in Dante's *Divine Comedy*: 'non ragioniam di lor, ma guarda e passa'.

[515] Archibald Douglas, fifth Earl of Angus. The phrase to 'bell the cat' comes from Aesop's Fable, 'The Mice in Council', and means a dangerous task that is undertaken for the benefit of all, but with a potentially dangerous outcome for the initiator.

He who possessed it (or was possessed by it), liked ever better, as he said, to hear the laverocks'[516] singing than the cheeping of the mouse. His hands were able, all his adventurous life, to keep his cheeks from scars, as he averred in Seville to the Spanish knight, who wondered at their absence from his face. Carrying a heart to Palestine, he fell, not in the Holy Land, but on the frontiers of Granada, that last outpost of the Eastern world. The heart he carried lies at Melrose, and his own, sealed fast in lead, soldered perhaps in some wild camp lost in the Ajarafe[517] of Sevilla, is the chief ornament of the grey chapel of his race.

Set like a ship, the chapel lies in the long waves of sullen hill and moor that roll away towards the south.

In its long voyage through the sea of time, crews of wild warriors have clung to it, as their one refuge from the spear of life. Each in their turn have fallen away, leaving it lonely, but still weather-tight and taut; a monument of faith, as some may think, or of good masonry and well-slaked lime, as the profane may say, still sailing on the billowy moors which stretch towards Muirkirk; so little altered that any one of those who in the past have prayed within its walls, if he returned to a changed world, would cling to it as the one thing he knew.

So it drifts on upon its voyage through time, bearing its freight of warriors to their port.

* * * * *

The following piece has a specific provenance. Five years after the sale of Gartmore House, Graham returned to Menteith to unpack some cases of pictures that a friend had kept for him. Later, he told Edward Garnett, 'As they came out one by one, it seemed that they were alive, and that I was buried.' He continued:

> In the Autumn, I went to the Lake of Menteith to get some things I left there, to look at the graves of many of my people in an island there. By the side of the lake, there lived two old sisters, ancient retainers of my family their people had been. The last had died not long ago. The cottage was shut and the garden deserted. I sat down on the doorstep in the evening, and smoked a cigarette. The tobacco was too bitter. I am trying to write about it, and cannot.[518]

---

[516] Scots: Skylarks.
[517] An extensive area of high ground to the north of Seville.
[518] Cunninghame Graham, letter to Edward Garnett, 26 December 1905. University of Texas.

Garnett, who believed that Graham was capable of more expressive writing, quickly replied, voicing his continuing frustration:

> Your words about Gartmore, and the island burying place give me all the feeling of the things inside you which you find it so impossible to express ... *Write it*, my dear Amigo, in a journal as if you were communicating with yourself ... Cast it in that loose and fluid form, and write it, so that something beautiful and tender may live for others out of all this passing away and coming to nothingness ... You have a great deal in you which as yet you have not fully expressed. I mean – in your books. The most *personal* and in that sense the most *preciously direct* from your life ... It is an instinct in you perhaps not to express those depth ... I want you to express yourself *fully* in literature ... I want you to think over what there is in yourself and life which you have shrunk from writing. Perhaps you don't see my meaning – but there are always deeper selves within us than we *know*.[519]

But he was aware that even in this piece, his most nostalgic so far for his ancestral home, he had failed to fully express his concealed emotions, and replied: 'I see I have not done what I feel, but that is impossible'.[520] This reticence may have had several causes. Firstly, it might simply have been fear of openly expressing feelings, a constraint that is not uncommon among men, (and, it may be said, common among Scottish men). It may also have been due to his upbringing, where any emotional display was frowned upon, or simply that he had no confidence in his abilities, as expressed in his Preface to *The Ipané* where he wrote, 'Few men know why they write, and most men are ashamed of what they do when once it stares them in the face in moulded type'.[521] However, there may be a more tangible reason. Graham remained deeply political, and, as we have seen, certainly during this period, he was still fighting campaigns, on and off the page, and no doubt adding new enemies to the old, or at least confirming the bad opinions of certain sections of society. This perhaps did not overly concern him, but displaying a softer side, or a suggestion of weakness, would have exposed a chink in his armour, and undermined his reputation, and the myth that he had so carefully cultivated, of the adventurous, fearless and incorruptible paladin, the

---

[519] Edward Garnett, letter to Cunninghame Graham, 2 December 1905. NLS.
[520] Cunninghame Graham, letter to Edward Garnett, 9 January 1906. University of Texas. Quoted in Smith, *The Uncommon Reader*, p. 108.
[521] Cunninghame Graham, Preface to *The Ipané* (London: Fisher Unwin, 1899), p. vi.

'Prince-Errant, and Evoker of Horizons', as his eulogist, Haymaker, called him.

This fear of emotional exposure eventually found voice in 1932 in the Preface to his anthology *Writ In Sand*, where he wrote 'It is the natural instinct in the majority of men to keep a secret garden in their souls, a something that they do not care to talk about, still less to set down, for other members of the herd to trample on'.[522] However, it was in his final anthology that we can perhaps find the clue to Graham's reserve, and his aversion to narrative 'invention'; that his imagination, which he considered 'the noblest faculty of the human mind',[523] was so vivid that he deliberately avoided dwelling upon it: 'To anybody cursed with imagination, the gift that makes life sometimes unbearable, it is infinitely sad.'[524] Here we can witness his reluctance to bare his soul in print, because, as a melancholic, he found his emotions too distressing to confront and brood upon.

It was also during this period that his wife Gabrielle became seriously ill. She would die seven months after this sketch was published.

HA TIL MI TULAIDH[525]

The Speaker, 17 February 1906, pp. 473–5.
Anthologised in *His People* (London: Duckworth, 1906), pp. 201–12.

ALL was unchanged, and Nature cared not, being occupied with sun and moon and stars, the tides, the mists, the dew, rain, snow, the fall and reproduction of the leaf, and the great mysteries, the cause of which evades and always has evaded man. She smiled, as she does sometimes at a funeral, sending a glimpse of sun upon a coffin-plate, so that the cold nipped mourners read the age of the deceased whilst they stand peering down into the grave, as in a blaze of light.

All was unchanged.

---

[522] Cunninghame Graham, Preface to *Writ In Sand* (London: Heinemann, 1932), p. xi.

[523] Cunninghame Graham, *Thirteen Stories*, (London: Duckworth, 1928), p. 130.

[524] Cunninghame Graham, *Mirages* (London: Heinemann, 1936), p. 159. The reference was to the imagined fate of many horses in the First World War, many of which he himself had purchased in South America.

[525] Gaelic: 'I Return No More'. The name of a song that Rob Roy MacGregor reputedly requested on his death-bed. Walter Scott has it as a song 'with which the emigrants bid farewell to their native shores'. Scott, *A Legend of Montrose* (Edinburgh: A. & C. Black), p. xxxvii.

The two tall lime trees towered above the rough field gate contrived of poles running through horseshoes wedged into their trunks.

The leaves just swept the roof, and in the evening air they seemed to sigh for the departed, who for so many years had watched them green in April bursting into life, and glorious in autumn as they fell carpeting the road, and piled upon the level doorstep with its concentric pattern drawn in chalk; the rush-thatched byre, upon whose roof grew fumitory and corydalis, looked just as it had looked for forty years, and the low door flanked by great tufts of golden-rod and of angelica, and painted blue, was shut for ever on its late owners and on me. Through it, from earliest childhood, as I passed, I led my ponies, tying them in the dark beside the cow to the tall uprights which in Highland cowsheds serve for stalls.

Two sisters, almost the last survivors of an ancient race, had lived for years in the old cottage by the reedy lake. Descendants of the retainer of a feudal chief, their ancestors had been hereditary ferry-men, for, in the days of old, caste, now confined to India and the East, was spread throughout the world.

In what rough coracle or boat their remote ancestors had ferried over to the island, men dressed in skins, no one can say, for from the dawn of history in Menteith marauding clansmen, coming with a creagh[526] from the laigh,[527] had been rowed over to the castle in the isle by some one of their race.

In the deep bay, rush-locked and clear, they or their father had constructed a rude pier of stones and wattles, to which a boat was tied, the paint all sun-cracked, and with an inch or two of water in the well.

So in the days gone by, in houses occupied by gentlemen whose pedigrees were longer than their purse, an antiquated carriage, used as a roosting-place by hens, slowly decayed in some gaunt coach-house, given up to damp.

Carriage and boat were evidence of better times, a link with days of glory long departed, drawing a smile or tear, according to the point from which the man who saw them looked upon the world.

So in the cottage the two sisters lived; relics of days when men were civil in their speech, had time and did not spare it in its use, they never travelled far, but, for all that, they knew the world in which they lived themselves in all its niceties. Constrained by poverty to work, the sisters yet appeared two ladies in distress, not fallen in

---

[526] Gaelic: Plunder.
[527] Scots: Low lying ground. The Lowlands.

fortunes, though their Potosi[528] was but the little croft and garden with "its hantle[529] of sour plumtrees," but, so to speak, having suffered wrong from Nature, which had not placed them free from all necessities at birth. Not that they lacked advancement either, for in their heart of hearts they held themselves the equals of the highest in the land; a tacit claim which all admitted, but their equals, in the old-fashioned district where they lived. Raw-boned and rather hard of feature, the oldest had the soft Highland voice and manner, which somehow seems not to belong to modern life, and places the possessor of them in a world outside the present age. The younger, gentle and delicate, had never married, must have been pretty in her youth, and lived her life subordinated to her sister, admiring her, and in her turn being admired and cherished by her in a half-tender and half-peremptory way.

Their father[530] was an ancient Celt who formed a link with olden times, being compounded of quite different essences and stronger simples than men of latter days. Born as he was, just where the Highlands and the Lowlands touch, he had amalgamated much of the characteristics of the two. His manners were all Highland, his knowledge of the world partly his own and partly that of the Low Country, as we style the realm of bogs and marshy fields that swells and billows like a sea up to the lumpy range of tawny hills that cuts them from the north, and, till the days of railways, formed a bar as strong and as insuperable as is a navigable river, or indeed the sea. Short, and in later years bent almost double, but to the last alert upon his legs, time and the rain, which when it ceases for a fortnight is the theme of prayers in church, had turned him a light fern colour, and his clothes, and hair – originally grey (for no one living could remember when his head was brown) – had weathered to a lichen-looking green, and his blue twinkling eyes, not bleared with age, could, as he said himself, "discern a gentleman almost a mile away." Gentry and gentlemen, by which he understood those of old family, for money could not make, nor the want of it mar, in his opinion, were the chief objects of his creed.

"The Queen can mak' a duke, she canna' mak' Lochiel,"[531] he would observe with pride, not that the limitation of the royal power rejoiced him, for he held, as do Mohammedans, that he who reigned

---

[528] Spanish: A colloquial term for 'great riches', derived from the wealth of the mines at the city of Potosi in Bolivia.
[529] Scots: A considerable number.
[530] The boatman Hugh Graham.
[531] Donald Cameron, third Lord Lochiel (c. 1700–48), popularly known as the 'Gentle Lochiel', was a Scottish Jacobite, and hereditary chief of Clan Cameron.

did so by right divine, but it seemed to him evident, or else the prayer for those "set over us and under Him" had been of no account.

Withal he was himself a gentleman, if natural good-breeding makes one, conjoined with courtesy in speech. Upon a visit, when he had showed you round his croft, with what an air he used to offer you fruit in a cabbage leaf, saying, "Will ye tak' berries, laird, or leddy," as the case might be, thus exercising hospitality in its best sense, by giving what he had without false shame or with excuses for his poverty. One ate them, listening all the time to local lore, distorted through the vision of his years, and rendered picturesque partly by want of education and partly by the way he touched his subject, embroidering and adorning it with sidelights of his own, just as an artist draws from what he sees in his own brain, and neither copies nor extenuates his theme.

Seated upon the gunwale of his boat, and talking volubly in the soft Highland accent, which makes you think that you knew Gaelic once upon a time, the landscape all unchanged, the scrubby oak copse straggling up the hill, the bracken yellowing in the autumn breeze, and leaves of sycamores, mottled and black, like trout in moorland burns, all falling softly round about, whilst the white mist crept up and hung the castle and the chapel in the air, making the great stag-headed chestnuts in the Isle of Rest[532] look like gigantic antlers thrown against the sky, the things and men of which he spoke became alive again and the long, broken link with the old world was welded into shape. You heard unmoved, and as a thing quite natural, and which it seemed had happened to yourself, how he had walked to Eglinton to see the tournament,[533] taking three days to do it, in the rain; had slept beneath the trees, had seen it all, especially the Emperor of the French, "Napoleon Third, ye ken," the Queen of Beauty carried through the mud, and then tramped back again.

Who, in these days of education and of common sense, made manifest and plain by copybook, would do the like, out of pure love of sport, lightness of heart, or the sheer devilment of youth?

All the old legends of the Borderland he knew; with much about Rob Roy, who as he used to say was "better in a tuilzie than a fight, for all his skill o' fence, and they long arms o' his, ye mind, he could untie the garters frae his hose without a stoop or hogging up his

---

[532] The island of Inchmahome, where Graham and his wife are buried.
[533] A huge medieval tournament mounted by the Earl of Eglinton at his castle in North Ayrshire in 1839. Despite heavy rain, it drew 100,000 spectators, and the young Prince Louis Napoleon, the future French Emperor, took part in the joust.

back."[534] He talked about the man just as he were alive, so naturally and without effort, having heard all he told you from his grandfather, that it would not have startled you on looking round to see Red Robert in the flesh come trotting down the hill, his target at his back, and his long Spanish "culbeir"[535] in his hand, humming a waulking song[536] or whistling a strathspey.

All the old legends of the district and his lore of times gone by he left his daughters, which, working in their minds and coming to the surface in their speech, stranded them lonely in the world, without a fellow, just as a glacier-carried boulder in a glen must feel deserted in the tall heather where it lies, far from the hills and stones.

The younger sister first departed, going on before to tell their father that the world was changed, and that no place was left for them or theirs, and that the osprey built no more in the old chestnuts which the monks had planted round the grey priory in the isle, and that the trees themselves were growing balder and more sere.[537] The elder lingered on alone, brisk but alert, driving her cow down to the mossy "park," and stepping east to church when it was fine, not following the road, but going through the fields (though it took longer by them), perhaps from the hereditary Highland habit of avoiding stones in days when every man made his own brogues at home. In summer time she took into her house artists and fishermen, and those whom the fine weather drives into the country for a time, and who lounge through their time smoking and bored, but conscious it is right to do as others do, and therefore satisfied. They thought her odd, and she esteemed them common, but "awfa' clever folk, ye ken, ane o' them painted me a bit picture o' ma sister from a fotygraph, ane o' they dagyriotypes,[538] ye mind them, done on glass, which I have by me since it was ta'en back aboot sixty-three, the time o' yon review at Paisla', the verra image o' her, laird, I'm tellin' ye." The effort of the limner's[539] art (to which even a "dagyriotype" on glass was preferable) hung in her little parlour, resplendent with megilp,[540] shining with poppy oil, and setting forth the patient with a grin upon her face, and with the clothes in fashion forty years ago, themselves not beautiful, rendered ridiculous by newness, just as a play of the same

---

[534] 'Better in a brawl than a fight, for all his skill at swordplay, and those long arms of his, he could untie the garters from his stockings without a stooping.'

[535] Cuilbheir = a Continental long-barrelled gun. Several thousand of them were imported into Scotland for the 1715 Jacobite Rising.

[536] A rhythmic work song, sung while 'waulking' or 'fulling' newly woven fabric.

[537] Dry and withered.

[538] Daguerreotype = an early photographic process.

[539] A painter.

[540] An oil medium for paint.

time appears to us absurd, not that our own are better, but because folly is a changing quantity and different in degree.

Our friendship, fast but intermittent, lasted many years, and the byre door through which my ponies used to pass became too small to lead my horse through, and so we generally talked outside the house, not that we said much, for she was growing deaf, and I knew all her stories years ago, but it pleased both of us, and when I mounted and rode off she used to stand, holding her hand above her eyes, after the fashion of a sailor on a pier, looking out seaward, even when not a sail is on the sea.

Her death was in the olden style, after the fashion she had lived; so to speak, not premeditated, but natural, just as a tree dies at the top, decaying downwards, till it is gone almost before those who have known it all their lives are well aware of its decease. The neighbours told me, for I was absent in that region which folks in Menteith call "up aboot England," that she was "travellin' from church, felt ill upon arriving at her house, took to her bed, and "sleepit bonnily awa'"[541] upon the following day. A man, that is a man who feels the ancient Highland spirit in his blood, would like to die with his boots on, but for a woman this was the nearest thing to sudden death, and quite became the last of an old violent race of men.

In the old churchyard by the lake, amongst the Grahams and the Macgregors, some of whom have swords upon their headstones, for all their trade-mark and memorial of their lives, she sleeps. With pride of race and Scottish thoughtfulness she left sufficient to erect a stone, in which is cut her name, her sister's, that of her father, and those of many of her clan. It stands in the wet grass, close to the wall of the kirkyard, a sort of landmark in the history of Menteith, showing a page turned down; a page on which but few could read, even before the book was shut for the last time. To bid her sleep in peace is but a work of supererogation, after full eighty years of life. Those who remain tossing and turning upon life's uneasy pillow stand more in need of such a wish.

So I "stepped west," and, coming to the Highland cottage by the lake, found the door shut, the hearthstone cold, the garden eaten up with weeds, the flauchtered feals upon the cowhouse roof fallen from the poles, and the old boat, hauled up upon the beach, paintless and blistering in the sun. No cow fed in the little rushy park, even the withies[542] which had once confined the gate were burst and swinging in the wind. The door was shut, shut against me, and shut upon the last of my old friends; so, sitting down upon the

---

[541] Slipped beautifully away.
[542] Branches of the willow, used for securing thatch, or in basketry.

step, on which no longer was a pattern laid in chalk, I smoked and meditated, seeing a long procession pass upon the road, all riding ponies which grew larger towards the end, until a man upon a horse brought up the rear. They stopped before the house, which seemed to have turned newer, and in which a fire of peats burned brightly on the hearth. Then, from the door … but … I will return no more (Ha til mi tuliadh); he who waits at the ferry long enough will get across some time.

Figure 11 The grave of Hugh Graham.

＊＊＊＊＊

The following sketch, which might have justifiably been called 'Laird Wallace', was wholly set within the district of Menteith, and is filled with nostalgia for 'types' who had disappeared, and customs which were now forgotten. These were local gentry who had retainers, and butlers, but who conversed in broad Scots, who were not the subjects of Kailyard novels, and, if Graham had not emphasised their Scottishness, could just as easily have fitted into English country houses.

It begins with a description of Graham's beloved Gartmore House, the loss of which continued to haunt him, moves on to a description of a fellow laird, Wallace of Gartchorrachan, before changing direction, and, using one of Graham's favourite techniques, the 'tale within a tale', whereby the Laird rather explicitly tells how he had 'encoffined' his spinster aunt, whom Graham had known in his youth. The Scots dialect is used judiciously, and only to reflect great emotion, ending with the storyteller leaving to return home, in a classic example of Graham's 'authorial silent finish'.[543] Walker believed that 'Christian Jean' was a relative of Graham's, but there is no family record of a maiden aunt who died in Scotland at this period, and in the text she only is referred to as Laird Wallace's aunt.

Figure 12 Dining room, Gartmore House.

MISS CHRISTIAN JEAN

Anthologised in *His People* (London: Duckworth, 1906), pp. 213–35.

Two pictures hang upon my study wall, faded and woolly, but well stippled up, the outlines of the hills just indicated with a fine reed pen, showing the water, coloured saffron, deepening to pink in the deep shadows of the lake. Although one picture is a sunset and the

---

[543] Watts & Davies, p. 157.

other done as it would seem at sunrise, they show a country which even yet is undefiled by any human step.

So accurately is the dark brown tree set in position on the border of the fleecy lake, one feels an artist, superior to mere nature, has been about the task. The castle on the mountain top, in one of the two masterpieces, is at the bottom of the hill in its compeer,[544] and in the two a clear blue sky throws a deep shadow over the unruffled water, on which float boats with tall white sails, progressing without wind.

Still, with their frames, which are but fricassees of gingerbread well gilt, to me they say a something all the art of all the masters leaves unsaid.

A masterpiece speaks of imagination in its maker; but those pale blue-grey hills and salmon-coloured pinkish lakes, castles which never could have been inhabited, boats sailing in a calm, and trees that seem to rustle without breeze, set me reflecting upon things gone by, and upon places of which I once was part, places which still ungratefully live on, whilst that of me which lived in them is dead.

A long low Georgian room, in which the pictures hung, with its high mantelpiece, its smell of damp and Indian curiosities, and window looking out on the sunk garden underneath the terraces, the sides of which were honeycombed by rabbits, rises in my view, making me wonder in what substance of the body or the mind they have been stamped.

How few such rooms remain, and how few houses such as that, to which the dark and dampish chamber, with its three outside walls, and deep-cut mouldings on the windows and the doors, was library. We called it "book-room," in the Scottish way, although the books were few and mostly had belonged to a dead uncle who had bought them all in India, and on their yellowing leaves were stains of insects from the East, and now and then a grass or flower from Hyderabad or Kolapur (as pencilled notes upon the margin said), transported children to a land so gorgeous that the like of it was never seen on earth. These books were all well chosen, and such as men read fifty years ago – Macaulay's Essays, with the Penny Cyclopaedia, Hume, Smollett, Captain Cook, The Life of Dost Mohammed, Elphinstone's Cabul Mission, with Burckhardt's Travels, enthralling Mungo Park,[545] and others of the kind that at hill stations in the rains, or in the plains during the summer, must have passed many an hour of boredom and of heat away for their dead purchaser. The rest were books of heraldry and matters of the kind, together with a set of Lever and of

---

[544] Something of equal rank or value.
[545] Mungo Park (1771–1806) was a Scottish explorer of West Africa.

Dickens, with plates by Cruikshank or by Hablot Brown.[546] One in particular set forth a man upon a horse, with a red fluttering cloak streaming out in the wind, galloping in the midst of buffaloes with a long knife between his teeth. But books and furniture and Indian curiosities, with the high Adams chimney-piece and portraits of the favourite hounds and horses of three generations, were, as it were, keyed up to the two water-colours, one of which hung up above a cabinet sunk far into the wall and glazed, the other over a low double door, deep as an embrasure.[547]

All through the house the smell of damp, of kingwood furniture, and roses dried in bowls, blended and formed a scent which I shall smell as long as life endures. This may, of course, have been mere fancy; but often in old houses some picture or some piece of furniture appears to give the keynote to the rest. But it seemed evident to me that, in some strange mysterious way, the pictures, outstanding in their badness, had stamped themselves upon the house more than the Reynoldses and Raeburns[548] on the walls, though they were pictures of my ancestors, and the two water-colours represented no known landscape upon earth. They entered into my ideas so strongly (though they were unobtrusive in themselves) that, looking from the window-seat in the deep bay of the sunk window in the dining-room, across the terraces, over the sea of laurels, beyond the rushy "parks," and out upon the moss and the low lumpy hills that ran down to the distant lake, almost divided into two by a peninsula set with dark pine trees and with planes, the landscape seemed unfinished and lacking interest without the castles and the chrome-laden skies of the twin masterpieces.

It may be, too, that the unnatural landscape caused me to form unnatural views of life, finding things interesting and people worthy of remark whom others found quite commonplace, merely upon their own account, and not from the surroundings of their lives. So every one connected with the house of the two works of art became mixed up somehow with them in a mysterious way, as well as things inanimate and trees, the vegetation and the white mist which half the year hung over moss and woods, shrouding the hills and everything in its unearthly folds, making them strange and half unreal, as is a landscape in a dream.

---

[546] Hablot Knight Browne (1815–82) was an English artist and illustrator who used the pseudonym 'Phiz'.

[547] A bevelled recess around a window or a door.

[548] Sir Joshua Reynolds PRA FRS FRSA (1723–92) was an English painter, specialising in portraits; Sir Henry Raeburn RA RSA FRSE (1756–1823) was a Scottish portrait painter.

Perhaps the fact that the house stood just at the point where Lowlands end and the great jumble of the Highland hills begins, and that the people were compounded of both simples, Saxon and Celtic mixed in equal parts, gave them and all the place an interest such as clings to borderlands the whole world over, for even forty years ago one talked of "up above the pass" as of a land distinct from where we lived. Down from those regions wandered men speaking a strange tongue, shaggy, and smelling of a mixture of raw wool and peat smoke, whose dogs obeyed them in a way in which no dog of any man quite civilized, broken to railways and refreshment-rooms, obeys his master's call. The bond of union may have been that both slept out in the wet dew, huddling together in the morning round the fire for warmth, or something else, the half-possession of some sense that we have lost, by means of which, all unknown to themselves, the drover and his dog communicated. Communion, very likely, is the word, the old communion of all living things, the lost connection between man and all the other animals, which modern life destroys.

But, be that as it may, the men and dogs seemed natives, and we who lived amongst the mosses and the hills seemed strangers, by lack of something or by excess of something else, according to your view.

The herds of ponies that the men drove before them on the road fell naturally into the scheme of nature; sorrels and yellow chestnuts, creams and duns, they blended with the scrubby woods and made no blot upon the shaggy hills. Instinctively they took the long-forgotten fords, crossing below the bridges, and standing knee-deep in the stream, the water dripping from their ropy tails and burdock-knotted manes. The herds of kyloes too have gone, which looked like animals of some race older than our own. The men who drove them, with their rough clothes of coarse grey wool, their hazel crooks, and plaids about their shoulders, whether the wind blew keenly or midges teased in August, all have disappeared. Their little camps upon the selvedge of the roads are all forgotten, although I know them still, by the bright grass that grows upon the ashes of the fires. Or have they gone, and are the hills brown, lumpy, heather-clad, and jewelled after rain by myriad streams, merely illusions; and is it really that I myself have gone, and they live on, deep down in the recesses of some fairy hill of which I am not free?

Men, too, like my friend Wallace of Gartchorrachan, have disappeared, and I am not quite sure if we should bless the Lord on that account. All through Menteith, and right "across the hill" as far as Callander and Doune, he was well known, and always styled Laird Wallace, for though our custom is to call men by the title of their lands, thus making them *adscripti glebæ*[549] to the very soul, the word Gartchorrachan stuck in our throats, although we readily twist and distort the Gaelic place-names in our talk just as the Spaniards muti-late the Arab words, smoothing their corners and their angles out in the strong current of their speech.

Dressed in grey tweed with bits of buckskin let into the shoulders of his coat, for no one ever saw him leave his house without a gun, he was about the age that farmers in the north seem to be born at – that is, for years he had been grey, but yet was vigorous, wore spectacles, and his thick curly hair was matted like the wool upon a ram, whilst from his ears and nostrils grew thick tufts of bristles, just as a growth of twigs springs from the trunk of an old oak tree, where it has got a wound.

His house was like himself, old, grey, and rambling, and smelt of gun oil, beeswax, and of camphor, for he was versed in entomology, and always had a case of specimens, at which he laboured with a glass stuck in his eye, reminding me of Cyclops or of Polyphemus,[550] or of an ogre in a story-book. Botany and conchology and generally those sciences which when pursued without a method soon became trifling and a pastime, were his joys, and he had cabinets in which the specimens reposed under a heavy coat of dust, but duly ticketed each with its Latin name.

He spoke good English as a general rule, and when unmoved, as was the custom with the people of his class and upbringing, but often used broad Scotch, which he employed after the fashion of a shield against the world, half in a joking way and half against the sin of self-revealment which we shun as the plague, passing our lives like pebbles in a brook, which rub against each other for an age, and yet remain apart.

In early life he had contracted what he called a "local liassong," the fruit of which had been a daughter whom he had educated, and who lived with him, half as his daughter, half as housekeeper. Her father loved her critically, and when she not infrequently swept china on the floor as she passed through the drawing-room (just as a tapir walks about a wood, breaking down all the saplings in its path), he would screw up one eye, and looking at her say, "That's what you get from breeding from a cart-mare, the filly's sure to throw back to the dam."

Withal he was a gentleman, having been in the army and travelled in his youth, but had not got much more by his experience than the raw youth of whom his father said, "Aye, Willie's been to Rome

---

[549] Latin: Joined to the land.
[550] Polyphemus (Greek: Πολύφημος): the name of a cyclops mentioned in the *Odyssey* and the *Aeneid*.

and back again, and a' he's learnt is but to cast his sark aince every day."[551] But still he was a kindly man, the prey of any one who had a specious story, the providence of all lame horses and of dogs quite useless for any kind of sport, all which he bought at prices far above the value of the most favoured members of their race.

His inner nature always seemed to be just struggling forth almost against his will, mastering his rough exterior, just as in pibrochs,[552] after the skirling of the pipes has died away, a tender melody breaks out, fitful and plaintive, speaking of islands lost in misty seas, of things forgotten and misunderstood, of the faint, swishing noise of heather in the rain moved by the breeze at night, and which through minor modulations and fantastic trills ends in a wild lament for some Fingalian hero, like the wind sighing through the pines.

Nothing was more congenial to his humour than to unpack his recollections of the past, seated before the fire, an oily black cigar which he chewed almost like a quid[553] between his teeth, and with a glass of whisky by his side.

After expatiating upon the excellencies of his lame, jibbing chestnut mare, that he had bought at Falkirk Tryst[554] from a quite honest dealer, but which had gone mysteriously so lame that even whisky for his groom had no effect in curing her, he usually used to lament upon the changes which the course of time had brought about. All was a grief to him, as it is really to all of us, if we all knew it, that some particular landmark of his life had disappeared. No one spoke Gaelic nowadays, although he never in his life had known a word of it. The use of "weepers"[555] and crape hat-bands by the country-folk on Sunday was quite discontinued, and no one took their collie dogs to church. Coffins were now no longer carried shoulder-high across the hills from lonely upland straths, as he remembered to have seen them in his youth. Did not some funeral party in his childhood, taking a short cut on a frozen loch, fall through and perish to a man? – a circumstance he naturally deplored, but still regretted, as men of older generations may have regretted highwaymen, as they sat safely by their fire. Although he never fished, he was quite certain no one now alive could busk a fly as well as a departed worthy of his youth, one Dan-a-Haltie, or make a withy basket or those osier loops which formerly were stuck between the "divots" in a dry stone dike, projecting

---

[551] Scots: 'Change his shirt every day'.

[552] A piece of bagpipe-music consisting of a theme and a series of variations.

[553] Something chewed, like tobacco.

[554] See below.

[555] A badge of mourning, such as a black hatband or veil, or perhaps a hired mourner.

outwards like a torpedo netting, to stop sheep jumping from a field. Words such as *flauchtered feal* and *laroch* were hardly understood; shepherds read newspapers as they lay out upon the hill, the Shorter Catechism had been miserably abridged, and the old fir-tree by the Shannochill was blasted at the top.

All these complaints he uttered philosophically, not in a plaintive way, but as a man who, at his birth, had entered as it were into a covenant with life just as it was, which he for his part had faithfully observed, but was deceived by fate.

Then when he had relieved his mind he used to laugh and, puffing out the smoke of his thick black cigar, which hung about the tufts which sprung out of his nostrils, just as the mist hangs dank above a bog, he would remark, "I'm haverin',"[556] as if he was afraid of having to explain himself to something in his mind. On these occasions, I used to let him sit a little, and usually he would begin again, after a look to see if I had noticed the gag he suddenly had put upon himself, and then start off again. "Ye mind my aunt, Miss Christian Jean?" I did, eating her sweetmeats in my youth, and trembling at her frown.

"Ye never heard me tell how it was I kisted[557] her," he said, and then again fell into contemplation, and once again began. "My aunt, Miss Christian Jean, was a survival of the fittest – aye, ye know I am in some things quite opposed to Darwin, the survival of the potter's wheel in the Fijis and several other things ... aye, haverin' again ... or the most unfitted to survive.

"She was a gentlewoman, ... yes, yes, the very word is now half ludicrous, ye need not smile, ... lady is a poor substitute. Tall, dark, and masculine, and with a down upon her upper lip that many a cornet of dragoons, for there were cornets[558] in those days, might well have envied, she was a sort of providence, jealous and swift in chastisement, but yet a providence to all the younger members of her race who came across her path.

"I see her now, her and her maid, old Katherine Sinclair, a tall, gaunt Highland woman, who might easily have walked straight from the pages of Rob Roy, and her old butler, Robert Cameron, grey and red-faced, and dressed eternally in a black suit, all stained with snuff, a pawky sort of chiel, religious and still with the spirit of revolt against all dogmatism which modern life and cheap and stereotyped instruction has quite stamped out to-day. My aunt kept order in her house, that is as far as others were concerned. Each day she read

---

[556] Scots: Talking nonsense.
[557] Scots: Put her in a chest (coffin).
[558] Formerly the lowest rank of a commissioned cavalry officer. Graham's father, William Bontine (1825–83) had been a cornet of horse in the Scots Greys.

her chapter, in what she styled the Book, not taking over heed how she selected it, so that the chapter once was duly read. It happened sometimes that when she came into the room where, as my cousin Andrew used to say – ye mind that he was drowned in one of those Green's ships,[559] fell from aloft whilst they were reefing topsails in a dark night somewhere about the Cape.

"I've heard him say he could come down the weather-leach of a topsail, just like a monkey, by the bolt ropes ... Where was I, eh? Aye, I mind, he used to say that my aunt's prayers reminded him of service in a ship, with all hands mustered; so as I said, my aunt would sometimes open up the book and come upon a chapter full of names, and how some one begat another body and sometimes upon things perfectly awesome for a maiden lady to read aloud, for 'twas all one to her.

"Then the old butler would put his hand up to his mouth and whisper, ' Mem, Miss Christian, Mem, ye're wandered,'[560] and she would close the book, or start again upon another chapter and maybe twice as long.

"My aunt and her two satellites kept such good order, that a visitor from England, seeing her neat and white-capped maids file in and take their seats facing the menservants, expressed her pleasure at the well ordered, comely worship, and received the answer, 'Yes, my dear, ye see at family prayers we have the separation of the sexes, but I understand when they meet afterwards at the stair foot, the kissing beats the cracking of a whip.'

"Poor Aunt Christian, I used to shiver at her nod, and well remember when a youth how she would flyte[561] me when I pinched the maids, and say, 'Laddie, I canna' have you making the girls squeal like Highland ponies; it is not decent, and decency comes next after morality, sometimes, I think, before it, for it can be attained, whereas the other is a counsel of perfection set up on high, but well out of our reach.'

"A pretty moraliser was my poor aunt, almost a heathen in her theory, guided by what she said were natural laws, and yet a Puritan in practice, whereas I always was a theoretic Puritan, but shaped my life exclusively by natural laws, as they appear to me.

"Let ministers just haver as they will, one line of conduct is not possible for nephews and for aunts. Take David, now, the man after the

---

[559] Ships built by the Green family at Blackwall (London), which sailed on the East Indies route and which were managed by Richard 'Dickie' Green (1803–63).
[560] See passim.
[561] Scots: Scold.

Lord's own heart, and ask yourself what would have happened if his aunt … aye, aye, I'm wandered from my tale … I ken I'm wandering.

"Well, well, it seemed as if my aunt might have gone on for ever, getting a little dryer and her face more peakit,[562] as the years went by and her old friends dropped off and left her all alone. That's what it is, ye see; it's got to come, although it seems impossible whilst we sit talking here and drinking – that is, I drinking and you listening to me talk. One wintry day I was just sitting wiping the cee-spring of a gun, and looking out upon the avenue, when, through the wreaths, I saw a boy on a bit yellow pony-beast come trotting through the snow.

"It was before the days of telegrams, and I jaloused[563] that there was something special, or no one would have sent the laddie out on such a day, with the snow drifted half a yard upon the ground, the trees all white with cranruch[564] like the sugar on a cake, and the frost keen enough to split a pudding stone and grind it into sand.

"I sent the laddie to the kitchen fire, and ripped the envelope, whilst the bit pony rooted round for grass and walked upon the reins. The letter told me that my aunt had had a fit, was signed by 'Robert Cameron, butler,' and was all daubed with snuff, and in a postscript I was asked to hurry, for the time was short, and to come straight across the hill as the low road was blocked by the snow drifting and nobody could pass. I harnessed up my mare – not the bit blooded chestnut I drive now" – this was the way in which he spoke of the lame cripple which had conveyed him to my house – "but a stout sort of Highland mouse-coloured beastie that I had, rather short backit,[565] a little hammer-headed, and with the hair upon the fetlocks like a Clydesdale … Maun, I think ye dinna' often see such sort of beasts the now." I mentally thanked God for it, and he again launched out into his tale.

"An awful drive, I'm tellin' ye! I hadna' got above Auchyle[566] ye mind, at the old bridge just where yon English tourist coupit his creels,[567] and gaed to heaven, maybe last summer – when I saw I had a job. The snow balled in the mare's feet as big as cabbages, and made her stotter in her gait, just like a drunken curler ettlin' to walk upon a rink.[568] I had to take her by the head till we got on the flat ground,

---

[562] Scots: Having a thin, drawn appearance, emaciated, angular, gaunt and ill-looking.

[563] Scots: Guessed, surmised

[564] Scots: A low creeping mist, or hoar-frost.

[565] Scots: Short backed.

[566] An estate near the Lake of Menteith.

[567] Scots: Did a somersault.

[568] Scots: Made her stumble in her stride, 'like a drunken player in a game of curling attempting to walk on an ice-rink'.

up about Rusky.[569] Man, it was arctic, and the little loch lay like a sheet of glass that had been breathed upon, with the dead bulrushes and reeds all sticking through the ice! The island in the loch seemed but a blob of white, and the old tower (I dinna' richtly mind if, at one time, it belonged to some of your own folk)[570] loomed up like Stirling Castle or like Doune in the keen frosty air. The little firwood on the east side of the old change-house – that one they called Wright, or some such name, once keepit – was full of roe, all sheltering like cows, so cold and starved they scarcely steered when I passed by and gave a shout to warm my lungs and hearten up the mare; and a cock capercailzie, moping and miserable, sat on a fir tree like a barn-door fowl. I plJoutered[571] on just to where there used to be a gate across the road, where ye see Uamh Var[572] and the great shoulder of Ben Ledi stretching up out by the pass of Leny and the old chapel of St. Bryde. It was fair awesome; I did not rightly know the landscape with the familiar features blotted out. I very nearly got myself wandered just in the straight above the Gart, for all the dikes were sunk beneath the snow, and the hedge-tops peeped up like box in an old cabbage-garden. At last I reached the avenue, the mare fair taigled,[573] and the ice hanging from her fetlocks and her mane and wagging to and fro. The evergreens were, so to speak, a-wash, and looked like beds of parsley or of greens, and underneath the trees the squirrels' footsteps in the snow seemed those of some strange birds, where they had melted and then frozen on the ground. Across the sky a crow or two flew slowly, flapping their wings as if the joint oil had been frozen in their bones and cawing[574] sullenly.

"On the high steps which led up to the door the butler met me, and as he took my coat, said, 'Laird, ye are welcome; your poor dear auntie's going. Hech,[575] sirs, 'twill be an awfu' nicht for the poor leddy to be fleein' naked through the air towards the judgment-seat. Will ye tak speerits or a dish o' tea after your coldsome drive, or will I tak' ye straight in to your aunt? I'm feared she willna' know you. But His will be done, though I could wish He micht hae held His hand a little longer; but we must not repine. I've just been readin' out

---

[569] A small local loch.
[570] Rusky Castle, home of Sir John Menteith (1275–1329), known as 'Fause Menteith' for his role in the capture of William Wallace during the Wars of Independence.
[571] Scots: Waded messily.
[572] A hillside and rock formation that features in Robert Louis Stevenson's *Kidnapped*.
[573] Scots: Weary.
[574] Scots: Turning or winding.
[575] Scots: Expressing sorrow or pain.

to her from the old Book, ye ken, passin' the time awa' and waitin' for the end."

"All day my aunt lay dozing, half-conscious and half-stupefied, and all the day the butler, sitting by the bed, read psalms and chapters, to which she sometimes seemed to pay attention, and at others lay so still we thought that she was dead. Now and again he stopped his reading, and peering at his mistress with his spectacles pushed up, wiped off the tears that trickled down his face with his red handkerchief, and, as if doubting he were reading to the living or the dead, said, 'Nod yer heid, Miss Christian,' which she did feebly, and he, satisfied she understood, mumbled on piously in a thick undertone.

"Just about morning she passed away quite quietly, the maids and butler standing round the bed, they crying silently, and he snorting in his red pocket-handkerchief, with the tears running down his face. The gaunt old Highland waiting-woman raised a high wail which echoed through the cold and silent house, causing the dogs to bark and the old parrot scream, and the butler stottered[576] from the room, muttering that he would go and see if tea was ready, closing the door behind him with his foot, as if he feared the figure on the bed would scold him, as she had often done during her life, if it slammed to and made a noise.

"All the week through it snowed, and my aunt's house was dismal, smelling of cheese and honey, yellow soap, of jam, of grease burnt in the fire, and with the dogs and cats uncared for rambling about and sleeping on the chairs. The cold was penetrating, and I wandered up and down the stairs quite aimlessly, feeling like Alexander Selkirk[577] in the melancholy house, which seemed an island cut off from the world by a white sea of snow. None of Aunt Christian's friends or relatives could come, as all the roads were blocked; even her coffin was not sent till a few hours before the funeral, the cart that brought it stalling in the snow, and the black-coated undertaker's men carrying it shoulder-high through the thick wreaths upon the avenue.

"The servants would not have a stranger touch the corpse, and the old butler and myself kisted my aunt, lifting her body from the bed between the two of us. A week had passed and she looked black and shrunken, and as I lifted her, the chill from the cold flesh struck me with horror, and welled into the bones. I could not kiss her as she lay like a mummy in the kist, for the shrunk face with the white clothes about the chin was not the same Aunt Christian's, whom I had loved

---

[576] Scots: Staggered.
[577] Alexander Selkirk (1676–1721) was a Scottish sailor who was castaway on a Pacific Island for four years, which inspired Daniel Defoe's *Robinson Crusoe*.

and before whom I trembled for so many years, but changed somehow and horrible to see.

"The butler did, looking at me, as I thought, half reproachfully as I stood silently, not once crying but half stupefied, and then as she lay shrunken and brown on the white satin lining of the kist, we stood and looked at one another, just as we had been partners in a crime, till they began to hammer down the lid. A drearsome sound it makes. One feels the nails are sticking in the flesh, and every time ye hear it, it just affects ye more than the last time, the same as an earthquake, as I mind I heard a traveller say one day in Edinburgh. What the old butler did, I do not mind; but I just dandered[578] out into the garden, and washed my hands in snow, not that I felt a skunner[579] at my poor Aunt Christian's flesh, but somehow I had to do it, for ye ken 'twas the first time."

Laird Wallace stopped just as a horse props suddenly when he is fresh and changes feet, then breaking into Scotch, said: "I have talked enough. That's how I kisted my Aunt Christian Jean, puir leddy, a sair job it was, and dreich.[580] ... Thank ye, nae soddy,[581] I'll tak' a drop of Lagavoulin."[582] Then lighting a cigar, he said, "Ring for my dog-cart, please," and when it came he clambered to the seat, and pointing to his spavined mare, said, "Man, a gran' beast, clean thorough-bred, fit to run for her life" (and this to me who knew her); then, bidding me good-night, drew his whip smartly on her scraggy flank, and vanished through the trees.

* * * * *

'In the moorlands between Trossachs and Aberfoyle,
a region made famous by Scott's *Rob Roy*, I have seen
atmospheric changes so sudden and so contrasted as to
appear marvellous.'[583]

This is Graham's description of Lochan Balloch[584] known locally as 'the Hidden Lochan', positioned high up to the south of Loch Venacher, below Ben Gullipen, to the west of the town of Callander.

---

[578] Scots: Walked aimlessly, wandered.
[579] Scots: Disgust.
[580] Scots: Miserable.
[581] See passim.
[582] A brand of Scotch whisky.
[583] Walter Evans Wentz, *The Fairy-Faith in Celtic Countries* (London and New York: H. Froude, 1911), p. 3.
[584] A corruption of the Gaelic 'Lochan Folaich' = the small concealed loch.

Figure 13 Lochan Balloch (photograph: Fiona McNicol).

LOCHAN FALLOCH

The Saturday Review, 4 January 1908, pp. 11–12.
Anthologised in *Faith* (London: Duckworth, 1906), pp. 101–7.

BROWN billowing woods spring from the rising ground beyond the lake. The lake itself is set in fir woods on three sides, and on the other bounded by a wild moor.

Almost all round it stretches a pebbly beach, broken by beds of bulrushes, which now and then rise from a mossy patch between the stones. Islands with ruins of the past stud its smooth surface, and are reflected upside down, as in a looking-glass reversed. The woods, chiefly of beech, appear like outworks thrown before the hills to guard their mysteries.

Rough, roaring burns here and there cut a passage to the lake and brawl between banks fringed with rowan trees and ash. After the woods are passed, a further outwork of wet boggy ground, in which grow willows and sweet-gale, extends.

This by degrees melts into a dull waste of ling,[585] strewed with great boulders of rough pudding-stone. The heath grows sparser higher up, where the wind sweeps upon it all the year. Then it gives place to tracts of stones. Lastly, the hill rising up steep from the last slope is reached, and following a burn, until it issues from a green mossy "well," you stand upon the ridge.

---

[585] Seaweed.

There, a panorama stretches out, studded with lakes, with woods, and interspersed with farms towards the west. Towards the east lies the brown Flanders Moss, an ancient sea, which even yet appears to roll in the white mist of evening. The whole is framed in ranges of long undulating hills, which guard the south.

Northwards, the Grampians, still mysterious and wild, tower up, in peaks, in castles, and in serrated ridges, through which the passes, now disused, formerly penetrated.

Standing upon the topmost ridge, and quite invisible from any other point, quite unsuspected, lost, almost forgotten by the outer world, is hid a little lake.

It is indeed a little hidden loch, lying so deep and unsuspected in its hollow between hills, that the first Kelt or Pict who came upon it, ages ago, must straight have hit upon the name it bears. Nature seems, now and then, to have suspected that a time would come when all her secrets would lie bare and open to the prying eye of vulgar curiosity, and to have hid away some of her chiefest beauties in places where they are in sanctuary, hallowed from human gaze, which at the same time worships and violates them. So, she set this her little gem, remote, hiding it as a hind conceals her young, deep in the heather, underneath the tallest bracken, and in a wilderness of hills. They tower on every side, bare, bald, and wind-swept, whilst in a corrie nestles the little lake, upon whose surface the wind scarcely or never preys, leaving it calm, mysterious, and unruffled, as if it held some secret, too natural for us to understand. If fairies still exist, they come, no doubt, from the Sith Bruach[586] which guards the Avon Dhu[587] at Aberfoyle, and sail their boats of acorn-cups and leaves on the black lakelet. Upon the little beach they run their craft ashore and dance on the broad ribbon of smooth sand which rings the lake, as a black mezzotint is edged around with white. But if the fairies come, they come unseen, leaving no token of their passage but a few turned-up leaves which they have used for boats, and the mysterious circlet of white foam they churn, which hangs between the fringe of bulrushes and the mimic surf in which float flies that have ventured further than their wings can bear them, and now wash up and down, as in some distant island of the South Seas, drowned mariners may drift upon the beach.

Sunk in its hollow far from the world, the tarn seems to have been left adrift, a derelict floated down to us from some older age, and with one's eyes closed one can see strange animals of monstrous size

---

[586] Gaelic: Fairy Bank (of a stream).
[587] Gaelic: Black River. A river that flows from Loch Ard (to the west of Aberfoyle) into the River Forth.

come down the steep hillsides and drink and play, throwing about the water as they stand knee-deep. Around its banks grows equisetum, as if to point back to a time when different vegetation, gigantic and distorted, towered by its edge, and in which harboured the strange beasts that must have been familiar to its shores.

Light-footed tribesmen, as they drove the "creagh" from the fat Lowlands to their hungry hills, must have stopped by the lake to slake their thirst, prone on their breasts their rough red beards floating like seaweed on the water as they drank. Even in summer, when bees hum in the heather, and the scent of peat fresh cast and left to dry perfumes the air, and little moss-trout bask in the tiny stream that issues from the lake, or dart amongst its stones, there broods an air as of aloofness from mankind. Over the corrie which the water fills, leaving but little ground between it and the hills except at one end, where a long-forgotten, perhaps Fingalian,[588] mountain trail is still half visible on the stones which lie amongst the ling, the wind sweeps softly, and the water-spiders, with greater faith than Peter's,[589] walk on the surface of the lake so lightly that they hardly leave a shadow as they pass.

In winter, when the wind laments aloud for the lost sun, and the dark water of the lochan turns to black ice, whilst the white foam congealed clings round the stalks of the dead bulrushes, and all the heather droops in the keen frost, the scene is wild and threatening, as if the spirits of the past kept watch over the last of their possessions that had remained untouched. Then, in spite of the keen cold, the birds and animals all venture out, certain that they are safe, at least from man, and leave strange tracks amongst the snow, which form a chart of them and of their habits, read-able but to those whose eyes have not been rendered dim by poring upon print.

Even in snow and cold, and when the wind drives all the grass and heather crouching to the ground, and when the little fish rise to the air-holes in the translucent ice to breathe, and nature seems to wither in the frost, there yet remains over the lochan dhu[590] an air as of content, amidst the desolation of the hills.

Whether the breeze just curls the water, or drives a dust of particles of frozen snow along the surface of the ice; whether the cotton-grass waves silkily and the bog-asphodels spring from the peat and the green "wells" are bright with mosses, or the field-mice play hide-and-seek between the stalks of the stiff frozen grasses, the lochlet seems to smile as enigmatically as does the Sphinx, showing itself in full communion

---

[588] Relating to the Ossianic hero, Fingal.
[589] Matthew 22:28–31
[590] Gaelic: Small black lake.

with the past. It smiles, like a fair woman who hides a guilty secret for knowledge, especially of happiness that is not shared with others, must be guilt, and to withhold it from us, who seek it all our lives, is surely criminal, that is, if the lake's secret were not beyond our reach, removed out of our ken, by its sheer innocence. As one looks down from the ridge, watching the black tarn sleeping in the heather, you see that what it holds is not for us, and that the sighing of the wind, which to it is a language comprehended, clear and sympathetic to its soul, to us serves but to stir the senses, and you turn away despairing, watching a heron or a gull enter at once into the fellowship, outside of which we stand.

It might be that at night, when the moon silvers all the waters, and mist enshrouds the hills, calling out from the grass and mosses their secret perfume; when roe steal from the copses browsing so timidly about the open patches of green herbage, scattered like islands through the heath; when dark grey moths flutter about the edges of the lake, that if a child dared venture up to the lone tarn, its eyes might open and behold a wondrous world of fairies, and it would understand all that the rustling of the wind amongst the heather really means. But if it did so, either it would turn rank poet and be damned amongst its fellows, or be snatched away to dwell for ever in some fairy hill, remote from man, seeing the world as in a camera obscura, with people running to and fro like ants, in a perpetual gloom. No child will venture; the spell will not be broken, and the black, little loch will remain hidden from men's hearts, lost in the mist, lost in forgetfulness, just as it was intended that it should be lost, by Nature, when she hid it in the hills.

* * * * *

As the observant reader will have noticed, mist is now making a regular appearance, and in this next piece, the word 'mist' is used five times, along with 'veil', 'a shroud of steam' (twice), 'billowy vapours', 'waves of vapour', 'gloom' and 'white dew'. Mist can be both obscuring and revealing; inside it, the normal world disappears; it blurs reality, both the physical and the temporal, and with our senses disarmed, we are thrown back on our own imaginings. It can also be revelatory when one is above it (as one often is at Gartmore); the vista is transformed into a sea (which Graham never tired of telling his readers it once was), or we might suspect, to his mind, a primordial landscape, 'undefiled by any human step', where the marks of civilisation are erased, and where the boundaries between past and present had been obliterated.

But this is no mere ghostly impression, for through the mist something very real appears. It is a companion piece to Graham's

'Introduction' to Morrison Davidson's *Scotland and the Scots*,[591] in which Graham meets a fellow Scot on the Argentinian pampa (without a suggestion of surprise), and now, out of the mists (again perhaps to break the other-worldly spell), there is an even more remarkable encounter, which takes him back to the town of Vigo, where he and Gabrielle had lived twenty-five years previously.

AT THE WARD TOLL

The Saturday Review, 7 November 1908, pp. 574–5.
Anthologised in *Faith* (London: Duckworth, 1909), pp. 108–17.

THE mist had blotted out the moss, leaving the Easter Hill, Gartur, and the three fir trees above Sanochil, rising like islands out of a dead sea. At times the waves of mist engulfed the islands, and again slowly fell back and left them clear, as if some tide, unseen and unsuspected, had ebbed and then had flowed again, or a volcano underneath the moss had been at first half doubtful of its works and shrouded it in steam till it had taken shape. Great drops of damp hung from the feathers of the larches in the long sheltering plantations on each side of the road. Damp filled up the interstices of spiders' webs that clung between the bents,[592] stretching like fairy rigging between the stems, as a triatic-stay stretches between a schooner's masts. It settled on the heads of grasses, enveloping them as in a veil, making each individual stem look like a little ghost of what it had been in the summer, when it was green with life. Where banks of rushes, now turning brown, emerged out of the shroud of steam, they looked like frozen water weeds protruding from the ice, by a pond's side, during a winter frost.

The perfume of the spruces and of the beds of moss and blae-berries hung in the moist atmosphere and filled the nostrils with a scent of something older than mankind, keen, subtle, vivifying, and which somehow connected man, by some unseen, uncomprehended essential oil or particle so small no microscope could make it manifest, with the whole universe.

Beyond the moss the five-fold hummocks of Ben Dhu ran out into the rolling waves of mist, as a great cape runs out into the sea. Far off in the interior ocean of the mist Ben Ledi showed its topmost ridge, just as the Peak of Tenerife rises among the fleecy clouds of the Trade Winds.

---

[591] *Scotland for the Scots: Scotland Revisited*, by John Morrison Davidson (Edinburgh: F. R. Henderson, 1902). See below.
[592] Scots: Rough grass.

The approaching evening added to the gloom, and night appeared to fall with double darkness on the wide valley of Menteith. My horse's feet fell with a hollow sound upon the road, and on his coat hung a dampness which looked as white as frost. Now and again out on the moor the crowing of a grouse was heard, and once an owl floated across the road as silently as thistledown is wafted through the air, like a gigantic moth. All was quiet and mysterious, one seemed to ride enveloped in a shroud which kept one from the world. The spirit of the north was in the air, intangible, haunting and vague, that make the dwellers of the north vague and intangible, poetic and averse to face the facts of life, yet leaves them practical in business, with a rind of hardness and a heart of sentiment. Shadowy forms rode in the billowy vapours upon one side, those Valkyrie which northern poets have discerned, either projected on the mist, as it did on that night, or else projected on the pia mater[593] of their brain, round which a mist of vapour always seemed to hang.

The shapes I seemed to see – or saw, for if a man sees visions with the interior sight he sees them, for himself at least, as surely as if he saw them with the outward eye – loomed lofty and gigantic, and peopled once again Menteith with riders, as it was peopled in the past. The shadowy and ill-starred earls, their armour always a decade out of fashion, and now and then surmounted by a Highland bonnet set with an eagle's feather, giving them the air half of the Saxon half of the Kelt, their horses lank and ill-groomed, their followers talking in shrill Gaelic, seemed to defile[594] along the road. Their blood was redder than the King's, their purses lighter than an empty bean-pod after harvest, and still they had an air of pride, but all looked "fey", as if misfortune had set its seal upon their race.

They passed and vanished into the mist they once had known so well, and it seemed to me that they all rode, just as if they knew the way as well as they had known it in their lives, towards the shadowy, ruined castle in the island of the rush-ringed lake.[595] I did not turn and ride with them, though had I done so I feel sure, upon arriving at the ferry-keeper's hut thatched thick with heather, out of which sprouted corydalis and on whose ridge grew tufts of ragweed, there would have been a place empty and waiting in the decaying, insubstantial boat. Highlanders, driving the "creagh" towards Balquhidder, passed, their moccasin-clad feet leaving as little impress on the mist as they had left in life upon the tussocks of bent-grass. They urged

---

[593] The membrane surrounding the brain.
[594] In this context, to ride or march in a straight line.
[595] The Lake of Menteith.

the shadowy cattle with the points of their Lochaber axes;[596] and, last of all, wrapped in his plaid, his thick hair curling close about his hard-lined features, passed one I knew at once by his great length of arm and red beard,[597] on which the damp hung in a frosty dew, just as it hung upon the coats of the West Highland kyloes that he drove before him on the road. Though for two hundred years he had slept well in the lone graveyard of the deserted church beside Loch Voil,[598] he seemed to know the road as perfectly as he had known it in his old foraying days. As he passed by he moved his target[599] forward and his hand stole to his sword, as if he recognised one of his ancient foes.[600] Then he was swallowed up by the same mist that had protected him so often in his life.

The gloom grew thicker, and in the clinging air fantastic noises hung as if the spirits of the hills, so long oppressed and overcome by modern life and by man's dominance of nature, were abroad and had resumed their sway. All the old legends appeared natural, the second sight a thing so evident, it seemed a madness to deny. The Bodach Glas[601] would not have been surprising had he appeared, his head averted and his plaid twisted about him in the ancient fashion of the Isles. London was a million miles off, lost in reality, and the true world was that I thought I saw on every side in the grey pall of mist. It seemed that I had ridden miles through the dark, steamy woods. The damp chilled to the bones, and if I put my hand upon my horse I left an imprint of my fingers in the white dew that clustered on his coat. Emerging from the woods, at least upon one side, where the rough woodland pasture stretches out towards the moss, close to the toll-house which stands at four cross-roads, four-square to all the winds, there is an island of old ash trees amongst the firs and spruces, which stands upon a knoll close to a gate. At all times the old trees look strange against the background of dark firs. Upon that evening they appeared gigantic, menacing, and magnified to twenty times their size. As I approached them, glad to have left the gloomy woods, my horse snorted and bounded half across the road. A voice in Spanish hailed me, and a figure moved from the shadow of the trees and stood, dew-damped and shivering, in his light southern clothes.

---

[596] The curved blade of the Lochaber axe was mounted on a pole topped by either a crook or spike.

[597] Rob Roy MacGregor.

[598] Balquhidder Parish Church.

[599] Round shield.

[600] The Grahams.

[601] 'The Old Grey Man' was a spirit that was believed to be a portent of death. In Walter Scott's first novel, *Waverley*, Fergus Mac-Ivor sees such an apparition, which foretells his death.

His olive face had turned an earthy colour with the cold, and it was rendered ghastly looking by a red sash tied like a comforter about his neck. He told me that at a village which he thought was called Bocliva [Buchlyvie], or something of that sort, he had been informed there lived a gentleman hard by who could speak Christian,[602] and he believed that I must be the man. He was, he said, "fasting from all but sin that day, and he esteemed his having come across me almost a miracle, for he felt saved as on a plank when he heard me speak".

He knew a "litel Inglis", which he would "spika so that I might hear". Then in that language he informed me that "he had lose the ship in Liz and walka Glasgo"; and then, turning again to Spanish, thanked me, and in particular for some cigarettes I gave him, which he declared "were better far than bread when the heart is empty and the feet sore, and that the scent of them was sweeter than the orange flower or than the incense in a church".

He came from Vigo,[603] so he said, and if I came there any time I had my house in Teis,[604] just past the blacksmith's, and he, though a poor man, was one who could appreciate. Then, after telling me that "Ildefonso Lopez was my servant, and God would pay me", he raised his battered hat and, starting off again upon the road to "walka Glasgow", disappeared into the night singing a tango in a high falsetto voice.

I rode into the open between the rough stone dykes that bound the road beyond the toll, passed the old-fashioned cast-iron milestone on which a hand is moulded pointing the way to Aberfoyle, and, riding cautiously down the stony brae, crossed the Ward bridge and came out on the moor.

White waves of vapour came surging up against the posts that marked the road, and foamed about them as the foam surges round a rock. Through the thick air the scent of the bog-myrtle penetrated, acrid and comforting, and on the banks of peat the willows trembled as my horse passed them, as if they floated on the moss.

All was as lonely and as northern as before, but the spell had been broken by Ildefonso Lopez in his brief apparition out of the mist and gloom of the October evening, and though I knew I rode along the road to the Kelty bridge, and marked unconsciously the junipers that

---

[602] Spanish colloquialism: "puede hablar Cristiano" = able to speak Spanish.

[603] An important port and fishing centre in north-west Spain, and a regular waypoint for ships going to South America. Graham and his wife Gabrielle lived there from 1881 to 1883, before returning to Scotland on the death of Graham's father.

[604] A fishing village, San Salvador de Teis, to the north of Vigo, which was undergoing development as a port when Graham lived in Vigo.

grow just by the iron gate that opens on the path towards the Carse,[605] it seemed somehow that I was entering Vigo, by the north channel between the Ciés[606] and the high land on which a clump of pine trees overhangs the sea.

The noble bay spread out between the hills, which ran down sheer, right to the water's edge, leaving at intervals just ground enough for a white little town with red-tiled roofs to lodge itself, half hidden amongst vines.

The fishing boats, brown and with sails as sharp as a shark's fins, dotted the water, and on a little tongue of land the town of Bouzas seemed to rock upon the sea, as it lay basking in the sun.

Vigo itself, with its steep winding streets, its dark-tree'd alameda,[607] its mouldering fort, and the decaying hulk of an old ship left derelict upon the sand, appeared just as I first had seen it thirty years ago. The castles, where the brass guns had sunk upon the ground beside the mouldering carriages, towered above the town.

Chestnut and pine woods almost met the houses, and from the beach the chattering of fishwives, in their bright red and yellow petticoats, sounded in my ears. Beyond the town the harbour narrowed, and the white oratory of La Guia crowned the pine-clad hill that rises up from the black point of the Cabron. Still narrowing till it seemed a lake, the harbour stretched towards the Lazaretto, where under piles of sand that clearly show on a still day, lie the galleons of Drake hunted up the bay until they sunk themselves to save the treasure that they held. It passed by Redondela, with its high bridge, and finished at San Payo, from whence as I looked backwards I seemed to see the islands at the harbour mouth float in a sunset, red and glorious, and crossed by bars of purple and black.

It all appeared to hang outlined and visible upon the vapour rising from the moss, just as a wood appears, hung in the air on the South Pampa on a misty morning, with its roots growing in the sky. Slowly it faded, and as I jogged along, passing the Kelty bridge and turning by the watering-trough into another belt of wood, I almost wondered whether Ildefonso Lopez had been a real man, or but an emanation from the mist from which he issued out so suddenly, and which had swallowed him again almost as suddenly, upon his lonely way.

*****

---

[605] The fertile valley along the River Forth to the west of Stirling.
[606] A group of islands across the mouth of the Vigo estuary.
[607] Spanish: A tree-lined avenue.

In the next sketch, Graham is clearly describing the small Hebridean island of Iona, which he claims as one of the "Vigias of the mind". In this descriptive piece we find his now familiar lament over progress and tourism, which he believes will ruin the unspoilt, mystical island. Thus, it is a vigia in as much as the island he describes will all too soon have vanished into the mists of the past.

A VIGIA

The Saturday Review, 30 November 1909, pp. 529–30.
Anthologised in *Hope* (London: Duckworth, 1910), pp. 53–60.

WHEN the old Spanish navigators, sailing in virgin seas, uncharted, undeflowered by keels, passed by some islet about which they were doubtful, seeing it dimly as in the mist lifted for a moment, or in the uncertain light of the false dawn, they called it a Vigia, a place to be looked out for,[608] and their old charts are dotted here and there with the Vigia of the Holy Spirit, the Trinity, the Immaculate Conception, or the Exaltation of the Cross.

Their followers, sailing with ampler knowledge but less faith, kept a look-out for the mysterious shoals or islets, not often finding them, unless they chanced to run upon them in the dark and perish with all hands. These were Vigias of the seas, but there exist Vigias of the mind, as shadowy and illusive, to the full, as any that Magellan, Juan de la Cosa,[609] or Sebastian Cabot marked upon their charts. We all know of such islands, low lying, almost awash, as it were, in the currents of the mind. On them we make our land-fall when we choose, without a pilot, except memory, to guide us in the darkest night. We land and roam about alone, always alone, for those who once inhabited them and welcomed us whenever we sailed in, are now all harboured. Commonly we stay but little there, for though the men we knew are dead, their ghosts so jostle us that we are glad to re-embark and sail again into a world of noise, that modern anæsthetic of the mind, still knowing that one day we must return and swell the shadowy procession that walks along the shores of their dead, saltless seas. There is an island, whose whereabouts I do not care precisely to reveal, although only a little strait divide it from a land of mist, of money-making, a land of faiths harder by far than facts, and yet, there it rides swaying on the sea like some great, prehistoric ship,

---

[608] More commonly, a look-out point or watchtower.

[609] A Castilian navigator (1450–1510). He was master of the *Santa Maria*, accompanying Columbus on his first and second voyages to the New World.

looking out westward in the flesh, and with interior vision straining its eyes to keep its recollection of the past fresh and undimmed. Green grass, white sands, limpid blue seas, with windows here and there of palest green in them, through which you look into the depths and count the stones, watch sea anemones unfold like flowers, and follow the minutest fish that play fathoms below your boat; these keep it fresh, old and uncontaminated. One likes to think of virgin souls, and so I like to think of this oasis in the desert of the sea as virgin, in spite of tourists, steamboats and the stream of those who go to worship and defile. They have the power to trample down the grass, to leave their sandwich papers and their broken bottles in the ling[610], but the fresh wind coming across a thousand leagues of sea eludes them. That they can never trample down. So may a woman in a brothel be the mattress of the vilest of mankind and keep some corner of the soul still pure; for it is dull, befitting only to the spirit of the so-called wise, to say the age of miracles is dead. Those who have kept their minds unclogged with knowledge know that they never cease.

So old my island is that it seems young – that is, it still preserves an air as of an older world, in which men laboured naturally just as the bee makes honey; a world where the chief occupation of mankind was to look round them as the Creator did in Eden and to find all things good. So they pass all the morning, meeting their fellows and saluting them, and in the afternoon re-pass and re-salute, then work a little in the fields, lifting up hay upon a fork with as much effort as an athlete in the circus raises a cannon in his teeth, till it is the time to sit down on a stone and watch the fishing-boats return upon the tides, the steersman sitting on the gunwale with his knee jammed against the tiller, and the sheet firmly knotted round a thwart. Just as of Avila, it might be said of my Vigia, that it is all made up of saints and stones, for not a stone is without its corresponding saint or saint without his stone. Thus in both places does the past so dwarf the present, that things which happened when the world was young seem just as probable as the incredible events we see before our eyes.

Upon a mound that looks out on a sandlocked bay the heathen crucified some of the new faith a thousand years ago, bringing as we might think their crosses with them ready made or rigging up a jury cross, fashioned from spars and oars, for not a tree grows, or has ever grown, upon the island where sheep feed peacefully on the short, wiry grass broken with clumps of flags.[611] A little further on fairies appeared the other day, not to a man herding sheep and dazed with solitude, but to a company of men who all declare they say the

---

[610] Scots: Coarse grass.
[611] Gravestones.

Little People sitting upon a mound. Fairies and martyrs both seem as natural as does the steamer landing its daily batch of tourists to hurry through the street where the kings sleep under their sculptured stones, gaze at the Keltic crosses and the grey, time-swept church which lies a little listed, as it were, to starboard, upon the grassy slope where once stood the wattled temple of the Apostle to the Isles. The mud-built church, where the Apostle chanted his last Mass, is nearer to us than the cathedral, now being killed with care. We see the saint lie dying, and his white, faithful horse approach and make its moan and, bowing down its head, ask for his blessing, as is recorded by the chronicler, with that old cheerful faith in the impossible that kept his world so young.

So standing on the Capitol, the Church, Popes, Cardinals and Saints, the glory of the Middle Ages, the empire, the republic and the kings, melt into mist and leave us, still holding, as our sure possession, to the two children suckled by the wolf.[612] Some men, like Ponce de Leon,[613] have sailed to find the fountain of eternal youth, landed upon some flowery land, left it, and died still searching, all unaware the object of their quest, had it been found, would have left paradise a waste. There in my island, whose longitude and latitude, for reasons of my own, I keep secret, there is, I think, some fountain in which those who bathe recover, not their youth, but the world's youth, and ever afterwards have their ear opened to the voices of the dead.

So, seated on the ground amongst the flowers that grow in miniature amongst the grass, bedstraw and tormentil, upon the cairn-topped hill from which the saint of Gartan[614] saw his vision, they see the history of the isle acted before them, as in an optic mirror of the mind. The setting still remains just as it was when the Summer Sailors[615] from the north fell on the peaceful monks one day in June, twelve hundred years ago, and sacrificed them and their prior to their offended gods. The thin, white road which cuts the level machar[616] in two, has probably replaced an earlier sheep track or footpath of the monks. The dazzling white houses, with their thatched roofs secured against the wind by stones slung in a rope, only require a little more neglect to fall again into the low, black Pictish huts. The swarthy

---

[612] In Roman mythology, Romulus the legendary funder of Rome and his twin brother Remus were suckled by a wolf.

[613] Juan Ponce de León (1474–1521) was a Spanish conquistador and explorer, the first to lead an expedition to Florida, who served as the first governor of Puerto Rico.

[614] A parish in County Donegal, Ireland, where Saint Columba was born.

[615] Viking raiders.

[616] Scots: Low-lying land next to the sand of the sea shore covered with grasses and used for rough grazing.

people, courteous and sauve, in whom you see a vein of subcutaneous sarcasm, as they lean up against a house, sizing the passing stranger up to the last tittle of a glance, would all look natural enough with glibs of matted hair,[617] long saffron Keltic shirts and the Isles kilt, made out of a long web of cloth, having the right arm bare.

Still in the Isle of Dreams remains the primitive familiarity between the animals and man, which only lingers on in the regions where no breath of modern life has set a bar between two branches of the same creation with talk about the soul. The still, soft rain yet blots the island from the world, just as it did of yore, and through its pall the mysterious voices of the sea sound just as menacing and hostile to mankind, as they did when the saint preached to the seals upon the reef. Perhaps – who knows? – he preached yet to those who have the gift of right hearing of the soft grating noise the pebbles make in receding wave upon the beach. The wind continues its perpetual monsoon, blowing across the unpolluted ocean for a thousand leagues. In the white coves the black sea-purses[618] which the tide throws up like necklaces of antique and prehistoric pattern are spread upon the sands, waiting the evening when mermaids issue from the waves and clasp them round their necks. Soft wind and purple sea, red cliffs and greenest grass, the echoing caves and mouldering ruins, with the air of peace, all make the islet dreamlike, sweet and satisfying.

To have seen it once, is to have seen it to the last day of one's life. The horses waiting at the rough pierhead to swim a mile of channel with its fierce, sweeping tide, the little street in which the houses spring from the living rock which crops up here and there and forms a reef right in the middle of the road, are not a memory, but a possession, as real as if you had the title-deeds duly engrossed and sealed. When all is said and done, the one secure and lasting property a man can own is an enchanted city such as one sees loom in the sky, above the deserted sands. That, when you once have seen it, is yours forever, and next comes a Vigia, which but appears for a brief moment, in the mind, as you sail past on some imaginary sea.

*****

Graham was a master of the obituary, and here is one of his funerary pieces, in which he describes, with affection, but without sentimentality, the mourning of a local ploughman. Set in a hamlet just to the south of Gartmore, his characters, who were likely his tenants, would have been readily recognisable to the folk in Menteith at the time he

---

[617] Historical: A mass of matted hair worn down over the eyes which was fashionable in Ireland.

[618] The egg case of skate or shark.

wrote, and his use of Scots in the tale has been favourably compared with that of Grassic Gibbon.

Again, roughly half is taken up with detailed descriptions of sights, sounds and smells of the countryside, and where the fairies make their increasingly familiar appearance. The awkward, abbreviated conversations between these men of the land, about the weather, their crops, their beasts, the state of the market, and their hesitant platitudes about the deceased, were expertly observed and related. 'At Dalmary' is an evocation of the ordinary, a scene without cynicism, except, we might suspect, at the words of the officiating minister, which Graham would have regarded as cant.[619] What is missing, however, and in all of Graham's vivid observations, is any deeper reflection on a wider community of relationships, of mutuality, of social intercourse, which, if he was aware of such relationships, might have mitigated his generally pessimistic view of the rural life. Perhaps it was because of his social position and distance that he was excluded from any such intimacies or participation, and his sojourns in Scotland, particularly after the sale of Gartmore House, were increasingly episodic.

Davies wrote that Graham was by nature, 'a good observer but a poor participator',[620] and in consequence, he remained an outsider, who has given us a very limited view of the reality of life in rural Scotland. The keen-eyed reader, however, will recognise echoes in the last sentences of Lilas Campbell of Gart-na-Cloich, wherein both widows distract their sorrow with household chores. In this case however, the widow might also be practising economy now that her bread winner has gone.

AT DALMARY

The Saturday Review, 4 December 1909, pp. 687–9.
Anthologised in *Hope* (London: Duckworth, 1910), pp. 61–3.

THE road led out upon an open moor, on which heather and wiry grass strove for the mastery. Here and there mossy patches, on which waved cotton grass, broke the grey surface of the stony waste, and

---

[619] 'The author [Graham] is a realist of the realists. His subtle compassion for his fellow men, his indignant tenderness for the weak, and his utter lack of sentimentality is, however, at the root of his charm.' *Academy & Literature*, 25 October 1902, p. 437.

[620] Davies, *R. B. Cunninghame Graham and the Concept of Impressionism*, DPhil diss., University of Sussex, 1972, p. 3.

here and there tufts of dwarf willow, showing the silvery backs of their grey leaves, rustled and bent before the wind.

The road, one of those ancient trails on which cattle and ponies were driven in old times down to the Lowland trysts, was now half covered up with grass. It struggled through the moor as if it chose to do so of its own accord, now twisting, for no apparent reason, and again going directly up a hill, just as the ponies and the kyloes must have straggled before the drovers' dogs. It crossed a shallow ford, in which the dark brown, moorland trout darted from stone to stone when the shadow of a passer-by startled them as they poised, their heads up stream, keeping themselves suspended, as it were, by an occasional wavering motion of their tails, just as a hawk hangs hovering in the air.

Beside the stream, a decaying wooden bridge, high pitched and shaky, reminded one that in winter, the burn, now singing its metallic little song between the stones, brown and pellucid,[621] with bubbles of white foam floating upon its tiny linns or racing down the stream, checking a little in an eddy, where a tuft of heavy ragweed dipped into the flood, was dangerous to cross.

The aromatic scent of the sweet gale came down the breeze, mixed with the acrid smoke of the peats. Hairbells [sic] danced in the gentle breeze, and bumble bees hummed noisily as they emerged, weighed down with honey, from the ling.

Across the moor, from farms and shielings, and from the grey and straggling village built on each side of the rough street, in which the living rock cropped up and ran in reefs across the road, came groups of men dressed in black clothes, creased and ill-fitting, with hats, grown brown with years of church-going and with following funerals in the rain; they walked along as if they missed the familiar spade and plough handle to keep them straight, just as a sailor walks uneasily ashore.

As they trudged on they looked professionally on the standing crops, or passed their criticisms on the cattle in the fields. Root crops, they thought, were back, taties [sic] not just exactly right, a thocht[622] short in the shaws, and every cow, a wee bit heigh abune the tail, for praise was just as difficult for them to give as blame was easy, for they were all aware their God was jealous, and it did not befit them to appear more generous than He. Hills towered and barred the north, and to the south the moors stretched until they met another range of hills,[623] and all the space between them was filled with a great

---

[621] Clear, translucent.
[622] Scots: A little bit.
[623] The Campsie Fells.

sea of moss, eyed here and there with dark, black pools on which a growth of water-lilies floated like fairies' boats. A wooded hill, which sloped down to a brawling river, was the fairies' court. Another to the south, steep rising from the moss, the Hill of the Crown received its name, back in the times of Fingal and Bran.[624] Gaps in the hills showed where, in times gone by, marauders from the north had come to harry and to slay. The names of every hill, lake, wood, or stream were Gaelic, and the whole country exhaled an air of a romantic past.

In it, the dour, black-coated men, although they thought themselves as much a part and parcel of the land as the grey rocks upon the moor, were strangers;[625] holding their property but on suffrance [sic] from the old owners, who named every stone, and left their impress even in the air.

It seemed the actual dwellers acted, as it were, a play, a sort of rough and clownish interlude, upon a stage set out for actors whom the surroundings would have graced.

Still, though they shared the land, just as we all do, by favour of the dead, they had set their mark upon it, running their rough stone walls across the moors, and to the topmost ridges of the hills, planting their four-square, slate-roofed houses in places where a thatched and whitewashed cottage, with red tropeolum growing on the corner of the byre, a plant of mullein[626] springing from a crevice in the wall, and flauchtered feals pegged to the thatch with birchen crockets, or kept down with stones, would have looked just as fitting, as theirs looked out of place. A land in which the older dwellers had replaced the nymphs and hamadryads[627] by the fairies, where, in the soft and ceaseless rain, the landscape wore a look of sadness, that the mist, creeping up the shoulders of the hills, at times turned menacing, was now delivered over to a race of men who knew no shadows, either in life or in belief. If they believed, they held each letter of "The Book" inspired and would have burned the man who sought to change a comma or a semicolon, and if they had rejected faith as an encumbrance they could do without, denied the very possibility of any god or power but mathematics, holding the world a mere gigantic counting-house in which they sat enthroned. The moaning birches and dark murmuring pines, the shaggy thickets by the streams, and the green hummocks under which tradition held Pictish and Keltic chiefs reposed, the embosomed corries over which the shadows ran,

---

[624] A Celtic mythological figure and his dog.
[625] Descendants of Lowlanders who had displaced the original Gaelic-speaking population centuries before.
[626] *Verbascum Thapsus.*
[627] A Greek mythological creature that dwelt in trees.

as imperceptibly as lizards run up a wall, turning the brown hillside to gold, which melted into green as it ran on, until it faded into a pale amethyst, faint and impalpable as is the colour in a dream, seemed to demand a race of men more fitted to its moods than those who walked along the road chatting about the crops. Still it may be that though the outward visible sign was so repellent, the unexpected and interior softness of the black-clothed and tall-hatted men was bred in them by the surroundings, for certainly their hard, material lives, and their black, narrow, anti-human faith could not have given it.

The road led on until on the south side of it a path, worn in the heather and the wiry grass, and winding in and out between the hillocks, crossed here and there by bands of rocks, outcropping, but smoothed down on the edge by the feet of centuries, broke off, not at right angles after the fashion of a modern road, but on the slant, just as a herd of driven animals slants off, stopping at intervals to graze.

The knots of black-clothed men, some followed by their dogs, slowly converged upon the path, and stood a minute talking, passing the time of day, exchanging bits of news and gossip in subdued voices, and mopping vigorously at their brows, oppressed with the unwonted weight of their tall hats.

"We've had a braw back end, McKerrachar", Borland[628] remarked. The worthy he addressed, a gaunt, cadaverous man, so deeply wrinkled that you could fancy in wet weather the rain ran in channels in his face, spat in a contemplative fashion, rejoining in a non-committal way:

"No just sae bad ... markets are back a wee." A nod of assent went round the group, and then another interjected:

"I dinna mind sae braw a back end for mony a year: aye, ou aye, I'll no deny markets are very conseederably back."

Having thus magnified his fellow, after the fashion of the stars, he looked a moment with apparent interest at his hat, which he held in his hand, and ventured the remark:

"A sair blow to the widow, Andra's death; he was a good man to her."

No one answering him, he qualified what he had said by adding:

"Aye, sort of middlin'", and glanced round warily, to see if he had overstepped the bounds by the too indiscriminating nature of his praise.

The house towards which the knots of men were all converging stood at the foot of a green, grassy mound, which looked as if it might have been the tumulus of some prehistoric chief. On it grew several

---

[628] The name of a nearby farm, and the tradition of naming farmers after their property.

wind-bent ash trees, and within twenty yards or so of the front door of the grey cottage, with its low thatched eaves, there ran a little burn. Two or three mulleins with flowers still clinging to their dying stalks, on which they stuck like vegetable warts, sprung from the crevices between the stones of the rough byre. A plant or two of ragweed grew on the midden on which a hen was scratching, and out of it in a green and oozy rivulet of slush filtered down to the stream. On one side was a garden, without a flower and with a growth of straggling cabbage, gooseberry bushes, and some neglected-looking raspberry canes, as the sole ornaments. In the potato patch a broken spade was stuck in the ground. All around the house some straggling plum trees, with their sour fruit half ripened and their leaves already turning brown, looking as if they had fought hard for life against the blast in the poor, stony soil, gave a peculiar air of desolation, imparting to the place a look as of an oasis just as unfruitful as the waste which stretched on every side. On one side of the door, but drawn a little on the grass, not to obstruct the way, there stood a cart, with a tall, white-faced and white-pasterned[629] horse between the shafts, held by a little boy. Peat smoke curled lazily out of the barrel stuck into the thatch that served as a chimney, and cocks and hens scratched in the mud before the door, bees hummed amongst the heather, and once again the groups of men in black struck a discordant note.

Inside the house, upon four wooden chairs was set the coffin of the dead ploughman, cheap and made in haste, just as his life had been lived cheaply and in haste, from the first day that he stood between the stilts,[630] until the evening when he had loosed his horses from the plough for the last time, his furrow finished and his cheek no more to be exposed to the November rain. Now in the roughly put-together kist he lay, his toil-worn hands crossed on his breast, and with his wrinkled, weather-beaten face, turned waxen and ennobled, set in its frame of wiry whisker, and his scant hair decently brushed forward on his brow. The peats burned brightly in the grate and sent out a white ash which covered everything inside the house, whitening the clothes of the black-coated men who stood about, munching great hunks of cake and slowly swallowing down the "speerits" which the afflicted widow pressed upon them, proud through her tears to say "Tak' it up, Borland", or "It will no hurt ye, Knockinshanock; ye ken there's plenty more".

The white peat ash fell on the coffin lid just as the summer's dust had fallen upon the hair of him who lay inside, and lay upon the polished surface of the thin brass plate, on which were superscribed

---

[629] The sloping part of a horse's foot between the fetlock and the hoof.
[630] The shafts of a plough.

the dates of the birth and of the death of the deceased, his only titles to the recollection of the race with whom his life had passed. Now and again the widow, snatching a moment from her hospitable cares, brushed off the dust abstractedly with her pocket-handkerchief, just as a man might stop upon the way to execution to put a chair straight or do any of the trifling actions of which life was composed. As she paused by the coffin the assembled men exchanged that furtive look of sympathy which in the North is the equivalent of the wild wailings, tears and self-abandonment of Southern folk, and perhaps stamps on the heart of the half-shamefaced sympathiser even a deeper line.

When all had drunk their "speerits" and drawn the backs of their rough hands across their mouths and shaken off the crumbs from their black clothes, the minister stood forth. Closing his eyes, he launched into his prayer with needless repetition, but with the feeling which the poor surroundings and the brave struggle against outward grief of the woman sitting by the fire in the old high-backed chair, in which her husband had sat so long, evoked, he dwelt upon the man's passage through the world.

Life was a breath, only a little dust, a shadow on the hills. It had pleased the Lord, for reasons of His Own, inscrutable, but against which 'twere impious to rebel, for a brief space to breathe life into the nostrils of this our brother, and here he made a motion of his hand towards the "kist", then to remove him to a better sphere after a spell of toil and trouble here on earth. Still we must not repine, as do the heathen, who gash themselves with knives, having no hope, whereas we who enjoy the blessings of being born to a sure faith in everlasting bliss should look on death as but a preparation for a better life. No doubt this hope consoled the speaker for all the ills humanity endures, for he proceeded to invoke a blessing on the widow, and as he prayed the rain beat on the narrow, bull's-eye window panes.[631] He called upon the Lord to bless her in her basket and her store, and to be with her in her outgoings and incomings, to strengthen her and send her resignation to His will. He finished with the defiance to humanity that must have wrung so many tears of blood from countless hearts, saying the Lord had given and that the Lord had taken, blessed be His Name.

All having thus been done that all our ingenuity can think of on such occasions, four stalwart neighbours, holding their hats in their left hands, hoisted the coffin on to their right shoulders and shuffled to the door. They stooped to let their burden pass beneath the eaves which overhung the entrance, and then emerging, dazed, into the light, their black clothes dusted over with white ashes from the fire,

---

[631] The cheapest form of glazing, being the centre boss of poured molten glass.

set down the coffin on the cart. Once more the men gathered into a circle and listened to a prayer, some with their heads bare to the rain, and others with their hats held on the slant to fend it off as it came swirling down the blast. A workman in his ordinary clothes took the tall white-faced horse close by the bit, and, with a jolt which made the kist shift up against the backboard, the cart set out, swaying amongst the ruts, with now and then a wheel running up high upon one side and now and then a jerk upon the trace-hooks, when the horse, cold with his long wait, strained wildly on the chains. The rain had blotted out the hills, the distant village with its rival kirks[632] had disappeared, and the grey sky appeared to touch the surface of the moor. A whitish dew hung on the grass and made the seeded plants appear gigantic in the gloom. Nothing was heard except the roaring of the burn and the sharp ringing of the high caulkins[633] on the horse as he struck fire amongst the stones on the steep, rocky road.

Leaning against the doorpost, the widow stood and gazed after the vanishing procession[634] till it had disappeared into the mist, her tears, which she had fought so bravely to keep back, now running down her face.

When the last sound of the cart-wheels and of the horse's feet amongst the stones had vanished into the thick air, she turned away and, sitting down before the fire, began mechanically to smoor[635] the peats and tidy up the hearth.

* * * * *

Here is another of Graham's tenants, possibly the one that most epitomises his "lost type". Graham's reminiscence forms a frank yet affectionate pen-portrait of a man he had known for many years, for whom he laments that "No one I know, is left in the whole world the least resembling him, so strange mixture of the present and the past". A critic in *The Academy* described this and other pen-portraits as 'so delicately limned that it is as if these people of a past age spoke from the printed page'.[636]

---

[632] Gartmore.

[633] The projections on a horseshoe.

[634] It was not customary for women, including wives, to attend funerals.

[635] Scots: Smother, extinguish. The suggestion is that the widow, now condemned to worse poverty, has put out the fire to save money.

[636] 'Scottish Stories', *The Academy*, 20 June 1914, p. 795.

A RETAINER

The English Review, July 1910, pp. 625–30.
Anthologised in *Hope* (London: Duckworth, 1910), pp. 175–85.

"LAIRD ye ken ane o' my forbears gaed to Bannockburn[637] wi' the
Græmes." Though my retainer always insisted that this forebear was
"nigh upon seven feet high," and used to add "men nowadays run
awfie small," he would himself with his inadequate six feet and four
or five inches have wielded a good spear.

Indeed, no man could possibly have had a better spearsman at his
back in the old days.

Tall, dark, and with a fell[638] of hair that grew down low upon his
forehead and met his curling beard, which grew so thick upon his
face, if you had dropped a pin upon it would have never touched the
skin, his twinkling grey eyes looked out suspiciously and yet with
humour on the world. His upper lip was always shaved, that is to say
upon "the Sabbath morn," and bore throughout the week a crop of
stubble upon it, so that, had it not been an article of faith with him to
shave it on the Sunday, he might as well have thrown away his razor,
though I can never fancy him with a moustache. He had, I think, a
vague idea that to have grown it would have been a sort of poaching
on the customs of the "gentry," though if a long descent can make
a gentleman, surely the fact of the grim forebear who had gone to
Bannockburn should have entitled him to be so styled, even though
the warrior ancestor may have been legendary. Most ancestors do not
bear looking at too closely, not only for their moral worth, but for
their authenticity, and my retainer's had done as much for him, as if
he had, after the manner of most Scottish worthies, hall-marked his
passage through the world by witnessing a charter, for he lived up to
him, according to his lights.

Born just before the railway penetrated the remoter districts, he
had, although he never knew it, preserved a flavour of an older world.

His speech was harsh and dialectic, but yet not vulgar, and in
his voice you heard that cadence, as of a Gaelic song, natural to
those born near the Highland line. Whether he ever knew it I know
not, but he appeared to me a little wasted in a world which had no
special function for such men as he was, to perform. Walking beside
a cart, towering above the horse, or sitting on the cramped iron
seat of some new reaper, cutting the corn upon his boggy fields, he
seemed a little out of place, too fine a figure for the work, not that

---

[637] The Battle of Bannockburn, 1314.
[638] Old English: A covering of rough hair.

he was especially intelligent, beyond a certain "pawky" humour,[639] the inheritance of nearly everyone who tills the soil in our bleak, kindly North, but because a manhood such as his imparts a dignity to its possessor, quite as impossible to explain as humour, but seen at the first glance.

Huge and athletic as he seemed to me in later life, in childhood he loomed gigantic, and illness, death, or age appeared in his case as impossible as they would have been to a mountain or to the world itself.

Seated beside his father, his very counterpart, but bent and grey, he used to keep my eyes focussed upon him, half against my will, during long hours in church. It seemed a miracle how his great hands, in which the soil had entered as it were below the skin and dyed them dark as peat, could "whummle o'er"[640] the pages in the "Book,"[641] and as I sat desperately waiting for the "saxteenthly and seventeenthly," and often cheated by the preacher, who always seemed to have "a few words in conclusion," extending over twenty minutes, in reserve, I used to envy his composure as he sat as little moved as is a rock upon a moor during a shower of rain. As I look back through the long vista of the years, it does not strike me that he was religious to a great degree, though such a constant worshipper in church. In fact, I think he was one of the class of commentators who would not give "five minutes of the clash of the Kirkyard,[642] for all the sermons in the world." It may be that in this I am unjust, for in things spiritual he did not venture an opinion, although on politics he thought that he was a Radical, that is, with reservations, as are most of us, for I remember that on one occasion he remarked he "was na sure ould Wully Gladstane[643] had done richt when he gave votes to the farm labourers," ... for, as he said, "yon class o' cattle is not eddicated up to it." It would have been a work of supererogation[644] to have told him was what was urged against his own class once upon a time, for he would certainly have answered: "Aye, ou aye, prejudice juist dies hard," or something of the sort, with the assurance of a man who knows that he is right.

---

[639] Scots: Having a mocking or cynical sense of humour.
[640] Scots: To turn over rapidly.
[641] The Bible.
[642] Scots: Talk, gossip, tittle-tattle, scandal.
[643] William Ewart Gladstone (1809–98), who was the Liberal Prime Minister of Great Britain four times between 1868 and 1894. Graham reputedly said, 'I sometimes wish I could believe in religion, for if I did, I could be sure that Gladstone was in hell.' Quoted in David Daiches, *A Companion to Scottish Literature* (London: Edward Arnold, 1981), p. 89.
[644] The performance of more work than duty requires, or needs.

His house, just on the edge of a wild moss, was suited to him, for certainly it had no outward sign of any inward grace,[645] as it stood gaunt and square, its grey stone walls and grey-green slates gave it an air of self-assertion, which I suppose it had to have to face the climate, just as a Scotchman who is lacking in it is a Scotchman lost.

Needless to say, no flowers climbed up the porch, no garden broke the look of sternness of the place.

The only sacrifice, that is, if sacrifice it could be called, upon the altar of æstheticism, were two small rowan trees which grew on each side of the iron gate which opened on the gravel path that led up to the house, and had been made to form an arch. I think that in his heart of hearts that my retainer looked upon this as foolishness and waste of time, for once when I directed his attention to it, he muttered "havers of the wife's," and turned the conversation with a remark that sheep "were back at the October Tryst," or something of the sort.

Though not a grumbler, or a man who ever asked for a reduction of his rent, my retainer never would allow that any season could be good for the crops. Markets were always "back,"[646] during the many years I knew him; potatoes always either were diseased or just were sickening for it; the "neeps"[647] had tae-and-finger,[648] and the hogs wintering upon his farm either had foot-rot[649] or fluke.[650]

None of these statements did he advance with an ulterior object, but simply threw them out, for what they might be worth, either as pleasant subjects to discourse upon, or as a sort of formula with which to enter into conversation in an agreeable way.

This habit, and his enormous hands, and feet encased in boots like barges, heavily soled and tacketed,[651] his homespun clothes and soft black hat (he lived before the age of caps), were but one side of him, the side that he turned outward to the world.

Not having the Gaelic, he had lost the gift of picturesque expression, the birthright, as it seems, of every Highlander, even the dullest of his race. Deep in his mind, however, there seemed to seethe a mixture of hard Lowland Scotch ideas, and a half Celtic spirit of

---

[645] An allusion to the definition of a sacrament in the Catechism of the Church of England (derived from St Augustine).

[646] Animal and crop prices were down.

[647] Scots: Turnips.

[648] Scots: 'Toe and finger', a colloquial name for *Plasmodiophora Brassicae*, a disease which affects cabbages, turnips, and other members of the order *Cruciferae*.

[649] An infection of the soft tissues between the claws often caused by *fusiformis* bacteria.

[650] A worm, *Fasciola hepatica*, which attacks the liver.

[651] See passim.

revolt, not against the powers that be, but against life as we all know it, striving for mastery.

This made him ever in hot water with his fellows, but, on the other hand, took him off into a fantastic world, not that of elves and fairies, of wraiths and second sight, but to a sphere in which all the occurrences of daily life were magnified till they became as interesting as they might well be, or perhaps really are, if we could see them his way.

During the whole course of his life he was, as he said, "sair ta'en up[652] wi' horse," and yet had the worst horses in the district on his farm.

Floods, frosts, and snows were deeper, fiercer, and more intense when he recounted them than anyone had ever known them, and yet in all his dealings with his fellows he was honest to a fault, so that it may have been he either was a poet without the gift of words, or that the spirit of the strange, wild district where he lived worked in his soul, whilst the affairs of life, sordid and commonplace, but yet compelling, influenced his mind.

The village, close to where he lived, was rent asunder by feuds between the Churches,[653] which, as the difference between them was infinitesimal, rendered their quarrels almost a bitter as those between the Spaniards and the Moors.

Often the battle raged on little matters, such as the appointment of a school-teacher, or the like, and my retainer, having taken as it were the shilling of the Free Kirk, duly embroiled himself with almost everybody, offending just as much his co-religionists, by too great violence, as he outraged his enemies by his attacks.

At last he found himself left all alone, the one sincere and honest man in the whole district branded as an intriguer and a liar.

So he retired to his marshy fields, and passed his time between the plough-stilts and his own ingle neuk,[654] but never missing kirk on Sundays, where he sat silently, his hair a little greyer, and his hands a little more like roots of trees, turning the criticising gaze of the old-fashioned members of his race upon the preacher and ostentatiously looking up all the texts he quoted, with a loud rustle of the pages, reminding one of dry leaves falling in a wood.

All the strange waifs and strays, goin' aboot bodies[655] and the like, who forty years ago travelled the upland districts in the North, drifted up to his farm, in the same way steel filings jump to a magnet, and he, although he bitterly complained about their presence and the small

---

[652] Scots: Heavily preoccupied.
[653] Gartmore.
[654] Scots: A domestic fireplace with a recess.
[655] Scots: A person of no fixed abode.

depredations that they made, was always ready to throw open barns and outhouses for them to pass the night.

Perhaps the district, with its wide mosses and enshrouding mists, its mouldering ruins of the past, mysterious-looking tarns lost in the hills, and its slow flowing, black-streamed river, upon whose bosom bubbles that seemed to rise up from the centre of the earth were ever bursting, was his chief friend, for no one could have pictured him in any other place. The great iron gin[656] he dug out of the moss, and which he called a wolf trap, and the claymore he found when casting peats, and which by a quite natural process soon became Rob Roy's, were his chief treasures. The one I have inherited, and the other which he sold to a travelling antiquary, was perhaps the sole occasion in which he got the best part of a bargain in his life. His all-embracing feuds, extending from his nearest neighbours, with every one of whom he had some question, either of "marches"[657] or of trespass, did not exclude the humblest from his wrath.

The parish gravedigger, he declared, should never bury him, for as he had not been consulted over his appointment, he used to say, "Yon Ramsey canna howk[658] a grave, he maks them mair like tattie pits,[659] no like a Christian grave."

Happening to meet him on the road one day long years ago, I asked him whether he had made it up with Ramsey, and received the answer, "Aye, ou aye, time is a sort o' healer. Aye, ou aye, ... when I dee, Ramsey wull just hae to sort me ... though he is sure to mak a bummle[660] o' the job!!"

Fate as it happened was not willing that his grave should be bungled in the way he feared, for, dying gin the North, a snow-storm caught the mourners and he was shoughed[661] as he himself would certainly have said, in a churchyard by a lake, where to this day his rough-hewn headstone moulders in the mist. All around him lie McFarlanes and McGregors, most of whose tombstones simply bear a sword upon them, thus setting forth the manner of their lives.

What he will think when he "spangs up" amongst them at the day of judgement, I cannot say, for in the days gone by they were sworn foes ... but, as he said himself, "time is a healer" ... and in the meanwhile the little wavelets of the lake break up against the wall of the wild graveyard where he lies, with a faint gurgling sound.

---

[656] A trap for catching small mammals.
[657] Boundaries.
[658] Scots: Dig up.
[659] Scots: A straw covered hole in the ground for storing potatoes.
[660] Scots: Bungle, botch.
[661] Scots: Put in a trench, buried.

No one I know, is left in the whole world the least resembling him, so strange mixture of the present and the past; on the one side a representative of the rough-footed Scots who harried and who reived, and, on the other, of the laborious race of ploughmen (loved of the seagulls) who have made Scotland what she is.

Roughness and kindness so struggled for the mastery in him that they seemed after a fashion of the spirit and the flesh to fight an everlasting battle for the predominance, leaving the struggle fortunately undetermined, so that he still appeared a man, weak and uncertain in his strength, an infant grafted on a giant, such no doubt was his fell[662] ancestor, who gaed to Bannockburn.

* * * * *

'Ces arbres qu'il plante et à l'ombre desquels il ne
s'assoira pas, il les aime pour eux-mêmes et pour ses
enfants, et pour les enfants de ses enfants, sur qui
s'étendront leurs rameaux'.[663]

'Hyacinthe' Loyson

The Crow Road is part of the B822 between Fintry and Lennoxtown, which cuts through the Campsie Hills, and is a popular route for cyclists. The name has nothing to do with crows as Graham implies; it was an old drovers', or 'drove' road, named for the Gaelic 'crodh', or male cattle. Subsequently, in a letter to *The Saturday Review*, Graham accepted this definition.[664]

Graham's second assertion that the road was 'unchanged, save for a sheep drain here and there, since the beginning of the world' was also incorrect. His relative, Peter Speirs, and his business partner Robert Dunmore, financed the realigning and regrading of the road to ease transport from their cotton mill in Fintry to the Forth and Clyde Canal at Kirkintilloch.

Although not without interest, this is an odd, bisected work. As if suddenly destitute of ideas, the evocative description of the lonely road becomes an excuse for another panegyric to his cousin Alexander Speirs of Culcreuch Castle, a virtual re-tread of his previous sketch 'A Veteran', written a mere ten years earlier. The castle itself, which is some distance from the isolated road, sits in sheltered and luxuriant surroundings compared to the bleak and treeless countryside he set out to describe.

---

[662] Cruel, ruthless.

[663] French: 'These trees which he plants, and under whose shade he shall never sit, he loves them for themselves, and for the sake of his children and his children's children, who will sit beneath the shadow of their spreading boughs'.

[664] Cunninghame Graham, 'The Craw Road', *Saturday Review*, 26 November 1910. In Scots popular parlance, 'away the Crow Road' = 'dead'.

Figure 14 (photograph courtesy of Hugh Edmond).

THE CRAW ROAD

The Saturday Review, 15 October 1910, pp. 479–80.
Anthologised in *Charity* (London: Duckworth, 1912), pp. 65–72.

ALL roads are said to lead to Rome. This may be so, of course, if a man follows them right around the world. Some, though, lead you to realms in which materialism of the City of the Seven Hills has not and never had a place.

Upon them no legionary in his caligulæ[665] and with his conquering spade upon his back has ever marched. The roads he traversed led straight to some place or another, over the tops of hills, across the

---

[665] Latin: Little boots.

rivers, passing morasses, cutting the valleys, and right across the plain, just as the State that paid him made its way to fame regardless of the feelings of the world. My road was traced originally by homing crows. Men saw them fly, and thought that where they came from there must be something worth their while to see. That was before the coming of the legionaries. The world was full of interest in these days, for fairies played upon the heathery knolls, elves sat upon the toadstools, and the white Caledonian cattle roamed the woods. The spirit of adventure was at least as strong as now, for anyone who left his home to travel, even a little way, where he had never been before, plunged into the unknown. To-day the difficulty is not, that there is not a sufficiency of roads, but that there are too many Romes. This difficulty did not beset the builders of the road I write about.

Following the flight of crows across the hills, they first of all laid a few faggots in the miry places, secured a coracle or two by streams too deep to cross, and, taking in their hands a club or a stone battle-axe, set out across the hills. Thus the road they traced in times gone by is made on other principles than those in use to-day. Winding round obstacles and in and out between the moors, skirting the base of hills, and now and then coming back upon itself in places where the first road makers no doubt sat down to rest, it takes its course.

Campseyan chiefs and then Fingalians[666] have passed along in their deerskin brogues. In places, short cuts, now long disused, still shine amongst the heath, showing the stones whitened and polished by feet, dead before Baliol and Bruce.[667] Into recesses of green hills, now out again and then running along the sides of streams, it winds. No road I know, not even between Mendoza and San Felipe de los Andes across the stony slopes of Uspallata,[668] where in the tempests stones roll along like leaves, is lonelier, more desolate, or looks more hostile to mankind.

By rights the road should lead to nowhere in particular, but finish off in some impenetrable morass or in some corrie of the hills. That would indeed be a crows' road, and far more interesting than the majority of roads that lead to places no one has any wish to go to, except the people who are born there and cannot get away. We are enjoined to practice virtue for its own sake and without hope of recompense.[669] What could be, then, more virtuous than to make a

---

[666] Graham was imagining tribal chiefs from around the Campsie Hills, and mythical Celts from the spurious tales of Ossian by James MacPherson.

[667] John Balliol (c. 1249–1314), was King of Scots from 1292 to 1296; Robert the Bruce (1274–1329) was King of Scots from 1306 until 1329.

[668] A route across the Andes from Argentina to Chile.

[669] This was undoubtedly borrowed from Thomas Carlyle's *Sartor Resartus*.

road to nowhere, thus giving people the opportunity to see science and money both expended for themselves, and have a road on which they all could walk, free from the feeling of ulterior motive, conscious of a high moral purpose, and confident that all was for the best?

Motors could whirr along it fifty miles an hour, or horses trot, cyclist enjoy the pleasures of the treadmill, without infringing any law to merit them, and then, when all had come to where the road stopped in a black peat-hag or up against a solid wall of rock, return rejoicing, pleased with the advance of science and with their victory over space. This is what the Craw Road should really be if it were perfect; but, as it is, it winds about the mist-filled hollows and wild hills, on which feed black-faced sheep, and passes now and then a lone farmhouse, white and four-square, with purple slates, its stack of peats at one end, cheese-stone before the door, its fank[670] for sheep of dry-stone walls, coped with a divot, and with a woman in a short striped petticoat washing eternally blankets in the burn. It leads through realms of heath and grass unchanged, save for a sheep-drain here and there, since the beginning of the world, until it reaches one of the rare old Scottish houses, left from an older age.

Miles from a railway station and jammed against the flank of a steep range of hills, between a melancholy little tarn, in which feed tench, and a thick wood, it stands. The grey peel-tower[671] with battlements either for defence or else to show its owner was a gentleman, stands sentinel beside a square grey house, with steep-pitched roof and corby steps,[672] and with a low front door set in a roll-and-fillet moulding, opening upon the road.

The stone above the door sets forth the year of grace in which the builders rested from their task. The narrow ribbon of grey flags in front is mossed and honeycombed by time. The grass which surges up, close to the avenue, leaving a narrow space in which to turn a carriage, right before the door, has that peculiar sour and scanty look of an old pasture only grazed by sheep. In the dank fields, which we in Scotland dignify as "parks", the trees are mostly all stag-headed, and the tall spruces on the weather side hold out bare arms, not dead, but stripped and polished by the blast. Moss has spread out over the avenue, not like a carpet, but with the look of a disease, and in the corner of the grounds the ribs and trucks of an old cotton mill, built

---

[670] Scots: A sheepfold.
[671] A fortified keep.
[672] Corbie, or 'crow' steps = ornamental steps on a gable, popular in northern Europe and Scotland.

as a speculation a hundred years ago,[673] add to the loneliness, by giving, as it were, an air of having perished in the fight.

The long, dank mill-head which once set the machinery astir is silted up, in places fallen in; and though long years have passed since it did anything but breed innumerable frogs, is still an eyesore, Nature having steadfastly refused to take it to herself and veil its ugliness.

Smoke curls unwillingly from the chimneys of the house, to be so soon absorbed in mist it leaves one doubtful whether it is smoke, or but damp floating from the trees. Squirrels and rabbits have come into their own, and look at you as on a trespasser, and from the woods even at midday roe venture forth and play. The heron's cry sounds lively, and the tinkling of the burn hidden beneath the bushes at the shrubbery almost oppressive in the noonday solitude. All must look magical in the silence of the stars, when the moon ghostens in the trees, and owls float noiselessly about or pass the time of night in their long melopy [sic], from hollybush to old Scots fir, their cries re-echoing from the turrets of the house and sounding on the lake.

Then the tall pine trees, which throng around the little urn bearing the inscription "Hæc loca cum peregrinis pinis exornavit, A. G. S."[674] and the date 1845, compare their notes about the flight of time. Hemlocks and Douglasses must then vie with one another, and the Sequoias vaunt their statures, whilst trembling Deodaras shyly claim the palm of grace. Long, tapering branches, looking fingerlike and human, must be agitated, waking the birds and squirrels by their movement; and if the raiser of the urn could see the trees he planted long years ago, now grown majestic in their age, he would indeed plume himself on his Latin and his faith in having planted them.

'Tis possible the planter of the trees never went out at night to watch their growth; but if he had, stranding beside his urn watching the moonbeams play on the scant and much-bethistled crop of oats which runs into a sort of bay on one side of the Pinetum,[675] he would have been a notable addition to the scene.

Time had been impotent to bow or mellow him; so he stood still defiant, like an ash grown on stony ground that stretches out its boughs to meet the wind. The suns of the Peninsula, in whose wars he passed his youth, the storms of politics and of religious controversy of his middle age, had but intensified his proud, unyielding soul. Perhaps the soft corner in his heart was to the trees, now grown so beautiful and so luxuriant (after he was dead), to whom, in sure and certain

---

[673] See 'A Veteran'.

[674] Latin: 'This spot adorned with exotic pines, Alexander Graham Speirs' (second of Culcreuch).

[675] An arboretum devoted to growing conifers.

hope that Nature would perform her unconscious miracle, he raised his little urn. One fain would hope that when at night, released from the presence of mankind, they whisper in the breeze, his memory is cherished, and that these foreign pines, which do indeed adorn the spot on which they grow, say now and then to one another "Do you remember the day, long ago, when we all lay together in a cart, and the stern, white-haired, eagle-eyed old man who set us upright in our places?". Meanwhile they wave and whisper, tall and beautiful, their branches covering the little burn which I remember in my youth running through a grass slope on which stood young trees, at varying intervals.

The hand that planted them is long decayed, and the old place sleeps in its corrie with something ghostly hanging over it, even in midday.

Through the rough hills, across the moors, passing the isolated white farmhouses, winds the way that leads to it; and overhead crows caw hoarsely, and seem to say to one another when a rare traveller passes by, "There goes a man upon the road".

1911–13

Despite being a world traveller, and maintaining residences in the most fashionable parts of London, Graham demonstrated an extraordinary ear for Scots dialect, and a knowledge of its folk etymology. Observant readers, however, will have already become aware of his repetitions: owls and crows frequently 'fabulate', 'the Moss' was once a sea, 'flauchtered feals' adorn many a roof and dyke, 'mist' makes an appearance in almost every sketch, sometimes several times, the fairies are increasingly present, and suddenly, for no apparent reason, the mood is broken by some Latin American reference. His themes, too, are becoming repetitive – a general feeling of loss and decay, and of nobler souls and worthy traditions, destroyed by 'the great drabness of prosperity which overspreads the world'. Nevertheless, Garnett believed that despite his occasional discords and lack of inventiveness, there was a central unity of purpose and expression:

> Everyday, commonplace, exceptional, or vanishing human figures, the Gaucho on the plains, mistress Campbell in Gart-na-Cloich, Heather Jock, or the Bristol skipper,[676] all remote from each other, all part of the great ridiculous common Human Family! [...] that a volume of such Sketches lives *through its very diversity*, (& through the author's strong Central view) a really connected harmonious picture of life – the *sketches fall into harmony* & form an artistic whole. The wider the range, the more powerful artistically does the volume become – with each fresh atmosphere the reader yields more & more to the eyes that saw, to the spirit that interpreted.[677]

For a writer who wrote almost entirely from life, and from his own experiences, finding the inspiration for this next tale has been challenging. However, by mentioning double eagles, he may have been giving a clue to the building that inspired it.

The only Scottish noble family to use a double eagle crest was Dunlop, and Dunlop Castle, near Stewarton in East Ayrshire, with its 'pepperpot' turrets perfectly fits architecturally his elvish castle. Moreover, Graham had a link to this location as it was the home of one of his great-uncles, Thomas Dunlop Douglas Cunninghame Graham of Dunlop (1817–84). Yet, its park does not fit the description in the tale, being very similar to that of another house with which Graham was well acquainted, Culcreuch Castle, home of another elderly relative, Alexander Speirs, whom we have now met twice before.

---

[676] Cunninghame Graham, 'Bristol Fashion', *Saturday Review*, 5 February 1898.
[677] Garnett, letter to Graham, 19–24 May 1898. Ibid., p. 212.

It seems likely that Graham created a composite of the two places with the imaginary adornment of eagles. Moreover, great-uncle Thomas, a life-long bachelor, who lived alone at Dunlop with a housekeeper, might have been the original model for the laird, though he was not a sailor and died peacefully in his bed. Perhaps, inspired by its architecture, it required a suitably Gothic occupant and ending, with both house and laird as conflated examples of 'the old Scotland which has sunk below the waves of Time'.

CAISTEAL-NA-SITHAN

The Saturday Review, 15 April 1911, pp. 454–6.
Anthologised in *Charity* (London: Duckworth, 1912), pp. 81–93.

IT was indeed a castle of elves. Over all, hung an air of melancholy. From the deserted lodge, behind the high, beech hedge, which shut the place off from the lake, the avenue led through a sea of billowy mounds, on which trees grew as thickly as in the tropics, some dead and some decaying, some broken off by storms and left to die or live just as they chose.

Moss had spread like a carpet over the deeply rutted road.

Here and there by its sides stood foreign shrubs, some of them growing rankly, and others which had died years ago, standing up dry and sere, inside their iron cages, as a dead body in a life-belt floats upon the sea. The bracken met the lower branches of the trees and formed a screen, through which rabbits had made their runs, like little railway tunnels.

They fed upon the mossy grass outside, retreating slowly when they were alarmed, conscious they were at home, and that a passer-by was an intruder into their domain. Where the trees fell, they lay and rotted, covered with lichens and with a growth of ferns that sprang from the dead bark.

The neglected woods seemed to have bred a strange and hostile air. Instinctively one looked around, as if some power of nature, which cultivation kills, was still unchecked, had just declared war upon mankind, and was about to open its attack.

The passing of a roe through the deep underwood, a passage ordinarily so fairy-like and light, there, sounded ominous, and the sharp cracking of a decaying twig under its flying feet, or the soft rustling of its body through the ferns, sent a thrill through the listener, as if some monstrous creature of a dream was going to appear.

Even in summer everything seemed dank, and in the peaty soil the water oozed beneath the footsteps, making the ground seem treacherous and false.

Sometimes at sunset, when the red gleam fell on the tops of oaks, turned all the bracken fiery, and lighted up the overhanging hills, which peeped above the tops of the high trees, the air of menace was dispelled and a breath of the outer world brought back security. When the last gleams had vanished, and a cold, chilly air, especially before an autumn frost, crept through the brakes and stirred the frozen tufts of bulrushes in the black, awful-looking ponds, fringed with dark rhododendrons, and set about upon one side with towering spruce firs, a panic seemed to creep into the soul.

The thick white mists that rose up from the pool hung in the trees, and seemed as if they were alive, so stealthily they crept about the branches, and twined like serpents, twisting and writhing in the air.

Owls floated like gigantic moths across the avenue, or sat and called to one another in the recesses of the woods. All was so silent and so still, you seemed to feel the waves of sound that floated from their call, just as one hears the whirring of an old clock before it strikes the bell. In the low park beyond the wood, through which the avenue led to the house, the dun or creamy coloured Highland cattle slept upon the hillocks, to shun the draughts of night. A chilly damp rose from the old bog-land, long since reclaimed, but showing black and peaty where moles had made their hills, which dotted the sour grass at intervals, and in the moonlight looked like animals asleep. A great moss ditch cut the low park in two, and in it the black, frozen water seemed like a stream of pitch. Birches and stunted oaks were set about the fields, their old, gnarled roots laid bare by winter rains, and by the stamping of the cattle in the summer, when they stood underneath the trees to shelter from the flies. Through the long, limb-like roots, rabbits had burrowed, and here and there a heavy stone was left, stuck in the crevices, looking like some lost weapon of the Stone Age or prehistoric club.

Just where the deep moss ditch crossed underneath the road, a high, iron, double gate barred off the avenue.

Beyond it stretched a gloomy road, winding between dark trees. At night, when you rode through it, your horse snorting occasionally when rabbits ran across the path, or birds stirred in the trees, it felt as if you were a thousand miles from help. In front, the dark road wound, as it seemed, interminably, through overhanging trees. Between you and the world was the half-mile or so of mysterious woods, and the black, sullen ponds.

At last, passing another gate, it led up to a shrubbery. A mossy burn fed a neglected duck-pond, upon whose water floated feathers, and round whose sides grew tufts of pampas grass. Tall bushes of wygelia [sic] and syringa, dead at the sides, but vigorous in the middle, with flowering currants, andromeda and rank-growing thickets of guelder-rose and dogwood, concealed the house from view.

The rabbit netting, nailed to the fence of the park, was broken here and there, and billowed like a sail. Through it the rabbits entered as they pleased, burrowing beneath the bushes, and leaving trails which led up to the lawn. Enormous beaches, and a sycamore or two, growing like cabbages, showed that at one time the neglected policies had been well cared for, and the decayed and mouldering rustic seats, set about here and there, recalled the time when children played upon the lawn, whilst nurses sat and watched them underneath the trees. The house itself, high and steep-roofed, with pepper boxes at the angles, and a wide flight of steps, upon whose parapet two great iron eagles, that once had been painted in the proper colours of the coat of arms of which they formed the crest, was desolate and drear. The rough-cast plaster, which at one time had covered all the walls, had fallen in patches here and there, leaving great blotches that looked like maps, upon its sides.

Right opposite the door, a roundel of rank grass, once closely shaven, but now rank and ill-tended, lay like an island in the road. Two whinstone posts, with eight-shaped irons at their sides, for hitching horses to in times gone by, just raised their heads above the turf.

The house door, left ajar, but yet made fast against the world by a confining chain, with the bolt running in a tube, gave just the touch of human interest required to accentuate the melancholy of the forlorn abode.

As one peeped through into the hall, covered with a well-worn oilcloth, and marked the absence of sticks, hats, umbrellas, and all that goes to give a hall a look of being the introduction to a comfortable home, one felt the owner was a solitary man, who in the summer evenings, when the owls hooted faintly in the recesses of the woods and swallows hawked at flies across the lawn, sat on the parapet of the tall flight of broken steps, between his iron eagles, and meditated on what might have been, had things gone differently.

Beyond the hall few ever penetrated, for an old woman, holding the door fast in her hand, used to peep out and answer, "The laird is oot", and then when the chance visitor had turned away disconsolate, flatten her nose against the window and watch him stumble down the road. The great, old Scottish stable, built around a courtyard, with the decaying clock upon its tower, one hand long lost, the other pointing eternally to twelve, stood, buried in the trees, whose branches swept the slates, showering them down upon the grass in gales, and dropping ceaselessly in rain, till a green lichen grew just underneath the drip.

Most of the doors had gone, and those that still fought on against the rain and wind were kept in place by pieces of coarse leather, roughly nailed on the jambs. Upon the wooden sheathing of the pump, hay seed had sprouted, giving a rank crop of grass, which in its turn had died, and hung all mildewed and with small drops of moisture oozing from the stems.

Such was the place, one of the last examples of the old Scotland which has sunk below the waves of Time. Perhaps not an example to be followed, but yet to be observed, remembered, even regretted in the great drabness of prosperity which overspreads the world.

Few people ever trod the avenue, and even tramps but rarely camped in the deserted woods, though fallen trees were plentiful, and none would have been wiser if they had stayed a week. The owner, an old sailor who had inherited the place in middle life, had by degrees become a recluse that sometimes weeks would pass without his being seen. Shut off from all the world, he lived with an old housekeeper, as it were in a wilderness, and if by chance he met a stranger on the road would dive behind the bushes to escape, like a wild animal. Now and then far-off relations would come down to shoot, stopping at some hotel, and now and then a neighbour would drive over, always to be received by the old housekeeper with the same formula, "The laird is oot".

Occasionally he left the country and went abroad, but always to some place near the seaside, where he would pass long hours looking at ships, though without making any friends. Lübeck and Kiel, Riga or Genoa were his favourite haunts, and those who met him at any of those ports used to report having seen him, dressed in his blue serge suit, and with the air of being the one man left in a depopulated world, in the same way that captains jot down in their log, "in such a latitude, in the first dog watch, passed a derelict".

By degrees his visits to far-off ports grew rarer, and at last he seldom passed the gates of his neglected grounds, except occasionally on Sunday, when he attended church, reserved and silent, speaking to none, but yet a little critical, after the fashion of a man who had read prayers on board his ship, and therefore should know something of the way in which a service ought to be carried on.

On these occasions he would stand a little in the churchyard, looking intently at a sort of pen, surrounded by a broken iron railing, in which his ancestors reposed.

Whether his thoughts ran on the unstability [sic] of life, or if he only tried to make a calculation of the probable expense he would incur if he embarked upon repairs, was never known to anyone, although some said he thought of neither, but merely leaned against the rails to pass the time until the congregation had dispersed, and left him free to set off home again.

Everyone speculated on his death, some saying that it would occur some day when he was quite alone, out in the woods, and others that he would be found dead in his chair, with the Pacific Pilot open in his hand. Not a bad book for an old sailor to have consulted, when just about to weigh his anchor; but as it happened he had to make his landfall, unassisted and alone.

A bitter frost, intense and black, had bound the district, congealing the dark waters of the lake into a sheet of glass. Trees groaned and cracked, and in the silent woods a shudder seemed to run through the gaunt trees as if they suffered from the cold. Crows winged their way, looking like notes of music on an old page of parchment, across the leaden sky.

High in the air passed strings of wild geese, and in the stillness of the frost their melancholy cry was heard, till they were almost out of sight.

All nature seemed engaged in a stern fight for life, with some calamity which had attacked it unawares. The little streams stood still to watch the progress of the battle, fast in their bonds of ice.

Somehow or other, after the fashion that in Africa news travels always a day or two ahead of the traveller, it got about the countryside the laird was missing from his home. As, in the little inn, the constable, "the post", one or two farmers, and the innkeeper were talking of the report, the housekeeper was seen hobbling along the road. Coughing and wheezing, she averred she "couldna bide alane, up in yon awfu' house". The laird, it seemed, upon the evening of the commencement of the frost, had gone out, as was usual, just before tea-time, but never had come back. She had waited for two days, setting his meals upon the table at the stated hours, and at night putting out a lantern at the front door to guide him to the house. A day and night had broken down her courage, and given her the strength to find her way alone through the deserted avenue, for, as she said, "If she had passed anither nicht alang wi' all they bogles and they howlets, she would have gone fair gyte".[678]

All search was useless. The woods and moors guarded their secret, and had not chance revealed it, the disappearance of the laird would have been put down as the last eccentricity of an eccentric life.

Fate was not willing that the laird's last resting-place should not be known, for as some boys were skating on one of the black ponds

---

[678] Scots: 'If she had passed another night with all those ghosts and owlets, she would have gone quite mad'.

they saw what they took for birds' feathers, frozen in the ice. When they came home, trembling and pale, they said the feathers turned out to be the hair of a man's head, and that below the ice they had seen something that looked just like a muckle fish.

At once the sparse inhabitants of the wild district proceeded to the place, entering the sacred grounds from which they had been debarred for years. Their lanterns, glimmering like glow-worms over the dark pond, and shedding a fantastic light on the black ice, outlining every branch upon the leafless trees, and playing on the clumps of rhododendrons on the bank, gave a strange air of unreality to the whole scene.

One of the boys pointed out the spot, and as the ice was frozen so intensely, on a clear, windless night, they saw beneath it the laird's body, in the same way that you can see a fish which has been taken by the frost.

When they had cut it out, framed in a square of ice, it looked so life-like, laid upon the bank, in the dim, quavering light of the horn lanterns, that those who saw it always used to say, "It was the first time that they had a richt sight of the laird, and he had been a bonny man".

* * * * *

This is another border-crossing tale of hybrid cultures, describing Argentinian families whose ancestors had left Scotland after the 1745 Jacobite Rebellion (which seems unlikely). After four generations, they still clung to the traditions of their past – a little Gaelic, and of course, inevitably, 'a belief in the fairies and the second sight still lingered in men's minds, with many a superstition more consonant with mountains and with mists, than the keen atmosphere and the material life of the wild southern plains'.

Here was a beautiful rendering of Graham's abiding interest in the past intruding into the present through the transmission of values and tradition, so that the past is kept alive.

SAN ANDRÉS

The English Review, July 1911, pp. 602–9.
Anthologised in *Charity* (London: Duckworth, 1912), pp. 116–32.

SOMEONE or other has said the dead have a being of their own, as we confess by saying such a one is dead, just as we say he is alive.

The author of the saying seems to have felt the dead had feelings and were not merely essences purified, quite separate and unapproachable by us. Few wish to see, even to think about, their dead "crowned with an aureole." We want them just as they were, just as we knew them, in their life. The rest is vanity, vanity of vanities,[679] and all the creeds are impotent to help. At best they are an anæsthetic, such as curare, which holds the suffering animal paralysed, so that the operator may not feel the pain that it endures or get his hands scratched. So we grieve on, watching the trees turn red and yellow in the fall, blossom again in spring, and be alive with bees in the summer, in winter swaying and cracking in the wind.

This is because we never really feel the dead have a distinct and real being of their own. In olden times, in Scotland, people thought differently, and it was held that too much grieving for the dead vexed them and broke their rest.

I remember once coming long years ago to an outlying settlement in the province of Buenos Aires, where all the people came, I think, from Inverness-shire; but, anyhow, once on a time they had been Scotch. Their names were Highland, but were pronounced by those who bore them after the Spanish way, as Camerón, and McIntryré, McLeán, Fergusón, and others, which they had altered in the current of their speech, so as to be unrecognisable except to those who spoke the language and knew the names under their proper forms.

None of these Scoto-Argentines spoke English, although some knew a few words of Gaelic, which I imagine they pronounced as badly as their names.

Four generations – for most of them had left their glens after Culloden – had wrought strange changes in the type. They all were dark, tall, sinewy men, riders before the Lord, and celebrated in the district where they lived as being "muy gaucho" – that is, adroit with bolas and with lasso, just as the Arabs say a man, is a right Arab, when they commend his skill in horsemanship. Having left Scotland after the Forty-Five,[680] most of their forebears had been Catholics, and their descendants naturally belonged to the same faith, though as there was no church in all their settlement, I fancy most of them believed rather in meat cooked in the hide and a good glass of Caña[681] or Carlón[682] than dogmas of their creed.

Horses stood nodding in the sun before the door of every house.

Packs of gaunt, yellow dogs slumbered, with one eye open, in the shade.

---

[679] A biblical allusion to Ecclesiastes 1:2
[680] The Jacobite rebellion of 1745, which ended with the Battle of Culloden.
[681] Caña Argentina (or Aguardiente de Caña) = a local rum.
[682] Carlón, a rough red wine.

The bones of the last cow killed lay in the little plaza of the settlement, and bullock-carts, with cumbrous high wheels and thatched like cottages, were left as islands here and there in the great sea of grass that surged up to the houses, without a garden or cultivated field to break in its billowing.

Two little stores, in which were piled up hides and sacks of wool, supplied the place with the few outside luxuries the people used, as sardines, Brazilian cigarettes, figs, raisins, bags of hard biscuits, sugar, red wine from Catalonia, and Caña from Brazil.[683]

Climate had proved a stronger force than race, and for the most part the descendants of the Gael were almost indistinguishable in looks from all the other dwellers on the plains. They themselves did not think so, and talked about their neighbours with fine scorn as "natives," and were paid back in kind by them with the nickname of "Protestantes," a most unjust reproach to the descendants of the men who lost their all for their old kings and faith.[684]

Protestants they certainly were not, nor for that matter very Catholic, for, as a general rule, people who dwell on plains, far from the world, have less religion than those who live in hills. Still, in the settlement of San Andrés – for the first settlers had called it after the patron saint of their old home – some of their racial traits still lingered fitfully. Born in a country where neither sweet religion nor her sister superstition ever had much influence upon the people (who ever saw a gaucho either religious or the least superstitious?), in San Andrés a belief in fairies and the second-sight still lingered in men's minds, with many a superstition more consonant with mountains and with mists, than the keen atmosphere and the material life of the wild southern plains.

Unlike the Gauchos and the Arabs, who bury, as it seems, in the most open place they can find, leaving the dead, as it were, always with the living, as if they thought the pressure of a passing foot somehow brought consolation to those lying beneath the ground, these Protestants railed off their little cemetery with a high fence of ñandubay.[685] The untrimmed posts stuck up knotty and gnarled just as they do in a corral, but all the graves had head and foot stones, mostly of hard and undecaying wood, giving an air as of a graveyard in Lochaber[686] by some deserted strath.

---

[683] Brazilian caña differs from the Argentinian in that it is made from the juice of the sugar cane instead of from molasses.

[684] The majority of the Highlanders involved in the Jacobite rebellions were nominally Protestant, although of the Episcopalian creed.

[685] A South American deciduous tree of the mimosa family, with very hard and durable reddish wood.

[686] A Scottish Highland region in south-west Inverness-shire.

There, "Anastasio McIntyre, killed by the Indians," rested in peace. "May God have mercy on him."

A little further on, "Cruz Camerón, assassinated by his friends," expected glory through the intermediation of the saints. "Passers-by, pray for him."

Amparo, widow of Rodrigo Chisholm, lost at sea, had reared a monument in stone, brought from the capital, on which was cut a schooner foundering, with a man praying on the poop. Her pious faith in his salvation and a due sense of local colour showed themselves in a few lines of verse in which the poet, whilst deploring the sad fate of Roderick, cut off so far away from wife and family, was confident that heaven was just as close at sea as on "tierra firme," and that the Lord High Admiral Christ watched over seafarers.

Such was the village, or, as the Gauchos used to say, the "pago",[687] for, for a league or two on every side, these Scoto-Argentines were the chief settlers upon the land. Indians occasionally harried their flocks and herds, and burned out-lying ranches, but nowhere found stouter resistance than from the dwellers in San Andrés, so that, as a general rule, they used to leave the settlement alone.

The patriarchal manners which their forefathers had brought from the Highlands, joined to the curious old-fashioned customs common in those days in Buenos Aires, had formed a race apart, in which Latin materialism strove with the Celtic fervour, and neither gained the day.

A grave sententiousness marked all the older men, whose speech was an amalgam of strange proverbs, drawn from their daily lives. They used to pass their evenings playing the guitar and improvising couplets, whilst the square bottle of trade gin went round, each sipping from the same glass and passing it along. "Never go to a house to ask for a fresh horse when you see that dogs are thin," one tall, red-bearded man would say, to which his fellow answered, "Arms are necessary, but no one can tell when." "A scabby calf lives all the winter and dies when spring comes in," and "When a poor man has a spree something is sure to turn out wrong with him," were specimens of their wit and humour, not much inferior, after all, to those recorded of much greater men than they in serious histories.

Sheep-shearings and cattle-markings were their festivities, and now and then, on their best horses, loaded down with plate, they tilted at the ring.[688] The grassy pampa, stretching like the sea on every side of them, but broken as with islands here and there by

---

[687] Latin: *pagus* = country, the traditional name given in South America to relatively small territories.

[688] Competing on horseback, spear or pole in hand, to carry off a suspended hoop or ring.

white estancia[689] houses set in their ring of peach groves, limited their horizon, just as a sailor's view is limited on board a ship to a scant league or two.

In that horizon all of them were born, and most of them had never passed outside of it, except some few who upon rare occasions had gone to Buenos Aires with a troop of cattle, and had returned to talk about its wonders for the remainder of their lives.

Still none of them were boors, but had the natural good manners both of the Gaucho and the Highlander. The forms of courtesy were long and ceremonious, and when friends met upon the plain, reining their horses in to show how sharply they were bitted, they used to ask minutely after each other's' health and of the state in which each member of the family found himself, and then, with an inquiry after a strayed colt, touching their stiff-brimmed hats with a brown, weather-beaten finger, just slack their reigns a little, and separate, each going at a slow canter through the grass, the wind blowing their ponchos out like sails, and making their long hair wave about like a great bunch of water-weeds moved by the current of a stream.

This was the settlement which no doubt long ago has turned into a town, with modern improvements, electric lights and drains, beggars and churches; and the few settlers of the older type have retired into the wilder districts or become millionaires by the increasing value of their lands.

There, though, the older spirit ruled, and the men who spoke Gaelic, or even those whose fathers had once spoken what they called "el Gaelico," were looked upon as the interpreters of the spirit of the race. Of these Don Alejandro Chisholm was the chief.

Tall and grey-bearded, he had the look of shagginess which marks the Highlander. Though he knew but a few words himself, his father used to croon old Gaelic songs, and all his childhood had been passed listening to the traditions which his people treasured in their minds. Somehow they looked upon them as their chief distinction, and seemed to feel by their possession that they were in some way or another superior to the rest of those with whom they lived, the men who passed their lives caring for nothing but the present, whilst they lived in the past.

Don Alejandro used to say: "A native has very little soul. When a friend dies he never thinks of him again, and still less sees him. We, on the other hand, have glimpses now and then of those who leave us, but whose spirits hover about the places they love."

---

[689] Spanish: ranches.

His daughter, Saturnina, a tall, dark girl, willowy and slight, had married Anacleto, her first cousin, and thus, as her father, with true Highland pride in lineage, used to observe, had never changed her name. Her husband, Anacleto, was an amalgam of the Scot and the Argentine. Speaking no word of English or of Gaelic, he yet esteemed himself as half a foreigner, although he was Gaucho to the core. He and his wife were married in a church, a circumstance which marked them out, and people speaking of them used to say they were the couple "married in Latin," which gave them much consideration and a sort of rank. Whether because of the unusual sanctity that blessed their union, from accident or natural causes, their marriage was so happy that throughout the settlement people spoke of a happy couple as being as well mated as "el matrimonio Chisholm," and looked on them with pride, as being somehow on a different plane from those who perhaps were married by some ambulatory priest after their children had been born.

They had no children, and perhaps on that account were more attached to one another than are those couples whose love is, as it were, dispersed, having more objects on which to spend itself.

There seemed to grow between them that curious identity of mind which comes to all women and all men who have lived long together, but in their case was so much marked that they divined beforehand each other's thoughts, and acted on them almost without words. On the long journeys which the husband took with cattle his wife used to declare she always knew all he was thinking of, and he, on his return, either to please her or because she had guessed right, always confirmed her words. The idea of death sometimes must have presented itself before their minds, but, like most happy people, probably only as a calamity, which might befall humanity in general, but could not touch themselves.

Don Alejandro, who in his long life had seen misfortunes, and was the last of all his race except his daughter, used to look sadly on them, and, shaking his head, say with a sigh; "God grant that I may not live to see the death of either of them. The children, though it is a bad comparison, Lord pardon me for likening Christians to brute beasts, remind me of two horses that I had that followed one another. One broke its neck out ostrich hunting, and the other never seemed right and pined in misery after its friend had died."

The inevitable came, when Anacleto was away, far on the southern frontier, out on the boleada,[690] beyond the Naposta.[691]

---

[690] Hunting with the bolas.
[691] Arroyo Naposta = a stream in Bahía Blanc.

Never before had he been so long separated from his wife. Three months had passed, and now, as he drew close to San Andrés, riding a tired horse, brown, dirty, and with the oppression that the north wind often brings in Buenos Aires weighing upon his mind, the well-known objects seemed to rise out of the plain, just as an island seems to rise out of the sea, although the men on board the ship know it is there, and have been laying off their course to make it, since the beginning of their voyage. He saw the peach montés[692] which he had known from childhood circling his neighbours' farms. He crossed the sluggish, muddy stream, bordered with dark, green sarandis, hitting the pass with the unerring accuracy of the man born upon the plains. Feeling his horse's mouth, he touched him with the spur, and struck into a lope. Passing the little inequalities of the ground, the swells and billows which the dwellers on the pampa know as lomas[693] or cuchillas,[694] and recollect as well as any Scotchmen recollect their hills, though they are almost imperceptible to strangers, he saw the well-remembered old ombú tree of the settlement. Eyes just as keen as were his own had seen him, too, and to his great surprise a horseman galloped out to meet him, and as he came a little nearer he recognised the well-known piebald of that Don Alejandro cherished as the apple of his eye. Sitting upright in the saddle, and swaying lightly, as if he had been five and twenty, to every movement of his horse, Don Alejandro rapidly drew near. Just about twenty yards from where his son-in-law was labouring along on his tired horse he checked the piebald, and stopped as if instantly turned to stone. "Welcome, my son," he said. "Your horse looks tired, but he will take you home soon enough."

The words froze on Anacleto's lips when he looked at the old man's countenance and saw how white and drawn he had become.

"Tell me at once!" he cried; "I see the tidings in your face of evil augury."

When they had drawn a little nearer Don Alejandro grasped his hand, and, after looking at the horse his son-in-law bestrode, pointed towards the little cemetery and said: "Let us go there, my son ... If we go slowly your horse can carry you."

Dismounting at the gate, they tied their horses to a post, and, entering, the old man led the traveller up to a little mound.

"Underneath this our treasure lies," he murmured gravely, and with the air of one who has got done with tears after long weeks of grief.

---

[692] Wild peach trees.
[693] Spanish: Hillocks.
[694] Spanish: Long sloping pieces of land.

They stood and gazed, holding each other's hands, until Don Alejandro said: "Weep, son, for God has given tears for the soul's health ... Laughter and tears are the two things that lift us higher than the beasts."

His son-in-law threw himself on the grave, driving his fingers into the black soil, and lay there tired, dirty, and unkempt, like a great wounded bird.

At last he felt a hand upon his shoulder, and heard a voice, which seemed to come from a great distance, saying: "Come, let us go now, and let our horses loose. In half an hour it will be night."

When they had reached their home they both unsaddled. The piebald, with a neigh, bounded away into the night, but Anacleto's horse stood for a moment, and then lay down and rolled, and, rising shook the dust out of his coat, just as a water-dog shakes himself after a long swim.

"He will do well," Don Alejandro said. "When a horse rolls like that after a journey it is a sign that he is strong."

Over the mate,[695] seated round the fire, on the low, solid wooden benches men used to use out on the pampa, the wanderer heard of how his wife had died.

Next day he passed seated upon her grave, silent and stupefied with grief.

Then for a day or two he lounged about, going down to the cemetery at intervals and looking through the posts like some wild animal.

Weeks passed, and he still roamed about, speaking to no one, but riding off across the plains, returning always just at sundown, to tie his horse up close to the cemetery gate and stand with his head pressed against the bars looking towards the grave. At last Don Alejandro, fearing that he was going mad, as they sat at the end of a hot day, began to speak to him, saying: "It is not well to grieve too long. It is, as we may say, a selfishness. My father, who knew the older generation, those who lost everything for their religion and their king, had listened in his youth to all the lore that they brought with them from that far region where, as they say, the mist blurs everything. My father spoke 'Gaelico'" – he said the word almost with reverence – "and those who spoke it always were versed in the traditions of our race. He used to tell me that to grieve for the dead beyond due measure disturbed them in their graves, and brought

---

[695] Yerba maté = an infusion made from the leaves of *Ilex paraguariensis* and drunk from a gourd through a straw. Graham had travelled to Paraguay in 1873 where he sought opportunities in cultivating it, but instead his explorations into the interior led to the 'discovery' of abandoned Jesuit missions, which he described in his book *A Vanished Arcadia* (1901).

their spirits weeping back again. So I have dried my tears." As he said this he drew his hand across his eyes, and, looking at it, saw it was dry.

"Grieve no more, Anacleto. We cannot call her back to us alive. To pain the spirit by our selfishness, that would be cowardly."

They sat till it was almost sunset, and then Don Alejandro went down to the corral to see the animals shut in, just in the way that he had gone each evening for the last forty years.

The sun set in a glare, the hot north wind blowing as from a furnace, making the cattle droop their heads, and bringing troops of horses, with a noise like thunder, down to the water-holes.

The teru-teros,[696] flying low, like gulls upon the sea, almost unseen in the fast-coming darkness, called uncannily. The tame chaja[697] screamed harshly behind the cattle-pens.

A boy, riding upon a sheepskin, drove the tame horses into the corral.

The sheep were folded, and in the dark leaves of the old ombú beside the door the fire-flies glistened, and from the pampa rose the acrid smell that the first freshness of the evening draws from the heated ground. Coming out of the rancho Anacleto looked across the plain.

His eyes were full of tears, but with a gulp he choked them, and muttering to himself, "No, it would be cowardly to break her rest, Don Alejandro says so; he had it from his father, who spoke Gaelico," he slowly lit a cigarette, and in the last rays of the light, watched the smoke curl up in the air, blue and impalpable.

* * * * *

The following piece, which recounts Graham's last day at Gartmore House, is undoubtedly one of the most touchingly autobiographical of his Scottish sketches. Written some twelve years after his departure, he seems to have found something of the personal depth that Garnett had demanded in 1905, and his sense of loss and guilt is evident, despite the passage of time and his artistic glosses. Whenever he returned to Menteith, Graham took various routes to avoid passing through Gartmore; even his funeral cortège went via Arnprior to by-pass his old home.

---

[696] *Vanellus chilensis lampronotus,* a bird common to all the central and northern plains of Argentina, usually found near rivers and lagoons.
[697] *Chauna Torquata,* a large bird unique to South America, which is related to swans and geese, and considered a symbol of the pampas.

Figure 15 Gartmore House, 1898.

A BRAW DAY

The English Review, November 1911, pp. 609–14.
Anthologised in *Charity* (London: Duckworth, 1912), pp. 133–45.

Never before, in the long years that had passed in the old place, had it appeared so much a part of his whole being, as on the day on which he signed the deed of sale.

Times had been bad for years, and a great load of debt had made the fight a foregone ending from the first. Still he felt like a murderer, as judges well may feel when they pronounce death sentences. Perhaps they feel it more than the prisoner, for things we do through fate, and by the virtue of circumstances that hedge our lives about with chains, often affect us more than actions which we perform impelled by no one but ourselves.

The long, white Georgian House, with its two flanking wings, set in its wide expanse of gravel, which, like a sea, flowed to a grassy, rising slope, looked dignified and sad. An air, as of belonging to a family of fallen fortunes, hung about the place. The long, dark avenue of beeches, underneath one of which stood the old gallows stone, looked as if no one ever used it, and on its sides the grassy edges had long ago all turned to moss, a moss so thick and velvety, you might have swept it with a broom.

The beech mast crackled underneath your feet as you passed up the natural cathedral aisle, and on the tops of the old trees the wind played dirges in the cold autumn nights, and murmured softly in the glad season "when the shaws are green."

The formal terraces were roughly mown and honeycombed by rabbits, the whinstone steps were grown with moss, and here and there were forced apart by a strong growing fern that pushed out to the light.

The seats about the garden were all blistered with sun and rain, and the old-fashioned coach-roofed greenhouse looked like a refrigerator, with its panes frosted by the damp. Under the arch, which led into the stable yard, stood two dilapidated dog kennels, disused, but with some links of rusty chain still hanging to them, as if they waited for the return of shadowy dogs, dead years ago.

The cedars on the slope below the terraces stretched out their long and human-looking branches, as they were fingers seeking to restrain and hold those whom they knew and loved.

All was serene and beautiful, with the enthralling beauty of decay. The fences were unmended, and slagging wires in places had been dragged by cattle into the middle of the fields; most of the gates were off their hinges, and weeds had covered up the gravel of the walks.

Nettles grew rankly in the grass, and clumps of dock with woody stems and feathery heads, stood up like bulrushes about the edges of a pond. Even at noonday, a light mist still clung about the lower fields below the house, marking out clearly where old "peat hags" had been reclaimed.

Such was the place at noonday; melancholy as regards the lack of care that want of means had brought about; but bright and sunny as it lay facing to the south, sheltered by groups of secular sycamores and beech.

At night a feeling as if one had been marooned upon some island, far away from men, grew on the inmates of the house.

Owls fabulated[698] from the tree tops, their long, quavering call seeming to jar the air and make it quiver, so still was everything.

The roes' metallic belling sounded below the windows, and the sharp chirping of the rabbits never ceased during summer nights, as they played in the grass.

When the long shadows, in the moonlight, crept across the lawn, it seemed as if they beckoned to the shadows of the dead, in the old eerie house. Those who had gone before had set their seal so firmly upon everything, planting the trees, and adding here a wing and there a staircase, that those who now possessed the house, dwelt in it, as it were, by the permission of the dead.

---

[698] Told invented stories.

One day remained to him whose ancestors had built the house; who had lived in the old ruined castle, in the grounds, and who had fought, and plundered, rugged and reived[699] after the fashion of their kind. All had been done that falls to a man's lot to do at such a time. The house stood gaunt and empty. By degrees, the familiar objects that time and sentiment make almost sacred and as if portions of ourselves, had been packed up, and on the walls, the pictures taken down, had left blank spaces that recalled each one, as perfectly as if it had been there.

Steps sounded hollow, in the emptiness and desolation on the stairs, and bits of straw and marks of hob-nailed boots showed where the workmen had been busy at their task.

Here and there marks of paint and varnish on a door showed where a heavy piece of furniture had touched in passing, as sometimes after a funeral you see the dent made by the coffin in the plaster of the passage, as it was carried to the heetse.[700]

A desolating smell of straw was everywhere. It permeated everything, even to the food, which an old servant cooked in the great, ungarnished kitchen, just as a tramp might cook his victuals at the corner of a road.

The polished staircase, which from their childhood had been a kind of fetish to the children of the house, shielded from vulgar footsteps by a thick drugget[701] and a protecting strip of Holland,[702] but bleached snowy white, was now all scratched and dirtied, as if it were no better than the steps which led to the back-yard.

The owner and his wife, after their years of struggle, had felt at first as if their ship had got into a port; and then as days went by, and by degrees the house which they had cared for more than their own lives, grew empty and more empty, till it was left a shell, now found their port had vanished, and they were left without an anchorage.

Still, there was one more day to pass. What then to do with it? The house was empty, the few old servants that remained, tearful and wandering to and fro, pleased to be idle and yet not knowing what to do with unaccustomed leisure, jostled each other on the stairs.

The horses had all been sold, all but one little old black pony; the dogs all sent away to friends.

Standing at the hall doorway, looking out on the sweep of gravel all cut up by carts, the owners stood a little while, dazed and not able

---

[699] Rustled cattle.
[700] Heese (*sic*) = hearse
[701] A coarse woollen fabric, felted or woven.
[702] The Holland cloth, or simply 'Holland' is a plain woven or dull-finish linen used as furniture covering.

to take in that twenty years had flown. It seemed but yesterday that they had driven up to the same door, young, full of expectation and of hope.

Now they were middle-aged and grey. The fight had gone against them; but still they had the recollection of the struggle, for all except the baser sort of men fight not to win, but simply for the fight.

Some call it duty, but the fight's the thing, for those who strive to win, become self-impressed, and that way lies the road to commonplace. Verily, they have their reward; but the reward soon overwhelms them, whilst the true fighters still fight on, with sinews unrelaxed.

At last, after having looked about in vain for sticks, but without finding one, for they had all been packed or given away as keepsakes, they walked out to the sundial in the great gravel sweep before the door. Though they had sat and smoked upon its steps a thousand times, watching the squirrels play at noon, the bats flit past at sundown, it seemed new to them, and strange. With interest they saw that it was half-past three in China, eight in the evening in New Orleans, and midnight in La Paz.

Somehow it seemed that they had never seen all this before, and that in future, time would be all the same the whole world over, or at least that it would not be marked by little brazen gnomons on a weather-beaten sab of slate. The garden, with the gardeners gone, and the gate open, seemed as strange as all the rest. The flowers that they had planted, and forgotten they had planted, in the course of time had come to be considered in the same way as the old castle just outside the garden walls, as things that had existed from the beginning of the world.

Weeds choked the gravel in the lower walk, bounded by a long hedge of laurel cut into castles at due intervals. They both agreed next week they should be hoed, and then stopped, smiled, and looked away, fearing to meet each other's eyes. The sun beat on the old stone wall, ripening the magnum bonum plums, for it was in September,[703] and both thought, they will be ripe in a few days, but feared to tell each other what they thought.

The tangled, terraced beds, where once had stood old vineries, all had been planted with herbaceous plants, which, from the want of care, had grown into a jungle; but a jungle unutterably beautiful, in which the taller plants, the coreopsis, bocconias, Japanese anemones,

---

[703] The Grahams' last day at Gartmore was, in reality, the 4 December 1900, thus, the plums were an artistic gloss.

Figure 16 Graham with 'Gabrielle' at the 'moondial' of Gartmore House, 1898.

and larkspurs stood up starkly, as palm trees rear themselves out of a wilderness of dwarf palmettoes, and of grass.

Over the garden gate, marauding ivy had run across the stone on which the arms of the decaying family were cut in hard grey whinstone, with the date 1666 in high relief, flanked by a monogram.

Upon a bench, from which the view stretched over the great moss that marked the limits of an ancient sea, and out of which a wooded hill rose like an island, the only thing that broke the level plain between the garden and the distant hills, they sat and let the sun beat on them, for the last time, as it had often done during their years of struggle and of fight.

Descending through a gate, which slagged a little on its hinges, and grated on the stone lintel as it opened after a heavy push, they passed into the curious long strip of extra garden, taken in as it were by afterthought, in the old Scottish fashion, which never seemed to have enough of garden laid about a house. They bade goodbye to the long line of *arbor vitae* clipped into cones which cast their shadows on the path, so clearly that you were half inclined to lift your feet to clear them, they looked so firm and round.

The curious moondial,[704] with its niches coloured blue and red, the burial ground[705] hidden away amongst the trees, and with a long, grass walk, mossy and damp, leading up to its old grey walls, they visited but did not see, as they were so familiar, that they had become impossible to look at, but as parts and parcels of themselves.

The day seemed never ending, and in the afternoon, to pass the time, seeing a water conduit underneath a road choked up with leaves, the departing owner of the place set about working hard to clear it, and having done so, congratulated himself on a good piece of work. To bid goodbye to buildings and familiar scenes seemed natural, as life is but a long farewell, but to look for the last time on trees – trees his ancestors had planted, and by which he himself recognised the seasons, as for example by the turning yellow of the horse-chestnuts, which he saw from his bedroom windows, or the first pinkish blush upon the broken larch, whose broken top was cased in lead – that seemed a treason to them, for they had always been so faithful, putting out their leaves in the spring, standing stark and rigid in the winter and murmuring in the breeze.

The whispering amongst their branches and the melodious tinkle of a little burn that crossed the avenue, were sounds which, on that last day, pervaded all the air and filled the soul with that deep-seated feeling of amazement that looks out, hopeless and heart-rending, from the eyes of dying animals.

The interminable day came to an end at last. The sun set, red and beautiful, over a low, flat moss, and disappeared behind the hills. The owls called shrilly from the trees, and the accustomed air of ghostliness, intensified a thousandfold by solitude, pervaded all the house.

The mysterious footstep which in the course of years had grown familiar, even in winter nights, as it passed up the corridor and stopped with a loud knock on the end bedroom door, again grew terrifying as it had been on the first night that they had heard it years ago.

From out the spaces where the pictures once had hung, the well-known faces seemed to peer, but unfamiliar-looking, with an air as of reproach.

---

[704] Now located in the Cayzer family burial ground in the kirkyard of Gartmore Parish Church.

[705] The burial ground, which is still owned by the Cunninghame Graham family, is the site of the graves of Graham's father, Willie Bontine, and many of his forebears, including Nicol Graham, who built the original house and founded the village of Gartmore, and his slave owning son, Robert Graham, who is the subject of a biography written by Graham in 1925, entitled *Doughty Deeds*.

The smallest footfall sounded as loud as if it were the trampling of a horse; and candles, stuck in bottles here and there, gave a dim, flickering light, casting dark shadows on the floor.

Long did the owners gaze into the night, watching the stars come out in their familiar places. The Bear hung right across the cedars, almost due north, for it was in November,[706] Alphecca close to the horizon, the square of Pegasus quite horizontal, and Fomalhaut in the south-west, athwart the corner of the Easter Hill.

A light, white frost turned all to silver, and the lake in the east middle distance lay like a sheet of burnished silver under the moon, its islands mirrored dimly and as if floating in the air. No leaf was stirring, and as they sat around a fire of logs, talking of were-wolves, fairies, and superstitions of another land, with their old Spanish friend and servant,[707] the night wore on so rapidly that it was daylight almost, as it appeared, before the sun went down.

Short preparations serve for those about to go, and when a few old servants and retainers took their leave, and a black pony slowly took their trunks down to the station, looking forlorn in the immensity of the beech avenue, they closed the door upon their house.

Quickly the trees rushed past, the pond with its tall islands looking like ships, the giant silver firs, the castle, which they beheld as in a dream, all floated by. Just at the cross roads which led into the park, beside the gate, a man stood there waiting for them.

He carried a hedgebill, and stood there waiting, as he had waited for the past twenty years, for orders for the day.

Now, he held out his hand, opened his mouth, but said nothing, and then, looking up with the air of one well learned in weather lore, said, "Laird, it looks like a braw day."

* * * * *

'A blend of Anglo-Saxon tenderness and sentiment, which leads him to write of "fallen" women, as most people in England write about flowers.'[708]

'Christie Christison' is a brilliantly told tale, similar in style to the less-endearing 'M'Kechnie v. Scaramanga'; full of obscure nautical allusions, and rich Scottish dialogue, and although set in an exotic location, the subject behaves and talks as if he had never left Aberdeenshire.

---

[706] Graham seems to have forgotten that he had earlier written, 'for it was in September'. The phrase is omitted in later versions for consistency.

[707] Peregrina Collazo, Gabrielle's Galician maid and travelling companion.

[708] 'Book of the Month' (*Charity*), *English Review*, April 1912, p. 163.

It is literally 'pornographic', ie. it depicts prostitution,[709] but despite the strictures and prohibitions of polite society, it was a subject that Graham did not shy away from. In fact, prostitutes appeared in other works such as 'Buta' (1900), 'Un Monsieur' (1910) and 'La Alcaldesa' (1910).

Graham despised 'respectability'[710] and considered Victorian morality false, hypocritical, bourgeois and an impediment to the reordering of society, with a legal system that turned married women into mere chattels – 'every institution, economic, social, political, and religious (especially religious) is designed, or has become without designing, a means to keep women dependent on men'.[711]

As a life-long supporter of women's rights and universal suffrage, he launched his most scathing attack in 1908 in the essay quoted above, in which he argued that society marriages were no better than sacramental prostitution: 'What can be more unjust than that a man who has run his course like twenty thousand bridegrooms rolled up into one should insist on marrying what he calls "A pure girl"?'

CHRISTIE CHRISTISON

Anthologised in *Charity* (London: Duckworth, 1912), pp. 177–95.

Of all the guests that used to come to Claraz's Hotel, there was none stranger, or more interesting than Christie Christison, a weather-beaten sailor, who still spoke his native dialect of Peterhead, despite his thirty years out in the Plate.[712] He used to bring an air into the room with him of old salt fish and rum, and of cold wintry nights in the low latitudes down by the Horn.[713] This, too, though it was years since he had been to sea.

Although the world had gone so well with him, and by degrees he had become one of the biggest merchants in the place, he yet preserved

---

[709] Greek: *Porné* = prostitute.
[710] 'Respectability! I hate respectability [...] What did respectability mean? Why, when respectability shut the door of its snug villa it showed humanity out.' *Edinburgh Evening News*, 18 March 1887, p. 3.
[711] 'The Real Equality of the Sexes', *New Age*, 11 July 1908, p. 207.
[712] The area surrounding the estuary between Argentina and Uruguay, including the cities of Buenos Aires and Montevideo.
[713] Cape Horn, the southernmost headland of the *Tierra del Fuego* region of Chile.

the speech and manners of a Greenland whaler, which calling he had followed in his youth.[714]

The Arctic cold and tropic suns during the years that he had traded up and down the coast, had turned his naturally fair complexion to a mottled hue, and whisky, or the sun, had touched his nose so fiercely that it furnished a great fund of witticism amongst the other guests.

Mansel[715] said that the skipper's nose reminded him of the port light[716] of an old sugar droger,[717] and Cossart had it that no chemist's window in Montmartre had any *flacon*,[718] bottle you call him, eh? of such resplendent hue. Most of them knew he had a history, but no one ever heard him tell it, although it was well known he had come out from Peterhead in the dark ages, when Rosas[719] terrorised the Plate, in his own schooner, the *Rosebud*, and piled her up at last, somewhere on the Patagonian coast, upon a trip down to the Falkland Islands. He used to talk about his schooner as if she had been one of the finest craft afloat; but an old Yankee skipper, who had known her, swore she was a bull-nosed, round-sterned sort of oyster-mouching vessel, with an old deck-house like a town hall, straight-sided, and with a lime-juice look about her that made him tired.

Whatever were her merits or her faults, she certainly had made her skipper's fortune, or at least laid the foundation of it; for, having started as a trader, he gradually began to act, half as carrier, half as mail-boat, going to Stanley[720] every three months or so with mail and letters, and coming back with wool.

Little by little, aided by his wife, a stout, hard-featured woman from his native town, he got a little capital into his hands.

When he was on a voyage, Jean used to search about to get a cargo for his next trip, so that when the inevitable came and the old *Rosebud* ran upon the reef down at San Julian, Christie was what he called "weel-daein,"[721] and forsook the sea for good.

He settled down in Buenos Aires as a wool-broker, and by degrees altered his clothes, to the full-skirted coat of Melton cloth, with

---

[714] Peterhead had long been the centre of the Scottish fishing and whaling industries.

[715] George Mansel, a former shipmate of Graham's brother, Charles, with whom Graham had ranched in Argentina, and to whom he dedicated his anthology *Thirteen Stories*.

[716] The red running light on the left side of a ship.

[717] A long-masted boat used in the West Indies.

[718] A glass perfume bottle.

[719] Juan Manuel de Rosas (1793–1877), a brutal tyrant who was dictator of Argentina (1829–52).

[720] Port Stanley, the capital of the Falkland Islands.

[721] Scots: Well-to-do/successful.

ample side-pockets, the heather-mixture trousers, and tall white hat with a black band, that formed his uniform up to his dying day. He wore a Newgate frill[722] of beard, and a blue necktie, which made a striking contrast with his face, browned by the sun and wind, and skin like a dried piece of mare's hide, through which the colour of his northern blood shone darkly, like the red in an old-fashioned cooking apple after a touch of frost.

Except a few objurgatory phrases, he had learned no Spanish, and his own speech remained the purest dialect of Aberdeenshire – coarse, rough and racy, and double-shotted with an infinity of oaths, relics of his old whaling days, when as he used to say he started life, like a young rook, up in the crow's-nest of a bluff-bowed and broad-beamed five-hundred barrel boat, sailing from Peterhead.

Things had gone well with him, and he had taken himself as partner a fellow-countryman, one Andrew Nicolson, who had passed all his youth in Edinburgh, in an insurance office. Quiet, unassuming, and yet not without traces of that pawky humour[723] which few Scots are born entirely lacking in, he had fallen by degrees into a sort of worship of his chief, whose sallies, rough and indecent as they often were, fairly convulsed him, making him laugh until tears ran down his face, as he exclaimed, "Hear to him, man, he's awfu' rich, I'm tellin' ye."

Christie took little notice of his adoration except to say, "Andra, man, dinna expose yourself," or something of the kind.

In fact, no one could understand how two such ill-assorted men came to be friends, except perhaps because they both were Scotchmen, or because Andrew's superior education and well-brushed black clothes appealed to Christison.

He himself could not write, but knew enough to sign his name, which feat he executed with many puffings, blowings, and an occasional oath.

Still, he was shrewd in business, which he executed almost entirely by telegram, refusing to avail himself of any code, saying, "he couldna stand them; some day ye lads will get a cargo of dolls' eyes, when ye have sent for maize. Language is gude enough for me, I hae no secrets. Damn yer monkey talk."

His house at Florés was the place of call of all the ship captains who visited the port. There they would sit and drink, talking about the want of lights on such and such a coast, of skippers who had lost their ships twenty or thirty years ago, the price of whale oil, and of things that interest their kind; whilst Mrs. Christison sat knitting,

---

[722] See passim.
[723] Scots: Dry humour, sly wit.

looking as if she never in her life had moved from Peterhead, in her grey gown and woollen shawl, fastened across her breast by a brooch, with a picture of her man, "in natural colouring." Their life was homely, and differed little from what it had been in the old days when they were poor, except that now and then they took the air in an old battered carriage – which Christison had taken for a debt – looking uncomfortable and stiff, dressed in their Sunday clothes. Their want of knowledge of the language of the place kept them apart from others of their class, and Christison, although he swore by Buenos Aires, which he had seen emerge from a provincial town to a great city, yet cursed the people, calling them a "damned set of natives," which term he generally applied to all but Englishmen.

Certainly nothing was more unlike a "native" than the ex-skipper now turned merchant, in his ways, speech, and dress. Courtesy, which was innate in natives of the place, was to him not only quite superfluous, but a thing to be avoided, whilst his strange habit of devouring bread fresh from the oven, washed down with sweet champagne, gained him the name of the "Scotch Ostrich," which nickname he accepted in good part as a just tribute to his digestive powers, remarking that "the Baptist, John, ye mind, aye[724] fed on locusts and wild honey, and a strong man aye liked strong meat, all the world o'er."

In the lives of the elderly Aberdeenshire couple, few would have looked for a romantic story, for the hard-featured merchant and his quiet home-keeping wife appeared so happy and contented in their snug villa on the Florés road. No one in Buenos Aires suspected anything, and most likely Christison would have died, remembered only by his tall white hat, had he not one day chosen to tell his tale.

A fierce pampero[725] had sprung up in an hour, the sky had turned that vivid green that mark storms from the south in Buenos Aires. Whirlfire[726] kept the sky lighted till an arch had formed in the southeast, and then the storm broke, blinding and terrible, with a strange seething noise. The wind, tearing along the narrow streets, forced everyone to fly for refuge.

People on foot darted into the nearest house, and horsemen, flying like birds before the storm, sought refuge anywhere they could, their horses, slipping and sliding on the rough, paved streets, sending out showers of sparks as they stopped suddenly, just as a skater sends out a spray of ice. The deep-cut streets, with their raised pavements, soon turned to watercourses, from three to four feet deep, through which the current ran so fiercely that it was quite impossible to pass on foot.

---

[724] Scots: Always.
[725] Strong south-westerly wind coming off the vast grassy plains (pampas).
[726] Lightning.

The horsemen, galloping for shelter, passed through them with the water banking up against their horses on the stream side, though they plied the whip and spurs.

After the first hour of the tempest, when a little light began to dawn towards the south, and the peals of thunder slacken a little in intensity, men's nerves became relaxed from the over-tension that a pampero brings with it, just as if nature had been overwound, and by degrees was paying out the chain.

Storm-stayed at Claraz's sat several men, Cossart, George Mansel, one Don José Hernandez[727] and Christie Christison. Perhaps the pampero had strung up his nerves, or perhaps the desire that all men feel at times to tell what is expedient they should keep concealed, impelled him; but at any rate he launched into the story of his life, to the amazement of his friends, who never thought he either had a story to impart, or if he had that it would ever issue from his lips.

"Ye mind the *Rosebud*?" he remarked.

None of the assembled men had ever seen her, although she still was well remembered on the coast.

"Weel, weel, I mind the time she was well kent,[728] a bonny craft. Old Andrew Reid o' Buckieside, he built her back in the fifties. When he went under, he had to sell his house of Buckieside. I bought her cheap.

"It's fifteen years and mair, come Martinmas, since I piled her up ... I canna think how I managed it, knowing the bay, San Julian, ye ken, sae weel.

"It was a bit hazy, but still I thought I could get in wi' the blue pigeon[729] going.

"I mind it yet, ye see you hae to keep the rocks where they say they ganakers[730] all congregate before they die, right in a line with yon bit island.

"I heard the water shoaling as the leadsman sung out the chains, but still kept on, feeling quite sure I knew the channel, when, bang she touches, grates a little, and sticks dead fast, wi' a long shiver o' her keel. Yon rocks must have been sharp as razors, for she began to fill at once.

---

[727] Very possibly the Argentinian journalist, poet, and politician, José Rafael Hernández (1834–86), best known as the author of the epic poem of the gauchos, *Martín Fierro*, which Graham loved, and from which he often quoted.

[728] Scots: Known.

[729] The affectionate nickname for the lead attached to the sounding line to test the depth of water.

[730] Christison's mispronunciation of the word "guanaco", a savage camelid native to South America, closely related to the llama.

"No chance for any help down in San Julian Bay in those days, nothing but ane o' they *pulperías*[731] kept by a Basque, a wee bit place, wi' a ditch and bank, and a small brass cannon stuck above the gate. I got what gear I could into the boat, and started for the beach.

"Jean, myself, three o' the men, and an old Dago[732] I carried with me as an interpreter.

"The other sailormen, and a big dog we had aboard, got into the other boat, and we all came ashore. Luckily it was calm, and the old *Rosebud* had not struck above two or three hundred yards from land. Man, San Julian was a dreich[733] place in they days, naething but the bit fortified *pulperia* I was tellin' ye aboot. The owner, old Don Augusty, a Basque, ye ken, just ca'ed his place the 'Rose of the South.' He micht as well have called it the Rose of Sharon. Deil[734] a rose for miles, or any other sort of flower.

"Well, men, the next day it just began to blow, and in a day or two knockit the old Rosebud fair to matchwood. Jean, she grat sair[735] to see her gae to bits, and I cursit a while, though I felt like greetin'[736] too, I'm tellin' ye. There we were sort o' marooned, a' the lot of us, without a chance of getting off maybe for months; for in these days devil a ship but an odd whaler now and then ever came nigh the place. By a special mercy Yanquetruz's band of they Pehuelches[737] happened to come to trade.

"Quiet enough folk yon Indians, and Yanquetruz himself had been brocht up in Buenos Aires in a mission school.

"Man, a braw fellow! Six foot six at least, and sat his horse just like a picture. We bought horses from him, and got a man to guide us up to the Welsh settlement at Chubut,[738] a hundred leagues away.

"Richt gude beasts they gave us, and we got through fine, though I almost thocht I had lost Jean.

"Yanquetruz spoke English pretty well, Spanish of course, and as I tellt ye, he was a bonny man.

---

[731] A small shop cum-bar-cum-trading post, where everyday items are sold, mainly groceries.

[732] A derogatory nickname for a Spaniard.

[733] See passim.

[734] Scots: Devil (meaning 'not').

[735] Scots: Wept bitterly.

[736] Scots: Crying.

[737] Probably José María Bulnes Yanquetruz, grandson of the famous Ranquel warrior, Yanquetruz (d. 1838), who fought the Europeans on the pampas. Graham wrongly attributed him to a rival indigenous tribe that lived in the region.

[738] A province in Patagonia where many Welsh-speakers had emigrated in the 1860s.

"Weel, he sort o' fell in love wi' Jean, and one day he came up to the *pulpería*, and getting off his horse, a braw black piebald wi an' eye like fire intil him, he asked to speak to me. First we had Caña,[739] and then Carlón,[740] then some more Caña, and yon Vino seco, and syne some more Carlón. I couldna richtly see what he was driving at. However, all of a sudden he says, 'Wife very pretty, Indian he like buy.'

"I told him Christians didna sell their wives, and we had some more Caña, and then he says, 'Indian like Christian woman, she more big, more white than Indian girl.'

"To make a long story short, he offered me his horse and fifty dollars, then several ganaker skins, they ca' them *guillapices*,[741] and finally in addition a mare and foal. Man, they were bonny beasts, both red roan piebalds, and to pick any Indian girl I liked. Not a bad price down there at San Julian, where the chief could hae cut all our throats had he been minded to.

" ... Na, na, we werna fou[742], just a wee miraculous.[743] Don Augusty was sort o' scared when he heard what Yanquetruz was saying, and got his pistol handy and a bit axe he keepit for emergencies behind the counter. Losh[744] me, yon Yanquetruz was that ceevil, a body couldna take fuff[745] at him.

"At last I told him I wasna on to trade, and we both had a tot of square-faced gin to clean our mouths a bit, and oot to the *palenque*,[746] where the chief's horse was tied.

"A bonny beastie, his mane hogged and cut into castles, like a clipped yew hedge, his tail plaited and tied with a piece of white mare's hide, and everything upon him solid silver, just like a dinner-service.

"The chief took his spear in his hand – it had been stuck into the ground – and leaning on it, loupit[747] on his horse. Ye ken they deevils mount frae the off-side. He gied a yell that fetched the Indians racing. They had killed a cow, and some of them were daubed with blood; for they folk dinna wait for cooking when they are sharp set.[748]

---

[739] See passim.
[740] A rough red wine.
[741] A covering made from the hides of guanaco worn as a poncho by the Indians.
[742] Scots: 'No, no, we weren't drunk, just a little tipsy.'
[743] Scots: Merrily drunk.
[744] Scots: A euphemism for 'Lord'.
[745] Scots: A sudden outburst of temper.
[746] An Argentinian hitching-post.
[747] Scots: Leapt.
[748] Scots: Hungry.

Others were three-parts drunk, and came stottering along with square-faced gin bottles[749] in their hands.

"Their horses werna tied, nor even hobbled. Na, na, they just stood waiting with the reins upon the ground. Soon as they saw the chief – I canna tell ye how the thing was done – they dinna mount, they didna loup, they just melted on their beasts, catching the spears out of the ground as they got up.

"Sirs me, they Indians just took flight like birds, raising sich yellochs, running their horses up against each other, twisting and turning and carrying on in sich a way, just like fishing-boats running for harbour at Buckie or Montrose.

"Our guide turned out a richt yin, and brocht us through, up to Chubut wi'out a scratch upon the paint.[750]

"A pairfect pilot, though he had naething in the wide world to guide him through they wild stony plains.

"That's how I lost the *Rosebud*, and noo, ma freens, I'll tell you how it was I got Jean, but that was years ago.

"In my youth up in Peterhead I was a sailorman. I went to sea in they North Sea whaling craft, Duff and McAlister's, ye ken. As time went on, I got rated as a harpooner … mony's the richt whale I hae fastened into. That was the time when everything was dune by hand. Nane of your harpoon guns, nane of your dynamite, naething but muscle and a keen eye. First strike yer whale, and then pull after him. Talk of yer fox hunts … set them up, indeed.

"Jean's father keepit a bit shop in Aberdeen, and when we had got acquaint, I cannot richtly mind the way of it. Her father and her mother were aye against our marryin', for ye ken I had naething but my pay, and that only when I could get a ship. Whiles,[751] too, I drinkit a wee bit. Naething to signify, but then Jean's father was an elder of the kirk[752] and maist particular.

"Jean was a bonny lassie then, awfu' high-spirited. I used to wonder whiles, if some day when her father had been oot at the kirk, someone hadna slippit in to tak tea with her mither … I ken I'm haverin'.[753]

"Weel, we were married, and though we lo'ed each other, we were aye bickerin'. Maistly aboot naething, but ye see, we were baith young and spirited. Jean liket admiration, which was natural enough at her age, and I liket speerits, so that ane night, after a word or two,

---

[749] Gordon's Dry Gin, called square-faced because of its bottle shape.
[750] Colloquial = undamaged.
[751] Scots: Occasionally.
[752] A person elected by the congregation to administer church affairs.
[753] Scots: 'I know I'm talking nonsense.'

I gi'ed her a bit daud or two,[754] maybe it was the speerits, for in the morning when I wakit, I felt about for Jean, intending to ask her pardon, and feelin' a bit shamed. There was no Jean, and I thocht that she was hidin' just to frichten me.

"I called, but naething, and pittin' on ma clothes, searchit the hoose, but there was naebody. She left no message for me, and nane of the neighbours kent anything aboot her.

"She hadna gone to Aberdeen, and though her father and me searchit up and doon, we got no tidings of her. Sort of unchancy, just for a day or two. However, there was naething to be done, and in a month or so I sold my furniture and shipped for a long cruise.

"Man, a along cruise it was, three months or more blocked in the ice, and then a month in Greenland trying to get the scurvy out of the ship's company, and so one way or another, about seven months slipped past before we sighted Peterhead. Seven months without the sight of any woman; for, men, they Esquimaux aye gied me a skunner[755] wi' their fur clothes and oily faces, they lookit to be baboons.

"We got in on a Sabbath,[756] and I'm just tellin' ye, as soon as I was free, maybe about three o' the afternoon, I fairly ran all the way richt up to Maggie Bauchop's.[757]

"I see the place the noo, up a bit wynd. The town was awfu' quiet, and no one cared to pass too close to the wynd foot in daylight, for fear o' the clash o' tongues.[758] I didna care a rap for that, if there had been a lion in the path, same as once happened to ane o' the prophets. Balaam, I think it was, in the Old Book.[759] I wouldna hae stood back a minute if there had been a woman on the other side.

"Weel, I went up to the door, and rappit[760] on it. Maggie came to it, and says she, 'Eh, Christie, is that you?' for she aye kent a customer. A braw, fat woman, Maggie Bauchop was. For years she had followed the old trade, till she had put awa' a little siller,[761] and started business for hersel'.

"Weel she kent a' the tricks o' it, and still she was sort of God-fearin' kind o' bitch … treated her lassies weel, and didna cheat them

---

[754] Scots: 'I struck her more than once'.
[755] Scots: 'those Eskimo women always disgusted me'.
[756] Sunday.
[757] A local whore-house.
[758] Gossip.
[759] The Bible. Christison misremembers the story of Balaam (Numbers 22:21–38) where it was an angel rather than a lion blocking the path.
[760] Scots: Knocked.
[761] See passim.

about their victuals[762] and their claithes. 'Come in' she says, 'Christie, my man. Where hae ye come from?'

"I tellt her, and says I, 'Maggie, gie us yer best. I've been seven months at sea.'

"'Hoot, man,' she says, 'the lassies arena[763] up. We had a fearfu' spate o' drink yestreen,[764] an awfu' lot of ships is in the port. Sit ye doon, Christie. Here's the Old Book to ye. Na, na, ye needna look at it like that. There's bonny pictures in it, o' the prophets … each wi' his lass ye ken.'

"When she went out, I looked a little at the book – man, a fine hot one, and then a time passed I started whistlin' a tune, something I had heard up aboot Hammerfest. The door flies open, and in walks Maggie, lookin' awfu' mad.

"'Christie,' she skirls, 'I'll hae nae whistlin' in ma hoose upon the Sabbath day. I canna hae my lassies learned sich ways, so stop it, or get out.'

"Man, I just lauch[765] at her, and I says, 'The lassies, woman; whistlin' can hardly hurt them, considerin' how they live.'

"Maggie just glowered at me, and 'Christie,['] she says, 'you and men like ye may defile their bodies; but whilst I live na one shall harm their souls, puir lambies, wi' whistlin' on His day. No, not in ma hoose, that's what I'm tellin' ye.'

"I laughed, and said, 'Weel, send us in ane o' your lambies! and turned to look at a picture of Queen Victoria's Albert picnickin' at Balmoral. When I looked round a girl had come into the room. She was dressed in a striped sort of petticoat and a white jacket, a blouse I think ye call the thing, and stood wi' her back to me as she was speaking to Maggie at the door.

"I drew her to me, and was pulling her towards the bed – seven months at sea ye ken – when we passed by a looking-glass. I saw her face in it, just for a minute, as we were sort o' strugglin'. Ma God, I lowsed[766] her quick enough, and stotterin'[767] backwards sat down upon a chair. 'Twas Jean, who had run off after the bit quarrel that we had more than a year ago. I didna speak, nor did Jean say a word.

"What's that ye say?

"Na, na, ma ain wife in sichlike place, hae ye no delicacy, man? I settled up wi Maggie, tellin' her Jean was an old friend o' mine,

---

[762] Food.
[763] Scots: Aren't.
[764] Scots: Yesterday.
[765] Scots: Laughed.
[766] Scots: Loosed/released.
[767] Scots: Staggering.

and took her by the hand. We gaed away to Edinburgh, and there I married her again. Sort of haversome[768] job, but Jean wanted it, ye ken. How she came there I never asked her.

"Judge not, the ould Book says, and after all 'twas me gien' her the daud. Weel, weel, things sort of prospered after that. I bought the *Rosebud*, and as ye know piled her up and down at San Julian, some fifteen years ago.

"I never raised ma hand on Jean again. Na, na, I'd suffered for it, and Jean, if so be she needed ony sort of purification, man, she got it standing at the wheel o' nichts on the old schooner wi' the spray flyin', on the passage out.

"Not a drop, thankye, Don Hosey. Good nicht, Mr. Mansel; bongsoir, Cossart, I'm just aff hame. Jean will be waiting for me."

* * * * *

Graham not only had an abiding interest in the clash of cultures, but in unusual graves and monuments, such as this one in Buckhaven, which allowed him to use another of his favourite techniques, what Walker called 'the "conjecture' approach".[769] Here he ponders on how a Polynesian princess came to be the wife of a Scottish mariner and came to be incongruously buried in an East Neuk kirkyard – a site that no longer exists.

A PRINCESS

Anthologised in *Charity* (London: Duckworth, 1912), pp. 196–207.

Nothing is wilder than the long stretch of sandy coast which runs from the East Neuk of Fife right up to Aberdeen.

Inland, the wind-swept fields, with their rough walls, without a kindly feal[770] upon the top, as in the west, look grim and uninviting in their well-farmed ugliness.

The trees are low and stunted, and grown twisted by the prevailing fierce east winds, all to one side just like the trees so often painted by the Japanese upon a fan.

The fields run down, until they lose themselves in sandy links, clothed with growth of bent.[771]

---

[768] Scots: Silly, bothersome.
[769] Walker, p. 28.
[770] See passim.
[771] Coarse grass.

After the links, there intervenes a shingly beach, protected here and there by a low reef of rocks, all honeycombed and limpet-ridden, from which streamers of dulse float in the ceaseless surge.

Then comes the sea, grey, sullen, always on the watch to swallow up the fishermen, whose little brown-sailed boats seem to be scudding ceaselessly before the easterly haar[772] towards some harbour's mouth.

Grey towns, with houses roofed with slabs of stone, cluster round little churches built so strongly that they have weathered reformations and the storms of centuries.

Grey sky, grey sullen sea, grey rocks, and a keen whistling wind that blows from the North Sea, which seems to turn the very air a steely grey, have given to the land a look of hardness not to be equalled on earth.

One sees at first sight that in the villages no children could have ever danced upon the green. No outward visible sign of any inward graces can be seen in the hard-featured people, whose flinty-looking cheeks seem to repel the mere idea of kisses, and yet down in whose hearts exists a vein of sentiment for which in other and more favoured lands a man might search in vain. As any district, country, or race of men must have its prototype, its spot or person that sums up and typifies the whole, so does this hard, grey land find its quintessence in the town of Buckiehaven [sic],[773] a windswept fisher village, built on a spit of sand.

Its little church is stumpier than all the other little churches of the coast. Its houses are more angular, their crowsteps[774] steeper, and the gnarled plane trees that have fought for life against its withering blasts, more dwarfish and ill-grown. The fisherfolk seem ruddier, squarer, and more uncouth than are their fellows.

Their little wave-washed harbour looks narrower and still more dangerous than the thousand other little harbours that dot the coast from Kinghorn to St. Forts.

Still in the churchyard in which the graves of mariners, of old sea-captains (who once sailed, drank, and suffered, where their descendants, now sail, drink and suffer), lie thick, each waiting for the pilot, the headstones looking to the sea, their Mecca, there is an air of rest. The graves all look out seawards, where their hearts lived, and yet most of the denizens returned to lay their bones in the old paroch where in their youth they must have run about, clattering like ponies on the grey causeway stones. Yet there are gravestones which relate

---

[772] See passim.
[773] Buckhaven (pronounced 'Buckhyne', which gave rise to the name of the local pub The Buck and Hind).
[774] See passim.

that Andrew Brodie or George Anstruther were buried in the deep, and that their monument was raised by Agnes, Janet, or some other sorrowing wife, in the full hope of their salvation, with a text drawn from the minor prophets[775] and unintelligible to any eyes but those of love and faith.

The lettering on the stones is cut so deeply that in mossless land it looks as fresh as when the widow and the local stonemason stood chaffering for its price, surrounded by her flaxen-haired children, whom in good time the sea would claim, taking them from her as relentlessly as it had claimed her man.

Only a little lichen here and there, yellow and looking like a stain, shows that time and the weather have both wrought their worst and failed to get a hold, so hard the whinstone, and so good the workmanship.

In the low, wiry grass the graves look like a flock of sheep, the rough-built wall keeps them from straying, and the squat cock upon the spire, that creaks so harshly in the wind, looks down upon them and does not crow, because it knows the inmates are asleep.

So they sleep on, sleeping a longer watch below than any that they ever had on earth, when the shrill boatswain's whistle roused each of them at each recurring period of four hours, or a shout called them all on deck to shorten sail.

All round the churchyard wall are old-world tombs, of worthies of the places – Brodies and Griersons, Selkirks and Anstruthers – adorned with emblems of their trades, as mallets, shears, and chisels, with a death's-head and crossbones crowning all, to show not only that the skeleton had sat unbidden at life's feast,[776] but after a full meal still lingered with his hosts.

The whinstone church, hardly distinguishable from the rocks beside the harbour in colour and in shape, the little burial-ground more like a sheep-pen than a cemetery, the high-pitched house-roofs in the steep stony staircases of streets, all give the idea of a corner of the world to which no stranger could have penetrated except by accident. If such a one there were, he must have felt himself indeed a foreigner in such an isolated spot.

Yet on the south side of the church, set perhaps by accident to catch the little sun that ever shines upon that drear East Neuk, there is a slab let in, or stuck against the wall.

---

[775] The twelve books of Old Testament prophecy from Hosea to Malachi whose writings are relatively brief. However, Graham incorrectly treats the 'minor' as if it meant of lesser importance.

[776] 'To the feasts of inferior men the good unbidden go.' Plato, after an ancient proverb.

Upon the granite tablet, edged round with a suppositious Gothic scroll, cut into flowers like pastry ornaments upon a pie, the letters poorly executed, showing up paltry in their shallowness, beside the lettering of the staunch old tombs amongst the grass, is written, "Here lies Sinakalula, Princess of Raratonga, the beloved wife of Andrew Brodie, Mariner."

What were the circumstances of their meeting the stone does not declare, only that the deceased had been a princess in her native land, and had died in the obscure east-country haven, and had been "beloved."

Nothing, but all – at least all that life has to give.

The simple idyll of the princess and Andrew Brodie, mariner, is writ on the red marble slab, in letters less enduring than their love, badly designed and poorly cut, and destined soon to disappear[777] in the cold rains and steely blasts of the East Neuk of Fife, and leave the stone a blank.

How they met, loved, and how the mariner brought home his island bride, perhaps to droop in the cold north, and how he laid her in the drear churchyard to wait the time when they should be reunited once again in some Elysian field, not unlike Polynesia, with the Tree of Life for palms, the selfsame opal-tinted sea, angels for tropic birds, and the same air of calm pervading all the air, only the mariner, if he still lives can say.

The princess, as Andrew Brodie first saw her, must have looked like the fair damsels Captain Cook[778] describes, with perhaps just a slight tincture of the missionary school, but not enough to take away her grace.

Dressed in a coloured and diaphanous sacque,[779] a wreath of red hibiscus round her head, her jet-black hair loose on her shoulders, bare arms and feet, redolent of oil of cocoanut, she must have seemed a being from another world to the rough mariner.

---

[777] The slab no longer exists as the church was demolished in the 1960s, along with the Old Town, and the rubble used to fill in the harbour.

[778] Captain James Cook (1728–79), explorer and cartographer, famous for his journeys in the Pacific and to Australia.

[779] Obscure eighteenth century: A dress with a loose back falling from shoulder to hem without a defined waistline

How he appeared to her is harder to determine, perhaps as did Cortés[780] to La Malinche,[781] or as did Soto[782] to the Indian queen amongst the Seminoles. True, we know what Cortés was like, how he rode like a centaur, was noble, generous, that he knew Latin, as Bernal Díaz says,[783] and Soto was designed by nature to capture every heart. The Scottish sailor possibly appeared as the representative of a strange race, harder and fiercer, but more tender at the heart than her compatriots.

His steel-blue eyes may have appeared to her as hardly mortal; his rough and hairy hands, symbols of strength embodified; his halting speech, a homage to her charms. Then as he must have been an honest and true-hearted man, approaching her with the same reverence with which he would have courted one of the hard-faced, red-headed women of his native place, not in the fashion of the trader or the beach-comber, it must have seemed as if a being, superior by its strength, had thrown strength aside, all for her love.

When his ship sailed, the sailor may have hidden in the hills, then when her topsails had sunk well beneath the waves, and he was sure the ship would not return, come out of hiding, and strolled timidly along the beach, until some trader or missionary came out and sheltered him.

Naturally, chiefs and missionaries and all the foreign population looked on his love as an infatuation; but he, setting to work, trading copra and bêche-de-mer,[784] in coral and the like, gradually made himself a man of consequence. Schooners would come consigned to him, and cargoes of his own lie heaped in *barracoons*,[785] thatched with banana leaves.

At last, when he had "gathered siller" and become a man of substance – for Brodie certainly was one of those who could not stoop to live upon his wife – he must have gone and seen the missionary. One sees him sweating in his long-shore togs, a palm-tree

---

[780] Hernán Cortés (1485–1547), the Spanish conquistador who defeated the Aztecs to win Mexico for Spain

[781] La Malinche, or Doña Marina, was an Indian princess who was Cortés' interpreter and mistress.

[782] Hernando de Soto (c. 1500–42), Spanish conquistador who took part in the conquests of Nicaragua, Peru, and his exploration of present-day US states of Georgia, the Carolinas, and Alabama, and his discovery of the Mississippi (1540–2).

[783] Bernal Díaz del Castillo (1492–1581), one of Cortés' captains, who wrote of the capture of Mexico in his *True History of the Conquest of New Spain*, which was published in 1632.

[784] The boiled and dried flesh of the sea-cucumber.

[785] A barracks used for the internment of slaves or criminals. It is unclear why Graham used it in this context.

hat upon his head, toiling along the beach, and rapping at the door. The missionary, most likely a compatriot, bids him come in, and lays the "Word," which he has been translating into Polynesian, upon the table and welcomes him.

"I'm glad to see ye, Andrew. How time goes on. Now you're a man of substance, and will be sending for a wife ... unless, indeed, you might think of Miss McKendrick, the new Bible-reader. A nice-like lass enough. No bonny, but then beauty, ye ken, is not enduring ... What, ye dinna say? I thocht ye had been cured o' all that foolishness. They island girls are a' like children. What sort of looking wife would she be to ye at hame, man Andrew?"

This may have passed, and then the wedding in the mission church, with the dusky catechumens[786] looking stiff and angular in the death-dealing clothes of Christianity, the bride listening to the old-fashioned Scottish exhortation on the duties of her new estate, what time the chief, her father, a converted pagan, thought with regret of the marriage ceremonies that he had witnessed in his youth, so different from these.

It may have been that for a year or two the ill-assorted pair lived happily, the husband trading and watching his men work in his garden, whilst his wife swung in a hammock underneath a tree. As time went by, the recollection of the grey village in East Fife would come back to the husband's mind and draw him northwards, whilst the wife wondered what it was he thought about, and why the steely eyes seemed to look through her as if they sought for something that she could never see.

At last would come the day when he first spoke of going home, timidly, and as if feeling somehow he was about to commit a crime. Her tears and expostulations can be imagined, and then her Ruth-like[787] resolution to follow him across the sea.

The voyage and the first touch of cold, the arrival in the bare and stormy land, the disappointment of poor Andrew, when he found he was forgotten by the great part of his friends, and that the rest despised him for having brought a coloured woman home, all follow naturally.

All the small jealousies and miseries of a provincial town, the horrors of the Scottish Sabbath, the ceaseless rain, the biting wind, the gloom and darkness of the winter, the disappointment of the brief northern summer, the sea, in which none but a walrus or a seal could

---

[786] See passim.
[787] Ruth 1:16–18. Ruth, a Moabitess, left her homeland to devotedly accompany her widowed mother-in-law, Naomi, as she returned to her hometown of Bethlehem.

bathe, must have done their worst upon the island princess, now become in very truth the wife of Andrew Brodie, mariner. One sees her in her unbecoming European clothes, simple and yet accustomed to respect, exposed to all the harshness of the land in which, though hearts are warm, they move so far beneath the surface that their pulsations hardly can be felt, except by those accustomed to their beat.

Then in the end consumption,[788] that consumption that usually attacks a monkey when it passes north of forty,[789] making its end so human and so pitiful, must have attacked her too.

Then the drear funeral, with Andrew and his friends in weepers[790] and tall hats, which the east wind brushed all awry, making them look like ferrets; the little coffin with outlandish name and date, and "in her thirtieth year" emblazoned on it in cheap brass lettering; and the sloping pile of shingly earth, so soon to be stamped down over the island flower.

Slowly the friends would go, after shaking Andrew by the hand. He feeling vaguely that he had murdered her whom he loved best, would linger, as a bird hovers for a time above the place where it had seen its mate fall, a mere mass of bloodstained feathers, to the gun.

When he was gone the island princess would be left alone with the wind sweeping across the sea, sounding around the Bass,[791] and whistling wearily above Inch Keith [sic][792] to sing her threnody.

* * * * *

In April 1913, Graham published 'Mist in Menteith', which drew us back into his mysterious realm, where the mists were again swirling, and transforming the landscape. This immersive quality, as we have seen, was a medium through which he could free his memories and desires. Graham seemed unable to break loose from the documentary form, unable to invoke the past, laden as it was with a supernatural atmosphere, without invoking some transformative medium. In her review of his anthology *Brought Forward* (1916), Amy Wellington wrote, 'His thought ends in a philosophical mist – in the poetic

---

[788] Tuberculosis. Graham's brother, Malise, died from the disease, aged twenty-five, in 1885.

[789] North of the fortieth parallel.

[790] White material added to the cuffs of coats, which could be used to wipe tears from the eyes of mourners.

[791] The Bass Rock, or simply 'the Bass', a precipitous volcanic plug in the outer part of the Firth of Forth.

[792] Inchkeith is a fortified island in the Firth of Forth, lying closer to Fife than to Midlothian. In Graham's day it was known for its lighthouse and mechanical foghorn.

invocation of Mist in Menteith, a study in lyrical prose which reveals, above all others, the quality of his literary genius'.[793]

MIST IN MENTEITH

The Saturday Review, 5 April 1913, pp. 420–1.
Anthologised in *A Hatchment* (London: Duckworth, 1913), pp. 104–13.

Some say the name Menteith meant a peat moss in Gaelic, and certainly peat mosses fill a third of the whole vale. However that may be, its chiefest attribute is mist. Shadows in summer play on the faces of the hills, and snow in winter spreads a cold carpet over the brown moss; but the mist stays longest with us, and under it the semi-Highland, semi-Lowland valley puts on its most familiar air.

When billowing waves wreath round the hills, and by degrees encroach upon the low, flat moors, they shroud the district from the world, as if they wished to keep it from prying eyes, safe and inviolate. Summer and spring and winter all have their charms, either when the faint green of the baulked vegetation of the north breaks out, tender yet vivid, or when the bees buzz in the heather in the long days of the short, nightless summer, or when the streams run noiselessly under their shroud of ice in a hard frost. Then comes the autumn, and brings the rain, soaking and blurring everything. Leaves blotch and blacken, then fall swirling down on to the sodden earth.

On trees and stones, from fences, from feals upon the tops of dykes, a beady moisture oozes, making them look as if they had been frosted. When all is ready for them, the mists sweep down and cover everything; from the interior of the darkness comes the cries of wild ducks, of herons as they sit upon the trees, and of geese passing overhead. Inside the wreaths of mist another world seems to have come into existence, something distinct from and antagonistic to mankind. When the mist once descends, blotting out the familiar features of the landscape, leaving perhaps the Rock of Stirling floating in the air, the three black trees upon the bare rock of the Fairy Hill growing from nothing, or the peak of the Cobbler,[794] seeming to peer above enormous mountain ranges, though in reality nothing more vast than

---

[793] Amy Wellington, 'An Artist-Fighter in English Prose: Cunninghame Graham', *Bookman* (New York), April 1918, p. 157.
[794] *Beinn Artair*, a mountain in Arrochar, at the western side of Loch Lomond. Its shape resembles a cobbler at his last.

the long shoulder of Ben Lomond intervenes, the change has come that gives Menteith its special character.

There are mists the world over, and in Scotland in particular; mists circling round the Western Islands, filling the glens and boiling in the corries of the hills, mists that creep out to sea or in towards the land from seawards, threatening and dreadful looking; but none like ours, so impalpable and strange, and yet so fitting to our low, flat mosses with our encircling hills. In older days they sheltered the marauders from the north, who in their gloom fell on the valley as if they had sprung from the night, plundered and burned and harried, and then retreated under cover of the mist, back to their fastnesses.

As they came through the glen of Glenny, or the old road behind Ben Dhu, which comes out just a little east of Invertrossachs, when the wind blew aside the sheltering wreaths of steam, and the rare gleams of sun fell on the shaggy band, striking upon the heads of their Lochaber axes, and again shifted and covered them from sight, they must have seemed a phantom army, seen in a dream, just between consciousness and sleep.

The lake, with its three islands,[795] its giant chestnuts, now stag-headed and about to fall, the mouldering priory, the long church with its built-up, five-light window,[796] the castle, overgrown with brushwood, and with a tree springing up from the middle hall,[797] the heronry, the rope of sand the fairies twisted, which would have made a causeway to the island had they not stopped in the nick of time, the single tree that marks the gallows, and the old churchyard of the Port,[798] all these the mist invests with a peculiar charm which they lack when the sun shines and shows them merely mouldering ruin and decaying trees.

So of the Flanders Moss. It, too, in mist seems to roll on for miles; its heathy surface turns to long waves that paly against the foot of the low range of hills, and beat upon Craigforth[799] as if it were an island in the sea. Through wreathes of steam, the sullen Forth[800] winds in and out between the peat hags, and when a slant of wind leaves it clear for an instant it looks mysterious and dark, as might a stream

---

[795] Scotland's only 'lake', The Lake of Menteith, with the islands of Inchmahome, Inchtalla and Inchcuin.

[796] The Priory of Inchmahome, where Graham and his wife are buried in 'the long church'.

[797] The castle, which was the seat of the Earls of Menteith, is on Inchtalla, which Graham owned.

[798] The hamlet of Port of Menteith.

[799] A rocky outcrop from the flat of the Forth Valley, near Stirling.

[800] The River Forth which rises close to Ben Lomond and enters the North Sea near Edinburgh.

of quicksilver[801] running down from a mine. When a fish leaps, the sound re-echoes like a bell, as it falls back into the water, and rings spread out till they are lost beneath the banks.

After a day or two of gloom life begins somehow or another to be charged with mystery; and, walking through the woods, instinctively you look about half in alarm as a roe bounds away, or from a fir-tree a capercailzie drums or flies off with a noise as if a moose was bursting through the trees.

Peat smoke floats through the air from cottages a mile away, acrid and penetrating, and fills the nostrils with its scent. The little streams run with a muffled tinkle as if they wished to hide away from sight; rank yellow ragweeds on their banks, bowed down with the thick moisture, all hang their heads as if they mourned for the lost sunshine and the day. Now and then leaves flutter down slowly to the ground like dying butterflies. Over the whole earth hangs, as it were, a sounding-board, intensifying everything, making the senses more acute, though at the same time carrying sounds as from a distance, focussed to the ear.

So through our mists, a shepherd's dog barking a mile off, is heard as loudly as if it were a yard or two away, although the sound comes slowly to the ear, as when old-fashioned guns hung fire and the report appeared to reach one through a veil. Thus does the past, with its wild legends, the raiders from the north, the Broken Men, the Saxon's Leap, the battles of the Grahams and the McGregors, come down to us veiled by the mist of time. In the lone churchyards, whose grass is always damp the whole year round, whose earth, when a new grave is dug, is always wet, so wet that not a stone rolls from it to the grass; the tombstones, with the lettering overgrown with lichens only preserve the names of the old enemies who now lie side by side in a faint shadowy way. The sword that marks the resting-place of men of the most turbulent of all the races of that border land, is usually only the shadow of a sword, so well the mist has done its work, rounding off edges and obliterating chisel marks.

Boats on the Loch o' Port, with oars muffled by the cloud of vapour that broods upon the lake, glide in and out of the thick curtain spread between the earth and sky, the figure of the standing fisher in the stern looming gigantic as he wields his rod in vain; for, in the calm, even the water-spiders leave a ripple as they run. In the low, mossy "parks" that lose themselves in beds of bulrushes before they join the lake, the Highland cattle stand and gaze, the damp congealing on their coats in whitish beadlets, and horses hang their heads disconsolately, for no matter in what climate they are born, horses are creatures of the sun.

---

[801] Mercury (Hg) is the only metallic element that is liquid at normal conditions.

Under the shroud of gloom it seems that something strange is going on, something impalpable that gives all the valley of Menteith its own peculiar air of sadness, as if no summer sun, no winter frost, no fierce March winds, or the chill cold of April, could ever really dry the tears of moisture that it lays up under the autumn mist. So all our walls are covered with a thick coating of crisp, grey lichen on the weather side that looks like flakes of leather, and on the lee side with a covering of bright, green moss.

Thatch moulders, and from it springs a growth of vegetation; a perpetual dripping from the eaves opens a little rill below it, in which the pebbles glisten as in a mountain stream.

Along the roads the scanty traffic rumbles fitfully, and on the Sabbath, down the steep path towards the little church, knots of fantastic figures seem to stalk like threatening phantoms. When they draw near, one sees that they were but the familiar faces of McKerrochar of Cullamoon, Graham of Tombreak, Campbell of Rinaclach, and Finlay Mitchell, dressed in their Sunday clothes. They pass the time of day, daunder[802] a little in the damp kirkyard, so heaped with graves they have to pick their way between them just as sheep pick their way and follow one another on a steep mountain path, or when they cross a burn.[803]

Although their talk runs on their daily life – the price of beasts at the last market or the tryst, upon bad seasons and the crops, all in the compassed and depreciatory vein characteristic of their calling and their race, they once have been fantastic figures towering above the dry-stone dykes that edge the road. That glory, nothing can take away from them, or from the valley where they live.

Nothing is stable. Snows melt and rain gives place to sun, and sun to rain again; spring melts into summer, then autumn blends insensibly with winter, and the year is out. Men come and go, the Saxon speech replaces Gaelic; even traditions insensibly are lost.

The trees decay and fall, then they lie prone like the great hollow chestnut trunks, blackened by tourists' fires, in Inchmahome. Our hills and valleys all have changed their shapes under the action either of fire or ice. Life, faiths, ideals, all have changed. The Flanders Moss that was a sea is now crossed by a railway and by innumerable roads. What then shall we, who have seen mists rising up all our lives, feared them as children, loved them in riper years, cling to, but mist?

Refuge of our wild ancestors, moulder of character, inspirer of the love of mystery, chief characteristic of the Keltic mind, spirit

---

[802] See passim.
[803] Scots: A stream.

that watches over the hills and valleys, lochs, clachans,[804] bealachs,[805] and shaggy baadans,[806] essence compounded of the water of the sky and earth, impalpable, dark and threatening, Fingal and Bran and Ossian,[807] and he who in outstretching Ardnamurchan[808] strung his harp to bless the birlinn[809] of Clanronald,[810] all have disappeared in thy gray folds.

Whether thou art death stealing amongst us, veiled, or life concealed behind curtain, or but an emanation from the ground, which the poor student, studying in Aberdeen, living on oatmeal, working by day upon the wharves and poring over books at night, can explain as easily as he can solve all other mysteries, with his science primer, who shall say?

All that I know is that when the mantle of the damp rolls down upon us, battling with the rough oak copse on Ben Dearch [sic][811] or Craigmore[812] till it is all swallowed up and a smooth surface stretches out over what, but half an hour before, was a thick wood of knarled and secular trees that stood like piles stand up in an embankment, eaten by the sea, the mist has conquered.

Somehow, I think its victory brings a sense of rest.

* * * * *

The subject of the next sketch, had made an earlier appearance in *Notes on the District of Menteith*, and it allowed Graham to flesh out and polish his earlier pen-portrait while displaying several of his major themes: the socially excluded "going aboot bodies"; the vulgarness of success; and unsentimentalised death.

---

[804] Gaelic: Small Highland villages.

[805] Gaelic: A narrow mountain pass.

[806] Gaelic: A wood.

[807] Fingal, who is based on the legendary Celtic hero Fionn mac Cunhail, is the hero of a poem of the same name in the spurious *Works of Ossian* which was published in 1760 and 1762 by James MacPherson. Ossian was supposedly Fionn's son, and Bran, his dog.

[808] Ardnamurchan (Scots Gaelic *Àird nam Murchan*: headland of the great seas) is a fifty-square-mile peninsula in the Lochaber region of the Western Highlands. The most westerly point of mainland Great Britain. *Corrachadh Mòr*, is in Ardnamurchan.

[809] In 1751, the Gaelic poet, Alexander MacDonald (Alasdair Mac Mhaighstir Alasdair) wrote a visionary poem, *Birlinn Clann Raghnaill* (The Boat of Clanranald), in which the Scottish Gaels returned to their roots in Ireland.

[810] Clanronald (more usually Clanranald: Scottish Gaelic: *Clann Raghnaill*) is a branch of Clan Donald, one of the largest Highland clans.

[811] Beinn Dearg (Red Mountain, pronounced 'jerach'), the highest of the Menteith Hills, lies between the Lake of Menteith and Loch Venachar.

[812] Craigmore is a prominent hill, 387 metres high, above the village of Aberfoyle, which is close to Graham's Gartmore estate.

'The Beggar Earl', William Graham by name, was the youngest son of William Graham of Gallingad, a Writer to the Signet,[813] and was an uncle of the Scottish miniaturist John Bogle. He was Graham's cousin five times removed and is one of the legendary characters of Cunninghame Graham family lore. Graham was clearly fascinated by him, perhaps because he was another eccentric who pursued his hopeless dreams.

William was born around 1704 and studied medicine at Edinburgh. In 1744, he took it into his head that he was rightful Earl of Menteith and accordingly presented himself at the election of Scottish peers claiming "the right to vote". He voted five times at the Election of Peers of Scotland between 1744 and 1761, after which, in 1762, his assumption of the dignities was prohibited by order of the House of Lords. Despite his claim being disallowed, he continued to use the title for the remainder of his life, and Graham romanticises his leaving Edinburgh by attributing it to weariness and disenchantment.

William died in a ditch at Bonhill in the Vale of Leven[814] on 30 June 1783, and typically, Graham, records his death without sentimentality, though he uses artistic licence to change the season from summer to winter to heighten the dramatic effect. Equally characteristically, he does not finish there as most authors would, but adds a couple of sentences about the Beggar Earl's old white pony.

Perhaps this was Graham's most complete 'Scottish' sketch, a touching portrait of eccentricity, without sentimentality, set in Menteith, it was tangibly historical, without the fantastical (or most of it). Even the scenes and atmospheres we are by now so used to feel like old friends, or at least, not out of place.

THE BEGGAR EARL

The English Review, July 1913, pp. 569–74.
Anthologised in *A Hatchment* (London: Duckworth, 1913), pp. 183–94.

Many a shadowy figure has flitted through the valley of Menteith. Just as the vale itself is full of shadows, shadows that leave no traces of their passage; but, whilst they last, seem just as real as are the

---

[813] Scots law = a Writer to the Signet is a solicitor who is widely recognised as signifying exceptional standards of competence and integrity and, thus, is permitted to conduct cases in the Court of Session.

[814] Ancestral home and birthplace of the 'Earl's' near contemporary, the historian and picaresque novelist Tobias Smollett (1721–71).

hills themselves, so not a few of those who have lived in it seem unsubstantial and as illusive [*sic*] as a ghost.

Perhaps less real, for if a man detects a spectre with that interior vision dear to the Highlanders and to all mystics, Highland or Lowland, or from whatever land they be, he has as surely seen it, for himself, as if the phantasm was pictured on the retina of the exterior eye.

Pixies, trolls, and fairies, the men of peace, the dwellers in the Fairy Hill[815] that opens upon Hallowe'en alone, and from which issues a long train, bringing with them our long-lost vicar Kirke of Aberfoyle,[816] True Thomas,[817] and the rest of all the mortals who forsook their porridge three times a day, for the love of some elf queen, and have remained as flies embedded in the amber of tradition, are in a way prosaic. Men have imagined them, enduing them with their own qualities, just as they have endued their gods, with jealousy and hate. Those born in the ordinary, but miraculous, fashion of mankind, who live apparently by bread alone,[818] and yet remain beings apart, not touched by praise, ambition, or any of the things that move their fellows, are the true fairies after all.

Such a one was the beggar earl. All his long life he lacked advancement, finding it only at the last, as he died, like a cadger's[819] pony, by a dykeside in the snow. That kind of death keeps a man's memory fresh.

Few can tell to-day where or in what manner died his ancestors – mail-clad knights who fought at Flodden, aided their kings, with half the Highland cunning of their race, and generally opposed the Southrons, who, impotent to conquer us in war, yet have filched from us most of our national character by the soft arts of peace. A mouldering slab of freestone here and there, a nameless statue of a Crusader with his crossed feet resting upon his dog, in the ebenezered cathedral of Dunblane;[820] a little castle on a little reedy island in a bulrush-circled lake, some time-stained parchments in old muniments[821]

---

[815] Doon Hill by Aberfoyle. See passim.

[816] The Reverend Robert Kirk. See passim.

[817] Sir Thomas de Ercildoun, better known as 'Thomas the Rhymer' (c. 1220–98), a Scottish laird, who was reputedly carried off by 'The Queen of Elfland', and returned having gained the gift of prophecy, and the inability to tell a lie.

[818] A biblical allusion to Matthew 4:4, in which Jesus cites Deuteronomy 8:3 to rebut Satan's temptation to turn stones into bread.

[819] A beggar.

[820] During the Reformation, Dunblane's cathedral was stripped of its sacred images, and over the next three centuries much of its architecture fell into ruin. 'Ebenezered' is Graham's own coinage, mocking the fondness of some Protestants for giving their chapels Biblical names. Eben-Ezer was a stone commemorating God's help in a battle against the Philistines (I Samuel. 7:12).

[821] A document or record, especially one kept in an archive.

preserve their memory, to those who care for memories, a futile and a disappearing race.

His is preserved in snow. Nothing is more enduring than the snow. It falls and straight all is transfigured. All suffers chromatic change: that which was black or red, brown, yellow, or dark-grey, is changed to white, so white that it remains forever stamped on the mind, and one recalls the landscape, with its fairy woods, its stiff, dead streams, its suffering trees and withered vegetation, as it was on that day.

So has the recollection of the beggar earl remained, a legend, and all his humble life, his struggles and his fixed, foolish purpose been forgotten; leaving his death, as it were embalmed, in something, of itself so perishable that it has had no time to die.

No mere success, the most vulgar thing that a man can endure,[822] would have been so lasting, for men resent success and strive to stifle it under their applause, lauding the result, the better to belittle all the means. His life was not especially eventful, still less mysterious, for the poor play out their part in public, and a greater mystic than himself has said, "the poor make no noise."

Someone who knew him said he was "a little man; a little clean man, that went round about through the country. He never saw him act wrong ... He was-just a man asking charity. He went into farm-houses and asked for victuals; what they would give him, and into gentlemen's houses."

This little picture, drawn unconsciously, shows us the man as he was after ill-fortune overtook him. For a brief season he had been well known in Edinburgh. In 1744, when he was studying medicine, he suddenly appeared at the election of a Scottish peer and told the assembly who he was, and claimed the right to vote.

From that time till his death, he never dropped his claim, attending all elections of a Scottish peer till he got weary of the game. Then disillusion fell on him, and he withdrew to beg his bread, and wander up and down his earldom and the neighbouring lands, until his death.

Once more he came into public view, in the year 1747, when he published his rare pamphlet, "The Fatal Consequences of Discord,"[823] dedicated to the Prince of Wales. In it he says "that there can be no true unity without religion and virtue in a State."

---

[822] A repeat of his sentiment expressed in his essay, 'The Failure of Success' (*Saturday Review*, 15 May 1902): 'Success, which touches nothing that it does not vulgarise, should be its own reward. In fact, *rewards of any kind are but vulgarities.*'

[823] 'The Fatal Consequences of National Discord or, a Political Address to the Noble and Rich Families of Great Britain'.

This marks him as a man designed by nature to be poor, for unity and virtue are not commodities that command a ready sale.

He had not any special gift but faith, and that perhaps sustained him in his wanderings, and perhaps he may have thought that he would sit some day in a celestial senate, and this belief consoled him for his rejection by an earthly house of peers. One thing is certain, even had the House of Lords, that disallowed his claim, although he voted several years in Edinburgh, approved him as a peer, it would not have convinced him of his right one atom more; for if a man is happy in conviction, he had it to the full.

It is said he bore about with him papers and pedigrees that he would never sell. No bartering of the crown for him, even for bread. A little, grey, clean-looking man, mounted upon an old white pony, falling by degrees into most abject poverty and still respected for his uprightness, and perhaps a little for his ancestry, for in those days that which to us is but a mockery, was real, just as some things which with us are valued, in those days would have been ridiculous.

So, through the valley of Menteith, along the Endrick, and by Loch Lomond side, past the old church at Kilmaronock,[824] through Gartocharn and up and down the Leven, he took his pilgrimage.[825]

Over the wild track on the Dumbarton moor, and past the waterfall at the head of the glen of Gallingad,[826] he and his pony must have wandered many times, reflecting that the lands he passed over should have been all his own, for he really was Earl of Menteith by right and descent, no matter though his fellow peers refused to recognise him. He talked at first, in any house he came to, of his rights, and people having little news to distract them in those days, were no doubt pleased to hear him and to inveigh against injustice in the way that those who had themselves received it all their lives are always pleased to talk.

So does a goaded ox lower his head and whisk his tail, and then, after a glance thrown at his fellow, strain once again upon the yoke. Then, when the novelty was over they would receive his stories with less interest, driving him back upon himself, until most likely he bore his wrongs about with him, just as a peddlar bears his pack, in silence, and alone. So did he, when the first efforts to obtain his title and his

---

[824] A parish to the south-east of Loch Lomond.

[825] Through the Beggar Earl's wanderings, Graham relived the ride from Gartmore to Ardoch that he knew so intimately; a ride which he not only no longer made, but which was avoided by his funeral cortège.

[826] Owned first by Graham's grandfather Walter, then his uncle Robert (Graham's six times great-grandfather) and finally by the Beggar Earl's own father.

rights had spent their force, quit Edinburgh as it had been a city of the plague when there was any election of a peer.

Whilst he was wandering up and down the parishes of Kilmaronock and of Port, Scotland was all convulsed with the late rising of the '45.[827] Parties of soldiers, and bands of Highlanders, retreating to the north, must have passed by him daily, and yet he never seems to have had the inclination to change sides.[828] Staunch in his allegiance to the Government, and with a faith well grounded in the Protestant Succession, as his pamphlet shows, most probably he was a Church and State man, as he would have said, up to his dying day.

Of such, as far as kings and rulers are concerned, are the elect, and thrones are founded on this unquestioning belief, more strongly than on armies or in Courts.

As the years passed, and he still wandered up and down Menteith, losing by degrees the little culture his studies had implanted in him when he attended the Edinburgh schools, the farmers must have begun to treat him, first as one of themselves, and then just as they would have treated any other wandering beggarman. Still, on a few occasions when he had to write a letter he always signed "Menteith," especially begging letters, and the signature, no doubt, consoled him many times for a refusal of his plea.

Few could have known all the traditions of the district as did the wandering earl; but he most probably, living amongst them, thought them not in the least remarkable, for it needs time and distance to make old legends interesting.

He and his pony must have been familiar figures on the roads, and when he came to a wild moorland farm, no doubt they welcomed him, expecting news from the outside world, and were a little disappointed when he sat silent in the settle, gazing into the smouldering peats, brooding upon his wrongs.

At such times, most likely he drew out his cherished papers from his wallet and pored upon them, though he must long ago have known them all by heart, and as he read them all his pride in his old lineage revived, and the long day upon hill tracks may have seemed light to him as he sat nodding by the fire. His hosts, with the old-fashioned hospitality of those times, would set before him a great bowl of porridge, which he must often only have eaten for good manners' sake, and then go off to sleep besides his pony on the straw.

---

[827] The Jacobite rebellion of 1745 to restore the British throne to the House of Stuart.

[828] Graham romantically ignored the fact that the Beggar Earl had published his pamphlet two years after the '45 and did not start his wanderings until almost two decades later.

How many years he wandered through the mosses and the hills, how many times he saw the shaws in April green upon the Fairy Hill, or the red glow upon the moor in autumn, is not quite clear; but all the time he never once forsook his wanderings. Offers were made him, by many of his friends, to settle down; but either the free life held something for him that no man dwelling in a house could give, or else he thought himself more likely to attain his object by being always on the road, travelling, as it were, like a Knight of the Holy Grail, towards some goal unseen that fascinated him, still always further on.

No doubt the darksome thickets by loch sides, in which he and his pony must have passed many summer nights, were pleasanter than a smoke-infested Highland shieling.[829] Sleeping alone in them he could hear all the mysterious voices of the night, hear wild ducks whirring overhead, the cries of herons in the early morning, and the splash made by rising trout, and watch the mist at dawn creeping upon the water as he lay huddled in his plaid.

All our old tracks, so long disused, but visible to those who look for such things, by their white stones, on which so many generations of brogue-clad feet have passed, and by the dark green grass that marks them as they meander across uplands or through the valleys, he must have known as well as did the drovers coming from the north.

Lone wells, that lie forgotten nowadays, but of which then the passers-by all knew and drank from, he too had drunk from, lying upon his chest, and with his beard floating like seaweed in the water as he lay.

Mists must have shrouded him, as he rode through the hills, and out of them strange faces must have peered, terrible and fantastic to a man alone and cut off from mankind.

Possibly to him the faces seemed familiar and more kindly than were those he generally saw upon his pilgrimage. If there were fairies seated on the green knolls, he must have seemed to them as one of themselves, for certainly he was a man of peace.

Cold, wind and rain and snow must have beat on him as they do upon a tree, but not for that did he once stay his wanderings up and down. As age drew on him it was observed that by degrees he seldom left his native parish of Kilmaronock, where he was known and understood by all.

There is a tract of moorland, high-lying and bleak, from which at the top you see Loch Lomond and its islands lying out as in a map beneath. Inch Cailleach,[830] high and grey-looking, and Inch Murren

---

[829] Scots: A hut or rude shelter, a temporary house of stones, sods, etc., occupied during summer pasturing.
[830] The subject of a later sketch by Graham. See below.

with its yews float in the foreground like hulks of ships, and the dark rock of Balmaha rises above the little reedy bay. Just at the bleakest part of the bare moor the wandering earl was seen by some returning drovers on a cold winter's night. Light snow was falling, and as they passed him on the wild track that leads down to the vale of Leven, huddled up on his pony, they spoke to him, but he returned no answer, and passed on into the storm. All night it snowed, and in the morning, when the heritors[831] were coming to the old kirk of Bonhill parish, they found him with his back to a dry stone dyke, and his beloved parchments in his hand.[832] Not far away his old white pony, with the reins dangling round his feet, stood shivering, and in the snow where he had thrust his muzzle deeply down to seek the grass, were some faint stains of blood.[833]

*****

For centuries the cattle of the Highland glens and coastal plains had found a ready market in the Lowlands, but it was the growth in demand from England following the union in 1707 which prompted the establishment of regular markets, or 'trysts'.[834] The largest was at Crieff near Perth, but after 1750 it went into decline, drovers preferring to take their beasts further south to sites around Falkirk.

The first Falkirk trysts were held on Reddingmuir, to the south of the town, but by the early 1770s enclosure of the common land forced a move to a second location at Rough Castle Roman Fort on the Antonine Wall. However, the construction of the Forth and Clyde canal forced them to move again, to Carmuirs, between Bonnybridge and Camelon, before finally settling at Stenhousemuir.

The big sale days were the first Tuesday of the months of August, September and October, where as many as 150,000 cattle, sheep and horses arrived from all corners of Scotland on the many 'drove' roads that criss-crossed the country, driven by 2,000 cattlemen and

---

[831] Scots: A landowner, a landed proprietor who had a liability to contribute to the upkeep of the parish church.

[832] 'The Beggar Earl' died on 30 June 1783, his burial in the Bonhill churchyard in July being paid for by his Bogle relatives, the receipt for which, dated 20 August, was signed by 'John Alexander, the Bonhill Kirk Session Clerk of the day'.

[833] What Graham is suggesting is unclear; however, there are resonances from a previous story – 'Snaekoll's Saga' (*Saturday Review*, 18 December 1897), where Graham inferred that a dead Icelander was eaten by his horse. In a letter to Graham, dated 7 January 1898, Conrad wrote: 'As to the Saga it confirms me in my conviction that you have a fiendish gift for showing the futility – the ghastly, jocular futility of life'.

[834] Prior to the Union, the importation of cattle into England from Scotland was prohibited.

Figure 17 Graham at Buchlyvie Public Hall, 28 July 1934.[835]

boys, who set up large tented townships around the site. Due to the growth of rail traffic, 'droving' and the market, went into decline at the end of the nineteenth century, and the site became an annual fairground.

In a speech at Buchlyvie Public Hall on 28 July 1934, Graham recalled the days when Highland cattle-drovers, on their way to Falkirk with their herds, slept by the road at night, leaving their dogs to watch over their charges: 'That would be as strange to the present generation as if a tribe of Indians came and camped by the roadside'.[836]

THE FALKIRK TRYST

Anthologised in *A Hatchment* (London: Duckworth, 1913), pp. 212–22.

In these days when every single vestige of old custom and old speech is being rapidly submerged in the dumb waves of progress, the word "Tryst" should be preserved by Act of Parliament. How well it figures in the Border Ballads – "Ate the Reidswire, the Tryst was set",[837]

---

[835] Graham had officially 'opened' the hall fifty years previously. The two gentlemen on the left, James Stewart, and John Harvie were Graham's former farm tenants, who had also been at the opening. Next to them is Colonel Archibald Stirling of Garden.

[836] 'Modern Progress', *Scotsman*, 31 July 1934, p. 13.

[837] 'The Raid of the Redeswire', also known as 'The Redeswire Fray', was a Border skirmish between English and Scottish soldiers on 7 July 1575. It took place at Carter Bar in Northumberland, the location of 'Truce Days', where

"Gailie she came to the Trysting Tree", and half a hundred other instances, show what a fine poetic word it is. None other in the language could supply its place, ... the trysting oak, at which Wallace is said to have convened his merry men in the Blane Valley, would sound poor enough, as poor as the Holy Scriptures, put into the modern vulgar tongue. Besides all this, it is a word that to Scotchmen (such as have no Gaelic) gives an air of superiority over the mere Englishman. Many years ago I crossed with a lady who always maintained that between English and Lowland Scots there was no difference, from the West Ferry to Dumbarton, in the ferry-boat.

It was raining cats and dogs, and, as we waited in the rain beside the rickety old pier below the castle, a cab drove slowly by. We eyed it curiously. I asked the driver to take us to the railway station. He rather surlily refused. Whereupon one of a host of long-shore youths who was standing heedless of the rain, watching a full-rigged ship being towed down the Clyde (being moved apparently by the air of discomfort which the lady who was with me showed), remarked, "Hurl them up, Jimmy." Jimmy relaxed his features, and answered in an apologetic way, "I canna, man, I'm trysted."

We tramped up to the station in the rain, but never afterwards did my companion maintain that the two languages were identical.

During my boyhood, Falkirk Tryst was an event to be looked forward to, for droves of ponies from the Islands and the north used to be driven down the pass by an old drove road which passed Aberfoyle.[838] Thin and wild-eyed, with ropy manes and tails that swept the ground, they strayed along.

Chestnuts and piebalds, duns with a black stripe down their back and markings like a tiger on the hocks, cream-colours with dark tails and manes, skewbalds[839] and bays (never a single roan), they used to remind me of troops of mustangs that I had read of in Mayne Reid.[840] Behind them on a pony, with his knees up to his mouth, a broken snaffle bridle, and in his hands a long, crooked hazel stick, the drover followed, always enveloped in a plaid.[841] A dog or two hung at his pony's heels, and in a language that was as strange to us as Telegu[842] he used to shout anathemas at beasts that lagged behind.

---

disputes between the two nations were usually settled without violence. 'The Raid of the Redeswire' appeared in the first edition of Walter Scott's *The Minstrelsy of the Scottish Border* in 1802.

[838] Not the Duke's Pass, but a steep track that descended to the east of the town, passing 'The Well of the Star'.

[839] Dappled white, black, and brown.

[840] Thomas Mayne Reid (1818–93), an Irish-American novelist.

[841] See passim.

[842] 'Telugu', a language spoken in the Indian subcontinent.

Slowly they trailed along, for time was what the driver had most at his command, stopping to crop the grass, or drink at the broad, shallow crossing of the mountain burns, standing about in knots knee-deep, and swishing with their tails, just as in after life [*sic*][843] I have seen wild horses do in both Americas. Foals trotted by their mothers' sides, and the whole road was blocked between its dry-stone dykes, mounted by their feals.[844]

Usually these herds of ponies, collected from the far Highlands and the Islands, were the first sign of the approaching Tryst. Sometimes, however, early in the morning if we were going out to fish, at one of those broad, grassy spaces, which in those days existed at the crossing of four roads, one used to come upon men lying round a fire. Wrapped in their plaids on which the frost showed white, or the dew shone just as it does upon a spider's web, their sticks laid near their hands, they slumbered peacefully. Around them grazed West Highland cattle, black, dun, or chestnut, their peaceful disposition belied by their long, curving horns and shaggy foreheads, and as you passed, one of the men was sure to rise upon his elbow, pull his plaid off his head, and after looking around to see the cattle had not strayed, throw wood upon the fire, and lie down to sleep again, after muttering a salutation either in Gaelic or in the sing-song English which in those days men of his kidney spoke. Great flocks of black-faced sheep were also to be met with coming southwards to the Tryst, driven by men who daundered[845] on behind them with that peculiar trailing step that only those who passed their lives upon the road were able to acquire. Generally two or three accompanied the herd, dressed usually in homespun tweeds, which smelt of wool and peat smoke, and were so thick that those who wore them looked like bears, as they lounged heavily along.

All of them had a collie, which if he was not trained, they led tied by a cord, without a collar around his neck, and fastened to a button on their coats. The dogs looked lean and wolfish, for it was long before the times when they were fashionable as pets, and at a sign, or in response to some deep guttural Gaelic order, they turned back straying sheep so dexterously, one used to wonder where the line that separated their instinct from their master's reason ended or began.

As the droves slowly took their passage through the land, the drovers would often sell a pony-beast, or a stot[846] that had gone

---

[843] Archaic = later life.
[844] On cultivated land, local farmers built low stone walls on either side of the 'drove' roads to keep the Highlanders and cattle from damaging their crops.
[845] See passim.
[846] Scots: A young castrated ox.

footsore, to farmers on the way. These sales were not concluded without expenditure of time and whisky and an infinity of talk.

Then the tired colt or calf was led into the byre, and the long line of ponies or of cattle started again, filling the road from side to side and leaving as it passed a wild, warm smell of mountain animals.

Such were the outward visible signs of Falkirk Tryst as I remember them, so many years ago, before the railways and the weekly sales reduced it to a mere cattle market, shorn of importance and of historic connection with the past. The country folks in upland farms and grazing districts looked on it as one of the important functions of the year.

"So many weeks from the October Tryst," "It would be aboot the Tryst that Andra married Jean," "I canna pay ye till the Tryst," were all familiar sayings, and the date itself was as well known to all, as Hallowe'en or Hogmanay, or even the New Year.

In those days Christmas was not held as a holiday except in districts such as Strathglass, Morar, or Moidart, or in the islands where the old faith prevailed, and where the phrases "if you please" and "thank you" were usual accidents of speech, which to a free and self-respecting man were not derogatory.

Mankind, however, must have festivals, and thus the Tryst had somehow crept into the Scottish Colin Clouts' Calendar.[847]

The drovers and droves, coming as they did from mysterious regions "above the pass," brought with them something of romance, and, in fact, as they strayed along our roads they always called to my recollection etchings by Callot[848] of the Hungarian gypsies which, bound in an old crushed morocco cover, used to lie in the drawing-room and be shown to us children on Sundays and wet afternoons.

It may be, too, that, unknown to themselves, the Lowland ploughmen working in the fields looked at the drovers as a man accustomed to office work looks on a sailor as he passes by, with feelings oscillating between contempt and envy of his adventurous life.

Certain it was that the old highland drovers would not have changed their mode of life for anything. To wake up on a bright morning in October, and shake the hoar frost from one's clothes, collect the cattle, and having sent the whisky bottle round,[849] once more to find oneself upon the road, with the scene changing constantly as you strolled along, must have been pleasanter by far than settled occupation with its dull daily round.

---

[847] A collection of essays by Grant Allen, published in London in 1883.

[848] Jacques Callot (1592–1635), a French etcher and print maker.

[849] The spirit was not usually swallowed, but cleaned the mouth after a night's sleep.

To travel round the Highlands buying a pony here, another there, three or four ewes or stots from one farm, and then setting out upon the trip to Falkirk, sleeping by the herd, and after perhaps a fortnight arriving at the Tryst, to find a booth set up, the other drovers gradually dropping in, exchanging notes on prices, and on the incidents of the march, produced a kind of that Scotland knows no more.

The "parks" by Larbert where the Tryst was held presented on the fateful day the aspect of a fair, with the tents and the crowd of country people.

Sheep bleated, and cows lowed, and, as it generally was raining, a smell of tar and wool hung in the air. Knots of men wrapped in plaids, their clothes showing signs of having camped by the roadside, their faces tanned and reddened by the sun, their beards as shaggy as the coats of the rough kyloes that they passed their lives with, chatted with Lowland shepherds from the Cheviots.

Dealers from England, better dressed but slower in their minds and speech than any Scotsman possibly can be, surveyed the animals, poking them with their sticks, and running down their points after the fashion of the intending buyer in every country in the world. Rough-looking lads, but with that air of supernatural cunning that commerce with the horse imparts, ran ponies up and down.

Beefy-faced cattle-dealers from the Midlands roared at Highlanders whose English was defective, thinking to make them understand by noise; and Highlanders, who themselves understood English as well as they did, and spoke it far more purely, pretended to mistake their meaning to get more time to think what they would say.

When, after an infinity of haggling, a price was reached, to which the seller gave assent, both parties would adjourn to one or other of the tents, to wet the bargain, and sit down at a white, deal table, placed upon the grass, and swallow whisky in a way that no one not connected with the cattle trade could possibly achieve. On them it had no more effect than milk, unless to make the fiery faces of the Yorkshire dealers a thought redder, and set the Highlanders a-talking still more fluently than when they had gone in.

Quarrels were rare, and drunkenness not common with such seasoned vessels; but on the rare occasions when the whisky had proved stronger than the head, they lay down peacefully to sleep it off, beside their animals, with their heads buried in their plaids.

The day wore on, amidst the lowing of the beasts and noise of bargaining, and towards evening the roads were full of strings of animals being driven off, either towards the railway, or on the way to their new homes. I often wondered if they missed the rough and shaggy men, so near to them in type, or thought about the upland pastures in the glens, or the sweet, waving grass of island "machars"[850] in the lush Lowland fields.

It pleases us and stills our conscience to say that animals know no such feeling, but yet "I hae my doots,"[851] and the wild winnyings and jerks back on the halter mean something, ... but after all they have no souls.

Not that such speculations ever entered anybody's head at Falkirk Tryst. Well, well, the Tryst, that is as I knew it in my boyhood, has slipped away into the realms of old, forgotten, far-away memories.

It formed a link between the modern world and times when kilted drovers with their targets[852] at their backs, girt with their claymores, their feet shod in the hairy brogues by which they gained the name of the Rough-Footed Scots, drove down their kyloes and their ponies through the very bealach[853] that I remember in my youth. They are all gone with the old world they lived in; but still the shadows fall upon the southern slopes and creep into the corries of the Ochils[854] that overlook the historic parks by Larbert in which the Tryst was held. Heavy-nailed boots now press the grass that once was brushed by the Highland brogues. No one now sleeps beside the roads, nor, rising with the dawn, wrings out the dewdrops from his plaid.

The life that once was real, now seems fantastic; not half as real as the shadows on the hills, and even they only endure whilst the sun shines, chasing one another up and down till it peeps in again.

---

[850] See passim.
[851] Scots: 'I have my doubts'.
[852] Round shields.
[853] Gaelic: A high gap or pass.
[854] The Ochil Hills, across the River Forth, in Clackmannanshire.

1915–33

There was a marked diminution in Graham's literary output during 1914, and no Scottish sketch at all. Surprisingly, for someone who had long held an anti-imperialist and an anti-war position,[855] and who six months earlier had described uniforms as 'a thing to be ashamed of',[856] within two weeks of the start of the Great War, at the age of sixty-two, he volunteered for unpaid military service, and in November it was reported that he had been given a commission by the War Office.[857] On 20 November, a letter from Graham appeared in *The Daily News & Leader* in which he said that Britain had been forced into war by Germany, and that 'we, perhaps by accident, have been forced into the right course, and that all smaller nationalities as Montenegro, Ireland, Poland, and the rest, would disappear on our defeat'.[858] Shortly afterwards, he departed for Montevideo where he spent eleven months buying horses for the war effort on behalf of the Government.[859] He returned to South America in February 1917 to report on cattle resources. The following story, however, was his only attempt in print to justify his belief that it was a people's war, not one for politicians and capitalists.[860]

BROUGHT FORWARD

The English Review, February 1915, pp. 285–9.
Anthologised in *Brought Forward* (London: Duckworth, 1916), pp. 1–10.

---

[855] Graham had invited Conrad to a pacifist meeting in London in early 1899, but Conrad declined the invitation, with the words, 'I am not a man of peace, nor a democrat'. Watts, *Joseph Conrad's Letters*, p. 116.

[856] Cunninghame Graham, 'Futurism', *Justice*, 30 April 1914, p. 9.

[857] *Glasgow Herald*, 4 November 1914, p. 6. Graham stated that he had been offered the rank of colonel, which he refused, 'thinking it ridiculous for a private citizen not a military man to hold such a title'. *Stirling Observer*, 2 December 1918, p. 3. Tschiffely wrote, however, that Graham had accepted the rank, but had refused to wear the uniform. Tschiffely, p. 361.

[858] *Daily News & Leader*, 20 November 1914, p. 4.

[859] *Glasgow Herald*, 11 August 1917, p. 4.

[860] At the war's end, Graham stood as the Liberal Candidate for West Stirlingshire in the 1918 General Election, on a home-rule and anti-German platform. His Labour opponent was his one-time supporter, future Secretary of State for Scotland, Thomas Johnston. Both were beaten by the Unionist, Sir Harry Hope, and Johnston believed that Hope won because he was even more bellicose over the war than Graham, and had a platform of hanging the Kaiser, and that the electorate believed that Graham 'would not pull the rope tightly enough'. Johnston, *Memories*, (London: Collins, 1952), p. 47.

The workshop in Parkhead was not inspiriting. From one week's end to another, all throughout the year, life was the same, almost without incident. In the long days of the Scotch summer the men walked cheerily to work, carrying their dinner in a little tin. In the dark winter mornings they tramped in the black fog, coughing and spitting, through the black mud of Glasgow streets, each with a woollen comforter, looking like a stocking, round his neck.

Outside the dreary quarter of the town, its rows of dingy, smoke-grimed streets and the mean houses, the one outstanding feature was Parkhead Forge, with its tall chimneys belching smoke into the air all day, and flames by night. Its glowing furnaces, its giant hammers, its little railway trucks in which men ran the blocks of white-hot iron which poured in streams out of the furnaces, flamed like the mouth of hell.

Inside the workshop, the dusty atmosphere made a stranger cough on entering the door. The benches with the rows of aproned men all bending at their work, not standing upright, with their bare, hairy chests exposed, after the fashion of Vulcans at the neighbouring forge, gave a half air of domesticity to the close stuffy room.

A semi-sedentary life quickened their intellect; for where men work together they are bound to talk about the topics of the day, especially in Scotland, where every man is a born politician and a controversialist. At meal-times, when they ate their "piece"[861] and drank their tea that they carried with them in tin flasks, each one was certain to draw out a newspaper from the pocket of his coat, and, after studying it from the Births, Deaths and Marriages, down to the editor's address on the last page, fall a-disputing upon politics. "Man, a gran' speech by Bonar Law[862] aboot Home Rule. They Irish, set them up, what do they make siccan a din aboot?[863] Ca' ye it Home Rule? I juist ca' it Rome Rule. A miserable, priest-ridden crew, the hale rick-ma-tick[864] o' them."

The reader then would pause and, looking round the shop, wait for the answer that he was sure would not be long in coming from amongst such a thrawn[865] lot of commentators. Usually one or another of his mates would fold his paper up, or perhaps point with an oil-stained finger to an article, and with the head-break in the voice, characteristic of the Scot about to plunge into an argument, ejaculate:

---

[861] Scots: A sandwich.
[862] Andrew Bonar Law (1858–1923), Canadian Conservative and Unionist politician who held numerous posts, including chancellor of the exchequer and prime minister.
[863] Scots: Such a fuss about.
[864] Scots: The whole lot or "caboodle".
[865] See passim.

"Bonar Law, ou aye, I kent[866] him when he was leader of the South Side Parliament.[867] He always was a dreary body, sort o' dreich[868] like; no that I'm saying the man's pairfectly illiterate, as some on his side o' the hoose, there in Westminster. I read his speech – the body is na blate,[869] sort o' quick at figures, but does na take the pains to verify. Verification is the soul of mathematics. Bonar Law, eh! Did ye see how Maister Asquith[870] trippit him handily in his tabulated figures on the jute business under Free Trade, showing that all he had advanced about protective tariffs and the drawback system was fair redeeklous ... as well as several errors in the total sum."

Then others would cut in and words be bandied to and fro, impugning the good faith and honour of every section of the House of Commons, who, by the showing of their own speeches, were held to be dishonourable rogues aiming at power and place, without a thought for anything but their own ends.

This charitable view of men and of affairs did not prevent any of the disputants from firing up if his own party was impugned; for in their heart and hearts the general denunciation was but a covert from which to attack the other side.

In such an ambient the war was sure to be discussed; some held the German Emperor was mad – "a daft-like thing to challenge the whole world, ye see; maist inconsiderate, and shows that the man's intellect is no weel balanced ... philosophy is whiles sort of unsettlin' ... the felly's mad ye ken."

Others saw method in his madness, and alleged that it was envy, "naething but sheer envy that had brought on this tramplin' upon natural rights, but for all that he may be thought to get his own again, with they indemnities."

Those who had studied economics "were of the opinion that his reasoning was wrong, built on false premises, for there can never be a royal road to wealth. Labour, ye see, is the sole creative element of riches." At once a Tory would rejoin, "And brains. Man, what an awfu' thing to leave out brains. Think of the marvellous creations of the human genius." The first would answer with, "I saw ye coming, man. I'll no deny that brains have their due place in the economic

---

[866] Scots: Knew.
[867] It is unclear to what this refers, but perhaps to when Bonar Law was leader of the opposition (1911–15), which sits on the south side of the House of Commons chamber.
[868] See passim.
[869] Scots: Dull, stupid.
[870] H. H. Asquith, prime minister from 1908 to 1916, and later Earl of Oxford. He was Graham's defence barrister following his arrest for his part in the 'Bloody Sunday' riot in Trafalgar Square on 13 November 1887.

state; but build me one of your Zeppelins and stick it in the middle of George Square without a crew to manage it, and how far will it fly? I do not say that brains did not devise it; but, after all, labour had to carry out the first design." This was a subject that opened up enormous vistas for debate, and for a time kept them from talking of the war.

Jimmy and Geordie, hammering away at one end of the room, took little part in the debate. Good workmen both of them, and friends, perhaps because of the difference in their temperaments, for Jimmy was the type of red-haired, blue-eyed, tall, lithe Scot, he of the *perfervidium ingenium*.[871] And Geordie was a thick-set, black-haired, dour[872] and silent man.

Both of them read the war news, and Jimmy, when he read, commented loudly, bringing down his fist upon the paper, exclaiming, "Weel done the Gordons!"[873] or that "was a richt gude charge by the Sutherlands."[874] Geordie would answer shortly, Aye, no sae bad," and go on hammering.

One morning after a reverse, Jimmy did not appear, and Geordie sat alone working away as usual, but if possible more dourly and silently. Towards midday it began to be whispered in the shop that Jimmy had enlisted, and the men turned to Geordie to ask if he knew anything about it, and the silent workman, brushing the sweat off his brow with his coat-sleeve rejoined: "Aye, ou aye, I went wi' him yestreen[875] to the headquarters of the Cameronians;[876] he's joined the kilties richt enough. Ye mind he was a sergeant in South Africa.[877] Then he bent over to his work and did not join in the general conversation that ensued.

Days passed, and weeks, and his fellow workmen, in the way men will, occasionally bantered Geordie, asking him if he was going to enlist, and whether he did not think shame to let his friend go off alone to fight. Geordie was silent under abuse and banter, as he had always been under the injustices of life, and by degrees withdrew into himself, and when he read his newspaper during the dinner-hour

---

[871] Latin: Of an ardent disposition.
[872] Scots: Sullen, gloomy.
[873] A Scottish regiment, the Gordon Highlanders, which saw action at the battles of Mons and Ypres.
[874] A Scottish regiment, the Argyll & Sutherland Highlanders, which saw action, like the Gordons, on the Western Front.
[875] Scots: Yesterday evening.
[876] A Scottish regiment, the Cameronians (Scottish Rifles), which saw action on the Western Front and at Gallipoli.
[877] South Africa. Jimmy had served, probably with the Cameronians, in the Second Anglo-Boer War (1899–1902).

made no remark, but folded it and put it quietly into the pocket of his coat.

Weeks passed, weeks of suspense, of flaring headlines in the press, of noise of regiments passing down the streets, of newsboys yelling hypothetic victories, and of tension of the nerves of men who know their country's destiny is hanging in the scales. Rumours of losses, of defeats, of victories, of checks and of advances, of naval battles, with hints of the dreadful slaughter, filled the air. Women in black were seen about, pale and with eyelids swollen with weeping, and people scanned the reports of killed and wounded with dry throats and hearts constricted as if they had been wrapped in whipcord, only relaxing when after a second look they had assured themselves the name they feared to see was absent from the list.

Long strings of Clydesdale horses ridden by men in ragged clothes, who sat them uneasily, as if they felt their situation keenly perched up in public view, passed through the streets. The massive caulkers[878] on their shoes struck fire occasionally upon the stones, and the great beasts, taught to rely on man as on a god from the time they gambolled in the fields, went to their doom unconsciously, the only mitigation of their fate. Regiments of young recruits, some in plain clothes and some in hastily made uniforms, marched with as martial an air as three weeks' training gave them, to the stations to entrain. Pale clerks, the elbows of their jackets shiny with the slavery of the desk, strode beside men whose hands were bent and scarred with gripping on the handles of the plough in February gales or wielding sledges at the forge.

All of them were young and resolute, and each was confident that he at least would come back safe to tell the tale. Men stopped and waved their hats, cheering their passage, and girls and women stood with flushed cheeks and straining eyes as the passed on for the first stage that took them towards the front. Boys ran beside them, hatless and barefooted, shouting out words that they had caught up on the drill-ground to the men who whistled as they marched a slow and grinding tune that sounded like a hymn.

Traffic was drawn up close to the kerbstone, and from the top of 'buses and carts men cheered, bringing a flush of pride to many a pale cheek in the ranks. They passed on; men resumed the business of their lives, few understanding that the half-trained, pale-faced regiment that had vanished through the great station gates had gone to make that business possible and safe.

---

[878] Caulkins or studs improve a horse's balance and grip over uneven or slippery ground.

Then came a time of waiting for the news, of contradictory paragraphs in newspapers, and then a telegram, the "enemy is giving ground on the left wing"; and instantly a feeling of relief that lightened every heart, as if its owner had been fighting and had stopped to wipe his brow before he started to pursue the flying enemy.

The workmen in the brassfitters' shop came to their work as usual on the day of the good news, and at the dinner-hour read out the accounts of the great battle, clustering upon each other's shoulders in their eagerness. At last one turned to scan the list of casualties. Cameron, Campbell, McAlister, Jardine, they read, as they ran down the list, checking the names off with a match. The reader stopped, and looked towards the corner where Geordie still sat working silently.

All eyes were turned towards him, for the rest seemed to divine even before they heard the name. "Geordie man, Jimmy's killed," the reader said, and as he spoke Geordie laid down his hammer, and, reaching for his coat, said, "Jimmy's killed, is he? Well, someone's got to account for it."

Then, opening the door, he walked out dourly, as if already he felt the knapsack on his back and the avenging rifle in his hand.

* * * * *

One of Graham's most significant political relationships was with Keir Hardie, whom he met in 1887, while fighting on behalf of the miners as a Liberal MP.[879] Influenced by the designer and socialist William Morris, Graham had envisaged a party of labour, and he set about grooming Hardie, a miner and journalist, to take up the leadership role.[880] According to Hardie's biographer, Caroline Benn, Hardie needed a mentor, to help him make the transition from regional to national stage, and while Hardie offered Graham an understanding of working-class life and needs, Graham offered Hardie 'an inside knowledge of how the governing classes really worked, and the courage to stand up to them'.[881] Subsequently, they founded the Scottish Parliamentary Labour Party, a precursor of the Independent Labour Party. By 1893, however, their relationship was fracturing, as Graham increasingly criticised what he saw as Labour's lack of direction and effectiveness.

---

[879] According to the socialist, Glasier, Hardie and Graham were close companions for six years, and they 'went about in harness'. Bruce Glasier, *James Keir Hardie: A Memorial* (Manchester: National Labour Press, 1919), p. 20.

[880] Hardie had been a committed Liberal, and had been reluctant to part from them.

[881] Ibid., p. 49.

Hardie died on 26 of September 1915, and was cremated at Maryhill cemetery on the 29th – 5,000 attended his memorial at Glasgow's St Andrews Hall. James Leatham wrote: 'Those of us who knew him best assert that he has veritably died of a broken heart at the shipwreck of all his ideals by the war.'[882]

It was at events such as this that Graham's observational and reflective skills were at their best, as first demonstrated in his description of Morris's funeral almost twenty years previously. The day after Morris's death, the publisher Frank Harris had commissioned Arthur Symons and George Bernard Shaw to write obituaries, and warned each to "stretch yourself", as Graham's "stuff would be hard to beat", whereby he believes that Shaw acknowledged Graham as 'a Master'.[883]

WITH THE NORTH-EAST WIND

The Nation, 23 October 1915, pp. 147–8.
Anthologised in *Brought Forward* (London: Duckworth, 1916), pp. 51–9.

A NORTH-EAST haar had hung the city with a pall of grey. It gave an air of hardness to the stone-built houses, blending them with the stone-paved streets, till you could scarce see where the houses ended and the street began. A thin grey dust hung in the air. It coloured everything, and people's faces all looked grey with the first touch of autumn cold. The wind, boisterous and gusty, whisked the soot-grimed city leaves about in the high suburb at the foot of a long range of hills, making one think it would be easy to have done with life on such an uncongenial day. Tramways were packed with people of the working class, all of them of the alert, quick-witted type only to be seen in the great city on the Clyde, in all our Empire, and comparable alone to the dwellers in Chicago for dry vivacity.

By the air they wore of chastened pleasure, all those who knew them saw that they were intent upon a funeral. To serious minded men such as are they, for all their quickness, nothing is so soul-filling, for it is of the nature of a fact that no one can deny. A wedding has its possibilities, for it may lead to children, or divorce, but funerals

---

[882] James Leatham, 'Some Memories of Keir Hardie', *Gateway*, vol. IV, October 1915.
[883] William E. Fredeman, 'William Morris's Funeral', *Journal of William Morris Studies*, Spring 1966, p. 29. Graham also wrote notable obituaries for Wilfrid Scawen Blunt, Joseph Conrad and Neil Munro (see below).

are in another category. At them the Scottish people is at its best, for never more than then does the deep underlying tenderness peep through the hardness of the rind. On foot and in the tramways, but most especially on foot, long lines of men and women, for the national prejudice that in years gone by thought it not decent for a wife to follow to the grave her husband's coffin, still holds a little in the north. Yet there was something in the crowd that showed it was to attend no common funeral, that they were "stepping west." No one wore black, except a minister or two, who looked a little like the belated rook you sometimes see amongst a flock of seagulls, in that vast ocean of grey tweed.

They tramped along, the whistling north-east wind pinching their features, making their eyes run, and as they went, almost unconsciously they fell into procession, for beyond the tramway line, a country lane that had not quite put on the graces of a street, though straggling houses were dotted here and there along it, received the crowd and marshalled it, as it were mechanically, without volition of its own. Kept in between the walls, and blocked in front by the hearse and a long procession of mourning coaches, the people slowly surged along. The greater portion of the crowd were townsmen, but there were miners washed and in their Sunday best, their faces showed the blue marks of healed-up scars into which coal dust or gunpowder had become tattooed [*sic*], scars gained in the battle of their lives down the pits, remembrances of falls of rock or of occasions when the mine had "fired upon them."

Many had known Keir Hardie in his youth, had "wrocht wi' him"[884] out-by, Blantyre, at Hamilton, in Ayrshire, and all of them had heard him speak a hundred times. Even to those who had not heard him, his name was as a household word. Miners predominated, but men of every trade were there. Many were members of that black-coated proletariat, whose narrow circumstances and daily struggle for appearances make their life harder to them, than is the life of any working men before he has had to dye his hair. Women tramped, too, for the dead leader had been a champion of their sex. They all respected him, loving him with that half-contemptuous gratitude that women often show to men who make the "woman question" the object of their lives.

After the Scottish fashion at a funeral, greetings were freely passed, and Reid, who hadna' seen his friend Mackinder since the time of the Mid-Lanark fight,[885] greeted him with "Ye mind when first Keir

---

[884] Scots: Laboured alongside him.
[885] The Mid-Lanark by-election of 1888 where Hardie, rejected by the Liberals as their candidate, stood as an Independent Labour candidate and was badly

Hardie was puttin' up for Parliament," and wrung his hand, hardened in the mine, with one as hardened, and instantly began to recall elections of the past.

"Ye mind yon Wishaw meeting?"

"Aye, ou aye; ye mean when a' they Irish wouldna hear John Ferguson.[886] Man, he almost grat[887] after the meeting aboot it."

"Aye, but they gied Hardie himself a maist respectful hearing ... aye, ou aye."

Others remembered him a boy, and others in his home at Cumnock, but all spoke of him with affection, holding him as something of their own, apart from other politicians, almost apart from men.

Old comrades who had been with him either at this election or that meeting, had helped or had intended to have helped at the crises of his life, fought their old battles over, as they tramped along, all shivering in the wind.

The procession reached a long dip in the road, and the head of it, full half-a-mile away, could be seen grouping themselves beside the hearse, outside the chapel of the crematorium, whose ominous tall chimney, through which the ashes, and perchance the souls of thousands have escaped towards some empyrean[888] or another, towered up starkly. At last all had arrived, and the small open space was crowded, the hearse and carriages appearing stuck amongst the people, like raisins in a cake, so thick they pressed upon them. The chapel, differing from the ordinary chapel of the faiths as much as does a motor driver from a cabman, had an air as of modernity about it, which contrasted strangely with the ordinary looking crowd, the adjacent hills, the decent mourning coaches and the black-coated undertakers who bore the coffin up the steps. Outside, the wind whistled and swayed the soot-stained trees about; but inside the chapel the heat was stifling.

When all was duly done, and long exordiums passed upon the man who in his life had been the target for the abuse of press and pulpit, the coffin slid away to its appointed place. One thought one heard the roaring of the flames, and somehow missed the familiar lowering of the body ... earth to earth ... to which the centuries of use and wont[889] have made us all familiar, though dust to dust in this case was the more appropriate.

---

beaten, leading directly, under Graham's guidance, to the establishment of the Scottish Parliamentary Labour Party (SPLP).

[886] John Ferguson (1836–1906) Ulster-born, Glaswegian, Irish nationalist and Labour supporter.

[887] Scots: Cried.

[888] The highest part of heaven.

[889] Accustomedness.

In either case, the book is closed for ever, and the familiar face is seen no more.

So standing just outside the chapel in the cold, waiting till all the usual greetings had been exchanged, I fell a musing on the man who I had known so well. I saw him as he was thirty years ago, outlined against a bing[890] or standing in a quarry in some mining village, and heard his once familiar address of "Men." He used no other in those days, to the immense disgust of legislators and other worthy but unimaginative men whom he might chance to meet. About him seemed to stand a shadowy band, most of whom are dead or lost to view, or have gone under in the fight.

John Ferguson was there, the old-time Irish leader, the friend of Davitt[891] and of Butt.[892] Tall and erect he stood, dressed in his long frock coat, his roll of papers in one hand, and with the other stuck into his breast, with all the air of being the last Roman left alive. Tom Mann,[893] with his black hair, his flashing eyes, and his tumultuous speech peppered with expletives. Beside him, Sandy Haddow, of Parkhead,[894] massive and Doric in his speech, with a grey woollen comforter rolled round his neck, and hands like panels of a door. Champion,[895] pale, slight, and interesting, still the artillery officer, in spite of Socialism. John Burns,[896] and Small,[897] the miners' agent, with his close brown beard and taste for literature. Smillie[898] stood near,

---

[890] Scots: A coalmine slagheap. Old Norse: *bingr* = a heap.

[891] Michael Davitt (1846–1906), an Irish republican activist who had served seven years in prison for gunrunning. In 1918, Graham claimed that he had stood on 'a thousand platforms' with Davitt and Charles Stuart Parnell, promoting Irish Home Rule. *Stirling Observer*, 26 November 1918, p. 5.

[892] Isaac Butt (1813–79), an Irish barrister, MP, and Conservative home-ruler.

[893] Thomas Mann (1856–1941). English trade unionist, and leading pioneer of the Labour movement.

[894] Alexander 'Sandy' Haddow (1851–1918). An early socialist pioneer in Scotland. Following his death, Graham paid tribute to, and unveiled a memorial to Haddow. *Glasgow Herald*, 14 August 1922, p. 10.

[895] Henry Hyde Champion (1859–1928). Born in India, and fought in the Afghan War. Later he became the editor of *Labour Elector*, to which Graham was a regular contributor.

[896] John Eliot Burns (1858–1943). An English trade-unionist of Scottish parentage, and a onetime close colleague of Graham. They were both arrested and imprisoned for charging police lines in Trafalgar Square during 'Bloody Sunday', in 1887. In 1892 he was elected Liberal MP for Battersea. He was briefly President of the Board of Trade, but resigned in protest at the First World War.

[897] William Small (1848–1903). A miners' organiser, and an original member of the SPLP and ILP.

[898] Robert Smillie (1857–1940). An early socialist pioneer in Scotland, and close colleague of Hardie and 'Sandy' Haddow. President of the Lanarkshire

he of the seven elections, and then check-weigher at a pit, either at Cadzow or Larkhall. There, too, was silver-tongued Shaw Maxwell[899] and Chisholm Robertson,[900] looking out darkly on the world through tinted spectacles; with him Bruce Glasier,[901] girt with a red sash and with an aureole of fair, curly hair, around his head, half-poet and half-revolutionary.

They were all young and ardent, and as I mused upon them and their fate, and upon those of them who had gone down into the oblivion that waits for those who live before their time, I shivered in the wind.

Had he, too, lived in vain, he whose scant ashes were no doubt by this time all collected in an urn, and did they really represent all that remained of him?

Standing amongst the band of shadowy comrades I had known, I saw him, simple and yet with something of the prophet in his air, and something of the seer. Effective and yet ineffectual, something there was about him that attracted little children to him, and I should think lost dogs. He made mistakes, but then those who make no mistakes seldom make anything. His life was one long battle, so it seemed to me that it was fitting that at his funeral the north-east wind should howl amongst the trees, tossing and twisting them as he himself was twisted and storm-tossed in his tempestuous passage through the world.

As the crowd moved away, and in the hearse and mourning coaches, the spavined[902] horses limped slowly down the road, a gleam of sunshine, such as had shone too little in his life, lighted up everything.

The swaying trees, and dark, grey houses of the ugly suburb of the town, were all transfigured for a moment. The chapel door was closed, and from the chimney of the crematorium a faint blue smoke was issuing, which, by degrees, faded into the atmosphere, just as the soul for all I know, may melt into the air.

Miners' Federation, President of the Miners' Federation of Great Britain, and MP for Morpeth, among many other positions.

[899] James Shaw Maxwell (1855–1928). An activist in the Scottish Land Restoration League, and a founder member of the Scottish Parliamentary Labour Party. He was elected a Glasgow city councillor in 1896, and was instrumental in the creation of free libraries in the city.

[900] Robert Chisholm Robertson (1861–1930). An active trade-unionist. President of the Scottish Miners' Association and Founding Secretary of the Scottish Miners' Federation.

[901] John Bruce Glasier (1859–1920). Glasgow-born socialist activist. Glasier had been selected to be Hardie's official biographer, but on his death, the role was given to William Stewart. In 1916, Graham and Glasier fell out over Graham's support for the First World War.

[902] See passim.

When the last stragglers had gone, and bits of paper scurried uneasily along before the wind, the world seemed empty, with nothing friendly in it, but the shoulder of Ben Lomond peeping shyly over the Kilpatrick Hills.

* * * * *

Next, Graham gives us a glimpse of a different ancestral area, that flanking the north bank of the River Clyde, where his great-great-grandfather, Robert Graham, who owned two sugar plantations in Jamaica, built a Jamaican style bungalow, Ardoch Cottage, for his Jamaican-born wife, Anne, in the early 1770s. Though the house had been sold in 1887, Graham and his wife managed to buy it back following the sale of Gartmore House, and it became his writing retreat.

The view Graham nostalgically evokes – nostalgically as the tale was most likely written while he was in Uruguay buying horses for the British Army – was less than an hour's walk from his study in the book room. It is the view from a small wood, called the Kellochy, which sits in the midst of the moor that crowns the hill behind Ardoch.

The laird's animal parable touchingly mirrored Graham's own situation a decade earlier: just as the curlew faithfully stood by its dying mate, so had he, equally helplessly but faithfully, succoured Gabriela in the last days of her life in Hendaye. His melancholy and his feelings of loss, voiced by the old laird, are extremely poignant.

The vignette, which true to life, closes without resolution, ends in what Neil Munro termed "a minor key"[903] and, characteristically for Graham, his "authorially silent finish".[904]

FIDELITY

The Nation, 27 November 1915, pp. 323–4.
Anthologised in *Brought Forward* (London: Duckworth, 1916), pp. 30–9.

My tall host knocked the ashes from his pipe, and crossing one leg over the other looked into the fire.

Outside the wind howled in the trees, and the rain beat upon the window panes. The firelight flickered on the grate, falling upon the polished furniture of the low-roofed, old-fashioned library, with its high Georgian overmantel, where in a deep recess there stood a clock,

---

[903] Neil Munro, p. 306.
[904] Watts & Davies, p. 157.

shaped like a cross, with eighteenth-century cupids carved in ivory fluttering around the base, and Time with a long scythe standing upon one side.

In the room hung the scent of an old country house, compounded of so many samples that it is difficult to enumerate them all. Beeswax and pot-pourri of roses, damp, and the scent of foreign woods in the old cabinets, tobacco and wood smoke, with the all-pervading smell of age, were some of them. The result was not unpleasant, and seemed the complement of the well-bound Georgian books standing demure upon their shelves, the blackening family portraits, and the skins of red deer and of roe scattered about the room.

The conversation languished, and we both sat listening to the storm that seemed to fill the world with noises strange and unearthly, for the house was far from railways, and the avenues that lead to it were long and dark. The solitude and the wild night seemed to have re-created the old world, long lost, and changed, but still remembered in that district just where the Highlands and the Lowlands meet.

At such times and in such houses the country really seems country once again, and not the gardened, game-keepered mixture of shooting ground and of fat fields tilled by machinery to which men now and then resort for sport, or to gather their rents, with which the whole world is familiar to-day.

My host seemed to be struggling with himself to tell me something, and as I looked at him, tall, strong, and upright, his face all mottled by the weather, his home-spun coat, patched on the shoulders with buckskin that once had been white, but now was fawn-coloured with wet and from the chafing of his gun, I felt the parturition of his speech would probably cost him a shrewd throe.[905]

So I said nothing, and he, after having filled his pipe, ramming the tobacco down with an old silver Indian seal, made as he told me in Kurachi, and brought home by a great-uncle fifty years ago,[906] slowly began to speak, not looking at me, but as it were delivering his thoughts aloud, almost unconsciously, looking now and then at me as if he felt, rather than knew, that I was there. As he spoke, the tall, stuffed hen-harrier, the little Neapolitan shrine in tortoise-shell and coral, set thick with saints, the flying dragons from Ceylon, spread out like butterflies in glazed case, the "poor's-box" on the shelf above the books with its four silver sides adorned with texts, the rows of blue books, and the row of Scott's Novels (the Roxburgh edition), together with the scent exuding from the Kingwood cabinet, the

[905] 'I felt the issuing of his next syllables would be painful to him.'
[906] Graham's own great-uncle, Mountstuart Elphinstone, brought many such things back from India, where he had been Governor of Bombay.

sprays of white Scotch rose, outlined against the window blinds, and the sporting prints and family tree, all neatly framed in oak, created the impression of being in a world remote, besquired and cut off from the century in which we live, by more than fifty years. Upon the rug before the fire, the sleeping spaniel whined uneasily, as if, though sleeping, it still scented game, and all the time the storm roared in the trees and whistled down the passages of the lone country house. One saw in fancy, deep in the recesses of the woods the roe standing sheltering, and the capercailzie sitting on the branches of the firs, wet and dejected, like chickens on a roost, and little birds sent along, battling for life against the storm. Upon such nights, in districts such as that in which the gaunt old house was situated, there is a feeling of compassion for the wild things in the woods that, stealing over one, bridges the gulf between them and ourselves in a mysterious way. Their lot and sufferings, joys, loves, and the epitome of their brief lives, come home to us with something irresistible, making us feel that our superiority is an unreal thing, and that in essentials we are one.

My host went on: "Some time ago I walked up to the little moor that overlooks the Clyde, from which you see ships far away lying at the Tail of the Bank, the smoke of Greenock and Port Glasgow, the estuary itself, though miles away, looking like a sheet of frosted silver or dark grey steel, according to the season, and in the distance the range of hills called Argyll's Bowling Green, with the deep gap that marks the entrance to the Holy Loch. Autumn had just begun to tinge the trees, birches were golden, and rowans red, the bents[907] were brown and dry. A few bog asphodels still showed amongst the heather, and bilberries, dark as blackcurrants, grew here and there amongst the carpet of green sphagnum and the stag's head moss. The heather was all rusty brown, but still there was, as it were, a recollection of summer in the air. Just the kind of day you feel inclined to sit down on the lee side of a dry-stone dyke, and smoke and look at some familiar self-sown birch that marks the flight of time, as you remember that it was but a year or two ago that it had first shot up above the grass.

"I remember two or three plants of tall hempagrimony still had their flower heads withered on the stalk, giving them a look of wearing wigs, and clumps of ragwort still had a few bees buzzing about them, rather faintly, with a belated air. I saw all this – not that I am a botanist, for you know I can hardly tell the difference between the cruciferæ and the umbelliferæ, but because when you live in the country some of the common plants seem to obtrude themselves upon you, and you have got to notice them in spite of you. So I walked on

---

[907] Scots: Common hair-grass.

till I came to a wrecked plantation of spruce and Scotch fir. A hurricane had struck it, turning it over almost in rows, as it was planted. The trees had withered in most cases, and in the open spaces round their upturned roots hundreds of rabbits burrowed, and had marked the adjoining field with little paths, just like the lines outside a railway station.

"I saw all this, not because I looked at it, for if you look with the idea of seeing everything, commonly everything escapes you, but because the lovely afternoon induced a feeling of well-being and contentment, and everything seemed to fall into its right proportion, so that you saw first the harmonious whole, and then the salient points most worth looking at.

"I walked along feeling exhilarated with the autumn air and the fresh breeze that blew up from the Clyde. I remember thinking I had hardly ever felt greater content, and as I walked it seemed impossible the world could be so full of rank injustice, or that the lot of three-fourths of its population could really be so hard. A pack of grouse flew past, skimming above the heather as a shoal of flying fish skims just above the waves. I heard their quacking cries as they alighted on some stooks[908] of oats, and noticed that the last bird to settle was an old hen, and that, even when all were down, I still could see her head, looking out warily above the yellow grain. Beyond the ruined wood there came the barking of a shepherd's dog, faint and subdued, almost musical.

"I sat so long smoking and looking at the view, that when I turned to go the sun was sinking and our long, northern twilight almost setting in.

"You know it," said my host, and I, who often had read by its light in summer and early autumn, nodded assent, wondering to myself what he was going to tell me, and he went on.

"It has the property of making all things look a little ghostly, deepening the shadows and altering their values, so that all that you see seems to acquire an extra significance, not so much to the eye as to the mind. Slowly I retraced my steps, walking under the high wall of rough piled stones till it ends, at the copse of willows, on the north side of the little moor to which I had seen the pack of grouse fly after it had left the stooks. I crossed into it, and began to walk towards home, knee-deep in bent grass and dwarf willows, with here and there a patch of heather and a patch of bilberries. The softness of the ground so dulled my footsteps that I appeared to walk as lightly as a roe upon the spongy surface of the moor. As I passed through a slight depression in which the grass grew rankly, I heard a wild cry

---

[908] Scots: A bundle of corn sheaves set up in the field to dry.

coming, it seemed, from just beneath my feet. Then came a rustling in the grass, and a large, dark-grey bird sprang out, repeating the wild cry, and ran off swiftly, trailing a broken wing.

"It paused upon a little hillock fifty yards away, repeating its strange note, and looking round as if it sought for something that it was certain was at hand. High in the air the cry, wilder and shriller, was repeated, and a great grey bird that I saw was a whaup,[909] slowly descended in decreasing circles, and settled down beside its mate.

"They seemed to talk, and then the wounded bird set off at a swift run, its fellow circling above its head and uttering its cry as if it guided it. I watched them disappear, feeling as if an iron belt was drawn tight around my heart, their cries growing fainter as the deepening shadows slowly closed upon the moor."

My host stopped, knocked the ashes from his pipe, and turning to me, said: –

"I watched them go to what must have been certain death for one of them, furious, with the feelings of a murderer towards the man whose thoughtless folly had been the cause of so much misery. Curse him! I watched them, impotent to help, for as you know the curlew is perhaps the wildest of our native birds; and even had I caught the wounded one to set its wing, it would have pined and died. One thing I could have done, had I but a gun and had the light been better, I might have shot them both, and had I done so I would have buried them beside each other.

"That's what I had on my mind to tell you. I think the storm and the wild noises of the struggling trees outside have brought it back to me, although it happened years ago. Sometimes, when people talk about fidelity, saying it is not to be found upon the earth, I smile, for I have seen it with my own eyes, and manifest, out on that little moor."

He filled his pipe, and sitting down in an old leather chair, much worn and rather greasy, silently gazed into the fire.

I, too, was silent, thinking upon the tragedy; then feeling that something was expected of me, looked up and murmured, "Yes."

* * * * *

The following story is a re-working of *A Survival*, which had been published in *The Saturday Review* two decades earlier, and anthologised in *Success* (London: Duckworth) in 1902. Both the farm and the Highlander remain unchanged, but the long, rambling diatribe against the Kailyard School has been dropped, allowing what Professor Walker called "the triple-headed monster of

---

[909] Scots: A curlew (*numenius arquata*).

civilisation-commerce-progress"[910] to take centre stage. As suggested earlier, five farms containing the name 'Offerance' were owned by Graham, so his friend 'Inverquharity' was most likely himself.

TRANSPLANTED IN VAIN

The Gateway,[911] September 1916, pp. 29–32.

Not far from where I live there dwells a worthy man, Scottissimus Scotorum,[912] a Scot of Scots, enriched by sweating of some sort, but still a kindly soul. Kindly, of course, in everything but trade, which is a thing apart and sacred, semi-divine, sent straight from God, and, like divinity, the teinds,[913] baptismal regeneration, and hell-fire, quite beyond argument. A Liberal, of the baser sort – that is a Liberal wishing to drag down all men over him – a Tory of the Tories to all below him, but yet a kindly, worthy, wealthy and not intolerable man. A moralist, if such a thing there be, thinking all sins but fornication venial. A teetotaller – that is for others – but he himself taking at times his glass of whisky for the reasons which have been so cogently set forth by St. Paul the Apostle to the Caledonians.

My friend lives in a house to which is joined a small estate called Inverquharity. Now though a Radical, nothing rejoices him so much as to be designated territorially as Inverquharity, and to give out that he is the third cousin of the Earl of Bishopbriggs.[914] These inconsistencies give zest to life, and go some way to redeeming even North Britain from the awful load of dreariness which Kailyarders depict.

One of the themes the worthy ex-sweater, now turned bonnet-laird,[915] delights to dwell on is, that race has little influence on a man. For take (he says) a Highlander and place him in the same conditions as a Lowland Scot, and he at once alters his mode of life, becomes industrious, and soon assimilates himself to those with whom he dwells. Nothing so difficult as to discuss such questions with my

---

[910] Walker, John (1985), 'The Scottish Writings of R. B. Cunninghame Graham', *Scottish Tradition*, vol. 13, p. 28.

[911] A monthly literary and political magazine, published by the Aberdonian socialist pioneer, James Leatham (1865–1945), between 1912 and Leatham's death. Regular contributors included William Morris's daughter, May, and Ramsay MacDonald.

[912] See passim.

[913] Scots: Payment derived from the produce of the land for the maintenance of the clergy.

[914] No such title exists.

[915] A petty landowner.

worthy friend. What the true Scotsman wants is argument, and it angers him as much if you agree with him as if you argue and confute his argument. If you agree you are a hypocrite, and arguing shows your narrow-mindedness, so that the safest way is to say nothing and be thought a fool.

Talking one day, he broached the theory that the crofters of the of the Hebrides were really fond of work, and that their idleness arose from a lack of opportunity. "See," he remarked, "in Manitoba how they improve in the new surroundings and without a landlord to rack-rent and oppress."

All landlords, in my friend's opinion, are rank tyrants, and though he likes to meet them individually, even to dine with them if they have titles, in the bulk they are accurst.

Of course there is no tyranny in trade, and if a strike takes place, why, who so loud as he to call for the police, to write for soldiers, and to complain that magistrates are weak, and that a whiff of melinite[916] is needed just to clean the air? – for commerce, as all know, came down from heaven, took root in Glasgow, and never can do wrong.

Talking of earls and dukes, and of the shameless immorality of countesses, the iniquity of game laws (though he himself preserves), stakes in the country and the state of trade, the villainy of servants, the rate of illegitimate births, and other things on which men placed as he is placed delight to dwell, he asked me if I knew of a farm known as the Offerance. I knew the spot, a little croft with a hideous little house, four windows and a door, with slated roof, and with two spruces ragged with the wind that sweeps over our favoured land, on either side of the "toon."[917] A little garden, in which grew "berries," as we style gooseberries and currants, and those sub-acid apples and plums which flourish in the north. A barn, a byre, and a horse-mill, with its mushroom-looking top, and four wide openings, contrived on purpose to give the horses cold when resting from their work; and over all that air of desolation which the lack of flowers and neatness, with the excess of wind and rain, impart to Scottish farms. Withal, not ill appointed, the fields well-drained and top-dressed, the fences in repair, and the whole place a thrifty, ugly, wire-fenced, and necessary blot upon the land. Though a small holding, nothing was done by hand, crops were scientifically dropped from machines into the ground, and then the harvest ready, as artfully manœuvred out, so that the acme of rural dullness and town desolation was attained.

---

[916] An explosive of great destructive power (picric acid), so called from its colour, which resembles honey.
[917] Scots: A farm, especially the farmhouse.

The tenant of this paradise was just about to leave, and Inverquharity announced that he was going to put his theory of environment into immediate execution, to get a crofter family down from the Hebrides to occupy the place. It seemed to me that if he must have Islanders, he might as well have got them from Tahiti as the Hebrides, but still I held my peace.

Time passed, and Inverquharity and I drifted apart, and Offerance, crofters, and theories of rent escaped my mind. Riding one day to visit a hill farm, I passed the Offerance. It looked a little unfamiliar, and seemed to have passed into a different state. Outside the door a fire of peats was burning, on which a kettle hung on three birchen poles, essayed to boil. Before the fire two ragged children sat, searching each other's heads[918] as diligently as if they had been scriptures. A different air of desolation brooded on the place. The fences were all broken, the ground untilled, and little zig-zag paths traversed the fields where short cuts had been made. The gates were off their hinges, lay on the ground or had been burnt, and in the gap a broken cart stood jammed into the hedge.

The stock was not extensive, and reminded one of that one sees outside an Arab's tent or Indian wigwam, mangy and full of ticks, and with the bones protruding through the hidebound skin. Two skinny ponies, with their feet hoppled[919] with withy ropes, which left the flesh all raw, were feeding on the weeds. Some Highland cattle and a goat or two, some scabby sheep, and a pack of sheep dogs and a lean, miserable cow, comprised the lot, and left me wondering if the owner ever expected to pay rent, or looked upon the Offerance as a fee simple given to him by Providence on which to put out all his agricultural lore, and teach the natives the Ossianic mode of carrying on a croft.

Close to the house a tall, athletic man, half drunk (but not as drunk as to have lost his wits), wrapped in a plaid and leaning on a stick, his fell of rough black hair descending to his small grey eyes, stood looking at a woman and a girl planting potatoes after the method known in the Highlands as the "lazy bed." That is, instead of plough- ing, you dig lightly with a spade, turning the turf a little over on one side, then put in the potatoes and rearrange the turf. The plan is excel- lent, and saves much work, manure is not required, or sweat of brow, and the soil is exhausted almost as quickly as a crofter can desire.

To see and understand took me but little time, and mentally I said, "This is the crofter family which my worthy friend has brought." On my horse fidgeting, the man looked up, came to the road unsteadily,

[918] Looking for lice and nits.
[919] A variation of hobbled.

and tried to seize my reins, then, taking off his hat, poured out a flood of compliments, all in the Gaelic tongue. I on my part caught a word here and there, learned he was glad to see me, and understood nothing particular, except the word "Tighearnas," which he repeated at the end of every phrase. It means a chief, and is used by Highlanders as gipsies use "captain" on a racecourse when they wish to flatter or delude.

The rain poured down, and he stood their [sic] bareheaded, talking and talking till I thought I should go mad. In a mixed jargon of broken Gaelic, and that sort of idiot English that we use to make our meaning clear to foreigners, I asked him to put on his hat and not to be a fool. He answered "Neffa," and though I found that he knew English pretty well, he beckoned to his wife to act as his interpreter.

"Donald," she said, "is out of Wester Ross, he does not like the digging, but Inverquharity is very pleased with him; for he puts up such a bonny prayer." This with the sing-song accent which all Highlanders affect.

Knowing the species, I was sure digging and ploughing, and every form of man-ennobling work, was not his style, and asked why he stood bareheaded, and if he liked the place.

"Och, aye," he said, "Offerance of Inverquharity is a pretty place, and a verra pretty name it has itself whatever."

Strange as it may appear, the uncouth syllables sounded quite different when pronounced by him. His wife, continuing, informed me that Donald never put his hat on when talking to one he thought a "chentleman," and though he cared but little for hard work, he was a "pretty gamekeeper," and a first-rate man to beat.

The semi-sacrament of whisky money having duly passed, I rode away amid a shower of what I took for blessings in the Ossianic tongue.

Turning, I saw the Offerance through the rain; black but uncomely,[920] ragged and wind-swept – a picture of old-world Scotland which has almost disappeared. Sloth was not altogether lovely, but prating progress worse.[921]

I might have left the place quite discontented even with mankind, had I not recollected that the world is to the young, and noted that the children's diligence had been rewarded, and that one was handing something to the other with quite an air of pride.

*****

---

[920] An example of Graham's wit in adapting quotations: Solomon's beloved says that she is 'black, but comely' (Song of Solomon 1:5).
[921] This paragraph is a word-for-word repeat from *A Survival*.

Graham had announced in the preface to *Brought Forward* (1916) that this was to be his last anthology: 'Tis meet and fitting to let free the horse or pen before death overtakes you, or before the gentle public turns its thumbs down and yells, "Away with him".'[922] A reviewer for *The Observer* included another sentence: 'So I shall write no more of these short stories, tales, sketches, or what you like to call them, for I perceive that in the writing of them I have written my life's story, and it can never be recalled.'[923] This sentence did not appear in the original 1916 edition or the 1917 reprint, but it may have appeared in a review copy, which might indicate that Graham considered it too final to be included in the final version. In 1927 he wrote, 'Thinking upon a vow I registered eleven years ago (Postume, Postume!)[924] not to write any more short stories',[925] confirming that this was indeed his original intention. Graham concluded his preface with the word *Vale* ('Farewell'), but he was still physically active, and it is not clear why he decided to stop at this point. The most obvious reason for this slowing down may simply be attributable to his age, which was undoubtedly a factor, but there was a less conspicuous reason. For a writer who wrote almost exclusively from his own experiences, his memories may have become exhausted, or perhaps too insubstantial or fleeting to be turned into sketches, and his life story had in fact been written.

In the few reviews of *Brought Forward*, each critic regretted Graham's decision to lay down his pen. Amy Wellington, for example, wrote in 1918 about the intended conclusion of Graham's literary career:

> With the North-East Wind [his sketch of Hardie's funeral] seems to close the book of Cunninghame Graham's own long and chivalrous fight for the despised and rejected of this earth; just as, a little later, he attaches his formal farewell as a writer to the preface of his final volume, *Brought Forward*. Both artist and fighter have grown a little cynical and very weary.[926]

Although his articles for journals greatly reduced, between 1916 and 1925, Graham published seven South American history books. But he was not entirely finished with the 'sketch' form, and 1925 saw his

---

[922] Cunninghame Graham, 'Preface' to *Brought Forward*, pp. x–xi.

[923] *The Observer*, 24 September 1916, p. 4.

[924] From Horace's ode, *Eheu Fugaces*: 'Alas … the years glide swiftly by, nor will righteousness give pause to wrinkles, to advancing age, or Death invincible.'

[925] Cunninghame Graham, Preface to *Redeemed* (London: Heinemann, 1927), p. 12.

[926] Wellington, p. 158.

re-engagement with *The Saturday Review*, with four pieces, rising to six the following year, then a final piece in 1931. His first 'ambient' Scottish sketch for twelve years was 'Inch Cailleach', an island in Loch Lomond, and return to his previous preoccupations, where the spirits of the past rose up from beneath the earth, and within the mist was another world, composed of mist, a world of the past, of ancient earls and warriors, which could, when conditions were right, re-impose itself on the present.

INCH CAILLEACH[927]

The Saturday Review, 5 September 1925, pp. 253–4.
Anthologised in *Redeemed* (London: Heinemann, 1927), pp. 103–9.

The Island of the Nuns lies like a stranded whale upon the waters of the loch, with its head pointing towards the red rocks of Balmaha.[928] Tradition tells of a Nunnery on the Island in times gone by, and certainly it must have been a fitting place to build a convent on. A deep, dark strait cuts it off from the world. No spot in the whole earth could be more fitted for a conventual life of meditation, or for the simple duties performed in simple faith, such as string out a life like beads upon a rosary, till the last prayer is said.

Fell[929] opportunity that has so often turned saints into sinners could have had no place upon the rocky islet in the lake. The voices of the sisters singing in the choir must have been scarce distinguishable from the lapping of the wavelets on the beach, or blending with them, made up a harmony, as if nature and man were joining in a pantheistic hymn. Nuns may have lived upon the Island with, or without, vocation, have eaten out their hearts with longing for their lost world, or, like the Saint of Avila,[930] in mystic ecstasy have striven to be one with the celestial spouse. All this may well have been, but the dim sisterhood has left no record of its passage upon earth, except the name Inch Cailleach, beautiful in its liquid likeness to the sound of the murmuring waves, and the wind sighing in the brackens and the bents.[931]

---

[927] Gaelic. In Celtic lore, a hag; more generally in Scots, an old woman; however, it can also refer to 'a veiled woman', i.e., a nun.

[928] A village on the eastern shore of Loch Lomond.

[929] Scots: Dire.

[930] St Teresa of Avila, whose life and works were the two-volume *magnum opus* of Graham's wife, Gabrielle.

[931] See passim.

Ben Lomond[932] towers above the wooded Island, with its outcrop of grey rocks, and in the distance Ben Vorlich,[933] Meall nan Caora[934] and Bein Chabhair[935] seem to protect it from all modern influences by their grim aspect and aloofness, for even their rare smiles when the sun hunts the shadows across their rocky faces still are stern. If the lone, wooded inchlet once sheltered Nuns, or if the name was merely given it to commemorate some ancient Highland Cailleach, who had retired there to gaze into the mists upon the hills, or dream of Fingal[936] and Cuchullin[937] as she sat nodding over a fire of peat, certain it is that nature must have put forth her best creative power to form so fitting a last resting place for the wild clan,[938] whose bones are laid beneath the mossy turf round the grey sculptured stones.

Right on top of a long shoulder of the Island, within the ruined walls of the old chapel whose broken pillars, moss-grown finials and grooved door jambs, lie in a growth of bilberries among the invading copse, Gregarach[939] for centuries have interred their dead. They and the wild McFarlanes – was not the moon known as McFarlanes' Bowat?[940] – rest from their labour at the sword. Quietly they lie, they who never knew a quiet hour in life. Equal in death and equal in misfortune when they lived, had they consulted all the heralds and their pursuivants[941] they could not have hit upon a better device more fitting than the cross-handled sword that is cut roughly on so many of their tombs. Bitterly they paid for the slaughter of Genfruin,[942] with two hundred years of outlawry,[943] and with the hand of every man against them.

---

[932] Gaelic: Beacon Mountain, a 974 m high mountain on the eastern shore of Loch Lomond, to the north of Inchcailleach.

[933] Gaelic: Hill of the Bay, a 985 m high mountain lying between Loch Earn and the Trossachs.

[934] Gaelic: Round Hill of the Sheep, a 717 m high mountain to the immediate south-west of Ben Vorlich.

[935] Gaelic: Hill of the Hawk, a 933 m high mountain situated to the north of Ben Lomond.

[936] See passim.

[937] Gaelic: 'Culann's Hound', a mythical demigod who is the hero of stories in Irish, Scots and Manx mythology.

[938] The Clan MacGregor.

[939] Ibid.

[940] Scots: A lantern.

[941] Officers of a College of Arms ranking below a herald.

[942] The Battle of Glen Fruin, 7 February 1603, in which the MacGregors inflicted heavy losses on their rivals, the Colquhouns of Luss.

[943] Following the slaughter at Glen Fruin, the clan was proscribed as outlaws and it became legal to hunt and kill MacGregors. Many took other surnames. It was not until 1784 that they were allowed to resume their own name and restored to all of the rights and privileges of British citizens.

Well did they deserve the title of the Clan Na Cheo,[944] for the mist rolling through the corries was their best hiding place, the natural smoke screen that protected all the Clan Gregor from their enemies. On the leafy Island in the great lake alone they found a resting place, and though long grey stones by which they swore are few in number, the grassy hillocks that dot the burial ground encircled by the ruined walls are numberless. Nowhere could men have found a spot so fitting for a long sleep after their foray in the world. The soughing wind among the thickets of scrub-oak, of hazel and of birch, the fresh damp scent of the sweet-gale and staghorn moss, the belling of the roe at evening, the strange, sweet wildness of the steep isolated island with its two headlands and its little plain, now buried deep in wood, must lull the resting children of the mist.

A steep and winding path leads from the pebbly beach, and crosses and recrosses a little rill, brown but transparent, as it wends its way towards the lake in miniature cascades and tiny linns, in which play minnows. It makes a tinkling music for the sleepers among the ruins of what was once Inch Cailleach parish church. It passes now and then a fir, whose bright red trunk stands out aflame among the copse, and bears the cones from which Clan Alpine took its badge. Here and there clumps of scarlet dockens mark the way, like stations of the Cross upon a Calvary. Hardly a footstep has beaten down the grass, for up above, in the lone circle of grey stones, lie men whose names were written in characters as evanescent as the smoke scrolls an aeroplane traces upon the sky. Clearly imprinted on the peaty soil, roe tracks call up the memory of men who passed the best part of their lives in following the deer. The silence of the woods is only broken by the flight of some great capercailzie, as its wings beat against the leaves when it first launches into flight, or by the cushats[945] cooing, deep and full-throated as the bell bird's[946] call in the Brazilian wilds.

The loneliness, the sense of isolation, although the world is just at hand, and tourist-laden steamers ply upon the loch, passing but a few hundred yards away and breaking up the picture of the wooded Island reflected in the lake, as in a mirage, with their paddles, are as absolute as if the Islet was situated in the outer [sic] Hebrides.

The very scent of the lush grass, set about thickly with the yellow tormentils, with scabious and bog asphodel, strikes one on the nostrils as from an older world, in which the reek of petrol and the noise of

---

[944] Gaelic: Children of the Mist.
[945] Scots: *Columba palumbus*: the ring-dove or wood-pigeon.
[946] *Procnias albus*, whose mating call is officially the loudest recorded birdsong.

factories was unknown. Many a procession of ragged warriors, in the past, their deerskin buskins[947] making scarce a sound upon the stones, must have toiled up the winding path to lay their dead within the little burial ground, and then, the ceremony over, stepped noiselessly away into the sheltering mist. The Nuns, McGregors and McFarlanes all have passed away, and are as if they never had been, and yet they have left an aura that still pervades the leafy Isle. Nothing is left of them but the vaguest memory, and yet they seem to live in every thicket, every copse, and as the burn runs brattling[948] to the lake it sings their threnody. When all is hushed at night and owls fly noiselessly, their flight hardly disturbing the still air, and the rare nocturnal animals that all destroying progress (or what you call the thing) has left alive, surely the spirits of the nameless sleepers under the mossy turf rise like vapour from their graves commune with Cuchullin and with Fingal, pat Bran's[949] rough head, and fight old battles once again; until at the first streak of dawn they glide back to their places, under the sculptured stones.

Let them sleep on. They have had their foray, they have chased the roe and followed the red deer. The very mists upon the mountains are more tangible that they are now. Let them rest within the ruined walls of the dismantled chapel buried in the copse, that has shown itself more durable than the stone walls that lie about its roots. Bracken and heather, bog myrtle, blaeberry and moss exhale their odours, sweeter than incense, over the graves where sleep the nameless men. The waves still murmur on the beach, the tiny burnlet whispers its coronach.[950] Under their rude tombstones men, whose feet shod in their deerskin brogues were once as light as fawns, are waiting till the shrill skirl[951] of the Piob Mor [sic][952] shall call them to the great gathering of the clans.

* * * * *

The theme of this next sketch, which is a short description of a Hebridean war memorial, concerns the transience of man and all his works which will be outlasted by the beauty of the natural world.

Walker believed the sketch to be ironic in tone, incorrectly translating *Euphrasia* as "cheerfulness".[953] However, he was trying to

---

[947] Calf-high or knee-high boots.
[948] Scots: To make a clashing or clattering noise, often used of a noisy stream.
[949] Fingal's faithful dog.
[950] See passim.
[951] Scots: To produce shrill sounds (on) a musical instrument, especially the bagpipes.
[952] Gaelic: Great pipes, i.e. the Highland bagpipes.
[953] Walker, p. 70.

be too scholarly, and missed the far simpler, true meaning, which was that *euphrasia* is the scientific name for the flower "eyebright", which grows widely in Scotland. This was clearly what Graham intended, as he mentions the flower in both his opening and final sentences.

As usual, Graham gives a detailed description of the setting before describing the war memorial with its Biblical text in Gaelic. He lists some of the names of the fallen, whose bones lie in foreign soil, noting that nearly all served in Scottish regiments and perceives them as warriors of the 'pre-Culloden type', who straddle the past and present.

Typical of his later pieces, in place of irony, there is a dreamy nostalgia, in this case for the mythology of the Ossianic heroes, from whom he imagines sprang the islemen who willingly gave their lives in battle, as their race had done for centuries. He pictures that the monument, long years after the War is forgotten, will still be watched over by "a million little eyes".

EUPHRASIA

The Saturday Review, 25 September 1926, p. 331.
Anthologised in *Redeemed* (London: Heinemann, 1927), pp. 172–5.

On a mound in an upland field, right in the middle of a waste of ragwort, black knapweed, and a sea of myriads of eyebright, there stands a War Memorial. The poorly carved Iona cross, and cast iron railings, with their gate looking as if bought at an ill country ironmongers, serve but to render its loneliness even more pathetic, contrasted with the overwhelming landscape. "Agus Bheannaich an Sluagh no [na] Daoine Uile a Therig iad Fein gu Toileach (Nehemiah xi, 2)"[954] runs the Gaelic text upon the plinth. Rendered in English it states, the men whose names are cut upon the stone gave their lives willingly. I do not doubt it, for they were born and passed their youth on the same soil and in the self-same atmosphere, sharp and

---

[954] 'And the people blessed all the men, that willingly offered themselves to dwell in Jerusalem' (Nehemiah 11:2, KJV). The Gaelic text omits the last four words. Graham's translation probably better reflects the intended sentiment of those who erected the memorial. NB 'Na daoine' should replace 'No daoine', to make sense of the quotation.

invigorating, tempered with the acrid reek[955] of peat, that nurtured Fingal,[956] Cuchullin,[957] Fergus[958] and the heroes the Celtic Homer[959] sang.

At the foot of the lean field where stands the cross, there winds a long sea loch with nothing upon its shores except a ruined castle, that man has sailed its waters since King Haco's[960] fleet visited it, six hundred years ago. As it was when he saw it from his rude birlinn,[961] with his oarsmen bending to their task, their shields ranged on the galley's sides, their swords bestowed beneath their feet on the vessels floor, so it remains to-day. The tide still leaves great fringes of brown kelp and yellow dulse[962] upon its slippery rocks; seals still bask on the islands; the dogfish hunts the shoals of herrings and the Atlantic clean, snell[963] air comes up between South Uist and Benbecula, just as the "Summer Sailors"[964] felt it on their tanned cheeks, stirring their yellow hair, in the days when in their long ships they scourged the Hebrides.

Green, flat-topped mountains tower up on the far side of the loch; great moors on which grow nothing but cotton grass, sweet gale and asphodel, stretch towards the fantastic range of the dark, purple mountains, to the east. Jagged and serrated, unearthly looking, shrouded in mists that boil and curl about their sides, they rise, looking as though they had something ominous about them, hostile to mankind.

The Ossianic Heroes still seem to stalk about their corries and peep out from the mists approvingly at their descendants, whose names are cut upon the little, lonely monument, set in its sea of wild flowers, opposite the loch. Far off Quiraing, Blaaven, and Bein a Cailleach; the unquiet tide rip opposite Kyle Rhea, Coruisk and Sligachan; all the wild myrtle-scented moors, the black peat haggs,[965] the air of wilderness and remoteness from the world that even the motors hooting on

---

[955] Scots: Smoke.

[956] See passim.

[957] Cuchullin (*Cú Chulainn*, Irish Gaelic) = a mythical demigod who is the hero of stories in Irish, Scots and Manx mythology.

[958] Fergus mac Echdach was king of Dál Riata from about 778 until 781.

[959] *The Poems of Ossian* by James MacPherson.

[960] The Norwegian king, Haakon IV, who, with his invading Norsemen, was defeated at the Battle of Largs by King Alexander II in 1263.

[961] Gaelic: A large rowing-boat or barge used in the West Highlands.

[962] Rounded fern weed (*osmundea osmunda*), more commonly known as 'Pepper Dulse'.

[963] Scots: Biting or piercing.

[964] Viking raiders.

[965] Scots: A soft marshy hollow piece of ground in a moor, e.g. where peats have been cut, or where it has naturally fissured.

the road, and charabancs with loads of tourists, four-beplussed,[966] shingled[967] and burberried[968] to the eyes, cannot dispel entirely, make a fit setting for a memorial to men bred and begotten in the isle. Most of them served in Scottish regiments, MacAskil Royal Scots, MacMillan London Scottish, McAlister Scottish South Africans, Galbraith New Zealand Infantry, MacPhee Black Watch, McKinnes Scots Guards, McDonald of the Rhodesian Rifles, and many more, all Skye men, whose bones moulder in battlefields far from the Winged Isle.[969]

That nothing should be wanting to connect the warriors with their sea-roving ancestors, Captain MacFarlane and Angus Cumming of the Mercantile Marine sleep with their slumber soothed by the waves above their heads, a fitting resting place for men born in an island into which sea-lochs bore into its very heart. Out of what sheilings,[970] with their little fields of oats and of potatoes that stretch like chess-boards on the hillsides, won from the uncongenial soil by the sweat of centuries of work, the humble warriors came, only their families can tell.

It matters little, reared as they were with one foot in the past, one hand on the "Caschrom"[971] the other on the handle of some up-to-date reaping machine from Birmingham. Those only who had gone out to the Colonies could have known much about the outside world, until the breaking out of the Great War,[972] in which they lost their lives. For them no placards, with their loud appeals to patriotism, could have been necessary. For a thousand years their ancestors had all been warriors, thronging to enlist in the Napoleonic wars, eager to join Montrose[973] and Claverhouse,[974] and fighting desperately among themselves when there was peace abroad. They fought their fight, giving up all that most of them possessed, their lives. And now, although their bodies are disintegrated in the four quarters of the

---

[966] A Graham neologism for wearing plus-fours = trousers that extend four inches below the knee.

[967] A women's hairstyle of evenly cut tapers that give a soft, sloping effect, which was popular when Graham wrote this.

[968] Wearing luxury coats from Burberry.

[969] English translation of Scots Gaelic *Eilean Sgitheanach* = the Isle of Skye.

[970] See passim.

[971] Scots: A crook-handled spade used by Highlanders.

[972] The Great War (to end all wars) was the original name of the First World War.

[973] James Graham, first Marquess of Montrose (known as 'the Great Montrose'), raised an army in Scotland in support of Charles I during the War of the Three Kingdoms and was captured and executed in 1650.

[974] See passim.

globe, it may be that their spirits have returned to some Valhalla in the mists that roll around Sligachan.

Seasons will come and go; the ragworts blossom in the fields where stands the monument, wither and die, and flower again next year. Time will roll on. The names carved upon the stone become forgotten. The cross may fall, and the cheap iron railings exfoliate away to nothing. The very wars in which the Islesmen fell become but a mere legend, as has happened to all other wars.

Men's eyes will turn more rarely to the memorial in the wind-swept field, and they will ask what it commemorates. Still, the wild hills will not forget, as they have not forgotten the story of the wars fought by the driver of the twin, thin-maned, high-mettled, swift-footed, and wide-nostriled steeds of the mountains, "Sithfada and Dusrongeal."[975] But if the eyes of men are turned no longer to the plinth, with its long list of names and Gaelic text, when the Spring comes, and once again the eyebright springs in the hungry field, the west wind sweeping up the loch will turn a million little eyes towards the cross.

* * * * *

In 1911, Graham inherited St Anne's Lodge, Ascog, on the Isle of Bute, from his cousin, Susan Henn, and lived there on occasion.[976] Given his penchant for unusual tombs, he naturally took an interest the grave of 'Reginald Montague' near one of the local kirkyards, the environs of which he skilfully paints for his readers.

This is another of Graham's 'conjecture sketches' in which he ponders the mystery of who Montague was; why he was buried outwith consecrated ground; who had designed the grave; and who, almost ninety years after his death, still placed flowers upon it?

The grave was in fact that of Montague Talbot Stanley A.R.S.A. (1809–44), an actor, landscape painter, poet, and evangelist, and contrary to Graham's assertion, quite a lot was known about him.[977] Stanley, who was born in Dundee, was taken to New York aged fourteen months, by his mother, before they moved to Nova Scotia, then Jamaica, then back to Britain in 1819. At the age of fifteen, he took up acting as a career, retiring from the stage at the age of thirty-one, because of his religious scruples, to become a successful landscape

---

[975] Cuchullin's chariot horses.
[976] See letter, *Glasgow Herald*, 8 September 1913, p. 5.
[977] Graham may simply have forgotten the gravestone's inscription. However, Stanley was famous enough to have his image recorded, using the early 'calotype' process, by Scotland's photographic pioneers, Robert Adamson and David Octavius Hill.

Figure 18 Montague Stanley, by Hill & Adamson, National Galleries of Scotland.

painter,[978] and married into a well-to-do Edinburgh family. In 1843, suffering from consumption, he settled in Ascog, but died the following summer, leaving a widow and seven children.

Kingarth United Free Church of Scotland, near where Montague is buried, was completed in 1843, one year before he died, and immediately following the 'Disruption', becoming what is claimed to be, the first Free Church building in Scotland. Why his grave was outside its precincts is not known, nor who still placed flowers upon it.

---

[978] After his death, almost all of Stanley's sketches and paintings, which were to be auctioned in Edinburgh, were destroyed by a spark from the locomotive, while being transported by train from Glasgow.

UP STAGE

The Cornhill Magazine, September 1933, pp. 284–6.
Anthologised in *Mirages* (London: Heinemann, 1936), pp. 147–53.

An iron railing with a locked gate surrounds a lonely grave on the lee side of a little church upon a rocky promontory jutting out to sea in a green island in the Firth of Clyde. There is no churchyard where the dead, stretched out in rows, so to speak keep each other company. I like to fancy that in the long nights of winter they are a consolation to each other, as they lie enduring rain, frost, snow, and the fierce north wind's blasts, the answering owls chanting their nightly threnody.

No one knows anything of the solitary dead, except his name – Reginald Montague – cut on the headstone, with the date 1844. A text by some friend, wife, mistress, or mother, to serve perhaps as passport to eternal bliss, or perhaps merely a last pathetic gesture of affection, is cut below the name.

Local tradition has it that the lonely tenant of the plot of ground, in mortmain,[979] who for so many years has lain beneath its well-mown turf, on which reposes, under a glass case, a white marble wreath of roses, was an actor.

No one knows any more of the alleged Thespian.

A bush of fuchsia grows at the corner of the little iron corral that guards the grave, in which the actor lies waiting the call-boy to summon him. Across the whitely gravelled path, where after weekly service the faithful daunder[980] for a few minutes of what in other parishes would be the clash o' the kirkyard,[981] sappier and more refreshing to the soul than all the sermons in the world, there is a wilderness of wiry grass, flecked here and there with tormentil and eyebright, and engayed[982] by harebells. Menacing fronds of bracken threaten to invade and overwhelm the little paradise. Two or three rowan-trees, ragged and stunted by the blast, stand round the ruins of a deserted salt-pan, hard by the church. Ivy has covered the soft red stone, biting into it, as the lianas[983] bite into the bark of some great ceiba[984] in the tropics, giving the mouldering stones an air as of a ruined castle.

---

[979] Medieval Latin: *mortua manus* = 'dead hand', referring to impersonal, inalienable ownership, usually by the church.
[980] See passim.
[981] See passim.
[982] A Graham neologism for 'made cheerful'.
[983] Climbing vines found in rainforests.
[984] Trees native to the American tropics.

The rocks upon the promontory are carpeted with dulse,[985] ware and sea tangle, whose tendrils float in the tide, coiling and recoiling like water snakes. Seals haunt the rocks, their round and human-looking heads bobbing up in the water, as they utter a sharp bark before they disappear into the depths.

The nightly owls, the seals, the lonely church, the wind-hacked trees, the moaning of the sea, the harsh cries of seagulls, and the honk-honk of the wild geese as they fly southward in a wedge, on winter nights, set the stage fittingly for the sleeper who no more shall tread the boards. Why he was buried in unconsecrated ground, outside the church, what made him lay his bones beside a fane[986] whose worshippers, Presbyterians of the strictest sect, who looked most likely on his art with contumely, holding it as a wile of Satan to entrap men's souls, no one remains to tell.

Who raised the well-wrought iron railing round the grave, planted the luxuriant fuchsia, and placed the marble wreath as if they knew, when they had passed away, it would remain to mourn, both for the sleeper and themselves, there is no record of them.

Almost a hundred years have passed since he was laid to rest. Was it a mother who came weeping to the grave, who placed the wreath, emblem of sempiternal[987] sorrow, on it?

Perhaps an actress of the company, mincing along in the full skirt of 1840, lace mittens on her hands; upon her feet low shoes with ribbons curling, like sandals, up her stockings, or as she might have said, a Greek cothurnus,[988] a curtained bonnet on her head tied beneath the chin with a silk ribbon, and carrying in her hand a much-flounced parasol, paid for the everlasting roses from her scant salary. She may have had what were called love passages in those days, with the member of the company who now was 'resting'[989] – a rest that no advertisement in the *Era*[990] will break with news of an engagement. Maybe a comrade who had acted, gambled and drank with him, put up the railing and the headstone, saying, 'Poor Reggie was a damned good fellow, and should not be forgotten like a dog, if he could help it.'

---

[985] Gaelic: A red seaweed (*palmaria palmata*) which is also known as 'sea lettuce'.

[986] Latin: *fanum* = a temple.

[987] Everlasting.

[988] A thick-soled, laced boot worn by Greek and Roman tragic actors.

[989] A theatrical euphemism for 'out of work'.

[990] A British weekly newspaper (1838–1939) which by the 1870s had become the leading theatrical journal. However, in the 1840s it was still a general newspaper.

But, then the wreath of roses and the text! Only a woman who had loved him could have thought of such a grave, so quiet, so romantic, and so like the resting-place the man would have desired.

He may himself have chosen his own burial-place; but what the devil brought him to the Isle of Bute?

There could have been no theatre in Rothesay in 1844, or if one had existed it must have been a place where only barnstormers strutted their little hour, and, the performance over, counted their exiguous gains. It is true that Edmund Kean[991] once owned a villa in the middle of the green Thule, by the borders of a lake. The unknown actor may have been a member of his company. Long Wolf sleeps in the Brompton Cemetery,[992] with his totem sculptured on his headstone, and such another wreath of artificial roses in a cracked glass case upon his grave, placed there by Colonel Cody,[993] ere he too passed to the happy hunting grounds.

Blondin,[994] his tight rope slackened and his balancing pole long ago chopped up for firewood, though once so certain of his equilibrium in mid-air, has found an even firmer footing in a London cemetery.

Reginald Montague, the name sounds somehow as if he had been, as goes the Spanish phrase, 'the son of somebody', and whosoever paid for the headstone and grave, and chose the spot, so well selected, with a southern aspect, and the waves always singing throbbing lullabies, must certainly have been a person of no ordinary taste.

After a life of grease paint, make-up, the petty jealousies and feuds of Thespian life, the triumphs, failures, and the constant doubt whether or not the 'ghost would walk'[995] on Saturday; all the discomforts of a strolling actor's life (if indeed he were an actor or a stroller), are done with, and he sleeps in a grave, fitting for any artist, poet, man

[991] Edmund Kean (1787–1833), a Shakespearean actor of short stature, as famous for his tumultuous life as for his acting.
[992] 'Long Wolf' or 'Schongamoneta Haska' (1844–92), was an Oglala Sioux chief, who died while touring with the Buffalo Bill's 'Wild West' show, and whose grave Graham wrote about in a sketch entitled *Long* Wolf in 1921. Graham's article was read by Elizabeth Knight of Worcestershire, who rediscovered the grave, and in 1997, after a long campaign, had his remains reinterred near the site of the Wounded Knee massacre.
[993] William Frederick 'Buffalo Bill' Cody (1846–1917) was an American soldier, bison hunter, and showman with whom Graham had become friends in Texas during the early 1880s. Graham took Cody to lunch in the Glasgow Art Club, on the show's second tour of Scotland, in 1904.
[994] Charles Blondin (1824–97), a French tightrope-walker, famed for crossing the Niagara Gorge in 1859. He is buried in Kensal Green Cemetery, London.
[995] A theatrical euphemism for 'pay-day'.

of letters, or anyone who in his life has been dependent on a fickle public, but now has reached his port.

Let him sleep on, the fuchsia every spring will put on its glad livery of green, and hang its scarlet flesh-like petals over the iron railings where he lies. The wind-seared trees will rustle in the breeze, the wavelets tinkle on the beach, and in the winter out on the rocks the seals will lie and sun themselves upon the dulse. At night the owls will call to one another, with their long quavering call to one another, with their long quavering Tu-whit, To-who, as if they asked a question that required no answer.

And the stage still waits.

Figure 19 Photograph: *Isle of Bute News.*

Introductions

Graham not only wrote his political articles, histories and sketches, he was much sought after as a writer of Introductions and Prefaces to the works of others, particularly for travel books, writing almost fifty during his long career. Joseph Conrad wrote to Graham saying, 'You are the Great Preface Writer of the Time.'[1] G. K. Chesterton reputedly called him the "Prince of Preface Writers".

The example below is a wonderful oddity, introducing a book by John Morrison Davidson, barrister, radical socialist, author, nationalist campaigner, and prolific pamphleteer. Tom Mann, the first Secretary of the Labour Party, described him as: 'a great character: he was terribly proud of being a Scotsman, and believed, or pretended to believe, that a very big share of all that was passable in the British Isles originated in Scotland'.[2]

In his Introduction, unable to control his gypsy impulses, in a book about Scotland, Graham whisked his readers off to the Argentinian *pampa*, where he related an extraordinary encounter; two ships that pass in the daylight, so to speak, telling us all we need to know about the wandering Scot, and, incidentally, again demonstrating Graham's mastery of the Scots language.

Age, nor class, nor ocean, are barriers to familiarity, and the unspoken bond between these strangers. Graham and his dishevelled compatriot share the sentiment expressed by Graham's friend and admirer Frederick Niven: 'We'll take Scotland with us, a kingdom of

---

[1] Joseph Conrad, letter to Graham, 14 January 1907.
[2] Tom Mann, *Memoirs* (London: MacGibbon & Kee, 1967), p. 123. Davidson claimed he had established that Graham, as a direct descendent of King Robert II, was *de jure* monarch of the United Kingdom. *Edinburgh Evening News*, 18 September 1895, p. 3. Ford Madox Ford recorded: 'Once driving with Mr. Graham from Roslyn Castle to Edinburgh I heard a politically minded lady say to him: "You ought Mr. Graham, to be the first president of a British Republic". "I ought madam, if I had my rights", he answered sardonically, "to be the king of this country. And what a three weeks that would be!" Ford Madox Ford, *Return To Yesterday* (London: Gollancz, 1931), p. 38.

the mind',[3] before we are removed to Graham's Arcadian, pre-Union, pre-Calvinist, pre-industrialised Scotland, which he forlornly hopes might one day be reclaimed.

Figure 20

INTRODUCTION: SCOTLAND FOR THE SCOTS: SCOTLAND REVISITED

by John Morrison Davidson (Edinburgh: F. R. Henderson, 1902).

Scottissimus Scotorum – Surely to no one more than to the author of "Scotland Revisited" does the above phrase apply. A Scot of Scots! although he apparently imagines that he has recently revisited Caledonia, I cannot think that he really left it for an hour.

Born in Buchan, perhaps to refute the saw,[4] 'there's rowth o' a'thing in Buchan haud awa' freet'[5] – he carries Buchan with him everywhere he goes.

---

[3] Frederick Niven, *The Flying Years* (London: Collins, 1935), p. 14.
[4] A saying.
[5] Obscure. Possibly 'there is an abundance of everything in Buchan, reject superstitious beliefs.' (Scots: freit = an omen.)

What is it that makes your true Scot, him I mean of the *perfer-vidum ingenium*,[6] so intensely national? It is, I think, because of those very qualities, the decay of which the Author bewails in his present book.

I remember once, in South America, having gone out to look for some strayed horses, and not having found them, that I ascended a little hill and sat me down to smoke. Below me rolled the Pampean ocean of brown grass: grass, grass, and still more grass: grass which the breeze from the south-west had set in motion in long waves: grass which, where rivers in the middle distance crossed it, was cut by strips of "Argentina," looking like silver bands: Grass in which deer and ostriches passed happy lives, so happy that the Gauchos knew the former as the "desert mirth": Brown waves of grass in which roamed cattle and sheep innumerable, and over which the Tero-Teros flew uttering their haunting cry.

And as I sat and smoked –

Upon a thin old chestnut horse, with a torn English saddle, over which a sheepskin had been laid, a man of about fifty years of age appeared. Dressed in a suit of Scottish homespun, such as our farmers wore, but twenty years ago, before the looms of Bradford and of Leeds had clothed them all in shoddy,[7] with a grey flannel shirt without a collar, and the whole man surmounted by a battered, flat straw-hat, which might have made an indifferent strawberry pottle,[8] I at once descried a brother Scot.[9] Dismounting and hobbling his horse, he drew a short clay pipe out of his pocket, capped with a tin cover that workmen in the North used to affect, in the pre-briar-root days, and greeting me in a strange Doric[10] Spanish, he sat down to smoke.

Some time he talked, till in compassion I said, "Friend, you appear to make but middling weather of it in the Spanish tongue." No sign he gave of the least astonishment, but between two draws, as he rammed the "dottle"[11] hard into his pipe, he said, "I see ye speak the English pretty well." I, though at the time, just at the age, when a man speaks, rides and shoots better than any other man in all the world, suppressed a smile, and said, "Yes; how do you like the view?"

---

[6] Latin: '*Perfervidum ingenium Scotorum*' = The intensely earnest character of the Scots.
[7] Clothing made of reconstituted woollen fibres.
[8] Scots: A conical punnet for fruit.
[9] For background into the Scots in Argentina, see: James Dodds, *Record of the Scottish Settlers in the River Plate and Their Churches* (1897).
[10] A distinctive dialect spoken in the north-east of Scotland.
[11] A plug of un-burnt tobacco.

"A bonny view, sir, aye, ou aye; I'd no say onything against the view: but man, maybe ye ken a hill – they ca' it the Dumyet[12] – just abune Brig o' Allan?"[13] I did so, having climbed it as a boy, and watched the Forth wind out, a silver ribbon towards Aberfoyle.[14]

"Weel, weel, if ye ken it, ye'll ken there's a far brawer view frae the Dumyet than frae the wee boranty[15] that we're sittin' on the noo."

When he had got upon his horse and schauchled[16] down the hill, I fancied that I could smell the heather and sweet gale, hear the whawps[17] calling on the moor, and in the towns see drucken folk a-stotterin'[18] from the public house.

Something of this compound essence of the North our Author has. Something of the pre-bawbean[19] times, something of those old shirtless Scottish scholars who, in the Middle-Ages, over-ran Europe, "gaun aboot bodies"[20] with a tattered Homer in their hand, Andrew Ferrara[21] on their hip and with a plenteous lack of pelf in the lean deer-skin pouch they carried at their side. So, naturally enough, the Scotland of to-day seems to him wersh,[22] the national character becoming moulded after the Southern form; the whisky no sae nippy in the mooth, religion turned but a dreich[23] Erastian affair, and even hell-fire merely a wee bit spunky in the lum.[24]

But he has put his finger on the blot, and pointed out (his bagpipe certainly gives no uncertain sound) our national vice of snobbism. Pity to see a Scot "attempt the English" and essay in havering[25] tones to clip the Doric, and, worst of all, to see our country clean despoiled of brains, and all her sons run off to London, for the gatherin' o' the gear. The Highlands too delivered over to the Yank, and the whole land become a cross between a rich man's playground and a

---

[12]   Dumyat ('Hillfort of the Maeatae tribe'). A hill to the north-east of Stirling, once the site of an Iron Age fort, commanding the River Forth.
[13]   Bridge of Allan, a fashionable spa town north of Stirling.
[14]   A small town adjacent to Graham's old estate at Gartmore.
[15]   Scots: A mound or tumulus. The diminutive of 'burian'.
[16]   Scots: Shambled.
[17]   Scots: Curlews.
[18]   Scots: Staggering.
[19]   Pre-materialistic.
[20]   Scots: Wanderers, travellers.
[21]   More correctly, 'Andrea Ferrara', the generic name for the Scottish basket-hilted broadsword.
[22]   Scots: See passim.
[23]   Scots: Dismal.
[24]   Scots: A small spark in the chimney. Spunkie = Will o' the Wisp.
[25]   Scots: Babbling, talking nonsense.

sweater's hell he marks with disapproval, and looks back to Fletcher, him of Saltoun,[26] who believed in the divine right of princes to be hanged.

He mourns our Scottish Parliament, that "lang auld sang" which Southern wiles and gold brought to an end, leaving the House disconsolate, and a mere stamping ground for Advocates, who, like the devil, walk to and fro seeking for those they may devour.[27]

Therefore he advocates Home Rule.

Not a return to those blithe days when in Auld Reekie[28] folks cried "Gardey-Loo,"[29] and on the causeway sword-and-buckler men fought for the "croon," whilst Highland chairmen carrying old gentlemen to routs,[30] paused not an instant though the bottom of the chair fell out, causing their fares desperately to run, and to exclaim on landing "that but for the honour o' the thing they had as lieve hae[31] walked."

But to return to a more national spirit and a revival of the ancient Scottish Type which ruled the roost before the Ten per Centlings[32] rose, making poor Scotland stink before the world with their base peddling ways.

*****

This next short, rambling work partially reflected Graham's commitment to an independent Scotland. In 1928, having been narrowly defeated by sitting prime minister, Stanley Baldwin, for the rectorship of Glasgow University as a Scottish nationalist, Graham was now the President of the National Party of Scotland.

Surprisingly, for someone who claimed descent from King Robert II, Graham failed to mention that 'The Wolf', Alexander Stewart, who was a robber and plunderer of cathedrals, was the king's 'natural' son, so if Graham's claim was correct, he and Alexander were very distant blood relatives.

---

[26] See passim.
[27] 1 Peter 5:8.
[28] Scots: 'Old smoky' = Edinburgh.
[29] French/Scots: 'Beware of the water'. A common cry from an upper storey, before a chamber pot was emptied onto the street below.
[30] Scots: Noisy hubbub.
[31] Scots: Might as well have.
[32] Capitalists.

INTRODUCTION: THE WOLF OF BADENOCH (1825)

by Thomas Dick Lauder (Stirling: Eneas Makay, 1930).

It is a sign of the times that there is a new edition of Sir Thomas Dick Lauder's[33] famous historical novel, THE WOLFE OF BADENOCH.[34] For a century Scotsmen have been content to remain pale copies of our "ancient enemy" from beyond the Tweed.[35] Some degenerate sons of Scotia, even to-day, attribute the economic progress of Scotland to the Act of Union[36] and forget their own share in the job.

Mesopotamia is a blessed word.[37] When you have said Act of Union there are still sporadic Scots who put on the same kind of long face as they assume on reading aloud the genealogy of King David.[38]

Mercifully they are becoming rare, as rare as those who think John Knox[39] invented Scotland, almost without assistance of the Deity. A new generation of race-conscious Scotsmen is arising,[40] and to it the republication of a Scottish novel that has stood the test of time will be a boon. THE WOLFE OF BADENOCH cannot be described as a work of genius, but it gives a picture of Scotland remote from modern times, a Scotland where wolves lurked in the mountain fastnesses, and the wild, white cattle grazed in the clearings of the woods.

With all the differences of setting, still in essentials Scotland was but little different at the core. The dividing line between the Highlands and the Lowlands seems to have been less sharply defined than it became in the course of the next two hundred years. Perhaps this was because the nobles were entrenched in their castles, and secure within their panoplies of Milan steel.[41] Moreover, in those days the

---

[33] Sir Thomas Dick Lauder (1784–1848), seventh Baronet of Fountainhall.

[34] Alexander Stewart, Earl of Buchan (1343–1405), third son of Robert II by his first marriage, was known as 'The Wolf of Badenoch' for his notorious cruelty and rapacity.

[35] The River Tweed, which, for a large part, separates Scotland from England.

[36] The 1707 Acts of Union united the Kingdoms of Scotland and England into the Kingdom of Great Britain.

[37] An allusion to the claim that a seventeenth-century lady found 'great support in that comfortable word Mesopotamia', when pronounced by the Methodist preacher George Whitfield (see *Brewer's Dictionary of Phrase and Fable*).

[38] The genealogy of King David is listed in the first book of Chronicles, Chapter 2.

[39] John Knox (c. 1514–72) was a Scottish minister and theologian who led the Reformation in Scotland and was a founder of the Presbyterian Church of Scotland.

[40] In a speech of October 1932, Graham asserted that 'Scotland has once again become race conscious'. 'The Awakening of a Nation', *Scots Independent*, October 1932, p. 184.

[41] A complete set of armour. Those by the armourers of Milan were the most sought after for their exquisiteness and exceptional quality.

Highlander by reason of inferior arms and discipline was never judged to be the equal of the Lowlander in fight. His superiority only grew in later years, when Lowlanders had changed the Scottish spear for the tradesman's yardstick, and the Celt had still remained a warrior. All this Sir Thomas Dick Lauder brings out well in the many thumbnail portraits scattered throughout his book.

That his romance had sterling qualities is shown by the fact that it appeared when the "Shirra's"[42] magic pen was at its best, and that it had to face comparison with several of his masterpieces.

The language is perhaps surcharged with archaisms. That was the fashion of the time, a fashion that Sir Walter Scott successfully avoided, even in such works as IVANHOE and THE TALISMAN.

Still those old dug-out, or dug-up words serve to mark an epoch in literary taste in the same way that Euphemism in England and Conceptism[43] in Spain marked epochs, or as a counterfeit coin of the Emperor Hadrian's time is sometimes as well worth preserving as a right, full weight denarius, from the Roman Mint.

Certainly Sir Thomas was a Scottish patriot, and that at a time when such vagaries could not have been popular, for all the fell[44] six hundred pages of his book breathe patriotism, and on the rare occasions when he speaks not through his characters, but straight to the reader, his point of view is widely different from that of anyone born on the wrong side of the Tweed.

The Wolfe himself is disappointing as I see the matter, for he repented, and repentant sinners, unless like Judas[45] they have the grace to hang themselves, were never to my mind.[46]

This is not the writer's fault, for he but follows history, and history clearly shows that after all the Wolfe was but a sheep in wolf's array, and though he harried and plundered Mother Church, he died a sad, good Christian at the heart, when his wild oats were reaped.

Life's fitful fever[47] over, he slept peacefully for at least two centuries in the Cathedral of Dunkeld, under a marble or perhaps a granite

---

[42] Scots: Sheriff = a reference to the novelist Walter Scott who, for thirty years, sat as Sheriff of Selkirkshire.

[43] A literary movement of the Baroque period of Spanish literature, which was dominant style during the Spanish Golden Age.

[44] Scots: Learned, profound.

[45] Judas Iscariot who betrayed Christ and later hanged himself (Matthew 27:5).

[46] Scots: Thought or imagination.

[47] 'After life's fitful fever he sleeps well.' *Macbeth* (III.2.23).

hearse.[48] A band of whey-faced western Whigs,[49] called Cameronians[50] in those days (perhaps for euphony), "dingit it doon,"[51] either because they thought the Wolfe was an Erastian,[52] or from antipathy to graven images that was the keystone of their faith.

*****

This very short Introduction allowed Graham to reflect once again on a place which was very dear to him, even more so following the death of his wife, Gabrielle, who is buried there, and where he would soon join her.

INTRODUCTION: INCHMAHOME[53] AND THE LAKE OF MENTEITH

by John A. Stewart (Printed privately, 1933).

The Lake of Menteith,[54] or the Loch o' the Port as we older residents most love to call it, seems to have the quality of calling forth an abundant literature. Soon its bibliography will extend to the dimensions of the Ragman Roll,[55] but with a difference. The signatories who affixed their names to that ill Roll, wrote themselves down thereby, false loons,[56] no true Scots, but henchmen to the Southron enemy.[57]

Those who write, have written, or still write, about "our Lake,"[58] are, of necessity, as Scottissimi Scotorum as were the mail-clad Stewarts who sleep in the choir of the great church that bears Saint

---

[48] Graham uses hearse in its earliest sense: a latticework canopy placed over the coffin (whilst in church) of a distinguished person.

[49] A seventeenth-century Scottish Presbyterian.

[50] A radical faction of Scottish Presbyterians who followed the teachings of Richard Cameron.

[51] Scots: Knocked down.

[52] One who advocates that the state is superior to the church in ecclesiastical matters.

[53] Gaelic: *Innis Mo Cholmaig* = 'The Island of My [St.] Colmac'. During and after the Second World War, the island was used as an ammunition dump, and the public banned.

[54] Scotland's only lake was originally called Loch Menteith until the 1830s. There are many theories as to what caused the change, none of which are definitive.

[55] A document signed by the nobility and gentry of Scotland in 1291 giving allegiance to Edward I of England.

[56] Scots: A rogue, rascal, scoundrel.

[57] England.

[58] This, of course, included Graham himself, his first book being *Notes on the District of Menteith* (1895).

Colmoc's[59] name. All of the writers from MacGregor Stirling[60] down to the latest bearer of the fess checky [*sic*],[61] write lovingly, even tenderly, of the island that contains the bones of so many of their ancestors. They seem to have been nurtured in their affection for the isle by the same soil that nurtured old oaks and the stag-headed chestnuts upon whose boughs the osprey nested in the days gone by.

This latest book of photographic views, armorial bearings, seals, tombs, trees, plants, "pikkis and perchis,"[62] the ruined castle of Inchtalla,[63] the "Dogge Islande,"[64] and the stately choir and splendid five-light east window in Saint Colmoc's Church, forms an epitome of all that has been written of the Isle of Inchmahome.

A clansman of the Red Cross Knight,[65] who with his Countess, their feet upon their "litel houndes," rests in the sacred earth after the labour and the perils shared with Sant Louis[66] in the Holy Land, has penned his latest tribute to the magic of the Lake.

We, Grahams and Stewarts, welcome the book and add it carefully to the bibliography of the Isle in which so many of our ancestors – their life's crusade achieved – await our coming.

ROBERTUS GRAHAM.
DE INCHTALLA IN TERRIS DE MENTETH[67]

* * * * *

---

[59] An Irish Saint and miracle worker (c. 500 ad). The priory of Austin Canons on Inchmahome was named for him.

[60] William Macgregor Stirling, who published his *Notes, Historical and Descriptive, on the Priory of Inchmahome* in 1815, was an antiquarian and Minister of the church at Port of Menteith.

[61] *Fess Chequy*. In heraldry, a chequered band that stretches horizontally across a shield, which in the case of the Stewarts is blue and white.

[62] Pikes and perches.

[63] See passim.

[64] Inchcuin, possibly a crannog, on which the Earls of Menteith kept their hounds.

[65] According to tradition, Walter 'Bailloch' Stewart, Earl of Menteith (*jure uxoris*), whose effigy (in the Priory of Inchmahome) Graham is describing, was a crusader who fought under the French banner (1258–9).

[66] Louis IX of France (1214–70) who led the seventh and eighth crusades, and who was canonised in 1297.

[67] Latin: 'Of Inchtalla in the Land of Menteith'. Following the sale of Gartmore, the caput for the feudal Barony was transferred to the island of Inchtalla, maintaining his link with the District of Menteith.

Figure 21 Robert Kirk's grave at Aberfoyle, with flowers and coins left in his memory.

The next Introduction was close to Graham's heart, as it dealt with the supernatural myths and legends, peculiar to the environs of Gartmore. In 1691, the minister of nearby Aberfoyle,[68] the Reverend Robert Kirk(e) (1644–92), wrote down one of the earliest and the most influential accounts of *An Sleagh Maith* – 'The Good People' in the English language – *The Secret Commonwealth*. Both banal and surreal, this little manuscript chronicled in detail the inhabitants of the subterranean world – fairies, elves, brownies, doppelgängers, and many more paranormal phenomena, seen by 'the middle-earth men' (those who occupy the realm between the subterranean world and heaven), who had the gift of second sight. But this was no mere account of superstitious beliefs in his frontier parishes among 'the low-country Scots'. Kirk was a true believer, and he presented his examples as living evidence, as scientific fact, stating that in the future, communication between the middle and lower world would be a normal occurrence. Local legend maintained that for divulging their secrets, Kirk was taken captive inside nearby Doon Hill, where he still remains, and a simulacrum of

---

[68] Kirk had previously been a minister at Balquhidder, and between these two parishes, would certainly have known Rob Roy and all the MacGregors.

his body was buried in his own churchyard, where his grave still attracts the oblations of pilgrims.

The Secret Commonwealth was not published until 1815, under the direction of (Sir) Walter Scott,[69] 124 years after it was first written down. Like Scott and Graham, Andrew Lang stood sponsor for it in 1893 under the title *The Secret Commonwealth of Elves, Fauns and Fairies*, and dedicated it to his old school-friend, Robert Louis Stevenson, and his love of Fairydom:

> We spoke of a rest in a Fairy hill of the north, but he
> Far from the firths of the east and the racing tides of the west
> Sleeps in the sight and the sound of the infinite southern sea,
> Weary and well content, in his grave on the Vaea crest.

Although no scholar like Lang, Graham was admirably suited to the task, being 'a descendent of men long domiciled within sight of the Fairy Hill', and since childhood, infused with the myths and legends of his native heath.

INTRODUCTION: THE SECRET COMMONWEALTH

by the Reverend Robert Kirk (Stirling: Eneas Mackay, 1933), pp. 11–18.

TO THE GOOD PEOPLE[70]

A seventh son[71] and born bi-lingual, having passed his life amongst the "Scottish-Irish," first in Balquhidder, and then in Aberfoyle, no one was better fitted to discourse upon the "Secret Commonwealth of Elves and Fairies," where since his last daunder[72] on the Fairy Hill,

---

[69] Scott described the locale and traditions in *Rob Roy* (1817), and the beliefs and misfortunes of Kirk[e] in his *Letters on Demonology and Witchcraft* (1830). Doon Hill is also a place of pilgrimage and oblation for those fascinated by fairy lore.

[70] The Fairies. Mortals deemed it advisable to maintain good relations with them, by giving them complimentary names. Scott referred to this practice in *Rob Roy*: 'They ca' them ... Daoine Sith, quhilk signifies, as I understand, men of peace, meaning thereby to make their gudewill. And we may e'en as well ca' them that too, Mr Osbaldistone, for *there's nae gude in speaking ill 'o the laird within his ain bounds*'. ('It can do no good miscalling the rightful owner, while passing through his territory'.)

[71] An allusion to the belief that the seventh son of a seventh son was blessed with 'second sight'.

[72] Scots: Stroll.

in 1692 (*circa*), he now resides, than was the writer of this book. The tomb that Walter Scott saw in the east neuk[73] of the kirkyard of Aberfoyle, so good a judge of fairydom as Andrew Lang[74] held for a mockery. It was inscribed "Robertus Kirk, M.A., Linguae Hibernæ Lumen," for the Reverend Kirk had more than a tincture of the Humanities, and to his English, and the Lingua Hibernica,[75] added Latin, and certainly had more Greek than Shakespeare, for he quotes from the Septuagint[76] (Job xxvi, 5) in the original.

Andrew Lang, steeped to the lips in all the lore of fairydom, of elves, of doublegangers,[77] pechts,[78] brownies,[79] banshees, and the second sight, stood sponsor for the edition of 1893.

I, though unworthy, a descendant of men long domiciled within sight of the Fairy Hill, the Sith Bruach[80] of the writer, stand sponsor, in a measure, for the reprint. I do so in full faith and admiration, though an infrequent worshipper of any kind of Gods, but with a lurking tenderness towards Gualichu,[81] having seen his tree in days gone by on the south Pampa below Bahía Blanca, adorned with bits of cast-off saddlery, ostrich feathers, and all the flotsam and jetsam of the Pampa Indians and Matrero Gauchos[82] (of those days), who being realists as are in general every race of plainsmen, offered to their deity those articles useless to themselves.

I sponsor it, because it is a monument in my opinion of a style of literature that long has disappeared, and has "a curiosa felicitas,"[83] that shows the writer to have been a man of parts and a believer, "quia impossiblis,"[84] in all he writes about. Faith it is said consists of the

---

[73] Scots: Corner.

[74] Andrew Lang (1844–1912) was a Scottish poet, novelist, literary critic and collector of folk and fairy tales.

[75] Irish Language = Gaelic.

[76] The second century bc Greek translation of the Hebrew Bible, widely adopted by the early Christian churches.

[77] An anglicised form of *doppelgänger*, a supposedly ghostly counterpart or double of a living person.

[78] Another name for the fairies, with strong connections to the ancient Pictish people, who occupied the Southern Highlands in the Iron Age.

[79] Small creatures who were attached to a family, and who came out at night when the household was asleep and completed the chores left undone. Both Scott and Stevenson referred to their 'brownies' as being the source of their subconscious inspiration, a thought-process known as 'creative incubation'.

[80] Gaelic: Fairy bank.

[81] An evil spirit or demon of the indigenous Tehuelche people of Patagonia, who was feared because every evil happening was attributed to him.

[82] Spanish: Gaucho bullfighters.

[83] Latin: (literally: careful felicity) = a studied appropriateness of expression.

[84] Latin: (literally: because it is impossible), an allusion to Tertullian: 'certum est, quia impossibile', *De Carne Christi* (c. 203–6), that stated that something

belief of something we know to be untrue. At least that was the way a child defined it, and from the mouths of babes and sucklings,[85] so we are informed, comes wisdom. Robertus Kirk, M.A., had the true faith that removes mountains,[86] though not sufficient in his case to move the Fairy Hill from its eternal anchorage, for which and for his book I am indebted to him, and recommend it to all painful readers (in the Elizabethan sense),[87] certain that they will find much in it worthy of being read, marked, learned and inwardly digested.[88]

Lang affixed some of his most characteristic Grass of Parnassus[89] to the edition of 1893.

It now appears to give a generation that seems to have lost faith, both in the Pentateuch[90] and the Apocalypse,[91] something that may be worthy of belief. In the old grey manse[92] of Aberfoyle, not beautiful in our author's time with the old Spanish chestnuts, brought from Inchmahome, as says tradition, by the Reverend Patrick Graham a few years after Kirk "went to his own herd"[93] he would have ample leisure to ponder on the fairy clan that in his time peopled the valley of Avondhu.[94] The weekly sermon, I conjecture, could not have given him much trouble, for I feel certain that he had the gift of words, and was not of that weak-backit, schaucle-kneed[95] breed of ministers, "sair confined to the paper,"[96] whose sermons, at the best, are mere cauld morality.[97] I like to picture him with his Geneva gown, neatly

---

was certain because it was impossible. This also reflected Kirk's concerns over sadduceedism; i.e., if one did not accept the existence of the supernatural, it was a step closer to denying the existence of God.

[85] An English proverb modified from Matthew 21:16 (in which Jesus quotes Psalm 8:2).

[86] An allusion to Matthew 17:20, '... If ye have faith as a grain of mustard seed, ye shall say unto this mountain, Remove hence to yonder place; and it shall remove ...'

[87] One who reads painstakingly or with great care.

[88] An allusion to the Collect (prayer of the day) for the Second Sunday in Advent from the Book of Common Prayer (1662).

[89] A book by Lang of *Rhymes Old and New*, published in 1888 by Longman, Green and Co.

[90] The Torah (Law of Moses), which forms the first five books of both the Tanakh (Jewish Scriptures) and the Christian Bible.

[91] The Apocalypse is an alternative name for the Book of Revelation, which is the last book in the Christian Bible.

[92] Scots: The house provided for the minister of a parish.

[93] To have returned to his own kind, but whether that be fairy or Christian must remain moot.

[94] See passim.

[95] Scots: Knock-kneed.

[96] Entirely reliant on reading the sermon.

[97] Scots: A moral discourse devoid of all evangelical fervour.

starched bands, and well sleekit pow,[98] after having waled[99] a text from Malachi or Nahum, drowsing along for a full hour by his sand glass, placed beside the Bible, to the contentment of his sleepy congregation. There could not have been many thrawn[100] commentators in his day in Aberfoyle, and almost every individual of the congregation must have preferred half-an-hours clash o' the kirkyard[101] to a' the sermons in the wurrld. If not, they were not the right progenitors of the men of Aberfoyle, that I remember when in the Inn, (it was not in those days called an Hotel), there hung an almanac in the entrance hall, containing the announcement, "12th August. Grouse shooting opens. Episcopacy abolished." All the above taken into consideration, it may well be that the Reverend Mr. Kirk was but a changeling[102] from his birth, a Leprechaun I think they call it, in the dialect of Erse,[103] spoken in Ireland, and sent on earth as ambassador from the Secret Commonwealth of Elves and Fairies, to make their ways and customs manifest to us, the grosser mortals, nurtured on beef and brose.[104]

That is one hypothesis, largely discounted, I must admit, by his knowledge of the classics, and his sacred calling, for the Good People could but have spoken Gaelic, or perhaps Pictish, and certainly, as Andrew Lang says in his verses, none of them could have kent[105] the Covenant o' Works,[106] frae that o' Grace.[107]

So perhaps after all the writer of this most curious book was but a mortal, mystical by nature, with his mysticism sublimated within the crucible of the Vale of Aberfoyle. Even to-day, in the half-light of autumn evenings, the vale takes on once more the air as of an older world.

Standing up sentinel above Loch Chon, Ben Lomond with the shadows of the evening creeping up its flanks, to join the fleecy clouds that mantle round its top, looms as gigantic as Aconcagua[108]

---

[98] Scots: A smooth head = bald.
[99] Scots: Chosen as most apposite.
[100] See passim.
[101] See passim.
[102] A fairy child, swapped for an unchristened human baby, which the fairies had stolen.
[103] Literally, 'Irish', i.e., the Gaelic language.
[104] A dish made by mixing boiling water or milk with oatmeal or peasemeal, and adding salt and butter.
[105] Scots: Known.
[106] God's promise of salvation in return for obedience to his laws.
[107] Salvation by means of the grace of God through faith in Jesus Christ.
[108] A mountain in Argentina, the highest in the Americas, which was sacred to the Incas.

or Puracé.[109] It seems to watch over the whole district and to domi-
nate it. No sound is heard, except the babbling of mountain streams
as they slip down over the smooth stones, or the sharp belling of
a roe in the thick alder copsewood that surrounds Loch Ard. The
little wavelets break upon the pebbly beaches, or plash[110] gently on
the rocks of the steep islet on which Duke Murdoch's ruined castle
stands. In Couligarten Bay, the bulrushes bend gently, as the homing
wild duck squatter down noiselessly amongst their stems, vanishing
as silently as a seal slips into the sea. The lime trees on the point below
the mansion of Alt Skeigh[111] look dark and menacing, as the light
fades gradually, blotting out the little pier, the beach, the high road,
and the ground they stand upon, leaving their tops suspended in the
air. All the names, hard to pronounce by the mere Sassenach,[112] fantastic looking on the map, Blairushinmore, Blairhulachan, Bofrishlie,
Glasnarichnich, Loch au Cheiard, and Blairachapuill, then lose their
harshness, becoming as inevitable as the great blocks of pudding-
stone balanced on the hillsides, and strewed upon the muirs.[113]

The district would be colourless without them, and they transplanted into different surroundings would rather sound like epithets
of opprobrium, than names expressive of the natural features of the
land. No doubt the congregation that the ingenuous minister served,
were most of them devout believers in the second-sight, in dreams,
in portents, will-o'-the-wisps,[114] fairy rings, and in corpse candles,[115]
being convinced of their reality in quite a different way from that in
which they held the dogmas of the fiery creed they were constrained
to listen to in church. These without doubt they all believed in, or at
least assented to, for in those days in Scotland, to doubt was to be
damned. The fairy lore they sucked in with their mother's milk, and
held, not by conviction, for they had never reasoned on it, but quite
naturally, as part and parcel of themselves.

In such surroundings it was not strange the writer of the book also
believed in them; at least in all the farrago of heterogenous learning,
he has brought together, he gives no indication that he doubted in
the least of the strange cases he discourses on. In fact all those who
doubted of what they thought they saw, came to untimely ends.

---

[109] One of the most active volcanoes in the Cordillera Central Range in Colombia.
[110] Scots: Splash.
[111] Named after *Allt na Sgeith*, a stream that discharges into Loch Ard.
[112] Gaelic: A Saxon; an English-speaking Lowland Scot.
[113] Scots: Moorland or fields.
[114] A phosphorescent light seen hovering or floating at night which is said to be a
mystical being who would lead travellers to their doom.
[115] Luminosity resembling the flame of a candle sometimes seen in churchyards
and thought to presage someone's death.

Thus, "as is notoriously known in Killin"[116] (a parroch[117] in country of the Scottish-Irish), "a yeoman that lived hard by, who coming into a companie within ane Ale-House, where a Seer sat at Table ... at the Sight of the Intrant Neighbour, the Seer starting rose to go out of the Hows; and being asked the Reason of his haste, told that the Intrant man would die within two days." It was a most unneighbourly prediction, and in no wise astonishes those who have lived among the Scottish-Irish that the Intrant, intending evidently to mak siccar,[118] in the old Scottish fashion, incontinently stabbed the Seer, and was himself executed in the Jedburgh fashion,[119] without suffering the law's delay. Thus was a prophecy fulfilled, a thing infrequent in our days, and the Seer justified of faith, to his own detriment. These Buddiel[120] and Aqua Vitae houses were the curse of the Highlands, for the Gael had not learned as Mr. Kirk avers the elves and fairies knew, "Aqua Vitae[121] (moderately taken)" both prolongs life, and if I apprehend the writer, nourishes the "aerial and ætherial parts"[122] (of human and elfin nature), "leaving the terrestrial behind."

Another case, most worthy of recording, was that of "a woman of fourtie years of age" whom the Reverend gentleman examined ("having another Clergie Man in my Companie"). This certainly showed his discretion, a quality rarely conspicuous amongst the clergy, who are too prone at times to examine ladies, even less than forty years of age, without a witness of their own cloth to testify that their intentions were innocuous.

The woman, close on the grand climacteric, her name, see the original M.S., not "in tyre,"[123] was as it seems a noctambule,[124] and "having tarried in the Fields over Night in seeking of her sheep, saw and conversed with a People she knew not, and slept upon the ground." This seeking of her sheep, may after all have been a pretext,

---

[116] A village in Perthshire. A misquote of Kirk's 'It is notoriously known that in Killin ...'

[117] Scots: A parish.

[118] Scots: Make sure. A reference to Sir Roger Kilpatrick, who was an attendant of Robert the Bruce when he killed John Comyn, chief of Clan Comyn, in the Greyfriars church at Dumfries in 1306. Kirkpatrick met the Bruce rushing out of the church exclaiming that he thought he had killed Comyn, and Kirkpatrick drew his dagger and re-entered the church with the words, 'I mak sikkar'.

[119] One in which execution precedes judgement.

[120] Gaelic: *Buideal* = bottle.

[121] Latin: Water of life = strong spirits/whisky.

[122] Physical and celestial parts.

[123] Complete.

[124] French: A night-owl.

for as Pope tells us, "women ben full of ragerie,"[125] and, as the writer says, but without comment, she had a "Child since that time and is still prettie melanchollyus and silent and never seen to laugh."

Death we are told on good authority, is the reward of sin,[126] a saying that is discounted as an apothegm, as it is also the reward of virtue, however rigorous.

The semi-Highland district was with its wealth of billowy little hills, covered by scrubby oak, with now and then an old Scotch fir clinging to an outcrop of rock, its trunk as red as a stripped cork tree in the Estremenian[127] glades, was a fit setting for the fairy minister. His flock, so quietly listening to time pass by, as plants must listen, for it is impossible that their sweetness does not minister to their own enjoyment of their brief lives, was an oasis in that wild Scotland, below and up above the Pass.[128] Rob Roy was in the vigour of his early manhood, looking no doubt as dour as in the print taken from the picture once owned by Buchanan of Arden, on Lochlomond side. In London, "Bobbing John," the Earl of Mar,[129] was a young cornet in the Horse Guards, famed for his swordsmanship, his perhaps too courteous manners, and for his flattering tongue. The memory of both Montrose[130] and Claverhouse,[131] was still revered by Gaelic-speaking men, from John o' Groats, down to the steep pitched bridge that spanned the Forth at Aberfoyle.[132] Beyond the bridge, for the dividing line is there (or thereabouts), dour Lowlanders with their blue bonnets and their love of quite a different kind of liberty – a liberty which left them free to dogmatize upon the Scriptures in their own fashion, but without the pride that bearing arms imparted to the Gael, girned[133] at the mention of their names. But if they girned, when near the Pass of Aberfoyle, they

---

[125] The first line of *In Imitation of Chaucer* by Alexander Pope. Ragerie: wantonness or lasciviousness, cf. Chaucer's *Prologue of the Wife of Bath's Tale*.

[126] A misquotation of the first part of Romans 6:23 'For the wages of sin is death; but the gift of God is eternal life through Jesus Christ our Lord'. (KJV)

[127] From the region of Estremadura in Spain.

[128] A steep road, built by the fifth Duke of Montrose, to link Aberfoyle with Brig o' Turk, and which is now known as the Duke's Pass.

[129] John Murray, sixth Earl of Mar, who earned the soubriquet 'Bobbing John' for his indecisiveness and shifting back and forth between one political faction and another.

[130] See passim.

[131] John Graham, seventh of Claverhouse, first Viscount Dundee, commander of James VII's forces in Scotland, who lost his life but won a victory at the Battle of Killiekrankie in 1689.

[132] Regarded by some as the demarcation between the Highlands and Lowlands in that part of the country.

[133] Scots: Grumbled.

did so inwardly, for as we know, his mourners dared not take the body of Stewart of Ardvoilich [*sic*], the slayer of Kilpont,[134] to its resting-place, "east by Dundura" but discreetly shoughed[135] it at Coilmore, "for there were many powerful families that were kin to the Menteiths, especially the Graems."[136]

For two and forty years did the good pastor sojourn in this vale of tears,[137] daundering[138] about his parish, from the manse to the Fielbaracan tree, round which the clachan[139] grew; occasionally, no doubt, dropping into the change-house,[140] for a crack[141] with his elders,[142] over that usquebagh,[143] that in his own words, should be imbibed with moderation. Often he must have passed long hours in his own study in the manse, collating all the various accounts of elves, droichs,[144] wraiths, and apparitions, during the composition of his veracious book. Oftener by far, during his wanderings up the steep path that leads to Gartmore, crossing the tawny burn,[145] with its deep, darkling linns,[146] on the flat stones beside the lochan on which float water lilies, as white as swans frozen into the ice in a hill tarn,[147] he must have communed with the Good People, seated on stones, on bulrushes and thistle stalks, decked in their fairy green. He saw them, for what we see we are convinced exists for us, as certainly as if we touched it, so that a man who is convinced that he has seen a ghost, has seen it actually – with the interior vision, that vision a thousand times more vivid than the exterior eye.

Wandering along, seeing each hillock peopled with the elves who must have nudged each other, laughing as they watched the passing of the elf-parson, who was designed, by fate, to be their chronicler, he found himself, just at the bottom of the Fairy Hill. Bees hummed

---

[134] Major James Stewart, second of Ardvoirlich, killed his closest friend, John, Lord Kilpont, only son and heir of William, seventh Earl of Menteith.

[135] Scots: Buried in a ditch.

[136] Note in text: 'See *Graham's Notes on the District of Menteith*, London 1895.'

[137] Note in text: 'Some commentators put his age at fifty. An examination of the archives of the fairy hill would settle the matter'.

[138] See passim.

[139] See passim.

[140] Scots: A small inn or alehouse.

[141] Scots: Free and easy conversation.

[142] In the Church of Scotland, one who is elected to assist the Minister in running church business.

[143] Gaelic (*uisge beatha*): 'Water of life'.

[144] Scots: A dwarf.

[145] Scots: A brook or stream.

[146] See passim.

[147] A small mountain lake.

in the air, and dragon-flies hawked just above the linns or hung suspended for an instant, like humming birds, upon a flower.

The wind soughed softly in the heather, ruffling the leaves of the sweet gale, and bending down the supple stems of the bog asphodel.

The rest is silence; but we the natives of the district are well assured that he was reft away,[148] and still lives in the recesses of the Fairy Hill, serving the fairy mass.

Does he, I wonder, have a longing once again to see the valley where he used to wander with one eye on his parishioner's and the other on his own true world of elfindom. There are delights, no doubt, in the unsubstantial world where he has a cure of tiny souls,[149] for once a minister, always a minister, that we cannot appreciate. Yet still, I fancy, sometimes he must have what in Portuguese is called "saudades,"[150] a sad half longing recollection of a life where on the moors, the blue Alexis and the meadow brown,[151] float with their wings fanning the rushes and the ling,[152] or swing on hare-bells awave in the south wind.

The Grey Mare's Tail[153] still thunders after a spate, into the foaming pot below, a miniature Niagara, and the grass grown Fingalian path above Ledard,[154] winds through the heather by Eas Chagill[155] down to Glasahoil. Above the waterfall of rocks, high on Craigmore,[156] hard to discern except by children, or in certain states of atmosphere, still the White Lady seems to kneel in prayer.

Could he return, he might expound to us if she has any real existence (stone or shadow), or is but a figment compounded in the brain of the old race that named the hills, the straths,[157] the corries,[158] all the copses and the burns, giving them names appropriate to them, just as in Eden, Adam named the beasts.[159] The Downans[160] is still sweet and green, its grass all flecked with eyebright[161] and with tormentil,

---

[148] Scots: to be taken away by force.

[149] The "Cure of Souls" comes from the Installation Service for Anglican clergy and refers to the priest's pastoral care of their parishioners.

[150] Portuguese: A feeling of longing, melancholy, or nostalgia, which is celebrated in Fado music.

[151] Butterflies.

[152] See passim.

[153] A picturesque waterfall on the Duke's Pass.

[154] A farm close to Loch Ard.

[155] A stream.

[156] The steep hill that rises behind Aberfoyle.

[157] Scots: A wide river valley.

[158] Scots: A hollow in a hillside; a hollow between hills.

[159] Genesis 2:19

[160] Scots: A green hillock.

[161] *Euphrasia.*

as fair as anything in fairyland. We know he once kept tryst[162] with Graham of Duchray, but though the fateful dagger was not cast that was to restore the pastor to the Scottish-Irish congregation,[163] it may be that, like Orpheus, he too looked back to his "owne herde" and so was lost.

Happier by far he must be with those green-clad little folk, who know no care, no envy, malice, hatred or un-charitableness and are always glad.

Cha Tille [sic] E Tuilleadh.[164]

* * * * *

---

[162] See passim.
[163] In the Reverend Kirk[e] legend, he appeared to a relative after his supposed death, to say that he would appear again, at a christening, and if a dagger was thrown above his spectral head he would be released back into the world. He duly appeared, but the congregation was so shocked, that the dagger was not thrown, and he returned to fairy captivity.
[164] See passim.

Other Pieces

'An Iron-Race the
Mountain-Cliffs maintain,
Foes to the gentler Genius of the Plain.
And while their rocky Ramparts round they see,
The rough abode of want and liberty.
(As lawless Force from Confidence will grow)
Insult the Plenty of the Vales below.'

Thomas Gray (1748).

'Mountaineers are thievish, because they are poor, and
having neither manufactures nor commerce, can grow
richer only by robbery.
They regularly plunder their neighbours, for their
neighbours are commonly their enemies; and having lost
that reverence for property, by which the order of civil
life is preserved, soon consider all as enemies, whom they
do not reckon as friends, and think themselves licensed to
invade whatever they are not obliged to protect.'

Samuel Johnson, *A Journey to
The Western Isles of Scotland* (1775).

The following piece is unique in the canon of Graham's works, being
an historical article written for an academic publication. Taken from
legal documents that were in his possession, it tells of a *creagh*, or
raid,[1] by Highlanders on a farm on the Gartmore Estate in 1698,

---

[1] When the raid took place, the Laird of Gartmore was Sir John Graham,
second Baronet, who had been 'cognosed insane', was in an asylum. He was
not a direct ancestor of Cunninghame Graham, being the nephew of his five
times great grandfather. Sir John died without issue in 1708 and the estate
passed to his niece, Mary Hodge, who disponed it to her first cousin once
removed, Robert Graham of Gallingad, on 9 February 1709.

and the lengthy inventory shows that the tenant, Isabell M'Cluckey, despite 'making a bad mouth' was relatively wealthy.

For Graham, it was a very personal piece, as his direct ancestors had owned the Barony of Gartmore since 1709, and Graham himself was Laird from 1883 to 1900, when he was obliged to sell (see 'A Braw Day' above). There is an obvious pleasure in his recording of these shenanigans, and despite being chock-full of witness statements, and pedantic and almost Chaucerian Scots legalese, it is an extraordinary record of late seventeenth-century life on what was a colonial frontier between the increasingly civilised Lowlands, and semi-barbaric Highlanders, where depredation was commonplace, and retribution swift and final.

Many of the place names, and some of the characters will now be familiar, as is the overall theme – the disappearance of a way of life, combining a love of his native district, and the romanticisation of the Highlanders, who seem comparable with Native Americans and Australian Aborigines, all of whom he perceived as vanished or vanishing races.

What Graham fails to mention (probably because he wasn't aware of it), was that by the time of the *creagh*, Scotland was three years into a terrible famine, known as 'The Seven Ill Years'. This was due to five consecutive failed harvests during a 'Little Ice Age', and an economic slump after the Nine Years War. Thousands starved to death, and this disaster (among others) hastened moves for a Union with England.

LOOSE AND BROKEN MEN

The Scottish Historical Review, January 1913, pp. 113–21.
Anthologised in *A Hatchment* (London: Duckworth, 1913), pp. 223–40.

I found the other day a bundle of papers docketed[2] as above in my own hand.

Many years ago I must have come upon them at Gartmore, and as in those days it was what the people called a "sort o' back-lying place,"[3] traditions of the doings of loose and broken men still survived, though vaguely and as in a mist. The loose and broken men, whose fame still echoed faintly in my youth, were those who after the

---

[2] Listed.
[3] Out of the way.

'Forty-five' either were not included in the general amnesty, or had become accustomed to a life of violence.[4]

Once walking down the avenue at Gartmore with my old relation Captain Speirs,[5] we passed three moss-grown lumps of pudding-stone that marked the ancient gallows-tree.[6] Turning to it he said:

"Many's the broken man your ancestor, old laird Nicol,[7] hangit up there after the Forty-five." He also told me, just as if he had been speaking about savages, 'When I was young, one day up by Loch Ard-side, I met a Hielandman, and when I spoke to him, he answered, "Cha neil sassenach;"[8] I felt inclined to lay my whip about his back.'

Even then I wondered why, but prudently refrained from saying anything, for the old Captain had served through the Peninsula Campaign, had been at Waterloo, and, as the country people used to say, he had 'an eye intil him like a hawk.'

This antipathy to Highland men which I have seen exhibited in my youth, even by educated men who lived near to the Highland Line, was the result of the exploits of the aforesaid loose and broken men, who had descended (unapostolically) from the old marauding clans.

The enemy came from 'above the pass'[9] to such as my old uncle, and all the glamour Scott had thrown upon the clans never removed the prejudice from their dour Lowland minds.

Perhaps if we had lived in those times we might have shared it too.

One of the documents in the bundle to which I have referred is docketted, "Information for Mr. Thomas Buchanan, Minister of Tullyallan, heritor of Goustan in Cashlie." Gouston is a farm on the Gartmore estate, on which I, in years gone by, have passed many long and wet hours measuring drains and listening to complaints. 'Laird, ma barn flures fair boss.' 'Ye ken a' the grips are fair wasted.' 'I havena got a gate in the whole farm,'[10] with much the same kind; complaints no doubt all justified, but difficult to satisfy without the Golconda or the Rand[11] to draw upon, are ever present in my mind.

---

[4]   More correctly, a general term in the Highlands for men who belonged to, or owed allegiance to, no particular clan, or whose clan no longer had a recognised chief.

[5]   See 'A Veteran' above.

[6]   A hanging tree near Gartmore House. It had fallen, or been felled, before Graham inherited Gartmore. A large 'pudding-stone' adjacent to the walled garden of Gartmore House, still marks its late location.

[7]   Graham's great-great-great-grandfather, Nicol Graham MP (1695–1775), fourth Laird of Gallingad, and from 1709, fifth of Gartmore.

[8]   Gaelic: 'I have no English'.

[9]   See passim.

[10] This refers to Gowston (Gouston) Farm, owned by Graham, in the parish of Balfron, tenanted by 'Andra' Graham. See 'A Traveller' above.

[11] A reference to riches, or rather lack of them.

The document itself, one of a bundle dealing with the case, written I should judge by a country writer (I have several documents drawn up by one who styles himself 'Writer in Garrachel,' a farm in Gartmore Barony), is on that thick and woolly, well-made paper used by our ancestors and unprocurable to-day. The writing is elegant, with something of a look of Arabic about its curving lines. It states that:

"Ewan Cameron, Donald M'Tavish in Glenco, Allen Mackay, in thair (in thair, seems what the French would call "un terre vague," but has a fine noncommittal flavour in a legal document), John and Arch. M'Ian, his brethren, Donald M'Ian, alias Donachar, also Paul Clerich, Dugald and Duncan M'Ferson in Craiguchty, Robert Dou M'Gregor and his brethren, John and Walter M'Watt, *alias* Forrester, in Ofference of Garrochyle belonging to the laird of Gartmore ... came violentlie under cloud of night to the dwelling house of Isabell M'Cluckey, relict of John Carrick, tenant in the town of Gouston with this party above mentioned and more, on December sixteen hundred (the date is blank, but it occurred in 1698), and then on that same night, it being the Lord's Day, broke open her house, stript [another document on the case says "struck," which seems more consonant to the character of the Highlanders] and bound herself and children contrarie to the authoritie of the nation, and took with them her whole insicht and plenishing,[12] utensils and domicil,[13] with the number of six horses and mares, sixteen great cows and their followers, item thirty-six great sheep and lambs and hogs equivalent, and carried them away violentlie, until they came to the said Craiguchty, where the said Ewan Cameron cohabited."

I fancy that in Craiguchty, which even in my youth was a wild-looking place, the 'authoritie of the nation' had little sway in those days. From another document in the bundle, it appears[:]

Ane particular List of what goods and geir utencills and domicills was taken and plundered from Issobell M'Luckey relict of the decest John Kerick by Eun Cameron and his Accomplices as it was given up by her self:

In primis there was Ane gray meir estat	040 00 0
Item other three meirs estat to 20 lib p.p. is	060 00 0
It Ane flecked horse and ane black horse estat to 24 lib p.p	048 00 0

---

[12] Note in text: 'The subjoined Inventory, dated 1698, shows how thoroughly the work was done. It also shows what a careful housewife Isabel M'Cluckey was, and that she was a past mistress of the science of making 'poor mouth' [complaining, or pleading poverty].

[13] All her personal household goods and furnishings.

It there was taken away 10 tidy Coues estat to p.p 24 lib is   240 00 0
It three forrow Cows giving milk estat to 20 lib p.p. is   060 00 0
It two yield Cowes estat to 12 lib p.p. is   024 00 0
It two twoyeirolds estat to 8 lib p.p. is   016 00 0
It there was taken away thirtietwo great southland Sheep estat
    to thre pound Scots p. pice is   096 00 0
It there was fourtein hogs estat to 2 lib 10 sh: p.p. is   021 00 0
It of Cloath and wolen yairn estat to   035 00 0
It Eight plyds viz four qrof double and four single estat to   048 00 0
It ane pair of wollen Clats estat to   001 16 0
It Ane pair of Cards estat to 2 mk is   001 06 8
It two heckles viz Ane fine & ane courser estat to   003 18 0
It of mead neŭ harn in shirts 30 elns estat to   012 00 0
It of neŭ Linning in Shirts 24 elns estat to   012 00 0
It ten petticoats estat to   030 00 0
It four westcoats for women estat to   004 06 0
It thre gouns for women estat to   012 00 0
It on ax two womals a borrall & a hamer estat to   002 10 0
It two brass pans estat   003 12 0
It two dozen & a half of spoons estat to   001 18 0
It on pair of sheetts & on air blanqwets estat to   005 00 0
It on Covering estat to   004 00 0
It two bibles estat to   003 10 0
It on pair of tongs estat to   000 10 0
It two pair shoes & two pairs stockings estat to   005 08 0
It two green aprons estat to   003 00 0
It Ane pair of plou Irons and plough graith estat to   012 00 0
It Ane pistol and ane firelock estat to   010 00 0
It of readie Cash   013 06 8
It ane buff belt   001 04 0
It two plyads estat to   016 00 0
It of Muslin and Lining and oyr fine close estat to   020 00 0
It ten elns of new black felt in yearns and wool   010 00 0
It Six Sack of tueling four elns each   008 00 0
It a canvass eight eln   002 13 4
It a quarter of Butter & half ston   002 00 0

———

1 flacked horse 4 year old
1 bell broun horse 3 whyt feet 8 year old
2 bell broun mares whyt foted whyt nosed year old
Merk of her sheep prope in ye far lug & only cloven in ye near lug -
Loss of 20 bols of red land whyt corn sowing   033 13 04
It a hundred cups of sheep muck   009 00 00

It Sixtie cups of cow muck   002 00 00
It of Silver Rent   060 00 00
It of Lorne meal ten bols   080 00 00
It of expenses wt. M'Luckie at several trysts   010 00 00
It of spy money   010 00 00

---

204 13 04

that, not content with driving off the stock and bearing away the "insicht and the plenishings," the complainants and their servants "were almost frichted from their Witts through the barbarous usadge of the said broken and loose men."

However, the "mad-herdsmen," as the phrase went then, drove the "creagh" towards Aberfoyle. The path by which they carried it was probably one that once I knew well.

It runs from Gartmore village, behind the Drum, out over a wild valley set with junipers and whins, until after crossing a little tinkling, brown burn, it enters a thick copse. Emerging from it, it leaves to cottages on the right hand, near which grow several rowans and an old holly, and once again it comes out upon a valley, but flatter than the last. In the middle of it runs a larger burn, its waters dark and mossy, with little linns in which occasionally a pike lies basking in the sun.

An old-world bridge is supported upon blocks of pudding-stone, the footway formed of slabs of whin, which from the remotest ages must have been used by countless generations of brogue-shod feet, it is so polished and worn smooth. Again, there is another little copse, surrounded by a dry-stone dyke, with hoops of withes[14] stuck into the feals, to keep back sheep, and then the track comes out upon the manse of Aberfoyle, with its long row of storm-swept Spanish chestnuts, planted by Dr. Patrick Graham, author of *Sketches of Perthshire*.[15] From this spot Ewan Cameron, M'Ian (*alias* Donachar) and Robert Dhu M'Gregor, might have seen, though of course they didn't look, being occupied with the creagh, the church and the ancient churchyard of Aberfoyle, and the high-pitched, two-arched bridge, under which flows the Avon-Dhu.

All this they might have seen as "Ewan Cameron cohabited at Craiguchty," near the Bridge of Aberfoyle. Had they but looked they would have seen the Clachan,[16] with its low, black huts, looking like boats set upside down, the smoke ascending from the wooden box-like

---

[14] Flexible branches of willow, used for tying, binding, basketry, or fencing.
[15] 1812.
[16] The town is often called 'The Clachan [small village] of Aberfoyle'.

chimneys, – these they did not mark, quite naturally, as they were the only chimneys they had ever seen; nor did the acrid peat-reek fill their nostrils, accustomed to its fumes, with the same smell of wildness as it does ours to-day.

Craigmore and its White Lady were nothing but a ruckle[17] of old stones to them, and if they thought of any natural feature, it may have been the Fairy Hill to which the Rev. Robert Kirke, their minister, had retired only six years before, to take up habitation with the Men of Peace.[18]

Most probably they only scrugged their bonnets, shifted their targets on their backs, called out to any lagging beast, or without stopping picked up a stone to throw at him. The retiring freebooters "lay there (Craiguchty) that first night." One can see them, going and coming about the little shieling, and Ewan Cameron's wife and children, with shaggy hair and uncouth look, coming out to meet them, just as the women of an Arab 'duar'[19] come out to meet a marauding party, raising their shrill cries.

Some of the men must have been on guard all night to keep the animals from straying and to guard against surprise, and as they walked about, blowing on their fingers to keep them warm, the cold December night must have seemed long to them.

They would sleep little, between the cold and fear of an attack. Long before daylight they would be astir, just as a war party of Indians, or cattle-men upon an expedition in America, who spend the colder hours before the morning seated around the fire, always rise before dawn to boil their coffee pots. We know what took the place of coffee with Ewan Cameron and his band, or can divine it at least.

Next night they reached Achray, "in the Earl of Menteith's land, and lay there in the town." By this time the "said hership" (that is, the stolen beasts) must have been rather troublesome to drive, as the old trail, now long disused, that ran by the birch copse above the west end of Loch Drunkie, was steep and rocky, and ill adapted for 'greate cowes.'

Both at Craiguchty and Achray they had begun to sell their booty, for the tenants there are reported as not having been "free of the hership."

In fact, "Walter and John M'Lachlin in Blairwosh" bought several of the animals. Their names seem not to have been concealed, and it appears that the transaction was looked upon as one quite natural.

---

17 Scots: A pile or heap. Also 'rickle'.
18 See above.
19 A camp or village of tents in Arabian countries.

One, Donald Stewart, "who dwells at the west end of Loch Achray," also "bought some of the geare," with "certaine" of the sheep, and 'thereafter transported them to the highland to the grass."

Almost unconsciously, with regard to these sheep, the Spanish proverb rises to the mind, that says, "a sardine that the cat has taken, seldom or never comes back to the plate."

So far, all is clear and above board. Ewan Cameron and his band of rogues broke in and stole and disposed of such of the booty as they could, sharing, one hopes, equitably between them the sum of "fiftie six pounds, six shillings and eight pennies" (Scots) that they found in the house, reserving naturally a small sum, in the nature of a bonus, to Ewan Cameron, for his skill in getting up the raid.

As I do not believe in the word "stripping," and am aware that if we substitute the homelier "striking" for it, no great harm would probably be done in age when the stage directions in a play frequently run "beats his servant John," when speaking of some fine, young spark, all hitherto seems to have been conducted in the best style of such business known on the Highland Line.

Now comes in one "Alexander Campbell, *alias* M'Grigor,' who "informs"; oh, what a falling off was there, in one of the Gregarach.[20]

This hereditary enemy of my own family, and it is chiefly upon that account that I want to speak dispassionately … "*sed magis amicus veritas*"[21] … informed, that is he condescended to give his moral support to laws made by the Sassenach, "that Duncan Stewart of Baad in Bochasteal, bought two of the said cowes." Whatever could have come into his head? Could not this Campbell, for I feel he could not have been of the sept of Dougal Ciar Mor, the hero who wrought such execution on the shaveling band[22] of clerks after Glen Fruin, have left the matter to the 'coir na claidheamh'?[23]

So far from this, the recreant M'Gregor, bound and obliged himself "to prove the same by four sufficient witnesses" – so quickly had he deteriorated from the true practice of his clan. His sufficient witnesses were, "John Grame and his sub-tenant in Ballanton, his

---

[20] The Clan MacGregor. *Gregorach*, Gaelic: *greighear* = 'herdsman'.

[21] Latin: (roughly), 'Truth is a better friend'.

[22] Note in text: 'I am well aware that gentlemen of Clan Gregor have indignantly denied that Dougal Ciar Mor was the author of the slaughter of the students in Glen Fruin. If though we hold him innocent, how is he to be justified in the eyes of fame, for he seems to have done nothing else of remark … except of course being the ancestor of Rob Roy, an entirely unconscious feat of arms on his part.'

[23] Gaelic: 'Crime of the sword'. For the alleged massacre of innocent bystanders (scholars) at the Battle of Glen Fruin in 1603, the name MacGregor was proscribed until 1784 (with a brief restoration between 1661 and 1693).

neighbour Finlay Dymoch, and John M'Adam, Ostelier in Offerance of Gartmore." A little leaven leaveneth the whole, and the bad example of this man soon bore its evil fruit.

We find that "Robert Grame in Ballanton" (that is not wonderful, for he was of a hostile clan and had received none of the spoil as justifiable hush money) also came forward, with what in his case I should soften into "testimony." Far more remains to tell. "Jean, spouse to the said Ewan Cameron," that very Ewan who so justly received a bonus as the rent of his ability, also came forward and informed. She deponed[24] "that Walter M'Watt was of the band," although we knew it all before.

It is painful to me to record that the said M'Watt "was tenant to said Laird of Gartmore," for it appears according to the evidence of Ewan Cameron's wife, that "he brocht the said rogues to the said house, went in at ane hole in the byre, which formerly he knew, opened the door and cutted the bands of the said cowes and horse." This man, who after all never made nor unmade kings, but only served his lord (Ewan Cameron), "got for his pains, two sheep, a plyde, a pair of tow-cards, two heckles and a pair of wool cleets, with ane maikle brass pan and several other thinges." The harrying of the luckless Isabell M'Clucky seems to have been done thoroughly enough, and in a business-like way. However, punishment possibly overtook the evil-doers, as Thomas M'Callum, "who changed the said brass pott for bute,"[25] testified in confirmation of the above.

"Item Janet Macneall giveth up that she saw him take the plough irons out of a moss hole the summer thereafter with ane pott when he flitted out of Offerance to the waird,[26] and that he sent the plaid and some other plenishings that he got to John Hunter his house in Corriegreenan for fear of being known. Item the said Walter M'Watt died tenant to the Laird of Gartmore and his spouse and the said John Hunter took and intromitted the whole geir.[27] Item Elizabeth Parland spouse to umquhile[28] George M'Muir, Moorherd in Gartmore, informs she being ane ostlere,[29] that they gave a cow that night they lifted the hership to Patrick Graeme in Middle Gartfarran in the byegoing betwixt him and his brother Alexander Graeme in Borland and also that the said Robert M'Grigor and his brethren with the said

---

[24] Gave testimony.
[25] Note in text: 'Bute = spoil or exchange'. Booty, possibly 'buit', Scots: recompense, or 'bunce'.
[26] Scots: Prison.
[27] Scots: Illegally handled and sold all the stolen goods.
[28] Scots: Onetime wife of.
[29] An innkeeper.

John M'Watt met them in the way, although they came not to the house.["]

"Item that they sold the rest of the geir at one Nicol M'Nicol's house in the Brae of Glenurchy and the said Nicol M'Nicol got a flecked horse for meat and drink from them and lastly Dugald M'Laren and his brother Alexander got aquaviti among them.[30] This is the true information of the said persons that I have endeavoured to get nottrie att,[31] and if they be not material bonds and grounds of pursuit in it I give it over, but as I think the most material point is in the third article."

So ends the document, leaving us in the dark as to what happened in the end, just as is usually the case in life.

The names of nearly all the witnesses, as Elizabeth Parlane, John Ffisher, Robert Carrick, Robert M'Laren, Tomas M'Millan, the pseudo-M'Gregor, and of course the Grames, were all familiar to me in the Gartmore of my youth.

All the place names remain unchanged, although a certain number of them have been forgotten, except by me, and various old semi-Highlanders interested in such things, or accustomed to their sound. Ballanton, Craiguchty, Cullochgairtane (now Cooligarten), Offrance of Garrachel, Gouston of Cashlie, Bochaistail, Gartfarran, Craigieneult, Boquhapple, Corriegreenan, and others which I have not set down, as Milltown of Aberfoyle, though they occur in one or the other of the documents, are household words to me.

What is changed entirely is the life. No one, I say it boldly, no one alive can reconstruct a Highlander of the class treated of in my document as Loose and Broken men.

Pictures may show us chiefs. Songs and tradition tell us tricks of manner; but Ewan Cameron, Robert Dou M'Grigor, and their bold companions elude us utterly. A print of Rob Roy, from the well-known picture once in the possession of the Buchanans of Arden, hangs above the mantlepiece just where I write these lines. He must have known many a "gallowglass"[32] of the Ewan Cameron breed; but even he was semi-civilised, and of a race different from all my friends. Long-haired, light (and rough) footed, wild-eyed, ragged carles[33] they must have been; keen on a trail as is an Indian or a Black-boy in North Queensland, pitiless, blood-thirsty, and yet apt at a bargain, as their disposal of "the particular goodes, to wit, four horses and two mares," the sheep and other "gear" goes far to prove.

---

[30] Drank whisky together.
[31] Information about.
[32] Mercenary warriors in both Scotland and Ireland.
[33] Scots: A common man.

The mares and horses are set down as being worth "thirttie six pound the piece overhead," and I'm certain that Ewan Cameron got full value for them, even although the price was paid in Scots, for sterling money in those days could not have been much used "above the pass." It must have been a more exciting life in Gartmore and in Aberfoyle than in our times, and have resembled that of Western Texas fifty years ago. In London, Addison was rising into fame, and had already translated Ovid's *Metamorphoses*. Prior was Secretary to the Embassy in Holland, Swift was a parish priest at Laracar, and in the very year (1698) in which Ewan Cameron drove his "creagh" past the Grey Mare's Tail, on the old road to Loch Achray, Defoe published his *Essay on Projects*, and two years later his *True Englishman*.

Roads must have been non-existent, or at least primitive in the district of Menteith. This is shown clearly by the separation, as of a whole world, between the farm of Gouston, near Buchlyvie, and the shores of Loch Achray, where it was safe to sell in open day, beasts stolen barely fifteen miles away.

Men, customs, crops, and in a measure even the face of the low country through which those loose and broken men passed, driving the stolen cows and sheep, have changed. If they returned, all that they would find unaltered would be the hills, Ben Dearg and Ben Dhu, Craig Vadh, Ben Ledi, Schiehallion, Ben Vorlich, distant Ben More, with its two peaks, and Ben Venue peeping up timidly above the road they travelled on that December night; the Rock of Stirling, the brown and billowy Flanders moss, and the white shrouding mists.

*****

This tribute to Graham's friend and fellow author, Neil Munro (1863–1930),[34] was published in *The Glasgow Evening News*.[35] It demonstrated Graham's consistency over almost forty years, as it contains many of his recurring themes: the difference between the Saxon and the Gael; the romanticised Highlander; mist; and even reprises his attacks on the Kailyard School of writing.

---

[34] Munro is now best remembered for his *Tales of Para Handy*. His historical fiction included *The Lost Pibroch* (1896), *John Splendid* (1898), *Doom Castle* (1901), which Graham mentions, and *The New Road* (1914).

[35] Munro was for many years a staff writer for *The Evening News*, which he had also briefly edited.

Figure 22 Neil Munro by William Strang, National Galleries of Scotland.

THE INSPIRATION OF NEIL MUNRO

The Evening Times (Glasgow), 23 December 1930.

The Evening News has received the following appreciation of the late Dr Neil Munro[36] from that other distinguished Scottish writer, Mr R. B. Cunninghame Graham. The Gaelic line Mr Cunninghame Graham has prefixed to his tribute mean, "I return no more," and is taken from the song or "spring" that Rob Roy asked for on his death-bed (see passim).

---

[36] Munro received an honorary LLD degree from the University of Edinburgh in October 1930.

"CHA TIL MI TUILIDH"

The death of Dr Neil Munro is a sad blow to Scottish letters.

In some ways he occupied a unique position. Born as he was, bilingual, he had a foot in both the Saxon and Celtic camps. Had he elected to be a Gaelic writer he might have been a worthy successor to Alister M'Donald of Ardnamurchan,[37] the last of the Scottish bards.

THE CELTIC SPIRIT

His poetic mind, I fancy, had he chosen to write in Gaelic, would have impelled him to write verse. As it is we owe him the "The Lost Pibroch",[38] perhaps the tale most inspired with Celtic Spirit written in modern times. Written in English, it yet is full of the nostalgia of the men who named our hills, our glens, our corries, and our lochs and straths, giving them names that for sonority are unequalled in the world.

His novels, especially "Doom Castle," were evidently thought in Gaelic, transmuted into English in his mind, and given to us, with something in them that no English-speaking Scot could have brought to them. Above all things he was a son of Inverary,[39] wielding his pen, as in old days his clansmen wielded the claymore, and skian dhu [sic], in defence of the Campbells and M'Calein Mhor.[40]

Without him, we would have had no type of Highlander except that of the men who fought and died for Prionsa Tearlach [sic][41] in the '15, and in the '45.

Besides the vein of poetry in his composition, he had a streak of the sly Celtic humour, a humour so deep seated that it is often missed by the Sassenach.[42] This was most evident in his "Jus Primæ Noctis,"[43]

---

[37] Alastair mac Mhaighstir (c. 1698–1770) was a schoolteacher in Ardnamurchan who is famed for writing a Gaelic/English Dictionary and his Gaelic poems, which range from the bawdy to the philosophical, many of which were passionately pro-Jacobite. He remains one of the most important writers in the history of Scottish Gaelic literature.

[38] *The Lost Pibroch and Other Sheiling Stories* by Neil Munro (1899).

[39] Inverary: a town on the western shore of Loch Fyne and the seat of the Dukes of Argyll.

[40] The Earls and Dukes of Argyll, hereditary chiefs of Clan Campbell, who style themselves *Mac Cailein Mór* (Son of Colin the Great), an allusion to their descent from the earliest recorded Campbell, Sir Colin Campbell (d. circa 1296).

[41] Gaelic: Prince Charles.

[42] See passim.

[43] Latin: (literally) 'right of the first night', or "*droit du seigneur*": was the mythical medieval legal right of a feudal lord to have sexual relations with lower-status women on their wedding night.

a story published privately, tragic at first sight, quite in the vein of Maupassant, but ending oddly, leaving the reader with his face contorted as if he had swallowed vinegar, thinking to drink wine – a fine unusual story, just trembling on the verge of tragedy, and Highland to the core, as were the drovers in the old days who drove down their kyloes to the Tryst at Eaglais Breac.[44]

JOURNALISTIC WORK

The exigencies of life bound him to journalism, but in all he wrote, there was a literary tang. And why for not, as some of his own characters might have said, for much of journalism is as good literature, as the greater part of epoch-making novels, that come out to-day as modern, and almost before they are ready for their bourne,[45] the dust-heap, have become antiquated. Still, I deplore that a talent meant to have produced so much enduring work should have been cramped by the necessity of fate.

Perhaps he was our finest Scottish writer; that is for Scots, for most Scottish writers write for the English public, limning[46] a snivelling, sentimental Scot that never existed, and I hope never will exist, until the Eildon Hills[47] join up again and the Tweed[48] flows backward, or as the old fisher saying had it, herrings climb up Largo Law.[49]

LIFE AND DEATH

Neil, for I think of him as I always thought of him in life, with his wavy hair, his fresh complexion, and his hearty salutation of "Ha, my hero" – a translation from his other tongue – had none of that about him. His characters were men, and men who wanted bread to be bread and wine and wine to be made of grapes[50] as men say in Spain when talking of an honest man.

Well, well, he has gone into the mist, that mist which shrouded so many of his clansmen in their forays, but in the end devoured them all.

---

[44] Gaelic: 'The Speckled Church' = Falkirk; 'Faw kirk' = 'The Speckled Church'.
[45] A limit or boundary.
[46] Portraying.
[47] A hill south of Melrose with three distinct 'tops', the highest of which is 422 m.
[48] The river which flows eastward through the borders of Scotland and England and into the North Sea.
[49] An ancient volcanic hill in the East Neuk of Fife.
[50] Al pan, pan, y al vino, vino is the Spanish equivalent of 'Call a spade a spade' = to speak frankly.

Some of his work should live, and that is all the best of us, the wielders of the brush or pen, can hope to be our lot.

Surely the "Lost Pibroch" will be immortal; that we have to leave to fate. It bears a freshness of all work men do in youth, and yet the sureness of touch speak of a craftsman born.

I like to think of him buried in Inverary in some old Highland churchyard, by the lochside, with a widespreading yew tree, stretching its whispering branches over his grave at night and the wild seafowl crying his coronach.[51]

---

[51] See passim.

Postscript

'Cunninghame Graham whose passing
Has left Scottish life
More mean and grey than ever before'.[1]

Described by Daiches as 'one of the puzzles of Scottish literary history',[2] and by Davies as 'a phantom of Scottish literature',[3] Graham's position in the pantheon of Scottish writers remains inconclusive, and his works have frequently been obscured by his adventurous life and romantic personality. Opinion was, and remains, divided. In 1910, a critic in *The Observer* wrote of his sketches, 'Judged upon their style, they rank among the best things ever written in this country ... little works of art that place the writer by the side of the great story-tellers of France and Russia',[4] while a biographer of Graham's great friend Conrad believed that Graham was never primarily a writer, let alone an artist.[5]

This contradictory reputation arose because, despite his undoubted eloquence, Graham wrote self-indulgently, for his own nostalgic satisfaction, ignoring the editorial conventions and disciplines of the professional writer, and peppering his already heavily nuanced works

---

[1] Hugh MacDiarmid, *In Memoriam James Joyce* (1955).

[2] David Daiches, 'Don Roberto', *London Review of Books*, vol. 5, no. 3, 1983, p. 17. Nancy Curme found Daiches's criticisms 'depressing': 'The debasement of Scottish culture must indeed have been accompanied by an addling of Scottish intelligence if the concept of bi-culturalism is so hard to comprehend by those who, after over 200 years, are themselves unable to decide whether they are Scots or just an inferior kind of English.' Nancy Curme, 'The Scottish Sketches of R. B. Cunninghame Graham', *Scottish Literary Journal Supplement*, 1983.

[3] Laurence Davies, 'R. B. Cunninghame Graham: The Kailyard and After', *Studies in Scottish Literature*, vol. XI:3, University of South Carolina, 1974, p. 156.

[4] *The Observer*, 16 October 1910, p. 5.

[5] Jocelyn Baines, *Joseph Conrad* (London: Weidenfeld & Nicolson, 1960), p. 203.

with obscure local and foreign details, that he alone cared about, some of which not one in a hundred of his readers would have understood. As John Galsworthy noted, with reference to Graham, the short story form required:

> An almost superhuman repression of the writer's self ... Very much of an artist, he is yet too much of a personality ever to be quite the pure artist; the individuality of the man will thrust its spear-head through the stuff of his creations.[6]

In 1924, Leslie Chaundy, who compiled the first bibliography of his writings, disclosed that Graham had told him that his works were written largely for his own amusement, since he was not a professional writer.[7] When he told Garnett that one of his pieces was 'an impression, nothing more, but that is all I can do',[8] he was being honest. Graham was not an Impressionist, he simply wrote impressions, which he usually wrapped around some central personal narrative or meditation.

In the final analysis, the most permanent legacy of Graham's Scottish sketches was not literary, but historical. He stands out in all of Scottish literature, not only for depicting the landscapes, atmospheres and characters of an area which many had considered a cultural backwater, but for depicting the vanished lives of a landed class, unvisited by any other Scottish writer. He was a documentarist, but a documentarist's primary concern is not the past, nor the present – but the future.

Graham had the good fortune to stand at the meeting-place of two worlds, and had the skills to reach into that older, lost world, and bring it back to us – almost intact. Frederick Watson described, more succinctly than Graham himself, the vanished Scotland that Graham knew:

> Old things have not decayed – they have collapsed – as when an axe fells the oak in its prime. There still clung, amongst the aged, ancient prejudices whose roots were buried deep in the past. Those silent hills were still haunted by the dim echo of forgotten feuds. These were the days when drovers still lay wrapped in their plaids before a smouldering peat fire, when men of eighty spoke of the tales their grandfathers had

---

[6] John Galsworthy, 'Notes on R. B. Cunninghame Graham,' *Forsytes Pendyces and Others* (London: Heinemann, 1935), pp. 273–4.
[7] Leslie Chaundy, *A Bibliography of the First Editions of the Works of R. B. Cunninghame Graham* (London: Dulan, 1924), p. 3.
[8] Cunninghame Graham, letter to Garnett, 27 August 1898.

quavered about Rob Roy, when the railroad was still struggling amongst the Northern hills. All this is not merely picturesque – it is important. I merely wish to emphasise the strange old world into which he [Graham] was born in the year 1852.[9]

But why were Graham's feelings of nostalgia so strong? What was his abiding interest in displaced princesses, forgotten actors, deluded eccentrics, dead aunts, and rustic farmers? Most persuasively, Watts found the source in Graham's humanity:

> Graham throughout his life was profoundly troubled by the idea that just as an individual may be lost without trace in the jungle, so men of the past, leading worthy lives, may be lost to history by the force of oblivion, and so people of the present may be ignored and forgotten for want of a due memorialist.[10]

This, however, was not the whole story, for when we examine Graham's subject matter, especially his evocations of the landscape and characters of Menteith, then a broader and more significant picture emerges; then the preoccupation with the death, decay and melancholy that pervade his works can be put in an historical context. Writing in 1927, the 'Tory nationalist' George Malcolm Thomson described it thus: 'The scent of death which Cunninghame Graham found in the Scottish countryside thirty years ago has drifted into the cities, and commerce grows feeble, rigid and cowardly in its miasma.'[11] What Graham was documenting, perhaps unconsciously, was a world of failure and erosion, including his own. Those of whom he wrote, both high and low, were the dying remnants of an economic boom of 100 years previously, who were now trapped, like flies in amber, unable to escape their deteriorating circumstances, in a rapidly changing world.

The enterprise of certain Scots after the 1707 Union with England, ambitious men on the make, some with questionable pedigrees, sharp wits, and few scruples, had led to the accumulation of great fortunes from the American and Caribbean Colonies, either from administration, or plantation ownership. This new wealth had supported the extraordinary flowering of the Scottish Enlightenment, and had

---

[9] Frederick Watson, 'R. B. Cunninghame Graham', *Bookman*, March 1916, p. 174.

[10] Watts, p. 41.

[11] G. M. Thomson, *Caledonia: Or the Future of the Scots* (London: Kegan Paul, 1927), p. 41. Thomson was instrumental in promoting 'The Scottish Party' – 'Nationalism for Tories, that's our proposal ... a synthesis of Toryism and nationalism'. It later amalgamated with the left-of-centre National Party of Scotland to form the SNP.

heralded an 'Augustan Age' in Scotland from the middle of the eighteenth century, when the estates of the old Jacobite families were acquired, and grand Palladian houses built, when the wealth-accumulators returned to their native soil, having purchased respectability.

Like the splendid but brief flowering of the 'planter aristocracy' in the antebellum 'Old South', another society built on slavery, this lifestyle, in the long term, was unsustainable, and as often as not, succeeding generations either lacked their predecessors' acquisitional skills, or no longer wished to indulge in the 'trade' on which their family fortunes had been built. Subsequently, they were obliged to live off the income from land-ownership, or subsist on their dwindling patrimony – rags-to-rags in three or four generations. This included 'useless sons' like Graham's 'Eccentric Uncle Tom' in 'A Relative' for whom 'No career was good enough ... so he, like a good son, remained without one to the last day of his existence'. Or Alexander Speirs in 'A Veteran', whose inheritance had come from the Glasgow tobacco monopoly, three generations earlier, but who was left to lead the lonely life of a country squire, because his own business enterprise had gone into bankruptcy. Or, like Graham himself, who, faced with enormous family debts, and whose South American business ventures had come to nothing, chose a career as an unpaid member of parliament, then an unpaid author, rather than increase the financial viability of his estate. But therein lay another unpleasant economic reality.

Incomes from land-ownership were declining, as the rural areas depopulated through mass emigration,[12] agricultural recession, new farming methods, and the attraction of better-paid work in the nearby cities. Although Graham's estate covered 12,000 acres, much of it was barren moor, and many of his farms were marginal, yielding little income.[13] Graham had confided to the publisher James Leatham, that he took less than £100 a year from his estate, and that 'I tremble in the presence of my poorest tenant'. 'This I took to mean that he was afraid the tenant might ask for repairs or improvements which he could not afford.'[14]

---

[12] The Registrar-General for Scotland recorded: 'No country on the continent of Europe had lost such a high proportion of her people as Scotland.' J. G. Kyd, *Scottish Population Statistics* (Edinburgh, 1952), p. xxii. John Foster wrote: 'The scale of the losses [in the Lowlands] dwarfed the Highland clearances of the early nineteenth century.' John Foster 'The Twentieth Century, 1914–1979', in R. A. Houston and W. W. J., eds, *The New Penguin History of Scotland* (London: 2001), p. 431.

[13] Polybaglot Farm, for example, only brought in a rent of £40 per annum. *Valuation Roll for the Parish of Drymen, Year 1895–96.*

[14] Leatham, *60 Years, of World Mending* (1940) (Turriff: Deveron Press, 2016), pp. 162–3. Graham's biographer, Alexander Maitland, wrote that the estate

A new kind of entrepreneur would soon take over the land-hold-ings, men of business, of industry, including the 'sweaters' whom Graham so despised. Self-made men like Sir Charles Cayzer, who bought Graham's estate, and who, ironically, as the founder of The Clan shipping line, had made his fortune in servicing the Empire that Graham had so vociferously attacked.

The paternalistic landed class were disappearing, along with their old-world retainers, and soon, after Graham's departure, the stub-born farmers that he so admired abandoned their meagre crofts, leaving a 'poor rickle of grey stones', and the reflective memoirs of their ould laird as their only memorials.

It was Graham, and Graham alone, who captured the moment.

---

made an annual profit of £660. However, much of this was taken up by house maintenance, and annuities to older relatives. Alexander Maitland, *Robert and Gabriela Cunninghame Graham* (Edinburgh: William Blackwood, 1983), p. 53.

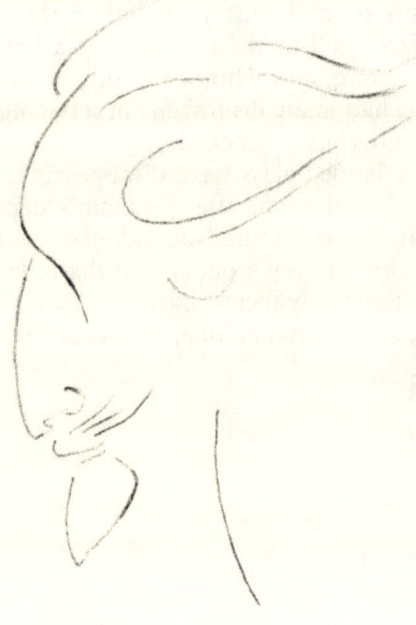

Mists of Menteith! Whose silvery mantle clings,
A dreamlike vesture round the resting place
Of him whose love and word of you still sings,
Though he is gone, last scion of his race.
                    Christian MacIntyre, *The Sacred Well* (1937)

Biography

Graham's career in the public eye demonstrated a remarkable longevity, spanning over fifty years: from an aristocratic 'cowboy-dandy' and radical *enfant terrible* of the British political establishment, a famed horseman and world traveller, he moved to a state of near veneration amongst every class in society. In 1927, the gossip columnist of *The Sunday Post* reported, 'There are few men nowadays so well known as Mr R. B. Cunninghame Graham',[1] and on his death in 1936, his early biographer, Aimé Tschiffely, believed that 'his name will surely grow'.[2] However, he quickly faded from both the academic and the public consciousness.

The quarter-Spanish Graham was born in London in 1852 to Anne Elizabeth Elphinstone Fleeming (1828–1925),[3] and Major William Cunningham Bontine [*sic*] (1825–83), scions of Scotland's landowning class. His principal family inheritance had come through his great-great-grandfather, Robert (Cunninghame) Graham of Gartmore (1735–97),[4] who had made his fortune in Jamaica, and who had inherited the estates of Gartmore, Ardoch and Finlaystone.[5]

Graham's father, William, who had received a severe head injury after falling from his horse whilst hunting during military service in Ireland,[6] slowly became more disturbed, and by the summer of 1866, after attacking his wife with a sword, he had been put under

---

[1] *Sunday Post*, 13 November 1927, p. 15.
[2] A. F. Tschiffely, *Fortnightly Review*, May 1936, p. 559.
[3] Daughter of Vice-Admiral the Hon. Charles Elphinstone Fleeming of Cumbernauld (1774–1840), and *Doña* Catalina Paulina Alesandro de Jiminez of Cadiz (1800–80), the daughter of a Spanish grandee family.
[4] Graham wrote a biography of Robert Graham, entitled *Doughty Deeds* (1925).
[5] Gartmore estate, which stretched from Aberfoyle to Kippen, had been in the family for 300 years. The other two estates faced each other across the River Clyde. Finlaystone was sold in the 1860s, and Graham bought back Ardoch in 1903, after Gartmore was sold in 1900 to pay off the family debts.
[6] A small fragment of skull had apparently lodged in his brain.

restraint. In an attempt to rescue his family's fortunes by cattle ranch-
ing, in 1870, at the age of seventeen, Graham, who had been educated at Harrow School and in Brussels, sailed for Argentina, but
found himself in the midst of a revolution. This was the first of three
abortive business ventures in South America. The second, in 1873,
found him Paraguay, where he sought opportunities in cultivating the
yerba-maté plant, the ingredient of a popular local infusion, but his
explorations into the interior led to the discovery of abandoned Jesuit
missions, which he described in his book *A Vanished Arcadia* (1901).

After his return to Europe in 1874, and further travels, in 1876
Graham sailed to Uruguay, with the intention of buying horses and
selling them to the Brazilian Army, described in his novella *Cruz Alta*
(1900).[7] This enterprise also came to nothing, but subsequently, back
in Europe, he met a young woman who styled herself 'Gabrielle Marie
de la Balmondière', a half-French Chilean poetess.[8] They married in a
London registry office[9] and sailed for the United States in an attempt
to set up a mule-breeding enterprise, but after a perilous journey into
Mexico by wagon train, their Texan ranch was apparently burned
down by Apaches. Returning to Europe in 1881, they lived quietly in
Spain and Hampshire, prior to inheriting the family seat of Gartmore
on William's death in 1883.

Like other Victorian gentleman-adventurers, throughout his varied
career, Graham remained a restless traveller, drawn particularly
to Hispanic regions, and to Morocco. In 1897, along with Syrian
and Moorish companions, he undertook a perilous reconnaissance
mission to the forbidden city of Taroudant in southern Morocco,
disguised as a Turkish doctor, but was captured and imprisoned. His
adventurers were recorded in his most celebrated book, *Mogreb-El-
Acksa* (1898), which MacDiarmid described as, 'one of the best travel
books ever written'.[10]

Graham's early experiences in wild and dangerous places, while
failing to bring financial security, provided him with a wealth of
material for his future literary career, but it also imbued him with a
particularly egalitarian and ecologically conscious world-view. This,
combined with strong moral convictions, and a predilection for fearless outspokenness, motivated him to become a Liberal member of

---

[7] Anthologised in *Thirteen Stories* (1900), pp. 1–84.
[8] Eighty years after her death, it was revealed that she was Caroline Horsfall,
the daughter of a Yorkshire doctor. Apparently, this fiction was concocted
and maintained because Graham's mother did not approve of her.
[9] The bride gave a false age and a false name.
[10] MacDiarmid, *Cunninghame Graham: A Centenary Study* (Glasgow:
Caledonian Press, 1952), p. 28.

parliament for the mining constituency of North-West Lanarkshire, espousing the nationalisation of land and the mines, universal suffrage, free school meals, the payment of MPs, the abolition of the House of Lords, and Irish and Scottish home rule.

Graham's words and behaviour, particularly his extraordinary maiden speech, brought him to the attention of the English textile designer, poet, and author, William Morris (1834–96), who converted him to socialism, and he was soon embraced by the denizens of London's radical demi-monde, which included Karl Marx's daughter Eleanor, Friedrich Engels, the anarchists Prince Pyotr Kropotkin and Sergey Stepnyak-Kravchinsky,[11] George Bernard Shaw, H. G. Wells and Oscar Wilde.[12]

Despite being a renowned orator, blessed with great charm, eloquence, and wit, which otherwise might have propelled him to high political office, Graham's brief time as an MP was marked by anger and frustration, when, for the first time, he was confronted with the realities of the lives of his mining constituents, and parliament's stubborn opposition to change, and on three occasions he was expelled from chamber for unparliamentary speech. Seemingly oblivious to his own political future, his erratic behaviour, and his campaigns on behalf of labour, quickly brought him national celebrity, particularly after he reputedly charged police lines in Trafalgar Square, in November 1887, was severely beaten, and sentenced to six weeks in prison.[13] Earlier that year, he had met the journalist-miner Keir Hardie, and in 1888 they founded Britain's first party of labour, the Scottish Parliamentary Labour Party. Graham, having resigned his parliamentary seat, failed to be elected as a 'Labour' candidate in 1892, but his political efforts did not cease, and he would re-emerge as an even more radical political activist, an outspoken supporter of women's rights, and an anti-imperialist, who would develop into a respected literary artist.

It was during his spell as an MP that Graham started writing for small socialist journals, including Morris's *Commonweal*, *The Labour Elector*, and *The People's Press*, but his writings stood out from the standard reports for their highly individual expressive declarations, particularly when they dealt with his overseas experiences, in what looked like the release of pent-up literary urges. His breakthrough

---

[11] Assassin of General Nokolai Mezentsov, Chief of the Tsar's secret police.
[12] Wilde and Morris rushed to Bow Street Magistrate's court after Graham's arrest, and Wilde's wife, Constance, attended every day of Graham's subsequent trial.
[13] At this time, Graham was a Justice of the Peace in Perthshire, Stirlingshire, and Deputy Lord Lieutenant of Dunbartonshire, positions which he retained, despite his incarceration.

came in 1895, however, with the publication of a guidebook entitled *Notes on the District of Menteith*, discussed above. As a direct
consequence, Graham was recruited to *The Saturday Review*, and
he remained an irregular contributor for thirty-six years. Hitherto,
his literary output had been marginal, and somewhat chaotic, but
now, writing for this prestigious periodical, which was described by
the *Manchester Guardian* as 'soaked in eighteenth-century Toryism',
undoubtedly lent a new kudos and respectability that he had lacked
in the eyes of the public and his peers. It was, nevertheless, an odd
partnership, the fiery communistic iconoclast, writing for the sedate
country house journal, and he was obliged to frame his radical views
discreetly for a politically conservative readership. Most, however,
were heavily disguised critiques of so-called 'progress', and the
advance of Empire, mediums for anger and nostalgia, which implicitly
regretted the destruction of natural environments, lifestyles, cultures
and traditions.

Graham was establishing himself as one of the most brilliant men
of the age,[14] and as Watts reminded us:

> His life was so picturesque as to resemble romantic fiction, and his rufous,
> swaggering, radical, patrician figure haunts the literature of the period.
> He appears as 'Mr. X' in Conrad's 'The Informer', as 'Mr. Courtier'
> in Galsworthy's *The Patrician*, and as 'Mr. Graham' in Wells's *When
> the Sleeper Wakes*; Professor Norman Sherry saw him in Charles Gould
> of *Nostromo*, while Professor Molly Mahood saw him as Etchingham
> Granger of *The Inheritors*.[15]

Despite his fame, Graham was still faced with insurmountable
debts,[16] and he was obliged to sell the family estate at Gartmore in
1900.[17] The estate had come to the family in the seventeenth century
and Graham keenly felt its loss and saw it as a betrayal of his

---

[14] In 1927, the gossip columnist in *The Sunday Post* reported: 'There are few
men nowadays so well known as Mr R. B. Cunninghame Graham'. *The
Sunday Post*, 13 November, 1927, p. 15.

[15] Watts, 'The Scottish Sketches of R. B. Cunninghame Graham', *Review of
English Studies*, vol. 36, no. 141, February 1985, p. 118.

[16] These had been incurred initially, by Graham's great-grandfather, William
Cunninghame Graham (1775–1845), known as 'Bad Willie the Swindler'. He
was part of a gang, along with his stepson, Alan Bogle, who swindled Glynn's
Bank out of £10,700. He was quickly arrested in Florence, but was never
prosecuted, although he was permanently barred from the Grand Duchy of
Tuscany.

[17] Recorded in 'A Braw Day', above. Graham had already sold off some
individual farms.

forebears. Then in 1906, 'Gabriela',[18] who had been a chain-smoker since their days in Texas, died from dysentery in Hendaye, France, at the age of forty-eight.[19] She was buried on the Island of Inchmahome in the Lake of Menteith. Graham, with the help of a family retainer, dug her grave, and her funeral was conducted by her brother, William Horsfall, a high-church Anglican priest. They had no children, and Graham never remarried.

Though a pacifist, Graham lost no time in trying to join up as a rough rider at the outbreak of the Great War. He was sixty-two years old and was naturally turned down. Undaunted, he petitioned his friends in the War Office, and was first put in charge of a section of the Remount, and later with the rank of brevet colonel was made president of a commission to purchase horses in the Argentine for the British Army. He spent the next eleven months riding with the gauchos as he had done in his youth. On his return voyage to England, his ship was torpedoed by a U-boat in the English Channel, but both he and the horses got safely ashore. However, he was promptly sent back to South America in January 1917 to report on beef cattle stocks in Colombia.

Graham had long been a supporter of Irish and Scottish home rule, and in 1886, along with Hardie,[20] was an original member of the first Scottish Home Rule Association (SHRA), and was elected its president.[21] After the war, having failed to be elected as the MP for Stirling West, in 1920 he joined the reformed SHRA, again as its president. In 1928 he was nominated as the 'nationalist' candidate for the Glasgow University rectorship, and with the assistance of Compton Mackenzie and Hugh MacDiarmid, was only narrowly defeated by the sitting prime minister, Stanley Baldwin. Directly after his defeat, there occurred another significant and unexpected outcome in Graham's later life, for his near-success had stimulated great enthusiasm among the home rule supporters, and a public meeting was arranged at St Andrew's Hall two days later, which attracted 3,000 Glasgow citizens. This consolidated the newly-formed National Party of Scotland (NPS), of which Graham had again been elected president, and he was regular speaker at the party's rallies in Stirling and Elderslie until a year before his death. He was subsequently a facilitator of the amalgamation of the NPS with the Scottish Party in 1934,

---

[18] By this time, she was using this form of her name.
[19] Not forty-five as Graham, and his biographer Tschiffely claimed.
[20] They did not meet until the following year.
[21] Hardie was secretary.

Figure 24 Graham's coffin being taken to the Buenos Aires dockside.

which was thereafter known as the Scottish National Party, and was elected honorary president.[22]

Despite his doctor's warnings that he was too ill to travel, Graham, who was suffering from bronchitis, insisted on visiting Argentina in early 1936. On his arrival he was fêted, but after visiting the birthplace of his friend, the renowned naturalist W. H. Hudson, at Quilmes, and a township named 'Don Roberto' in his honour, he developed pneumonia and he died in the Plaza Hotel, Buenos Aires, on 20 March 1936, aged eighty-three. His body lay in state in the Casa del Teatro where thousands came to pay their respects, as did the President of the Argentine Republic. The funeral procession to the docks was long and included the two horses that his friend Tschiffely had ridden from Buenos Aires to Washington DC. He had planned to return home on the *Almeda Star*[23] on 26 March, and so he did.

He was buried alongside 'Gabriela' in the ruined chancel of the Priory of Inchmahome under a rough-cut stone that bears his Argentine cattle brand. A year later, a memorial to him was unveiled at Castlehill in Dumbarton (later removed to Gartmore). It contained stones from Argentina, Paraguay and Uruguay – the countries of his youthful adventures, and a medallion by Alexander Proudfoot RSA, with the inscription:

'Robert Bontine Cunninghame Graham 1852–1936 – Famous Author – Traveller and Horseman – Patriotic Scot and Citizen of the World – As Betokened by the Stones above. Died in Argentina, interred in Inchamahome – He Was a Master of Life – A King Among Men'.

---

[22] The presidency went to his kinsman, the Duke of Montrose.
[23] The ship was sunk in enemy action five years later.

EU representative:
Easy Access System Europe
Mustamäe tee 50, 10621 Tallinn, Estonia
Gpsr.requests@easproject.com

www.ingramcontent.com/pod-product-compliance
Lightning Source LLC
Chambersburg PA
CBHW060225030726
47499CB00004B/1198